The hard hand of war

The Hard Hand of War explores the Union army's policy of destructive attacks on Southern property and civilian morale – how it evolved, what it was like in practice. From an initial policy of deliberate restraint, extending even to the active protection of Southerners' property and constitutional rights, Union armies gradually adopted measures that were expressly intended to demoralize Southern civilians and to ruin the Confederate economy. Yet the ultimate "hard war" policy was far from the indiscriminate fury of legend. Union policymakers promoted a program of directed severity – and Professor Grimsley demonstrates how and why it worked.

The Hard Hand of War fits into an emerging interpretation of the Civil War that questions its status as a "total war" and emphasizes instead the survival of political logic and control even in the midst of a sweeping struggle for the nation's future. The primary goal of the Federal government remained the restoration of the Union, not the devastation of the South. Intertwined with a political logic, and sometimes indistinguishable from it, was also a deep sense of moral justice – a belief that whatever the claims of military necessity, the innocent deserved some pity, and that even the guilty should suffer in rough proportion to the extent of their sins. Through comparisons with earlier European wars and the testimony of Union soldiers and Southern civilians alike, Grimsley shows that Union soldiers exercised restraint even as they made war against the Confederate civilian population.

The hard hand of war
Union military policy toward Southern civilians, 1861–1865

MARK GRIMSLEY

The Ohio State University

CAMBRIDGE
UNIVERSITY PRESS

Published by the Press Syndicate of the University of Cambridge
The Pitt Building, Trumpington Street, Cambridge CB2 1RP
40 West 20th Street, New York, NY 10011-4211, USA
10 Stamford Road, Oakleigh, Melbourne 3166, Australia

First published 1995
Reprinted 1996

Printed in the United States of America

Library of Congress Cataloging-in-Publication Data is available

A catalogue record for this book is available from the British Library

ISBN 0-521-46257-6 hardback

For my teachers:
Billie Cranford, Inez Curry,
and Williamson Murray

Contents

Contents

Acknowledgments

Many people helped with this book. Allan R. Millett and Williamson Murray of The Ohio State University, who jointly directed the dissertation on which it is based, gave me both warm encouragement and a large degree of independence. James M. McPherson took time from his demanding schedule to serve on the dissertation committee. Timothy S. Hartley and Peter Maslowski read the completed dissertation and offered keen criticisms that greatly assisted me in turning it into a book. Two reviewers refereed the manuscript for Cambridge University Press and made useful suggestions. To them, my thanks. Chapter 6 benefited from a faculty workshop organized by Michael Les Benedict of The Ohio State University.

One of the most helpful ways to approach this subject was by a comparative look at the wars of late medieval and early modern Europe. As the reader will see, this perspective suggested a somewhat different picture of the Federal "hard war" policy than the one most commonly portrayed. For guidance to these European antecedents, I am grateful to John A. Lynn, Geoffrey Parker, and Clifford J. Rogers.

No significant Civil War research could be accomplished without the patience and dedication of the people who administer the major libraries and archives of the United States. I would like to thank the staffs of the National Archives and Library of Congress in Washington, D.C.; the Ohio Historical Society, Columbus; the Western Reserve Historical Society, Cleveland; the U.S. Army Military History Institute, Carlisle Barracks, Pennsylvania; the Virginia Historical Society, Richmond; the Manuscripts Reading Room, William Perkins Library, Duke University, Durham, North Carolina; and the Southern Historical Collection, University of North Carolina, Chapel Hill. Nor could serious research be done without time and money. A dissertation fellowship and later a faculty Seed Grant, both awarded by The Ohio State University, provided me with both, as did a research grant from the Virginia Historical Society.

Then too it is useful to have access to the research notes and collections of one's fellow historians. Stephen W. Sears generously made available a microfilm roll of McClellan-related correspondence. James M. McPherson culled his extensive notes for manuscript material that might be helpful to me. And Todd D. Miller permitted me to use several Civil War letters from his personal collection.

Acknowledgments

As the book moved into production, I received cordial and highly professional assistance from several quarters. Ronald McLean of The Ohio State University prepared the excellent maps that accompany the text. Dyon Stephanon of *Civil War Times Illustrated* took time from his regular work to help me secure most of the illustrations. Ronald Cohen did a most capable job of copyediting the manuscript. And Frank Smith of Cambridge University Press has been the sort of editor every author appreciates.

Finally, I want to thank three individuals without whose early support I would long ago have begun to earn a decent living, albeit in some line of work less satisfying than the one they gave me the courage to pursue. At age twenty, I promised myself that I would dedicate my first book to Billie Cranford, Inez Curry, and Williamson Murray. Many others have helped me generously in the years since then. Some of them are mentioned here. But these three came before anyone else. They were the ones who shaped my desire, first to become a writer, then to become a historian. As my ninth grade English teacher, Billie Cranford supported both my writing and historical interests, encouraged me to think in terms of publication, and even excused me from regular assignments to undertake an independent writing project that formed my first attempt to grapple with the sweep of the Civil War. In my senior year in high school, Inez Curry's creative writing class sharpened my love for shaping thoughts and images on paper. She also helped me with what would become my first published article, and for years thereafter read a number of my other manuscripts with a practiced, discerning eye. Williamson Murray took a freshman political science major, convinced him that "you think like a historian, not a social scientist" – whatever that meant – and spent the next decade patiently waiting for that distracted undergraduate to settle down to serious study. The debt I owe each of these people is incalculable. I am profoundly grateful for the difference they have made in my life.

Maps and Illustrations

Abbreviations Used in Footnotes

CWMC   Civil War Miscellaneous Collection (USAMHI)
CWTIC   Civil War Times Illustrated Collection (USAMHI)
DUL   Special Collections, Perkins Library, Duke University, Durham,
          North Carolina
HCWRTC   Harrisburg Civil War Round Table Collection (USAMHI)
HEHL   Henry E. Huntington Library, San Marino, California
ILHS   Illinois Historical Society, Springfield
LC   Library of Congress, Washington, D.C.
MNHS   Minnesota Historical Society, St. Paul
MOHS   Missouri Historical Society, Saint Louis
NYHS   New York Historical Society, New York
OHS   Ohio Historical Society, Columbus
OR   *War of the Rebellion: A Compilation of the Official Records of the Union
          and Confederate Armies,* 128 vols. Washington: Government
          Printing Office, 1880–1901
SHC   Southern Historical Collection, Wilson Library, University of
          North Carolina at Chapel Hill
USAMHI   U. S. Army Military History Institute, Carlisle Barracks,
          Pennsylvania
UW   University of Washington, Seattle
VHS   Virginia Historical Society, Richmond
WRHS   Western Reserve Historical Society, Cleveland

Introduction

On a raw Christmas Day in 1864, fifteen-year old William Nalle rushed to his grandmother's farm in Culpeper County, Virginia. Federal cavalrymen had just swept through the neighborhood. William knew some of them personally; they had wintered near his home the previous year. Now they had come back, and in the words of the horsemen's commander, "thoroughly cleaned [the countryside] of stock and forage." They had done more than that. Reaching his grandmother's home, young Nalle beheld "a spectacle I shall not shortly forget." The farm had indeed been stripped of stock and forage; in the process, some of the doors had been wrenched off and the entire place ransacked as Union troopers had searched for provisions. Some of them, William recorded in his diary, had even grabbed his grandmother by the collar and unsuccessfully demanded money. Others had stolen clothing from the slaves living on the farm and forced "an old colored man (whom they had stripped) [to] stand out and try to dance." All in all, the experience had been terrifying. And, William noted, "every body within three or four miles of the road on which the yankees passed was treated just as bad and in [a] great many cases much worse."[1]

The fate that befell William's grandmother, her slaves, and her neighbors was shared by thousands of Southern civilians during the American Civil War. Then and later, white Southerners recalled the fear and humiliation of their ordeal with a bitterness that still resonates after more than a century. Even in 1994 – 130 years after William T. Sherman began his famous March to the Sea – the North Carolina Secretary of Cultural Resources could still threaten to block a proposed monument to Sherman's soldiers at Bentonville, the state's principal Civil War battleground. The troops, she said, had been commanded by a man "more evil than Ivan the Terrible or Genghis Khan." The state commander of the Sons of Confederate Veterans agreed: "Monuments should be erected to heroes. These were no heroes. They were thieves, murderers, rapists, arsonists, trespassers."[2]

[1]Report of Maj. Gen. Alfred T. A. Torbert, December 28, 1864, U.S. War Department, *War of the Rebellion: A Compilation of the Official Records of the Union and Confederate Armies*, 128 vols. (Washington: Government Printing Office, 1880–1901), Series I, vol. 43, pt. 1, p. 679. Cited hereafter as OR. (Unless noted, all citations are to Series I.) Entry for December 25, 1864, William Nalle Diary, VHS. A list of abbreviations used in the footnotes is on page xii.

[2]"New Bentonville Battle Pits History, Memories," *Raleigh* (N.C.) *News and Observer,* May 29, 1994.

It is easy to chuckle at such unreconstructed sentiments. Yet they remain a cultural artifact of considerable power, and have helped to shape a view of Union military policy toward Southern civilians that distorts as much as it illuminates. The actual picture was considerably more complex. For example, sprinkled among scathing Southern descriptions of the coming of the Yankees one can also find accounts like that of John Brown, a judge living in Camden, Arkansas. He headed his diary entry for April 15, 1864, "THE AWFUL DAY OF ALL DAYS," as Union troops swept into town and carted off bacon, hams, and other foodstuffs. The loss of his provisions was bad enough, but far worse was the prospect of "what might and indeed was likely to happen, the sacking of my house and . . . probably personal violence and insults to my family. . . ." By evening, however, this apocalypse had yet to materialize, and after nine full days of Federal occupation Brown reported, "As good order as could be expected is preserved in the City – Indeed, better than I had expected." When the Federals departed, Brown estimated his losses at "about $1000 per day for the 12 days," a figure that included the value of several slaves who left with the Union armies. On the whole, however, he felt "quite easy" about his losses. His slaves had departed, his garden had been trampled, but no "personal violence or indignity" had occurred, and he still had enough provisions to feed his family.[3]

Brown was unusually philosophical about his experience. Yet although less traumatic than that of William Nalle's grandmother, his encounter with the Yankees was not wholly dissimilar. Both civilians had seen their food larders ransacked. Both had suffered damage and losses. But both had survived, their lives and homes intact. A Southern partisan might argue that they had nevertheless suffered needless trauma. A Northern partisan could respond that they got off lightly. And each could debate endlessly the typicality of either experience. From a historical perspective, however, it is less interesting to distribute praise or blame than to note the obvious combination of severity and restraint, and to ask what such a phenomenon can mean.

In this book, I will argue that it suggests the continual working of political logic even in a circumstance as volatile as the unleashing of armed men against a hostile population. Intertwined with the political logic, and sometimes indistinguishable from it, was also a deep sense of moral justice: a belief that whatever the claims of military necessity the innocent and helpless deserved some pity, and that even the guilty should suffer in rough proportion to the extent of their sins. As one might expect, such convictions were sometimes observed in the breach, and certainly what transpired as Union armies ranged the American South could be highly destructive even when carried out with discrimination. But it was seldom the wanton, wholesale fury of legend.

The North's ultimate "hard war" policy was very far from the program with which it had begun the conflict. In fact, initially the Federal government deliberately sought to exempt white Southerners from the burdens of war. Their constitutional rights were to be respected; their property was not to be touched. The Lincoln administra-

[3]Entries for April 15, 24, and 28, 1864, John Brown Diary, HCWRTC, USAMHI.

tion specifically renounced any intention of attacking slavery. The central assumption underlying the early policy was a faith that most white Southerners were lukewarm about secession, and if handled with forbearance, would withdraw their allegiance from the Confederacy once Union armies entered their midst. Not all Northern generals embraced this conciliatory policy, but most did, and it remained the dominant posture toward Southern civilians until the summer of 1862.

At that point, a series of Union military reversals convinced many Northerners to abandon conciliation. The Lincoln administration encouraged field commanders to seize Southern property that might be useful to their operations. In September 1862 it issued its preliminary Emancipation Proclamation. The decision to free Confederate slaves firmly repudiated the conciliatory policy; it also signaled that the war thenceforth would be prosecuted with less regard for its effect on Southern society. Some feared it would unleash a racial war of outright extermination. But the Federal government maintained political control over the situation; its primary objective remained the restoration of the Union, not the devastation of the South.

Although the issuance of the Emancipation Proclamation destroyed conciliation as a major Federal policy, it did not immediately herald the birth of the hard war program of 1864–1865. The classic hard war operations that historians have found so striking had at least two main attributes. First, they were actions against Southern civilians and property made expressly in order to demoralize Southern civilians and ruin the Confederate economy, particularly its industries and transportation infrastructure. Second, they involved the allocation of substantial military resources to accomplish the job. Operations fitting these basic criteria did not surface in the western theater until at least April 1863. In the East and along the coast, they seldom made their appearance until much later – indeed, not until Grant became General-in-Chief and was able to impose his western concepts of warfare on commanders in the Virginia theater.

The conciliatory and hard war policies both possessed a strategic dimension. Each sought to detach Southern civilians from their allegiance to the Confederate government – the first through respect and magnanimity, the second through intimidation and fear. Between the conciliatory and hard war phases a third period intervened, a pragmatic interlude in which Union policy toward noncombatants had little strategic purpose. During this period, Union commanders sought victory exclusively on the battlefield; their stance toward civilians tended to be whatever seemed best calculated to produce operational success. They foraged when they needed to forage and retaliated when beset by guerrillas, but otherwise viewed civilians as peripheral to their concerns. This did not mean, however, that the political dimension was wholly lost. Official policy during this period came to discriminate between three kinds of Southern civilians – overt secessionists, neutral or passive individuals, and persons known to sympathize with the Union – and prescribed different treatments for each.

One must of course use care in imposing conceptions like conciliation, pragmatism, and hard war on a struggle that sprawled across thousands of miles of varied terrain, involved millions of individuals, and took four years to fight. Elements of all three policies were present from the war's outset, and remnants lingered to its conclusion. The shift should not be thought of in absolute terms, but rather in degree of emphasis. Conciliation was the primary policy from April 1861 until June 1862; pragmatism from July 1862 until about January 1864; and hard war from February 1864 until the war's end. Even then, the difference between the pragmatic policy and the subsequent hard war policy was never so clearly distinct as between conciliation and its competitors. Indeed in the western theater, where the pragmatic policy formed the crucible of subsequent hard war measures, the distinction tends to blur. It holds up better in the eastern theater, where commanders, particularly in the Army of the Potomac, clung to a conservative style of warfare much longer than did their western counterparts.

By the beginning of 1864, the Union high command had embraced a "strategy of raids" in which the Confederate economic infrastructure became a major target. Here too, however, political calculations persisted. The Northern armies continued to distinguish between Unionist, passive, and secessionist civilians. The hard hand of war descended most heavily on public property and the property of private persons who supported the Confederacy, especially the wealthy.

This three-way division among Southern civilians remained to the end of the conflict. So did orders that forbade wanton acts of destruction. And although much needless destruction occurred, it is remarkable that generally the policy held up. The war on Southern civilians did not degenerate into savagery compared with past European experience or white America's war on the Indians. The policy worked in part because statesmen and generals wished it so. But that was only part of the story. It also survived because tens of thousands of Union soldiers – toughened by war, hungry for creature comforts, and often angry at the civilians in their midst – nevertheless understood the logic and abided by it.

Indeed, throughout the war, the evolution of Union policy toward Southern civilians cannot be understood simply by looking at the prescriptions of high public officials. One must instead examine the interplay between formal directives issued at the top; informal attitudes held by Northern generals, private soldiers, and civilians; and the actions of Union forces in the field. This interplay helped shape and reshape Federal policy toward Southern civilians as it moved toward the hard war of the conflict's final years.

The phrase I have chosen to express this final stage – "hard war" – requires some explanation. I have preferred it to "total war," the term more frequently employed, for several reasons. First, although total war does connote the destructiveness of attacks on the economic resources of an enemy society, strictly speaking it embodies important other dimensions, such as the extensive mobilization of manpower and resources, which lie outside the scope of this book. A second reason to use an expression distinct from total war was so that I might emphasize the substantial continuities between Federal strategy and previous practice without having to apply total war to describe everything from the Hundred Years War to World War Two. Third, other historians

4

have used hard war to describe this form of warfare, which saved me the embarrassment of creating a completely novel label. Then too, the phrase had at least a limited contemporaneous usage, as in one observer's characterization of William T. Sherman: "He believes in hard war."[4]

Finally, the term hard war was expressive but not too exact. I needed something flexible enough to include operations aimed at the destruction of enemy economic resources (whether publicly or privately owned), forced evacuations, or confiscation of property without recompense. As will be seen, the range of operations that fit this description was too wide to conform easily to a more precise label. But most of these operations had one common element: the erosion of the enemy's will to resist by deliberately or concomitantly subjecting the civilian population to the pressures of war.

This book is a study of how the North came to choose such a policy, and what that policy was like in action. It does not, therefore, touch on all aspects of Union military policy toward Southern civilians. The Federal army's role in military government, wartime Reconstruction, and emancipation is a worthy subject I hope to explore in another book. But it lies outside the scope of this one, which confines itself to Federal military policy toward Southern civilians and property within the zone of active hostilities.

The book is not overtly concerned with ethical judgment or prescription. I am not interested in assessing the extent to which Federal units behaved legitimately, or the degree to which their actions swerved outside the bounds of accepted conduct. My purpose is different: I want to describe what was done, and examine the human web of decisions and attitudes that made it possible. Nevertheless, the issue of military attacks on noncombatants is, as it should be, a matter of grave moral concern. I believe I owe it to readers, when addressing a subject as fraught with moral implications as this, to briefly offer my personal perspective and thus alert them to my potential biases.

I believe in restraint in the conduct of war. It is sometimes tempting to echo Leo Tolstoy's scathing contempt toward those who "prate about the rules of warfare." "War," he makes Prince Andrei declare in *War and Peace*, "is not a polite recreation but the vilest thing in life, and we ought to understand that and not play at war." Nevertheless, however naive or even offensive the "ethics of war" may seem, in practice they are not dreamy ideals but simple reality. Those who wage war routinely seek to justify themselves on moral grounds, something they would hardly bother to do if moral claims did not matter. Union commanders and soldiers alike accepted those claims. Grant spoke of the destruction of civilian property as a "humane" policy that ultimately saved the lives of Federals and Confederates alike; Sherman said in

---

[4]For examples of the term "hard war," see Bruce Catton, *Grant Moves South* (Boston: Little, Brown and Company, 1960), 294, and James M. McPherson, *Battle Cry of Freedom: The Civil War Era* (New York and Oxford: Oxford University Press, 1988), 779. The quote is from Burke Davis, *Sherman's March* (New York: Random House, 1980), 9.

defense of his order exiling the citizens of Atlanta: "God will judge . . . whether it be more humane to fight with a town of women at our back or to remove them in time to places of safety among their own people."[5]

Above all, I believe in the principle of noncombatant immunity, the distinction drawn between the fighting man, who is a proper object for attack, and the civilian, who usually is not. This too is a distinction that soldiers in the Civil War period accepted and generally observed. At the same time, however, I do not believe that this principle can be made absolute. If military organizations are to be expected to conform to rules in warfare, those rules must provide them scope to perform their duties effectively; the rules must, in short, permit them to do what is truly necessary to win. Sometimes military necessity requires attacks of a kind that expose civilians to risk or their property to destruction. When such attacks are required, some sort of mediating principle is needed to reconcile the imperatives of noncombatant immunity and military necessity. I regard the principle of "double effect" as the most workable and satisfactory guideline. This is an old idea that goes back to the Catholic scholastics of the sixteenth century, but Michael Walzer has offered a good modern definition: "The intention of the actor is good, that is, he aims narrowly at the acceptable effect [i.e., a legitimate act of war]; the evil effect [death or severe hardship to noncombatants] is not one of his ends, nor is it a means to his ends, and, aware of the evil involved, he seeks to minimize it, accepting costs to himself."[6]

These are my own views. They are by no means universally shared, and they do not always coincide with those held by the actors in the Civil War. I have not consciously tried to impose them on the events described in these pages, although I have attempted to ascertain and express the moral beliefs actually held by participants in the conflict. Readers may judge for themselves how well I have succeeded.

[5]Leo Tolstoy, *War and Peace,* trans. Rosemary Edwards, 2 vols. (Harmondsworth, Middlesex, England: Penguin, 1957), vol. 2, p. 922; Ulysses S. Grant, *Personal Memoirs of U.S. Grant,* 2 vols. (New York: Charles Webster, 1885) vol. 1, p. 369. William T. Sherman, *Memoirs of General William T. Sherman,* 2 vols. in 1 (reprint edition; Westport, CT: Greenwood, 1974 [1875]), vol. 2, p. 125.

[6]Michael Walzer, *Just and Unjust Wars: A Moral Argument with Historical Illustrations* (paperback edition; Harmondsworth, Middlesex, England: Penguin, 1980 [1977]), 155.

The roots of a policy

"A reckless and unprincipled tyrant has invaded your soil," the proclamation raged. Heedless of moral and constitutional restraint, Abraham Lincoln had hurled his "abolition hosts" into northern Virginia, murdering civilians, seizing private property, "and committing other acts of violence and outrage too shocking and revolting to humanity to be enumerated." The Northern invaders had abandoned all rules of civilized warfare. "[T]hey proclaim by their acts, if not on their banners, that their war-cry is 'Beauty and booty.'"[1]

Addressed to the people of northern Virginia and dated June 5, 1861, this purple missive took flight from the pen of Confederate General P.G.T. Beauregard, hero of Fort Sumter and newly appointed commander of the defenses at Manassas Junction. In the innocent morning of the American Civil War – the bombardment of the fort had killed no one, and scarcely anyone had perished since – such grotesqueries were not uncommon. Few, however, were more thoroughly out of tune with reality. Twenty-five miles from Manassas, the leader of the "abolition hosts," Brigadier General Irvin McDowell, had a very different sense of his purpose and methods. He had made his headquarters in the shade of a mansion on Arlington Heights. Far from pillaging the handsome residence, he had composed a polite letter to its owner, the wife of Confederate General Robert E. Lee. A guard had been placed around the house, McDowell assured her, and an officer was living on the lower floor to insure its being respected. As for himself, "I am here temporarily in camp on the grounds, preferring this to sleeping in the house, under the circumstances which the painful state of the country places me with respect to its proprietors."[2]

It was a chivalrous letter, but much more than chivalry was at work. Beauregard's blandishments to the contrary, McDowell's government sought not only to embrace but to exceed the rules of civilized warfare, and thereby demonstrate that Southern civilians had nothing to fear from Northern armies. As an order to Union soldiers put it in worthy counterpoint to the indignant charges of the rebel commander, a "turbulent faction" had seized control of Virginia and sought to inaugurate a "reign of

[1]"To the good People of the Counties of Loudoun, Fairfax, and Prince William," June 5, 1861, OR 2:907.
[2]Irvin McDowell to Mrs. R.E. Lee, May 30, 1861, ibid., 655.

terror" over loyal citizens. "You are going on American soil . . . ," the order counseled. "You must bear in mind that you are going for the good of the whole country, and that while it is your duty to punish sedition, you must protect the loyal, and, should occasion offer, at once suppress servile insurrection." And they would go gently. For property damaged by unruly soldiers, McDowell established a system to indemnify the owners; for houses occupied for military use and wood cut for soldiers' campfires he asked the War Department to pay rent and compensation.[3]

The logic behind such a policy was simple. Shakespeare put it succinctly in *Henry V*: "[W]hen lenity and cruelty play for a kingdom, the gentlest gamester is the soonest winner." Each Union soldier, declared a Boston newspaper, "can exert incalculable influence in favor of a permanent peace after the shock of battle has subsided, by his demeanor toward belligerents. It will not be too much to say that the length of the war will be determined, as much by the behavior of the loyal forces, when not employed in actual fighting, as on the field of strife." In 1861, many Northerners thought such a posture made excellent sense. The perceived nature of the rebellion, the status of contemporary legal prescription, and the inheritance of previous American military experience all testified to its wisdom.[4]

THE NATURE OF THE REBELLION

Perhaps the principal reason Northerners resisted the idea of making war on Southern civilians was that it seemed unnecessary, even counterproductive, to do so. Few thought the Confederacy enjoyed widespread support; most believed that pockets of staunch Unionism still existed throughout the South, and that the majority of those who professed loyalty to the Confederate government were either lukewarm in their support or else ignorant and deluded. "Wrongly or rightly," noted one foreign observer in September 1861, "[the Northern people] affect to believe that the South has been led astray by the conspiracy of only a few leaders, for whom they reserve all their anger." If this were true, Union armies could expect to be welcomed by a sizeable element of the Southern population. Cowed into submission or seduced by the apparent triumph of secession, these wayward countrymen would recover their loyalty as soon as the Federal government demonstrated its resolve to maintain the Constitution and enforce the law.[5]

In some respects, the faith in widespread Southern Unionism seemed difficult to support. The seceded states, after all, had withdrawn by the expressed will of popularly elected state legislatures and conventions. That certainly implied a broad foun-

[3]"To the United States Troops of this Department," June 3, 1861, ibid., 662; McDowell to E.D. Townsend, May 29, 1861, ibid., 653.

[4]*Boston Evening Transcript,* July 19, 1861.

[5]Entry for September 16, 1861, Comte de Paris Journal, typescript copy in the possession of the author. The original journal is in the possession of the Fondation Saint-Louis, Amboise, France. A typescript copy may be consulted at the U.S. Army Military History Institute, Carlisle Barracks, Pennsylvania.

dation of approval, as Northerners sympathetic to the South pointed out to their more bloody-minded peers. But many Northerners – and most Republicans – subscribed to the theory that the South had been hoodwinked into secession by a comparative handful of men, a wealthy slaveholding aristocracy styled, in the melodramatic political rhetoric of the period, the Slave Power Conspiracy. According to this view, the wealthiest slaveholders in the South, although a small minority of its white population, controlled the balance through their domination of social and political life. "One class of citizens is accustomed to rule," declared Carl Schurz in 1858, "and the other to obey."[6]

Although this was a gross simplification of political conditions in the South, it formed a staple component of Northern political perceptions in the antebellum period. The Nullification Crisis, the War with Mexico, the filibuster expeditions to Central America, the Ostend Manifesto, Kansas-Nebraska Act, Lecompton Constitution, and Dred Scott decision all had seemed to confirm the existence of a minority faction that through control of the national government, had regularly imposed its will upon a passive majority. Now, apparently stymied by the election of a free soil President, the same conspiracy had used its control of the state governments in the South to secede from the Union and establish an illegitimate, despotic Confederacy.[7]

The pervasiveness of the Slave Power myth made plausible the idea that most Southerners had enjoyed little voice in the decision to leave the Union and simply accepted it as a fait accompli engineered by their social betters. Lincoln himself subscribed to this theory. As late as July 1861 he maintained, "It may well be doubted whether there is, to-day, a majority of the legally qualified voters of any State, except perhaps South Carolina, in favor of disunion. There is much reason to believe that the Union men are the majority in many, if not in every other one, of the so-called seceded States." The nature of the conflict, then, was not really a contest between two mobilized, committed societies. Rather, as Representative James M. Ashley of Ohio insisted, it was a "struggle between the people on one side, and a privileged class on the other."[8]

Given this view, it seemed pointless to invade the South with fire and sword. The notion that the soul of the rebellion reposed in a planter aristocracy made clear where the blade of vengeance should be thrust. James Shields, an Illinois Congressman turned general, summed up the popular view in a letter to Union General-in-Chief George B. McClellan in January 1862. "The Southern Government," Shields lectured, "is a military oligarchy. The head of the oligarchy is in Richmond, and when the head

---

[6]Carl Schurz, *Speeches of Carl Schurz* (Philadelphia: Lippincott, 1865), 11–12.

[7]For background on the belief in a Slave Power Conspiracy, see David Brion Davis, *The Slave Power Conspiracy and the Paranoid Style* (Baton Rouge: Louisiana State University Press, 1969), passim.; and Eric Foner, *Free Soil, Free Labor, Free Men: The Ideology of the Republican Party Before the Civil War* (New York and London: Oxford University Press, 1970), 88–102.

[8]"Message to Congress in Special Session," July 4, 1861, Roy P. Basler (ed.), *The Collected Works of Abraham Lincoln*, 8 volumes and index (New Brunswick, NJ: Rutgers University Press, 1953), vol. 4, p. 437. Ashley's statement is quoted in Kenneth M. Stampp, *And the War Came: The North and the Secession Crisis, 1860–1861* (Baton Rouge: Louisiana State University Press, 1950), 254.

falls a Union sentiment will be bound to burst forth in the South, which will soon entomb the body of this foul conspiracy."[9]

Shields was a Democrat, not a Republican, and his characterization of the Confederate government as a "military oligarchy," coupled with his prediction of a massive outpouring of Union sentiment in the South, indicated how extensive was the belief among Northerners that the rebellion lacked popular support. Many others held that such support as did exist was brittle and could be readily overthrown. Edward Bates, Lincoln's Attorney General and a prominent conservative, thought an effective naval blockade would suffice to defeat the Confederacy. "Their people are high spirited and ready enough to fight," he told the President in April 1861, "but impatient of control and unable to bear the steady and persistent pressure which we can easily impose and which they have no means to resist."[10]

As a conservative, Bates was also suspicious of the sweeping changes that might accompany a destructive invasion, particularly the specter of a murderous slave uprising. He hoped "to conduct the war [so] as to give the least occasion for social and servile war, in the extreme Southern States, and to disturb as little as possible the accustomed occupations of the people." Other conservatives agreed and argued, moreover, that severe measures would only provoke the South to greater resistance. Speaking out against a proposed confiscation bill in August 1861, Senator John Crittenden of Kentucky insisted that "these laws will have no efficacy in war. Their only effect will be to stimulate your adversaries to still more desperate measures. . . . The experiment has been tried by other countries. England tried it upon Ireland, and she reaped the reward of it in hundreds of years of intestine war." Union Brigadier General George G. Meade concurred. "Let the ultras on both sides be repudiated," he wrote his wife, "and the masses of conservative and moderate men may compromise and settle the difficulty."[11]

The antislavery "ultras," of course, felt differently. In their minds, it made little sense to oppose a rebellion without also attacking the institution that lay at the heart of it. Unlike their more moderate colleagues, however, they believed – or at least affected to believe – that such a step would not stiffen Confederate resistance. A policy of emancipation would hardly be conciliatory. Even so it did not require Union armies to sweep into Southern territory and devastate the region's economy. Indeed, during the war's first year the Radical Republicans advocated such a policy no more than anyone else, although they frequently voiced their readiness for harsh measures if necessary. What they wanted from Union commanders was prompt, vigorous military action – but action aimed at destroying rebel armies and seizing rebel cities, not the visitation of deliberate hardship on Southern civilians.

[9]Shields to McClellan, January 28, 1862, OR 5:700–702.

[10]"Memorandum," April 15, 1861, Howard K. Beale, ed., *The Diary of Edward Bates, 1859–1866,* American Historical Association Report, 1930 (Washington: Government Printing Office, 1933), 183.

[11]Ibid; U.S. Congress, *Congressional Globe,* 37th Congress, 1st session (Washington: Government Printing Office, 1861), 412; Meade to Mrs. Meade, November 24, 1861, in George Gordon Meade, ed., *The Life and Letters of George Gordon Meade,* 2 vols. (New York: Charles Scribner's Sons, 1913), vol. 1, pp. 230–231.

The supposed existence of a Slave Power Conspiracy not only offered insight into the apparent nature of the rebellion, and therefore into the measures appropriate for its suppression, but also served as a powerful ideological tool to vindicate the justice of Northern efforts to subdue it. Misguided as many Northerners perceived the Southern rebellion to be, like all Americans they had imbibed from childhood an unquestioned belief in the right of revolution. It had after all been vindicated with the blood of their ancestors and enshrined in the Declaration of Independence. When Southerners deployed the right of revolution to justify their own rebellion, Northerners found it slightly baffling. At a visceral level, most rejected it out of hand, but on a rational plane it remained an awkward assertion to rebut. That was one reason the Lincoln administration insisted on drawing a distinction – obscure to the vanishing point but nevertheless useful – between crude "coercion," which had the taint of tyranny, and just enforcement of the laws. When Union men joined the colors, they often did so with this distinction in mind. The belief that a Southern aristocracy had engineered the rebellion was not only an estimate of the nature of the rebellion, but also an important instrument for assuring Northern men that their cause was ideologically pure. They were not coercing an entire people that had consciously and deliberately exercised its right of revolution, but rather were preserving the Union against the machinations of a dark conspiracy. They could even imagine themselves acting on behalf of the common people of the South – who were, after all, the ignorant, deluded pawns of a planter aristocracy.[12]

LEGAL PRESCRIPTION

Domestic and international law formed a second, obvious guide for military conduct toward Southern civilians, although at first it was hard to decide what sort of law to apply. Was the conflict an insurrection like the 1794 Whiskey Rebellion, albeit on a far greater scale? The Federal government sometimes liked to portray it that way. Lincoln, in the proclamation issued after the firing on Fort Sumter, called for 75,000 troops to subdue "combinations too powerful to be suppressed by the ordinary course of judicial proceedings, or by the powers vested in the Marshals by law." Under such circumstances, the Constitution logically remained in full force, and thereby the protections extended to all citizens – Southerners as well as Northerners – under the due process clause of the Fifth Amendment. The war's primary object, Lincoln said, was simply the reoccupation of the government installations seized from the Union. He explicitly promised that "the utmost care will be observed, consistently with the objects aforesaid, to avoid any devastation, any destruction of, or interference with,

[12]"Proclamation Calling Forth Militia and Convening Congress," April 15, 1861, Basler (ed.), *Collected Works of Lincoln* 4:331–332. On the importance of this issue to Northerners, see Earl J. Hess, *Liberty, Virtue, and Progress: Northerners and Their War for the Union* (New York and London: New York University Press, 1988), 18–31.

property, or any disturbance of peaceful citizens in *any* part of the country."[13] [Emphasis supplied]

Taken literally, of course, such statements had a surreal quality about them. By June 1861, eleven states – a geographical expanse the size of western Europe with a white population of 5.5 million – had left the Union, inaugurated a new government, and fielded a large, well-equipped army. In most respects the ensuing warfare resembled a contest between two sovereign nations rather than a rebellion in the ordinary sense, and many thought it should be regarded as such, notwithstanding the Federal government's refusal to accept the legal existence of the Confederate States of America.

Vigorous debates on this issue fill the record of the United States Congress during the war's early years, especially its deliberations on two bills to confiscate rebel property. These debates on the proper characterization of the war, and whether the Constitution or the laws of war should have primacy in conducting it, were of more than academic import to the Union commanders charged with winning the conflict. They illustrated the powerful, often contradictory political currents with which they had to come to terms, currents that precipitated more than one general to an early retirement.

Conservatives as well as many moderates urged that whatever the technical status of the Confederacy, the conflict should be regarded as a struggle between two de facto nations. "A body of men can do in fact that which they have no right [i.e., secede and establish a separate nation]," argued a Republican Congressman from Pennsylvania. "An admission that they have done the unlawful act is no acknowledgement of its being right." A colleague from the Keystone State agreed. Since the South had organized a functional government and fielded a conventional army, "we are compelled to act, in most respects, towards them as if they were a foreign government of a thousand years' existence, between whom and us hostilities have broken out."[14]

Most advanced Republicans, however, insisted that the Constitution must continue to apply to Southerners. When Senator Lyman Trumbull, a Radical Republican from Illinois, introduced in December 1861 a "bill for confiscating the property, and giving freedom to the slaves, of rebels," he argued explicitly that the plea of military necessity was "the plea of tyrants. . . . I hold that under the Constitution the military is as much subject to the control of the civil power in war as in peace." Such a stance was necessary in order to provide a logical basis for the passage of laws designed to punish traitors, emancipate slaves, and confiscate property in such a way as to break the power of the planter aristocracy. Radical Republicans sought to enact legislation during wartime that would enable them to reconstruct Southern society once the war had ended.[15]

Conservatives, aware of the radicals' agenda, insisted that the executive branch

---

[13]"Proclamation Calling Forth Militia and Convening Congress," April 15, 1861, Basler (ed.), *Collected Works of Lincoln* 4:332. The wording was carefully chosen to conform to the Militia Act of 1792.

[14]*Congressional Globe*, 37th Congress, 2d session, pt. 4, appendix, p. 168; ibid., pt. 3, p. 2299.

[15]Ibid., pt. 1, p. 18.

already enjoyed full authority to confiscate property through operation of its war powers and the plea of military necessity; Congress thus had no legitimate role to play. And they sometimes waxed eloquent in depicting the terrors that might be loosed in the name of military necessity. According to Senator Orville Browning, a conservative Republican from Illinois:

It may become a military necessity, as an army marches through the enemy's country, to waste and devastate it, and leave only ruin and desolation behind to signalize its passage. It may become a military necessity, upon the surrender of a beleaguered city, to give it up to pillage and plunder, or to wrap it in flames and reduce it to a smoldering and blackened heap of ruin. . . . It may become a military necessity to refuse quarter in battle, or to put to the sword all the prisoners who may be captured.

Browning, of course, neither believed nor desired that Federal commanders would pursue such a heartless policy. His real point was to deny that Congress had any right to pass legislation concerning what might or might not be done to Southern civilians: "These necessities can be determined only by the military commander, and to him the Constitution has intrusted the prerogative of judging of them."[16]

Thus, in their characterizations of the struggle, conservatives and radicals found themselves espousing doctrines that, taken at face value, ran counter to the way they really desired the war to be fought. Conservatives, hoping for a conflict that would be limited in its impact on the South, preferred an interpretation that actually gave Union commanders wide latitude to wreak havoc on Southern society if military necessity seemed to require it. Radicals, who wanted bold, vigorous, determined action, insisted on a characterization that left the Constitution in full force.

As the tangled Reconstruction experience would eventually underscore, Union statesmen never entirely settled the precise legal status of the rebellion. It is therefore not surprising that many officers adopted informal guidelines that weaved back and forth between the acknowledgement of certain Constitutional protections, extending at least to demonstrably loyal Southern civilians; and policies built largely on the basis of military necessity.

Even so, as a practical matter the war did resemble a conflict between two sovereign nations, and in many respects the Federal government treated it as such. From the outset of the conflict, despite its firm insistence that the Confederacy enjoyed no legal existence, it behaved as if the Southern nation enjoyed belligerent rights. Union commanders granted prisoner-of-war status to captured rebel soldiers and sailors, arranged battlefield truces with their Confederate counterparts, and even negotiated a cartel for the regular exchange of military captives. Both sides asserted repeatedly that they were conducting the struggle according to the established laws and usages of war (usually in the course of accusing the other side of violating those same norms). It thus seemed natural, as a corollary, for Union commanders to regard Southern civilians as de facto subjects of a foreign government, at least concerning the sort of military measures that might be permissible against them. Although numerous commentaries

[16]Ibid., pt. 4, p. 2918.

on the laws of war were available, Congressmen and generals generally consulted the work of the Swiss jurist Emmerich de Vattel. First published in 1758, his magnum opus, *The Law of Nations,* still remained a standard authority on the subject.

Legal scholars in the field of international law draw a distinction between *lex lata* – the law as it is, expressed through treaties and protocols, and *lex ferenda* – the law as it ought to be. In relation to the law of land warfare, the first category acquired no substantial body of material until the Hague Conventions of 1899. Vattel's work, like that of other commentators, fell largely into the second category. Less a compendium of binding international agreements than a lengthy essay in practical moral philosophy, its influence derived from the belief, dating back to classical times, that certain fundamental moral ideas were self-evident. Societal prohibitions against murder, theft, and dishonesty, for example, did not necessarily derive from a specific religious world-view; they were universally valid ethical precepts that could be deduced from the social order. Most educated persons, until the so-called "collapse of moral consensus" in the twentieth century, accepted this view without question. These precepts, when modified to take into account the qualities that distinguished political states from individual persons, became the "law of peoples" – the Latin *jus gentium* or, as the term appeared in English translation, the "law of nations."[17]

About a quarter of Vattel's book dealt specifically with the law of nations as it related to warfare. Anyone consulting it for the most appropriate characterization of the Southern rebellion would have come upon this passage: "When a nation becomes divided into two parties absolutely independent, and no longer acknowledging a common superior, the state is dissolved, and the war between the two parties stands on the same ground, in every respect, as a public war." (A Republican Congressman, in fact, quoted this passage in a speech on the House floor, adding, "This is in reality the principle now governing the case.") What implications did this have for the treatment of Southern civilians?[18]

In theory, Vattel considered the subjects of an enemy state to be enemies themselves, albeit noncombatants. As such, their persons were not inviolate, and military commanders could subject them to "every measure" calculated to weaken the enemy state, "provided they be not of an odious kind, nor unjustifiable in themselves, and prohibited by the law of nature." But Vattel quickly excepted "women, children, feeble old men, and sick persons." These, he said, "are enemies who make no resistance; and consequently we have no right to mistreat their persons, or use any violence against them, much less to take away their lives."[19]

---

[17]For a discussion of *lex ferenda* and *lex lata,* see James Turner Johnson, *Just War Tradition and the Restraint of War: A Moral and Historical Inquiry* (Princeton, NJ: Princeton University Press, 1981), 86–88. Barrie Paskins, *The Ethics of War* (London: Duckworth, 1979), 202–208, critiques the concept of natural law. (See also Johnson, *Just War Tradition,* 85–120.) Definitions of the "law of nations" vary. The one used here is Vattel's own. See Emmerich de Vattel, *The Law of Nations, or, Principles of the Law of Nature Applied to the Conduct and Affairs of Nations and Sovereigns* (revised edition; London: G.G. and J. Robinson, 1797), iii–xx.

[18]Ibid., 427. Book III, Ch. 28, para. 295; *Congressional Globe,* 37th Congress, 2d session, pt. 1, p. 82.

[19]Vattel, *Law of Nations,* 321 (Book III, Ch. 5, paras. 69–70); ibid., p. 347 (Book III, Ch. 8, para. 138; ibid., 351–52 (Book III, ch. 8, para. 145).

Vattel then went on to extend this exception to other noncombatants as well. The normative state of affairs in his own time, he wrote, was for war to be carried on only by regular troops:

[T]he people, the peasants, the citizens, take no part in it, and generally have nothing to fear from the sword of the enemy. Provided the inhabitants submit to him who is master of the country, pay the contributions imposed, and refrain from all hostilities, they live in as perfect safety as if they were friends: they even continue in possession of what belongs to them.

Such forbearance, he continued, had practical advantages for the occupying commander who, by protecting noncombatants and keeping his troops well-disciplined, "procures an easy subsistence for his army, and avoids many evils and dangers."[20]

Concerning the property of enemy civilians, Vattel permitted greater latitude than was the case with enemy lives. "We have a right to deprive our enemy of his possessions, of every thing which may augment his strength and enable him to make war." This right extended both to the levying of forced contributions and the waste and destruction of provisions within a locality in order to deny them to the enemy. Even so, the right of devastation was not absolute: "Those who tear up the vines and cut down the fruit trees, are looked upon as savage barbarians. . . . They desolate a country for many years to come, and beyond what their own safety requires. Such a conduct is not dictated by prudence, but by hatred and fury."[21]

In general, then, Vattel enjoined a code of conduct that exempted enemy civilians, as far as possible, from the severities of war. The exemption, as it affected property, was ultimately utilitarian in nature. "If you once open a door for continual accusations of outrageous excess in hostilities," he warned, "you will only augment the number of complaints, and inflame the minds of the contending parties with increasing animosity: fresh injuries will be perpetually springing up; and the sword will never be sheathed till one of the parties be utterly destroyed."[22]

The mild treatment accorded civilians, however, hinged on the fact that although they were enemies in a technical sense, they played no role in the struggle. If the general population committed any hostilities, the invader was entitled to show them no mercy, and could hang them "as he would so many robbers or banditti." Vattel's injunction thus forbade guerrilla warfare carried on by private citizens.[23]

In addition to Vattel's *Law of Nations,* anyone interested might also have turned to a fat new volume, just published in May 1861, entitled *International Law; or, Rules Regulating the Intercourse of States in Peace and War.* The author was Henry Wager Halleck, a San Francisco lawyer and former army officer. Returning to active duty when the war broke out, Halleck acquired a major general's commission, and became General-in-Chief of the Union armies in July 1862. Hence, *International Law* offers a

---

[20]Ibid., 352–53 (para. 147).
[21]Ibid., 364. Ch. 9, para. 161.
[22]Ibid., 369. Bk. III, ch. 9, para. 173; ibid., 367. para. 166.
[23]Ibid. Ch. 15, para. 226.

wealth of insight into the views of one of the Federal army's most important commanders.[24]

According to Halleck's taxonomy of war, the Civil War readily qualified as a "war of revolution" – similar to that undertaken by the American colonists in 1776 or by the Italians in 1860 – by virtue of its aim, "the dismemberment of the state." The conflict, however, also readily qualified as a "national war" because both the established and insurgent governments possessed established territories and deployed regularly constituted armies. He made it clear that "where such insurgent militia are called into the field, they are entitled to all the rights of war, and are subject to its duties and responsibilities." But Halleck offered no scope for guerrilla activity outside the authority of a belligerent state. Self-constituted partisan bands enjoyed none of the rights of war. "Their acts are unlawful; and, when captured, they are not treated as prisoners of war, but as criminals, subject to the punishment due to their crimes."[25]

Heavily indebted to Vattel, Halleck agreed with him that the subjects of an enemy government, although technically enemies, should be exempt from the severities of war as far as possible. This exemption extended not only to the lives of noncombatants but also to private property – which, he wrote, "is now, as a general rule, exempt from seizure or confiscation; and this general exemption extends even to cases of absolute and unqualified conquest. . . ." Private property could not be taken without compensation except in three specified instances: "1st, confiscations or seizures by way of penalty for military offenses; 2d, forced contributions for the support of the invading armies, or as indemnity for the expenses of maintaining order, and affording protection to the conquered inhabitants; and 3d, property taken on the field of battle, or in storming a fortress or town."[26]

Throughout the Civil War, Halleck as well as numerous other commanders would make use of the first exception in order to punish communities for guerrilla activities committed in their midst. Although he thought it best to discover and punish only the guilty individuals when possible, it was still a general law of war that communities were to be held accountable for the acts of their individual members. This, he explained, "makes it the interest of all to discover the guilty persons, and deliver them up to justice." (Interestingly, Halleck specified that monetary contributions were the usual punishment to be imposed on a community in such instances. He said nothing about the taking of hostages or the burning of private houses – remedies frequently employed by Union forces.[27])

While Halleck acknowledged the right of military commanders to seize contributions from the countryside for subsistence or to permit their troops simply to live off the land, he regarded both expedients with distaste, especially large-scale foraging. It

---

[24]Henry W. Halleck, *International Law; or, Rules Regulating the Intercourse of States in Peace and War* (New York: D. Van Nostrand, 1861).

[25]Halleck, *International Law,* 331. Ch. XIV, para. 5. Ibid., 334. para. 10. Ibid., 386–387. Ch. XVI, para. 8.

[26]Ibid., 446. Ch. XIX, para. 1. Ibid., 456. para. 12.Ibid., 457. para. 13.

[27]Ibid., 458. para. 14.

inevitably degenerated into out-and-out pillaging, with the result that ordinarily peaceful civilians were converted into "bitter and implacable enemies. The system is, therefore, regarded as both impolitic and unjust, and is coming into general disuse among the most civilized nations."[28]

In short, both Vattel and Halleck, while conceding that armies had the option of foraging from civilians and destroying their property, viewed such practices as throwbacks to an older, less enlightened time. As understood in 1861, therefore, the laws and usages of war served as strong reinforcement for a civilian policy based on conciliation.

HISTORICAL EXPERIENCE

As proof of the danger of expedients such as foraging, Halleck pointed to the disasters that had accompanied their use by Napoleon's armies in Spain during the period 1808–1813. On that occasion, the Spanish people had risen up in a large-scale guerrilla war that harried the French at every turn, bled the Grand Army heavily, and ultimately played a signal role in the ejection of the Napoleonic regime from the Spanish throne. Although not well-understood even fifty years later, the memory of this people's war horrified professional officers, who warned against unleashing such savagery in the future. Baron Antoine de Jomini, the foremost military analyst of the day, warned that such conflicts "are the most formidable of all." Their consequences, he continued, "are so terrible that, for the sake of humanity, we ought to hope never to see it."[29]

Historical experiences of this kind were the third element that shaped Union policy toward Southern civilians at the war's outset. In forming their ideas about warfare, Federal commanders looked primarily to three major conflicts: the War for American Independence, the Napoleonic Wars, and the War with Mexico. Together these struggles constituted the basic model of expectations for what should transpire in military operations. Each example seemed to suggest, for different reasons, that successful warmaking should concentrate on the battlefield. They provided little indication that a hard war strategy was either required or efficacious.

At first glance this seems surprising. An uncommonly fearsome variety of hard war characterized colonial warfare against the Amerindian population. In this respect, as John Shy and others have argued, American practice significantly diverged from contemporary European standards – although even Old World standards were not as mild as sometimes believed. Complete elimination of the Amerindian threat was the preferred goal of the colonists, and one they occasionally managed to achieve, as in King Philip's War of 1675–1676. The desire for complete annihilation frequently extended to the threats posed by the French and Spanish colonies as well. Yet despite

[28]Ibid., 459. para. 15.
[29]Baron Henri Jomini, *The Art of War,* trans. by G.H. Mendell and W.P. Craighill (Reprint Edition; Westport, CT: Greenwood Press, 1971 [1862]), 29.

the totality of the desired objective in conflicts with both Amerindians and rival colonists, American military practice differed markedly in the means permissible to achieve this end. Race was the determining factor. Where Amerindians were concerned, colonists seldom hesitated to visit complete destruction on villages; they often killed women and children as well as warriors. In their struggles with the French and Spanish, however, Americans generally followed contemporary European practice: They concentrated their efforts on the opposing military forces, employed orthodox tactics, and left the civilian population more or less alone.[30]

The persistence of this two-tier American way of war can be confirmed by even the most cursory glance at the Federal government's handling of Native American uprisings during the Civil War. In October 1862, for example, the commander of the Department of New Mexico, intent upon curbing the Mescalero Apache in his district, matter-of-factly instructed one of his colonels that "all men of that tribe are to be killed whenever and wherever found." Soon afterward, in the wake of a major Sioux revolt in Minnesota, more than 1,700 Santee Indians – mostly women and children – were taken prisoner, and later assaulted by civilian mobs while being marched into captivity. Thirty-eight ringleaders of the Sioux uprising were tried and hanged. (The department commander wanted to hang more than 300.) And in 1864, over 200 Cheyenne and Arapaho men, women, and children were slaughtered in the infamous Sand Creek Massacre. To equate such viciously lethal actions with those meted out to Southern civilians would be completely inappropriate.[31]

Instead, Union norms of conduct were guided much more by those adopted by American colonists during the War of Independence. Although in many respects this was truly a "people's war" without European parallel until a generation or so later, the revolutionaries consciously eschewed a strategy based on guerrilla warfare and relied as far as possible on a conventional force organized, equipped, and trained along the lines of the British army. This militarily conservative strategy served primarily to emphasize the American government's claim to legitimacy, but it also avoided the sort of partisan struggle that might unleash a destructive, punitive British response against civilians and private property. To be sure, fighting of a guerrilla character did occur, and Southerners in particular treasured the memory of "men who left the plow at the enemy's approach and returned to it when he had been driven back." But

---

[30]See John Shy, "The American Military Experience: History and Learning," in his *A People Numerous and Armed: Reflections on the Military Struggle for American Independence* (New York and London: Oxford University Press, 1976), 227–254; and Don Higginbotham, "The Early American Way of War: Reconnaissance and Appraisal," *William and Mary Quarterly*, 3rd Series, Vol. 49, pp. 230–273. Allan R. Millett and Peter Maslowski, *For the Common Defense: A Military History of the United States of America* (New York: Free Press, 1983), 14–18; Francis Jennings, *The Invasion of America: Indians, Colonialism, and the Cant of Conquest* (New York: W.W. Norton, 1976 [1975]), *passim.*, esp. 146–170 and 202–227. The best account of the colonial wars is Ian K. Steele, *Warpaths: Invasions of North America* (New York and Oxford: Oxford University Press, 1994).

[31]Brig. Gen. James H. Carleton to Col. Christopher Carson, October 12, 1862, OR 15:579. A good brief account of Amerindian warfare during the Civil War years is Robert M. Utley, *Frontiersmen in Blue: The United States Army and the Indian, 1848–1865* (New York: Macmillan, 1967), 219–340.

Americans believed that independence had been won mainly by the efforts of the Continental Army and the militia, not by guerrillas.[32]

Following the American lead, the British employed a conservative strategy that targeted the rebel army, not the civilian population. Their rationale was similar to that of the Northern administration at the outbreak of the Civil War. Like Lincoln, the British government believed that most of the colonial population was loyal and that the revolution was largely the product of a few hotheads. "I never had an idea of subduing the Americans," one British general explained; "I meant to assist the good Americans to subdue the bad ones." Given this estimate of the situation, a conciliatory policy promised to extinguish the insurrection without producing undue bitterness on the part of the colonists. The Howe brothers in particular pursued this strategy, even to the point of permitting Washington's beaten army to escape after the battles around New York and offering generous pardons to rebels who gave themselves up. Although conciliation eventually proved ineffective, the British never moved, as did the North, to a hard war strategy.[33]

Even so, a number of episodes occurred that did display some of the elements of such a strategy. British forces burned a number of coastal towns and partly destroyed Richmond, Virginia, in 1781. Other British and mercenary troops, in their pursuit of Washington's retreating army across the New Jersey plains in the autumn of 1776, indulged in an orgy of pillaging that alienated the local population and scandalized their own officers. In South Carolina, Lieutenant Colonel Banastre Tarleton burned the homes and crops of Whig families, while Whigs and Tories grappled with one another in a savage, atrocity-strewn civil war. Along the western frontier, the use of Amerindian allies by the British produced a number of outrages that called forth a vengeful, relentless Whig response. In 1777, British-led Amerindian forces burned and pillaged hundreds of homes and fields in the Wyoming Valley of Pennsylvania. Two years later, the colonists returned the favor by leveling forty Amerindian villages, burning orchards, and destroying about 160,000 bushels of corn. Yet most of these operations, however fierce, had little military purpose. They reflected the ideological fury of a people's contest, not deliberate strategic choices.[34]

Even in the realm of logistics, the War of Independence displayed an unusually

[32]See Russell F. Weigley, *The American Way of War: A History of United States Military Strategy and Policy* (paperback edition, Bloomington: Indiana University Press, 1977), 3–17; Brigadier General Daniel Ruggles, CSA, to Major General Benjamin Butler, USA, July 15, 1862, OR 15:519–520.

[33]Sir William Howe, quoted in Troyer Steele Anderson, *The Command of the Howe Brothers During the American Revolution* (New York and London: Oxford University Press, 1936), 145; ibid., 134–135, 160–163. See also Maldwyn A. Jones, "Sir William Howe: Conventional Strategist," and Ira D. Gruber, "Richard Lord Howe: Admiral as Peacemaker," both in George Athan Billias, ed., *George Washington's Opponents: British Generals and Admirals in the American Revolution* (New York: William Morrow, 1969), 39–72, 233–259.

[34]Richard B. Morris, *Forging of the Union, 1781–1789* (New York: Harper and Row, 1987), 4; Don Higginbotham, *The War of American Independence: Military Attitudes, Policies and Practice, 1763–1789* (New York: MacMillan, 1971), 377; ibid, 164–165; [New York] Division of Archives and History, *The Sullivan-Clinton Campaign in 1779: Chronology and Selected Documents* (Albany: State University of New York, 1929), 159–168.

mild character. The British, despite an urgent need to supply themselves from the countryside, followed a policy of respect for civilian property in the interests of conciliation. Although it sometimes became necessary to requisition food, forage, and transportation from unwilling colonists, British officers paid for what they took and reverted to a system of voluntary supply as soon as practicable. American forces followed a similar system, although emergencies and a lack of hard currency often forced them to supply their wants by impressment.[35]

In one respect, however, the British did employ a measure whose adoption by Federal armies during the Civil War was taken to signal the onset of a "war of extermination": They attempted to liberate slaves or turn them against their masters. Nothing frightened Southern colonists more profoundly. James Madison considered it "the only part in which this Colony [Virginia] is vulnerable; & if we should be subdued, we shall fall like Achilles by the hand of one that knows the secret." Once the war broke out, the British tried to fulfill Madison's prediction by encouraging bondsmen to run away and by offering black men places in their irregular forces – a step the Lincoln administration avoided until the Civil War had raged for nearly eighteen months. They even went the North one better by actively courting the possibility of a large-scale slave revolt – after all, they would not have to live quite so close to the consequences. Surprisingly little came of these efforts, however. Although a considerable number of bondsmen left their masters during the conflict or even fought for the British, no slave insurrection of consequence erupted, and American slavery survived the war with scant harm. In this, as in other respects, the War of Independence lacked the obvious attributes of a truly hard war.[36]

Ultimately, when Americans looked back on the conflict, they saw it as having been decided by open combat on the battlefield, not by the destruction of economic resources or attacks on the civilian population. This perception is of critical importance, for despite the interposition of other military contests between the War of Independence and the Civil War, the glorious struggle of 1775–1783 retained a priority on American imagination and perceptions concerning the nature of war.[37]

Second in importance to the generation that fought the Civil War – and perhaps first to the professional officer corps who dominated the top commands – were the wars of Napoleon. The campaigns of the great Emperor, lovingly studied by a few West Pointers and vaguely worshipped by all, offered the promise of decisive battlefield success to any general who mastered the trick of Napoleonic maneuver. Here

---

[35]R. Arthur Bowler, *Logistics and the Failure of the British Army in America, 1775–1783* (Princeton, NJ: Princeton University Press, 1975), 78–81; Erna Risch, *Supplying Washington's Army.* Center of Military History, Special Studies (Washington, Government Printing Office, 1981), 20–23; E. Wayne Carp, *To Starve the Army at Pleasure: Continental Army Administration and American Political Culture, 1775–1783* (Chapel Hill: University of North Carolina Press, 1984), 53–98.

[36]Madison to William Bradford, June 19, 1775, in William T. Hutchinson and William M.E. Rachals (eds.), *The Papers of James Madison,* 16 vols. to date (Charlottesville: University Press of Virginia, 1962), vol. 1, p. 153; Sidney Kaplan, "The 'Domestic Insurrections' and the Declaration of Independence," *Journal of Negro History* 61 (1976):250–251.

[37]See Shy, "The American Military Experience," 238–240.

again, attacks on civilian persons and property seemed unnecessary and beside the point. Many American officers, however, missed one critical element of Napoleonic warfare. Despite the emphasis placed on audacious maneuver and shattering combat, the success of Napoleonic armies ultimately depended on their ability to derive sustenance from the countryside through which they passed. Hence the burden they placed on the civilians in their path was far from light, although Napoleon did make limited efforts to inaugurate a regularized system of supply. The resultant foraging operations were frequently disorderly and not readily distinguishable (from a civilian point of view) from the pillaging the authorities denigrated. Even so, this gritty reality remained very much the underside of the Napoleonic system, often overlooked amid the seductive prospect of the Austerlitz-style battle of annihilation. Once again, the battlefield seemed the quickest and most obvious route to victory.[38]

The third example available to Civil War commanders was that of the recently concluded conflict with Mexico, a struggle in which a sizeable number of them had been personally engaged. Here too – and far more consistently than in either the War of Independence or the Napoleonic Wars – the general policy had been one of restraint toward the civilian population. President James K. Polk initially endorsed such a policy as well-calculated to drive a wedge between the Mexican government and its people. Continued Mexican resistance after the early campaigns caused him to harden his stance somewhat, and his preferred policy went from liberal payment for supplies to one of contributions and outright seizure. However, his major field commanders, Generals Zachary Taylor and Winfield Scott, continued to follow a de facto policy of generous treatment. Scott in particular treated the native populations with kid gloves. In his decisive campaign against the Mexican capital, he followed a policy of painstaking restraint toward the civilian populations he encountered along his army's line of march. Scott's rationale stemmed less from excessive scrupulousness than from the prudent recognition that his lines of communication were both lengthy and tenuous. He could not afford an active partisan resistance in his rear. Hoping to avoid this, he bent every effort toward making his troops as inoffensive toward Mexican civilians as possible, even requiring his soldiers to salute local officials. The basis for Scott's military rules, General Order No. 20, emphasized an even-handed system of justice that sought as far as possible to preserve peacetime standards of order.[39] Such was the example that Scott's junior officers saw and frequently emulated, at least initially, when they assumed major assignments during the Civil War.

Yet, as in previous instances, the Mexican War experience also offered illustrations of a harsher policy. Despite the deliberate mildness of the American occupation, a few guerrilla outbreaks did occur, and when they did the Americans responded harshly. Taylor made Mexican citizens responsible for all such outrages committed in their

[38]See Martin van Creveld, *Supplying War: Logistics from Wallenstein to Patton* (Cambridge: Cambridge University Press, 1977), 40–74.

[39]Justin H. Smith, "American Rule in Mexico," *American Historical Review* 23 (January 1918):287, 292; Ralph H. Gabriel, "American Experience with Military Government," *American Historical Review* 49 (July 1944):633–37.

midst. He forced the people of Jalapa, for example, to pay $300 for every murder and meet the value of destroyed property. In Mexico City, when Scott's troops were sniped at, Scott threatened to level the city block from which fire was received. General John Worth did use his artillery in this fashion: "I caused the heavy guns to be turned against every house [from which a shot was fired] . . . and after a few hours of such appliance, not regarding where or who it hit, quelled the dastardly villains." Then too, after the end of hostilities, Scott imposed a $150,000 contribution on Mexico City, and also collected the usual taxes in every locale under American control.[40]

Even so, one can hardly regard even the more stringent American measures during the Mexican conflict as examples of hard war, and they had little influence beyond the moment. When American officers looked back on the conflict, they remembered Buena Vista and Cerro Gordo, not Worth's punitive bombardment, just as Americans in general recalled Saratoga and Yorktown when they thought of the War of Independence, and Marengo and Jena-Auerstadt when they remembered Napoleon. The need to resort to massive attacks on economic resources thus came to them as something of a surprise.

Taken together, perception of the rebellion's nature, the status of the laws of war, and the inheritance of previous military experience all reinforced an initial belief that Southern civilians should not be subjected to the direct burdens of war. The widespread opinion that a slaveholding aristocracy had engineered secession made attacks on the Southern yeoman seem unwise and counterproductive. The works of Vattel and Halleck made them seem unjust and uncivilized. The legacies of the American Revolution, Napoleonic campaigns, and Mexican War made such attacks seem unnecessary.

Yet beneath the surface, each of these factors had a darker, less encouraging message. Exempting Southern civilians from the burdens of war made political sense only if their support for the Confederacy was indeed shallow and if they remained passive in the face of Union armies. The mild policy made legal sense only if there were no compelling military necessity to forage for supplies or destroy resources the enemy was using to continue his war effort. It made military sense only if victory could be won exclusively on the battlefield. One by one, the actual course of the Civil War challenged each of these perceptions.

[40]Smith, "American Rule in Mexico," 291–293.

2

Conciliation and its challenges

Conciliation formed the dominant Union policy for the first fifteen months of the war. It not only characterized the way in which Federal forces were to deal with Southern civilians, it also shaped the Federal strategy to defeat the Confederacy. Northern officials instinctively grasped the truth of Treitschke's statement that "Again and again, it has been proved that it is war which turns a people into a nation." The slave-holding aristocrats had made a rebellion; they must be not allowed to make a nation. Conciliation on the one hand, and a sweeping military effort on the other, seemed the keys to preventing this. Together these two approaches would sap Southern resistance and make possible an early victory.[1]

It was a rational, even enlightened policy. But in war, events are not easily controlled, and from the outset, conciliation faced two major challenges. The first stemmed from the mere existence of a competing policy hatched in Missouri. The second, more serious challenge came from the soldiers in the ranks. Even as the senior Union leadership formulated the conciliatory policy, forces were already at work that significantly undercut it.

CONCILIATION ESPOUSED

Two commanders, Brevet Lieutenant General Winfield Scott and Major General George B. McClellan, epitomized the conciliatory policy at the war's outset. McClellan had served on Scott's staff during the Mexican War, had noted the General-in-Chief's enlightened attitude toward Mexican civilians, and had been greatly impressed by Scott's magisterial personality and consummate military skill. Although destined to clash on other issues, both officers shared identical opinions about the nature of the rebellion, which they regarded as the product of extremism on both sides. Temperamentally, Scott and McClellan possessed the instinctive moderation of the gentleman, not the fiery passion of the ideologue. They displayed a persistent faith

---

[1]Quoted in Boyd C. Shafer, *Nationalism: Myth and Reality* (New York, Harcourt, Brace, 1955), 45.

Lieut. Gen. Winfield Scott sought to avoid the bloodshed and bitterness that would accompany a major Union offensive. If the North merely isolated the South and waited, he argued, "the Union spirit will assert itself; those who are on the fence will descend on the Union side, and I will guarantee that in one year from this time all difficulties will be settled." If, on the other hand, the North launched a major invasion, "I will guarantee that at the end of a year you will be further from a settlement than you are now." (Courtesy, Civil War Times Illustrated Collection, Harrisburg, Pennsylvania)

Maj. Gen. George B. McClellan, shown here with his staff, argued forcefully that Northern forces must respect Southern property and avoid any entanglement with slavery. "I have not come here to wage war upon the defenseless, upon private property, nor upon the domestic institutions of the land," he informed a Virginia planter. "I and the Army I command are fighting to secure the Union & to maintain its Constitution & laws – for no other purpose." (Courtesy, Civil War Times Illustrated Collection)

in the power of sweet reason, voiced with dignified firmness, to overcome most human problems.

"Of all manifestations of power," wrote Thucydides in the fifth century B.C., "the quality that most impresses men is restraint." Winfield Scott may never have read the Greek historian's observation, but he clearly understood the principle and spent much of his career illustrating it. Tact and patience marked his behavior toward the volunteer troops he commanded during the War of 1812. Afterward he managed to avoid a violent war with the Cherokee Nation in 1836–1838, through negotiations in which he convinced them to accept the forced removal from their Georgia lands to the Indian Territory. On at least two subsequent occasions, his diplomatic gifts helped to avert potential strife with Great Britain: first over conflicting claims to a chunk of northern Maine in 1838–1839, and then in 1859 over a disputed island in Puget Sound along the border with British North America. His policy of careful restraint during the Mexico City campaign in 1847 has already been discussed.[2]

Finally – and this experience surely influenced him in the spring of 1861 – he had also managed to defuse tensions during the Nullification Crisis of 1832–1833. On that occasion, he had ventured to South Carolina, quietly arranged for the strengthening of Federal posts in the region, and treated the malcontents with enormous aplomb. Although the Nullifiers were "on the road to treason," he told his troops, they remained fellow countrymen and might be turned from "that great crime by respect and kindness on our part." He firmly ordered his men to ignore insults and "even a few brickbats." When a Charleston sugar refinery caught fire, he sent an unarmed detachment into the city with orders to offer itself to the city authorities and, if asked, to help fight the blaze. A Virginian who witnessed Scott's conduct during the crisis wrote that "nothing could have been more judicious. . . . From the beginning to the end, his conduct was as conciliatory as it was firm and sincere."[3]

Thus restraint, in Scott's experience, paid great dividends. When the secession crisis erupted, it became his watchword. Even before Lincoln's election in 1860 he urged a policy of utmost moderation should any of the Southern states attempt to leave the Union. The Federal government, he wrote President James Buchanan, should hold the military posts of the Deep South in such force as to make any attempt to seize them appear "ridiculous," but otherwise attempt no invasion of any states that might secede. Instead, the government should assert its continued authority by the symbolic device of stationing warships off Southern ports to continue the collection of import duties. Scott's entire proposal aimed at avoiding war in the hope that an eventual compromise might be reached. If war began, however, he was pessimistic. He thought it unlikely that the country could be reunified without exchanging the existing republic for a severe despotism. He even suggested to Buchanan that if a rift

[2]On these matters, see Charles Winslow Elliott, *Winfield Scott: The Soldier and the Man* (New York: MacMillan, 1937), 345–366, 665–671.

[3]Winfield Scott, *Memoirs of Lieut.-General Scott,* 2 vols. (New York: Sheldon and Company, 1864), vol. 1, p. 248; Elliott, *Winfield Scott,* 284; Benjamin Watkins Leigh to Edward Mansfield, no date; quoted in Scott, *Memoirs* 1:256.

seemed inevitable, it would be better to let the Union divide into four new confederacies split along commercial and geographic lines.[4]

That extraordinary proposal – a manifestation of the aging general's occasional flights of fancy – was not far short of idiotic, but his belief in a policy of nonconfrontation had many adherents, not least of whom was the incoming Secretary of State, William H. Seward. A long-time friend and political ally of Scott, Seward felt sure that if military confrontation could be avoided, latent Unionist sentiment in the Deep South would resurface and the seceded states would return to the Union voluntarily. Throughout the winter of 1860–1861, he and Scott worked harmoniously to impress this course on Lincoln.[5]

On the eve of Lincoln's inauguration, Scott drafted a memorandum to Seward. Ostensibly an eyes-only document, it was widely published in an obvious bid to attract support for Seward's conciliatory stance. In it, Scott noted that the incoming Lincoln administration had four potential courses of action. First, it could initiate a full-scale invasion of the South, but Scott painted this option in tones of bleakest gray:

No doubt this might be done in two or three years by a young and able general – a Wolfe, a Desaix, or a Hoche, with 300,000 disciplined men, estimating a third for garrisons, and the loss of yet a greater number by skirmishes, sieges, battles and Southern fevers. The destruction of life and property on the other side would be frightful, however perfect the moral discipline of the invaders.

The conquest completed at that enormous waste of human life to the North and Northwest, with at least $250,000,000 added thereto, and *cui bono?* Fifteen devastated provinces! not to be brought into harmony with their conquerors, but to be held for generations, with heavy garrisons, at an expense quadruple the net duties or taxes which it would be possible to extort from them, followed by a protector or an emperor.

Clearly some less draconian policy would be preferable. As a second possibility, the incoming administration might adopt the Crittenden compromise or some other conciliatory formula. If so, "my life upon it, we shall have no new case of secession, but, on the contrary, an early return of many, if not all, the States which have already broken off from the Union." A third option, if the administration preferred not to compromise, was to close Southern ports and collect the duties on foreign goods from warships stationed off the blockaded harbors. Finally, in words that quickly became notorious, Scott suggested that the North might simply "[s]ay to the seceded States, Wayward Sisters, depart in peace!"[6]

The Confederate bombardment of Fort Sumter on April 12, 1861, ended the possibility of a peaceful solution to the crisis. Lincoln promptly summoned 75,000 volunteers to suppress the rebellion. His firm action brought cheers from much of the

[4]Scott to Buchanan, October 29, 1860, in [Jeremiah Black], *Mr. Buchanan's Administration on the Eve of Rebellion* (New York: D. Appleton, 1865), 287–288.

[5]On this point, see Glyndon G. Van Deusen, *William Henry Seward* (New York: Oxford University Press, 1967), 238–254, 269–287; and David M. Potter, *Lincoln and His Party in the Secession Crisis* (New Haven: Yale University Press, 1942), passim.

[6]Scott, *Memoirs* 2:625–628.

North but triggered a second wave of secession in April and May as the four states of the Upper South cast their lot with the Confederacy. Although General-in-Chief Scott did not advocate acquiescence in secession, as some critics asserted, he did continue to recommend against a full-scale invasion of the South. In May 1861, he began to sketch a design that he thought might defeat the Confederacy without the bloodshed, devastation, and bitterness that would accompany a major offensive. First, Scott argued, blockade the Southern coastline. Second, send a strong column down from Cairo, Illinois, to secure the Mississippi River. Third, wait. If the North did these things, Scott maintained, it "will thus cut off the luxuries to which the people are accustomed; and when they feel the pressure, not having been exasperated by attacks made on them within their respective States, the Union spirit will assert itself; those who are on the fence will descend on the Union side, and I will guarantee that in one year from this time all difficulties will be settled." If, on the other hand, Federal armies invaded the South at any point, "I will guarantee that at the end of a year you will be further from a settlement than you are now."[7]

Although these views remained relatively private, both the Northern press and men of influence soon acquired a fairly good idea of Scott's proposals and the assumptions on which he based them. On May 18, for example, the *Boston Evening Transcript* reported that "General Scott's plan is said to consist in hemming in the rebels on all sides." Two days later, the New York worthy George Templeton Strong recorded his conversation with two notables just back from Washington, "where they have been in conference with General Scott, Seward, Lincoln, and other magnates." They understood that the summer would be devoted to the "assemblage and organization of great masses of men at suitable points from Cairo [Illinois] to Washington." Then, once autumn had overtaken the steaming Southern summer, "two great columns" would advance down the Mississippi Valley and along the Atlantic seaboard. "The program," Strong noted, "looks sensible and promising." By the end of June, the entire country understood the basics of Scott's proposal. Emphasizing the slow squeeze it would place on the Southern people as opposed to a single, swift stroke, the press dubbed it "the Anaconda Plan."[8]

For several weeks, the Northern press accepted Scott's generalship with unquestioning confidence, partly because patriotism seemed to dictate a supportive stance, partly because rumors also circulated that Scott's deliberation would extend no further than mid-July at the latest, and partly because many Northerners retained faith in the possibility of a settlement without much bloodshed. Such criticism as did materialize

---

[7]Scott never crystalized these ideas into a single, concrete proposal. That he entertained them may be gleaned from an exchange of letters between McClellan and himself. See McClellan to Scott, April 27, 1861, especially the endorsement Scott wrote when forwarding the letter to Lincoln, OR 51, pt 1:338–339; Scott to McClellan, May 3, 1861, ibid., pp. 369–370; Scott to McClellan, May 21, 1861, ibid., 386–387; and E.D. Townsend, *Anecdotes of the Civil War in the United States* (New York: D. Appleton, 1884), 55–56.

[8]*Boston Evening Transcript,* May 18, 1861; entry for May 20, 1861, Allan Nevins and Milton Halsey Thomas (eds.), *The Diary of George Templeton Strong,* 4 vols. (New York: MacMillan, 1952), vol. 3, p. 144; *Cincinnati Commercial,* June 26, 1861; *Chicago Tribune,* June 28, 1861.

came, not from men who rejected Scott's faith in latent Southern Unionism, but rather from those with different ideas concerning the best way to tap it. Scott believed that prompt, bloody action would extinguish Southern Unionist sentiment in a flood of indignation and resentment. Others thought the opposite. To them, only quick action could ignite Southern Unionists; delay would leave them correspondingly discouraged.

In mid-May 1861, for example, Seward asked Montgomery C. Meigs, a well-regarded army captain, to prepare a memorandum on the war in general and the Virginia situation in particular. When Meigs endorsed Scott's view that the government should defer action until the army was better trained, Postmaster General Montgomery Blair blasted the waiting game. Meigs, Blair wrote Lincoln, was making the same error as Scott and most other regular army officers. Such men grossly overestimated the strength of secessionist spirit in the South. "This," he declared, "is a fundamental and fatal error and if our military movements are predicated on it & we fail to go to the relief of the people of the South they will be subjugated and the state of consolidation now falsely assumed will be produced." If that occurred, Blair warned, the Union could not be preserved without the complete conquest of the South. Immediate action, on the other hand, would be "hailed with joy by the people of the South everywhere" and it could be accomplished by a very small portion of the army.

Blair considered Scott incapable of grasping the true state of affairs and therefore unlikely to adopt sound military measures. While he did not mean to impugn Scott's patriotism, he concluded, the President should adopt a policy independently of the General-in-Chief. The thrust of Blair's letter left no doubt about what that policy should be.[9]

For the time being, Lincoln continued to accept Scott's policy of deliberation. But as the weeks dragged by without significant offensive action, portions of the Northern press began to adopt Blair's belief that prompt military action was imperative. Much of it stemmed from simple frustration over a variety of minor disasters, among them the secessionist capture of the Gosport Naval Yard at Norfolk, the seizure of the Federal arsenal at Harpers Ferry, and the defeat of Union forces in a militarily insignificant but humiliating skirmish at Big Bethel, Virginia. On June 26, the *New York Tribune* raised what it called "The Nation's War Cry":

Forward to Richmond! Forward to Richmond! The Rebel Congress must not be allowed to meet there on the 20th of July! BY THAT DATE THE PLACE MUST BE HELD BY THE NATIONAL ARMY!

A second major Republican organ, the *Chicago Tribune,* adopted the same slogan the following day, and both papers carried "The Nation's War Cry" for several days thereafter. The Chicago paper also printed a number of articles attacking Scott's "Anaconda Plan," basing its objections squarely on the same argument that Blair had

---

[9]Russell F. Weigley, *Quartermaster General of the Union Army: A Biography of M.C. Meigs* (New York: Columbia University Press, 1959), 159. Blair to Lincoln, May 16, 1861, Robert Todd Lincoln Collection of the Papers of Abraham Lincoln, LC.

presented to Lincoln: "The Union men of the South, to whose relief the loyal army is marching, will be crushed out, or forced into cooperation with the rebels, long before the anaconda has got the whole country enveloped in its coils."[10]

The "Forward to Richmond" campaign is often portrayed as triggering an irresistible lust in the Northern press for immediate action. In fact, however, a substantial portion of the Union's major newspapers ridiculed the impatience of the two *Tribunes* and continued to endorse Scott's policy. The conservative *Boston Evening Transcript* continued to adhere to the line it had adopted on June 22. "Gen. Scott," asserted its lead editorial, "has undertaken the suppression of the rebellion at a minimum waste of human life," and it applauded his deliberate policy while chiding his critics. On June 27, the *New York Times* ran an article that termed "erroneous" other reports that Scott had changed his plan and intended to "commence active operations" at once. "From an authoritative source," wrote its Washington-based correspondent, "I have learned the general outlines of his plan of the campaign." Scott did not intend to bring on a major battle. He intended, first, to concentrate such large numbers in Virginia and the border states as to "make it madness for the rebels to attempt to attack." The main purpose here was political: "While thus intimidating them, the presence of our forces will encourage the loyal citizens to rise in sufficient numbers to prevent any further outrages, to cut off their resources, increase the dissatisfaction in their camps and cause desertion, and by thus harassing them, ultimately demoralize the rebel forces and drive them from the Border States." That, Scott thought, would insure the loyalty of the border states, after which he would land strong naval forces at a variety of points along the Southern coast in the expectation that the individual Southern states would then recall their own troops and thus fragment the Confederacy's "grand army and make it powerless for any offensive movement." "By January," the correspondent concluded, "he [Scott] thinks that the rebellion will be entirely defeated, and the Union reconstructed."[11]

The conciliatory nature of this plan was well understood. When a letter to the editor on June 29 termed the proposed campaign "strange and unnatural" and called for an immediate advance, the *New York Times* printed a lengthy rebuttal two days later that concluded: "The South must be made to feel *full* respect for the power and *honor* of the North: she must be humbled, but not debased by a forfeiture of self-respect, if we wish to retain our motto – *E pluribus unum* – and claim for the whole United States the respect of the world."[12]

With public opinion on its efficacy still divided, the popular notion that Lincoln was somehow forced into launching an immediate offensive is untenable. It is much more likely that the President himself embraced the Blair thesis that an early offensive offered the best way to encourage the Southern Unionist sentiment that, he hoped, would then overwhelm the slaveholding aristocracy. On June 29, he met with Scott,

---

[10]*New York Tribune,* June 26, 1861; *Chicago Tribune,* June 28, 29, 1861.

[11]*Boston Evening Transcript,* June 22, 1861. *New York Times,* June 27, 1861. The correspondent's report is dated June 25.

[12]*New York Times,* June 29, 1861; ibid., July 1, 1861.

the Cabinet, and Brigadier General Irvin McDowell, commander of the field army being gathered around Washington. At the conference, Lincoln insisted on an advance on Manassas within three or four weeks. Scott objected, and continued to champion his own plan, but yielded gracefully when the President pressed his case. By July 8, Lincoln issued positive orders for McDowell to launch an offensive; eight days later McDowell set his forces in motion.[13]

At this time, both Northern civilians and Union policymakers believed that even aggressive action should be undertaken solely against Confederate combatants. In southeastern Virginia, Major General Benjamin F. Butler threatened summary punishment to soldiers who despoiled private property. En route to meet the enemy at Bull Run, McDowell instructed his troops that they must conduct themselves "with as much forbearance and propriety as if they were at their own homes." Although deploring reports of Southern sabotage and bushwhacking against McDowell's column, the *Boston Evening Transcript* nevertheless insisted that Federal troops should bear in mind that each soldier "can exert incalculable influence in favor of a permanent peace after the shock of battle has subsided, by his demeanor toward belligerents. It will not be too much to say that the length of the war will be determined, as much by the behavior of the loyal forces, when not employed in actual fighting, as on the field of strife." This view enjoyed wide acceptance among Northern opinion-makers, regardless of their views on the prosecution of the war. Even the *New York Tribune,* learning of "outrages" perpetrated by Union soldiers near Fort Monroe, Virginia, called for the summary execution of "scoundrels who disgrace the flag of the Union by robbery and wanton destruction of private property."[14]

Unfortunately for the Union cause, McDowell's army suffered humiliating failure in its maiden offensive. Meeting a Confederate army near Manassas Junction on July 21, 1861, it was beaten and routed after a grueling all-day battle. The defeat ended any hopes of a rapid Confederate collapse. It also destroyed whatever promise the Anaconda plan had held out, for the South had been further united by the nationalistic pride generated by the victory. Stunned by this defeat, Lincoln summoned to Washington Major General George Brinton McClellan, whose recent victories in western Virginia marked him as a commander of apparent energy and brilliance.

Starved for a hero, the Northern press lionized McClellan as "the Napoleon of the present war" and accepted at face value his claim that his Union force had "annihilated two armies . . . entrenched in mountain fastnesses fortified at their leisure." His presence in the nation's capital seemed to promise swift military action. What McClellan brought with him, however, was a perspective on the war more nearly akin to Scott's than Lincoln's, although in some respects he combined their viewpoints. Like Scott, McClellan saw the need for a crafted, conciliatory strategy that would woo Unionist sentiment and above all avoid driving Southerners further into the grip of

---

[13]William C. Davis, *Battle at Bull Run: A History of the First Major Campaign of the Civil War* (Garden City, NY: Doubleday, 1977), 69–89.
[14]General Orders No. 2, May 28, 1861, OR 2:664; General Orders No. 18, July 18, 1861, ibid., 744; *Boston Evening Transcript,* July 19, 1861; *New York Tribune,* June 27, 1861.

the Slave Power. Like Lincoln, however, he recognized that the Union could not afford to wait several years for an Anaconda-type plan to work. McClellan offered his views to Lincoln in a detailed memorandum, personally handed to the President on August 2 and read before the assembled Cabinet the following morning.[15]

The task facing the Union, McClellan insisted, was not simply to defeat the Confederacy's field armies, but also "to display such an overwhelming strength, as will convince all our antagonists, especially those of the governing aristocratic class, of the utter impossibility of resistance." The recent defeat at Bull Run was doubly regrettable because it had doubtless consolidated the nationalist sentiment of the Southern people. "Had we been successful in the recent battle," he wrote, "it is possible that we might have been spared the labor and expense of a great effort." As things stood, however, the North had no alternative: The Southern success "will enable the political leaders of the rebels to convince the mass of their people that we are inferior to them in force and courage, and to command all their resources." In McClellan's view, the idea that the slaveholding aristocracy formed the major foe was, for the moment at least, no longer the case. "The contest began with a class; now it is with a people" – and only military success could divide the people from the slavocracy. A strategy of crushing, complete military success, combined with "a rigidly protective policy as to private property and unarmed persons, and a lenient course as to common soldiers" was the best (in McClellan's mind the only) way to achieve this.[16]

McClellan went on to outline the military component of this strategy. In the western theater, he suggested the deployment of a number of columns: "a strong movement" to be made on the Mississippi River, another force to secure Missouri, and a third force to be sent into Unionist east Tennessee as soon as Kentucky – then observing a precarious and extra-legal "neutrality" – entered firmly into the Union fold. McClellan recommended a similar advance into western Texas, which, like east Tennessee, was said to contain substantial Unionist sentiment. Other forces would hold western Virginia and Fort Monroe. He also alluded to the creation of a substantial amphibious force to land, or threaten to land, at various points along the Southern coast.[17]

The goal of these operations was not so much to gain important objectives as it was to support the main offensive McClellan had in mind: a massive thrust against Richmond, followed by an advance into the Deep South that would eventually result in the capture of Charleston, Savannah, Montgomery, Pensacola, Mobile, and New Orleans. For this herculean operation McClellan proposed to use an army of 273,000 troops and 600 pieces of artillery – or, to put it in perspective, an army twenty times the size of the one that had taken Mexico City in 1847. McClellan fully understood

---

[15]*New York Herald,* July 16, 1861; McClellan to the "Army of the West," July 16, 1861, OR 2:236.

[16]Stephen W. Sears (ed.), *The Civil War Papers of George B. McClellan: Selected Correspondence, 1860–1865* (New York: Ticknor & Fields, 1989), 71–72 [Cited hereafter as Sears (ed.), *McClellan Papers*]. See also the letter (misdated August 4, 1861) in OR 5:6–8.

[17]Ibid., 73.

that the force he had in mind was far larger than any that had ever been deployed on the North American continent. That was precisely the point: "The question to be decided is simply this; shall we crush the rebellion at one blow, terminate the war in one campaign, or shall we leave it as a legacy for our descendants?"[18]

Historians seldom take McClellan's August memorandum seriously. T. Harry Williams, for example, scored it as "rambling . . . defective . . . fundamentally wrong" and a "fantasia." But Joseph Harsh is surely correct in his insistence that whatever its merits or deficiencies, the August memorandum clearly embodied the strategy that McClellan actually tried to carry out. Critical to that strategy was the effect it would have on Southern civilians; indeed, McClellan's conceptions make little sense without it. As the whole thrust of his memorandum makes clear, he had two ultimate objectives in mind: first, the detachment of the bulk of the Southern population from its presumably weak loyalty to the "political leaders of the rebels"; second, a convincing demonstration to the "governing aristocratic class" that successful resistance to Federal authority was futile. Achievement of the first goal required the avoidance of any further major Union setbacks and a lenient policy that would not utterly alienate ordinary Southerners from their former flag. To accomplish the second, McClellan planned – as he informed his wife in a letter written the same day as his memorandum to Lincoln – to "carry this thing on 'En grand' & crush the rebels in one campaign." Any other course, he feared, would drive Southerners more deeply into the arms of the Confederacy, either by the severe treatment they might receive at the hands of Union troops, or by a bloody and indecisive stalemate – which would increase the stakes of independence by raising hopes for eventual Southern victory.[19]

McClellan had every reason to think that this proposed strategy enjoyed a reasonable prospect for success. He had already given it an apparently successful trial run during his western Virginia campaign. There he had gathered his forces until he enjoyed a sizeable numerical advantage over his opponents. Only then had he advanced, assuring the local population that his troops would rigorously respect their private property – including their slaves – and would crush any attempt at a slave insurrection. To all appearances, this policy had worked quite well. Unionist sentiment had come to the fore, a loyal government had been created, and western Virginia

[18]Ibid., 74–75.

[19]T. Harry Williams, *Lincoln and His Generals* (New York: Alfred A. Knopf, 1952), 30–31; Joseph L. Harsh, "George Brinton McClellan and the Forgotten Alternative: An Introduction to the Conservative Strategy in the Civil War: April-August 1861" (unpublished diss., Rice University, 1970), 194. Harsh's dissertation, unfortunately never published, is a stimulating attempt to take McClellan seriously as a strategist. I benefited substantially from it in preparing this section. In addition, see also the following three articles by Harsh: "On the McClellan-Go-Round," *Civil War History* 19 (June 1973):101–118; "Battlesword and Rapier: Clausewitz, Jomini, and the American Civil War," *Military Affairs* 38 (December 1974):133–138; and "Lincoln's Tarnished Brass: Conservative Strategies and the Attempt to Fight the Early Civil War as a Limited War," in Roman J. Heleniak and Lawrence L. Hewitt, eds., *The Confederate High Command & Related Topics: Themes in Honor of T. Harry Williams* (Shippensburg, PA: White Mane Publishing, 1988), 124–141. McClellan to Mary Ellen McClellan, August 2, 1861, Sears (ed.), *McClellan Papers*, 75.

had been well-launched on the path that would eventually end in the creation of the separate, loyalist state of West Virginia in June 1863.[20]

McClellan made a serious mistake, however, in failing to make his commitment to this strategy and his reasons for pursuing it clear to the Washington policymakers, and the country as a whole. Instead he permitted himself to be characterized as a commander dedicated to prompt, vigorous, decisive action. His reluctance to make his program plain was, in some respects, quite understandable. He was almost certainly correct in his belief that the advanced wing of the Republican party would not have accepted a carefully limited campaign. His willingness to be seen as a man of action allowed him to retain the support of that group significantly longer than he might otherwise have done. It also gave him a decisive tactical advantage in his growing feud with Winfield Scott, who strongly disagreed with McClellan over a variety of issues unconnected with the conciliatory policy or military strategy.[21]

When in October 1861, for example, several Radical Republican senators visited McClellan, determined to "worry the administration into a battle," McClellan implied that the delays in embarking on an active campaign stemmed from Scott's intransigence, not his own belief in the necessity for the creation and husbanding of overwhelming strength prior to any major offensive. The senators, believing him, pressured Lincoln to remove Scott and appoint McClellan as General-in-Chief in his place. This paid dividends in the short run, but McClellan's duplicity added the bitterness of betrayal to the radicals' opposition when it finally did materialize. Then, because McClellan had done so poor a job of explaining and defending his strategic ideas, the radicals were able to successfully portray him as a timid, incompetent, and possibly disloyal commander who had no business being in charge of an army. Such charges placed McClellan's supporters permanently on the defensive, and because they frequently lacked a clear understanding of McClellan's plans, the issue quickly narrowed to McClellan himself. His conservative strategy went largely undiscussed.[22]

In the meantime, McClellan did succeed Scott as General-in-Chief, and when he did he pressed his conciliatory views on each of the Union army's major commanders. His instructions habitually reflected the political objective to be attained. "We shall most readily suppress the rebellion and restore the authority of the Government by religiously respecting the Constitutional rights of all . . . ," ran a typical passage. "Preserve the strictest discipline, among the troops, and while employing the utmost

---

[20]McClellan to the Union Men of Western Virginia, May 26, 1861, and to the Inhabitants of Western Virginia, June 23, 1861, both in ibid., 26 and 34–35 respectively. See also OR 2:48–49, 196.

[21]Scott resented McClellan's undue influence with, and access to, the Lincoln Cabinet. He also opposed the younger general's plans for organizing the Army of the Potomac, and disagreed with him on the degree of risk to which the Federal capital was exposed. On the power struggle between the two men, see Mark Grimsley, "Overthrown: The Truth Behind the McClellan-Scott Feud," *Civil War Times Illustrated* 19 (November 1980):20–29.

[22]John Hay, Diary, entry for October 26, 1861, in Tyler Dennett (ed.), *Lincoln and the Civil War: The Diaries and Letters of John Hay* (New York: Dodd, Mead & Company, 1939), 31; Mary Karl George, *Zachariah Chandler, A Political Biography* (East Lansing: University of Michigan Press, 1969), 55–56.

energy in military movements, be careful so to treat the unarmed inhabitants as to contract, not widen, the breach existing between us & the rebels."[23]

McClellan was not fatuous enough to believe that Southern civilians posed no threat at all. Sometimes their sympathy for the Confederacy expressed itself through direct assistance to the rebel government. On those occasions, he informed one commander, "it is of course necessary to arrest them." But McClellan warned that Federal officers should avoid causing "unnecessary irritation by causeless arrests and persecution of individuals." Overzealous subordinates often made such arrests on mere suspicion. In any event, he concluded, "It should be our constant aim to make it apparent to all that their property, their comfort, and their personal safety will be best preserved by adhering to the cause of the Union."[24]

CONCILIATION REJECTED

Although Scott and McClellan preferred a conciliatory policy, this did not automatically mean that their desires controlled military conduct in every zone of operations. The area of hostilities was too far-flung, the Federal government too small, and political power too diffuse to permit a rigidly responsive system of command and control. The Lincoln administration therefore had to improvise. About the best it could do, as hundreds of thousands of volunteer soldiers coalesced under the command of erstwhile captains, lawyers, and railroad executives, was to provide general guidelines, correct really serious policy mistakes, and otherwise let the military commanders formulate their own policy for conduct toward civilians.

Lincoln, indeed, consciously employed a managerial style that lent itself to a decentralized system of decision-making. "My policy," he often declared, "is to have no policy." He habitually avoided committing himself to any particular doctrine, permitted Cabinet members and other officials substantial latitude in pursuing courses of action, and usually endorsed whatever course seemed to prove most effective. This further ensured that subordinates who wanted to pursue an independent line could often get away with it. Concerning Union conduct toward Southern civilians, then, it is more appropriate to think of a constellation of policies rather than a single policy. It so happened that during the first year of the war, most Federal commanders embraced conciliation, but those who did not found themselves free to pursue a more draconian course.[25]

A case in point was Missouri. Although the state never left the Union and seventy-

[23]McClellan to Don Carlos Buell, November 7, 12, 1861, OR 4:342, 355–356.
[24]McClellan to Buell, November 12, 1861, ibid., 356.
[25]See David Donald's essay, "Abraham Lincoln and the American Pragmatic Tradition" in his *Lincoln Reconsidered: Essays on the Civil War Era* (2nd Edition; New York: Alfred A. Knopf, 1956), 128–143. The quotation appears on p. 131.

five percent of Missourians who bore arms during the Civil War wore Federal blue, in many respects the Union army treated the region as if it were enemy country, and indeed enemy country of a particularly virulent kind. The one attempt at conciliation was aborted early on and then repudiated; afterward, no truly conciliatory policy was ever mounted again. In some respects what happened in Missouri during 1861 looks quite as severe as what happened in the South fully three years later.

Much of the responsibility for this can be laid at the doorstep of two individuals, Nathaniel Lyon and Francis P. Blair, Jr. Although affairs in Missouri might have turned out as they did even without their intervention, it remains incontestable that these men played a signal role in creating the situation that in fact developed. Their machinations during the spring of 1861 cut the props out from under the conciliatory policy even before it had much of a trial.

Both men were in Saint Louis when the war broke out, Lyon as a captain of regular infantry and Blair as a recently elected U.S. Congressman. Lyon had strong antislavery proclivities and a stormy hatred for secessionists; so too did Blair, whose brother Montgomery was Lincoln's postmaster general and an early proponent of a prompt, vigorous military effort. Both suspected the loyalty of the military commander of the region, Major General William S. Harney, and both thought he treated the less-than-completely loyal Missouri state government with too much delicacy.

In Harney's opinion, delicacy was precisely the thing required. The governor of the state, Claiborne Jackson, had roared defiance at Lincoln's call for troops, and was clearly bent on adding Missouri to the Confederacy, but the state legislature and a specially appointed convention had already voted against secession, and by substantial margins. A veteran of the sectional antagonism – as commander of the Department of the West he had dealt closely with opposing factions during the "Bleeding Kansas" crisis – Harney thought he understood the emotions that animated Missourians. While most of them were proslavery, a substantial number were not, and although they looked with disfavor on Federal coercion of the Southern states, the majority wanted to remain in the Union.

To Lyon and Blair, Harney's conciliatory manner indicated gullible weakness at best and disloyalty to the Union cause at worst. Blair began using his family's considerable influence, first to get Lyon placed in charge of the important Federal arsenal at St. Louis, where the captain quietly and extra-legally began to arm Unionist home guard units; and second to get Harney removed from command. His efforts on the latter score created enough doubts to get Harney called to Washington temporarily. During his absence, Lyon moved against Camp Jackson, a large Missouri militia encampment just outside St. Louis. Although the militia was largely pro-Confederate in sympathy – its camp streets bore such revealing names as Beauregard and Davis – its legal right to assemble was unquestioned since Missouri had never left the Union. Lyon nevertheless surrounded the camp with Union home guards, disarmed the suspect militiamen, and paraded them ignominiously through the streets of Saint Louis. His impetuous action brought forth a mob of pro-Southern sympathizers in the city who hurled insults and brickbats at the home guardsmen. A full-scale riot broke out. The Unionists opened fire, and in the ensuing violence two soldiers and twenty-eight civilians were killed and dozens of others wounded.

The attack on Camp Jackson, coupled with the bloodshed in St. Louis, convinced many conditional Unionists in Missouri that secession was the best and most honorable choice remaining. Even so, Governor Jackson and militia general Sterling Price attempted a compromise arrangement with Lyon and Blair. Lyon, by now a brigadier general in the Union army, threw away this possibility by erupting in fury at the thought that a mere state might "dictate" to the Federal government on any matter. Rather than concede such a thing, he told Jackson, "I would see you . . . and every man, woman, and child in the State, dead and buried. *This means war.*"[26]

Soon afterward, Harney returned from Washington to discover the tension his subordinate's stance had wrought. More loyal to the Union than Lyon and Blair supposed, he refused to repudiate Lyon's policy. To do so, he believed, would suggest weak indecision on the part of the Federal government. But he did attempt one last try at a more moderate, conciliatory policy. On May 20 he met with Price and hammered out an agreement whereby Missouri would continue to remain "neutral" in the struggle between North and South. It would neither contribute troops to a Federal invasion of the Confederacy nor extend assistance to the Confederacy. The state would take responsibility for maintaining order within its boundaries, and as long as it did so effectively, Harney would avoid any action that might create a confrontation between Missouri troops and Union forces.[27]

For ten days the agreement remained in force. Tensions eased, the Missouri press largely applauded, and Harney believed he had secured a "bloodless victory" for the Union cause. But Lyon and Blair were certain Harney had been duped. And unbeknownst to Harney, Lincoln had entrusted Blair with an order relieving the general from command, to be used at Blair's discretion. Blair did so at the first opportunity. Harney was removed; Lyon briefly assumed charge of the department pending a permanent replacement.[28]

The uncompromising policy of Blair and Lyon almost immediately sparked a bloody guerrilla warfare that plagued Missouri to the end of the conflict. The irregular bands that quickly gathered created a situation in which a conciliatory policy seemed to reflect not moderation but impotence. Unable to strike directly at the bushwhackers, Union authorities quickly decided to make the civilian community responsible for their depredations. Most of these decisions were made ad hoc, without guidance from Washington.

---

[26]The story of Lyon's actions in Missouri is well-known. Good secondary accounts include Allan Nevins, *War for the Union,* 4 vols. (New York: Charles Scribner's Sons, 1959–1971), vol. 1, pp. 120–129; McPherson, *Battle Cry of Freedom,* 290–292; and especially Christopher Phillips, *Damned Yankee: The Life of General Nathaniel Lyon* (London and Columbia: Missouri University Press, 1990), 129–214. The quotation is in Thomas Snead, *The Fight for Missouri from the Election of Lincoln to the Death of Lyon* (New York: Charles Scribner's Sons, 1886), 199–200.

[27]Harney to E.D. Townsend, May 29, 1861, OR 3:376; Harney to Lorenzo Thomas, June 5, 1861, ibid., 383.

[28]Harney to Lorenzo Thomas, May 31, 1861, ibid., 381.

Lyon's general orders regarding conduct toward civilians were similar to most at that period of the war. He condemned pillaging and urged that private property should remain unmolested, whatever the owners' political views, provided they remained quiet. But against active secessionists he was notably harsh, a stance that encouraged similar toughness on the part of subordinates. In the District of North Missouri – known as "Little Dixie" because of the many plantations and slaves in the region – the local commander, Brigadier General John Pope, quickly introduced policies similar to those that would earn him such notoriety in Virginia a year later.[29]

On July 21, Pope issued a proclamation to the civilians in his district. Bushwhackers had repeatedly damaged the bridges and culverts of a strategic railroad in the region, but the local population professed to know nothing about it. Pope did not believe them. He thought the people could "easily" protect the railroad from destruction, "and it is my purpose to give them strong inducements to do so." He therefore informed area communities that they would be made to pay for any damage to the track within a five-mile radius. They could escape the penalty only by furnishing "conclusive proof" that they had resisted the saboteurs, or by giving prompt information to Union authorities. Union officers were ordered to visit each community in question, identify prominent citizens – the proper county officials were to be preferred if available – and appoint five people to create a "committee of public safety." In a letter to one of his subordinates, Pope specified that at least two of the committee members should be "worthy and prominent" secessionists. "It is the service of the secessionists I specially require," Pope continued, "and I desire that you will give them plainly to understand that unless peace is preserved, their property will be immediately levied upon, and their contribution collected at once in any kind of property at hand."[30]

Although this policy scarcely seemed conciliatory – by the standard of the time it was positively draconian – it reflected the assumptions underlying the mild policy. Pope did not regard the entire population as hostile; instead he believed that they were cowed into submission by the secessionists in their midst. The wealthy disunionists, he assumed, enjoyed great influence and could halt attacks on the railroad if they chose to do so. He also considered this the mildest policy available to him. His first object, Pope informed a civilian critic, was to restore peace and safety "with the least bloodshed, the least distress to quiet persons, and the least exasperation of feeling among the people." He could have dispatched troops to root out the guerrillas directly, but that would have led to bloody fighting, house-to-house searches, and the arrest of potentially innocent persons. He preferred to believe that the local population was able, if properly motivated, to keep the peace by itself.[31]

[29]Orders No. – , July 26, 1861, OR 3:407.

[30]"Notice," July 21, 1861, OR 3:404. General Order No. 3, July 31, 1861, ibid., 418. Pope to Commanding Officer Iowa Forces, Keokuk, Iowa, August 2, 1861, ibid., 422. See also Pope to Col. Cyrus Bussey, August 10, 1861, ibid., 435–436. On Pope's Missouri policy, see Wallace J. Schutz and Walter N. Trenerry, *Abandoned by Lincoln: A Military Biography of General John Pope* (Urbana and Chicago: University of Illinois Press, 1990), 66–69.

[31]Pope to J.H. Sturgeon, August 3, 1861, ibid., 423–424.

Pope was confident that once the guerrillas understood the citizens of the area did not sympathize with them and saw that their forays against railroad property jeopardized the property of their families and friends, they would stop such attacks. The tactic seemed effective. He soon made an example of Marion County and its principal town, Palmyra, for guerrilla activity in the area, and levied contributions of $10,000 and $5,000, respectively, on the offending communities. After that he had no further trouble with damage to the railroads in his zone of responsibility.[32]

Other Union officers in Missouri followed a similar line. In mid-August, Major John McDonald of the 8th Missouri (Union) Infantry informed the citizens of St. Genevieve that persons in any way connected with outrages upon Unionist civilians or troops "will be held individually responsible, both in their persons and property. . . . When reliably informed of such [outrages], I will not hesitate to return to this city and retaliate in the most summary manner. It will be no excuse that they did not assist the rebels. They must prevent any outrages on Union men or take the consequences."[33]

THE VIEW FROM THE RANKS

The more rigorous Missouri policy partially eclipsed the message of conciliation being broadcast elsewhere. The most compelling strain on the mild policy came not from competing programs but from the bald fact that the average Union soldier never accepted it. For him it was always something forced on him from above, just one of many foolish orders imposed by a military hierarchy whose capacity for arbitrary decision-making was impossible to fathom. The failure of the private soldier to embrace conciliation must be counted among the most important reasons for its eventual failure. If the fact of armed coercion against them made rapprochement with the Southern population a ticklish business, acts of pillaging and vandalism by private soldiers threatened to destroy the possibility of such a thing altogether.

A few soldiers opposed conciliation on principle. "I believe, generally, there is no remission of sin without the shedding of blood," wrote one Ohio soldier; "and the sin of rebellion is no exception. True here as very often, the blood of the innocent must mingle their blood with the guilty." But for the most part, the soldiers' rejection of conciliation stemmed from more practical concerns, chief among them the quest for creature comforts. Practically every military order touching on soldiers' conduct toward civilians emphasized that they were neither to steal property nor enter Southern homes without permission. Actions of this kind were not only bad for military discipline in the abstract, but could quite quickly alienate and embitter the local population beyond hope of restoring good relations. Cold, wet, and famished Union soldiers, however, generally found this logic less than persuasive. It seemed to them that they were being asked to risk wounds and death on the battlefield or fatal illness

---

[32]Ibid., 424; Pope to [Palmyra, Missouri] Mayor and Authorities, August 19, 1861, ibid., 135.
[33]McDonald to the Citizens of St. Genevieve, Missouri, August 15, 1861, ibid., 133.

in crowded, unsanitary camps; that their country was calling on them to endure privation, discomfort, and bad food on a daily basis. The least it could do, in their collective opinion, was to let them take a few things that might make life more bearable.[34]

Thus, when the Fourth Minnesota Volunteers arrived at the deserted hamlet of Farmington, Tennessee, they quickly and quite literally took the place apart, but not from any rancor toward the vanished inhabitants. The regiment's historian was matter-of-fact about it: "The boys needed lumber for their tents, floors, etc., and made short work of the buildings, which were vacant, and there were only a few of them." Other soldiers regularly stole fence rails, despite the protests of officers and farmers alike. "There was never anything invented in the shape of wood," vowed one Massachusetts man, "that would make a better or quicker fire than a fence rail."[35]

The desire for a home-cooked meal sometimes led soldiers to pressure local civilians to feed them, despite standing orders against entering private houses. Usually their mere armed presence sufficed to wring a square meal from the reluctant families. Private Leander Stilwell and a companion found it perplexing that having asked two isolated women for a meal and having offered to pay for it, their benefactors seemed less than happy about their presence at their table. "[T]hey looked daggers," Stilwell remembered years afterward. Then, when the soldiers finished their dinner – "a splendid meal, consisting of corn bread, new Irish potatoes, boiled bacon and greens, butter and buttermilk" – the women refused to accept their proffered payment of Union greenbacks. The two men went away satiated but perplexed, and Stilwell asserted in his reminiscences, "[I]n my entire sojourn in the South during the war, the women were found to be more intensely bitter and malignant against the old government of the United States, and the national cause in general, than were the men." He found this difficult to understand. A more detached observer, watching these begrimed strangers, rifles in hand, extort a meal from two frightened women, might find the explanation easier to grasp.[36]

Back home, of course, few men would have dismantled houses, stolen fence rails, or coerced meals from unwilling hosts. Army life, however, changed things. The usual rules did not apply, and as a result men often did things as soldiers they would never have contemplated in civilian life. A minister who served with the Fifth Maine explained that "[s]tripped of all the restrictions and influences of home, of society and immediate friends, the natural inclinations and characteristics of a man are sure to speedily develop themselves. . . ." Men seemed to feel they could do just as they pleased, animated by nothing but the gratification of their own desires. "I know of no surer test upon which to apply a man's character," he concluded, "than to place him in

[34]Charles Pendleton Bowler to his brother, August 14, 1861, Bowler Family Papers, VHS.

[35]Alonzo L. Brown, *History of the Fourth Regiment of Minnesota Infantry Volunteers During the Great Rebellion, 1861–1865* (St. Paul: Pioneer Press, 1892), 49; Charles E. Davis, Jr., *Three Years in the Army: The Story of the Thirteenth Massachusetts Volunteers from July 16, 1861, to August 1, 1864* (Boston: Estes and Laurie, 1894), 41–42.

[36]Leander Stilwell, *The Story of a Common Soldier* (Kansas City, MO: Franklin Hudson, 1920), 83. A similar incident is recounted in Davis, *Three Years in the Army*, 78.

a volunteer army." An Ohio clergyman agreed. While visiting Rolla, Missouri, he saw the town overrun by hundreds of Iowa troops, "drinking and swearing and tearing about to the great annoyance of most of the people and to the great risk of damage to person[s] as well as property. . . . Their Officers seem to care but little what they do and have but little control over them. O! what a school is war. It is the field of Satan. . . ."[37]

Most Northern units at least waited to reach rebel soil before commencing careers of petty vandalism and theft. But some got an early start. Of his own regiment, the 19th Illinois, one soldier recalled that "a more mischievous crowd was never gotten together in all the war." While still encamped outside their state capital, Springfield, "they made it warm for the officers and citizens. . . . They learned to forage early and a rooster was not safe to come within a mile of camp at night." Similarly, in early December 1861, soldiers training at Camp Goddard, just outside Zanesville, Ohio, destroyed numerous sheds belonging to an agricultural society that had operated on the site before it became a military encampment. The soldiers used the sheds, worth thousands of dollars, for kindling. A few soldiers also insulted women on the streets of Zanesville and two recruits robbed one man on a downtown corner.[38]

Frequent breakdowns in regular supply added the spur of necessity to the temptations that soldiers already faced. Sometimes troops waited until their officers gave them permission to forage. More often, soldiers who deemed their normal rations inadequate turned to foraging on their own. Some Illinois soldiers, worried about the debilitating effects of camp life and convinced that fresh milk might relieve their chronic poor health, regularly stole it from the milch cows of a Tennessee family. One of them recalled the episode without apology: "After a few days the owners of the dairy discovered that someone had kindly milked their cows for them, so they laid in watch for us one night and caught us at it. High words followed but they knew better than to meddle with us. . . . Milk we wanted and milk we would have. We were sick and it was a military necessity and they had to submit."[39]

Regardless of whether foraging was authorized, it almost invariably provoked a

[37]George W. Bicknell, *History of the Fifth Maine Volunteers* (Portland, ME: K.L. Davis, 1871), 72–73. Entries for January 13, March 3, 1862, Lyman D. Ames Diary, OHS. For similar observations about the dissolute effects of military life, see Bell Irvin Wiley, *The Life of Billy Yank: The Common Soldier of the Union* (Indianapolis and New York: Bobbs-Merrill, 1951), 247–249; and James I. Robertson, Jr., *Soldiers Blue and Gray* (Columbia: University of South Carolina Press, 1988), 81–82.

[38]MS. recollections, James Fenton Papers, Regimental Papers of the Civil War, WRHS. *Zanesville (Ohio) Courier,* December 3, 1861; *Zanesville City Times,* December 7, 1861; both cited in Brett Barker, "The Forgotten Majority: The Northern Homefront During the Civil War, Zanesville, Ohio, 1860–1865" (unpub. M.A. thesis, The Ohio State University, 1989), 76–77. There was nothing unusual about such acts of petty vandalism against the soldiers' own people. Much the same thing had occurred during the War for Independence. See Charles Royster, *A Revolutionary People at War: The Continental Army and the American Character, 1775–1783* (paperback edition; New York: Norton, 1979), 72–74.

[39]Lucius W. Barber, *Army Memoirs of Lucius W. Barber, Company "D," 15th Illinois Volunteer Infantry* (Chicago: J.M.W. Jones, 1894), 64. For instances of authorized foraging, see Charles M. Clark, *The History of the Thirty-ninth Regiment, Illinois Volunteer Veteran Infantry (Yates Phalanx) in the War of the Rebellion, 1861–1865* (Chicago: n.p., 1889), 76; Henry R. Pyne, *Ride to War: The History of the First New Jersey Cavalry,* ed. by Earl Schenck Miers (New Brunswick, NJ: Rutgers University Press, 1961), 33–34.

bitter response from the civilians whose goods were taken. In early November 1861, a Union brigadier general in eastern Kentucky lamented that he could not supply himself in his present position and was forced to subsist his troops on the countryside. Despite his policy of issuing vouchers for all goods taken, he wrote, "the utmost dissatisfaction prevails among the inhabitants." The Confederates had already plundered the region to a large extent, "and we are at this time virtually plundering the people of what little they have left. Our promises to pay are looked upon by the people as a mere sham, amounting to nothing. We are taking at the point of the bayonet what the citizens really need for the support of their families, without returning to them anything available therefor; thus turning against us a public sentiment we should endeavor to cherish."[40]

It would be wrong, however, to suggest that Union soldiers regarded the civilians in their midst simply as potential sources of food and fuel. They quickly developed strong personal feelings about them as well. Sometimes these feelings were positive in nature; more usually they were hostile. Many grew to resent civilians, not so much for their presumed disloyalty as for their sharp practice and general ingratitude.

While still in Unionist western Maryland, for example, a soldier in the 13th Massachusetts reported that the local farmers, discovering that the troops had plenty of money, promptly raised the price of watermelons from two cents to twenty-five cents each, with corresponding price increases for butter, eggs, and other items. Once south of the Potomac, a soldier in another regiment found that the Virginians indulged in the same brand of price gouging. A farmer near their camp, he wrote, "used to supply pure Virginia corn-cakes at a quarter apiece, probably making twenty-four cents clear profit." A decade later he was still fuming about it: "I know the papers used to talk a great deal about Union people in Virginia, and their love for their country and our soldiers. It never happened to be our fortune to see any of those exceptions to Southern character, but we were duly impressed with the truth, that their love consisted chiefly in swindling the soldiers out of their money, and getting *a shot at them at night*. Possibly that may seem a hard statement, but it is not so hard as was the reality."[41]

Soldiers did not take this sort of thing passively if they could help it. In Campbellsville, Kentucky, the Ninth Ohio discovered a large strawstack in a field near their encampment. "At once we planned to demolish it for bedding," the regimental historian wrote, but in keeping with the conciliatory policy a guard was established over the strawstack instead. When the soldiers discovered a cache of apples hidden in the stack, the farmer decided to make what profit he could from them and began selling them to the soldiers "for filthy lucre." This exasperated the soldiers. "Suddenly" wrote the regiment's historian, "the stack burst into flame, by spontaneous combustion of course! We got the apples already roasted and for nothing —

[40]Brigadier General A. Schoepf to Captain George E. Flynt (Assistant Adjutant General to Brigadier General George H. Thomas), November 2, 1862, OR 4:329.
[41]Davis, *Three Years in the Army*, 9; Bicknell, *Fifth Maine*, 69.

certainly healthier and cheaper than buying them from the would-be sly Kentuckian."[42]

By far the largest source of soldiers' complaints toward civilians, however, stemmed from the stubborn hostility they encountered even when attempting to safeguard private property. During the occupation of Winchester, Virginia, for example, a protective guard was placed over the home of James Mason, a Confederate diplomat made famous by his recent capture during the *Trent* affair. It had little effect on his family, however. "Their sentiments were of the rabid kind," wrote a Massachusetts soldier. "They believed a dead Yankee was the best kind of Yankee. We did our best, by good nature and politeness, to remove their impressions; but it was no go, as the gangrene of contempt had too deeply affected their minds to allow a change of heart."[43]

Such ingratitude sometimes produced reprisals from exasperated Northern troops. While in the lower Shenandoah Valley, for example, a known secessionist farmer approached the colonel of the 1st Pennsylvania Cavalry for protection; the colonel obligingly posted a number of guards. But when he asked if he and his staff could sleep in the farmer's house overnight, the farmer curtly refused. The colonel then withdrew the guards and "told the boys to help themselves." The soldiers swarmed over the place, slaughtering livestock and seizing smoked meats and grain. "Yes, we helped ourselves," one trooper recalled, "and the whole staff of officers stayed all night too. After twelve hundred of us had helped ourselves, there wasn't much left. . . ."[44]

Sometimes such incidents came in retaliation for Confederate depredations upon Southern Unionist families. In August 1861, the Sixth Ohio, stationed near Beverly, Virginia, learned that a force of rebel cavalry had been confiscating the cattle herds of local Unionists. The regiment sent an expedition in pursuit. Frustrated in their efforts to bring the perpetrators to bay, they contented themselves with burning the homes of "two or three notorious rebels." In May 1862, the men of the Tenth Maine learned from Unionist merchants in Martinsburg, Virginia, that some of Stonewall Jackson's troops had gutted their stores. "It was not long," wrote Captain John Gould Mead, "before the soldiers . . . returned the compliment upon a rebel shopkeeper. . . ."[45]

The conciliatory policy left scant room for any such acts against civilians, and some

---

[42]Constantin Grebner, *We Were the Ninth: A History of the Ninth Regiment, Ohio Volunteer Infantry, April 17, 1861, to June 7, 1864,* trans. and ed. by Frederic Trautmann (Kent, OH and London: Kent State University Press, 1987 [1897]), 82.

[43]Davis, *Three Years in the Army,* 35. See also "Anti-Rebel" [pseudonym of Wilbur Fisk] to Editor, *Freeman,* May 20, 1862, Wilbur Fisk Papers, LC.

[44]Aaron E. Bachman typescript memoir, HCWRTC, USAMHI. For similar accounts, see S. F. Horrall, *History of the Forty-second Indiana Volunteer Regiment* (Chicago: Donahue and Henneberry, 1892), 114–115; and Hartwell Osborn, *Trials and Triumphs: The Record of the Fifty-fifth Ohio Volunteer Infantry* (Chicago: A.C. McClurg, 1904), 40, 42.

[45]E. Hannaford, *The Story of a Regiment; A History of the Campaigns . . . of the Sixth Regiment, Ohio Volunteer Infantry* (Cincinnati: n.p., 1868), 95–97. John Gould Mead, *History of the First-Tenth-Twenty-ninth Maine Regiment* (Portland, ME: S. Berry, 1871), 146. Mead himself was ambivalent about the reprisal and carefully noted that it was done "at the instigation of some worthless local characters."

officers made stringent efforts to prevent them. Writing from Missouri in March 1862, Colonel Hans W. Heg assured his wife that despite certain knowledge that a local plantation owner was secessionist in his sympathies, "I have protected his property so far, and not allowed the soldiers to destroy any thing." In the Shenandoah Valley, Captain Marcus M. Spiegel was proud of the control he maintained over his men. In a letter home he wrote that despite his cordiality toward "the boys," he felt certain that "there is no Captain in the Service that has more the respect and moral as well as military power over his boys than I have." As proof he offered the following: "Over 900 of the Refugees have returned to their homes and fireside since the advance of the Union troops, and still they come. Although when the Sesesh troops were here it was not safe for Union families to be here, but during the stay of the Union troops the Sesesh families are as much protected as Union, if they only behave themselves, and this is truly just as it should be."[46]

It took a gifted leader, however, to secure circumspect conduct from his troops while retaining their goodwill. More often, an officer who tried to enforce noninterference with civilian property courted much resentment. A Ninth Ohio captain with more zeal than sense attempted to forbid his company from using the straw found in a barn, despite the fact that the men were freezing from the brutal January cold. The troops, wrote the unit historian, "did not exactly obey with alacrity his order to leave the straw and come to the empty floor below and lie on the bare ground there." Undaunted, the captain probed the cracks in the loft's planking with the point of his sword to enforce the directive. Far from regarding this devotion to orders as virtuous, the historian considered it sheer "madness."[47]

West Pointers tended to be the strictest disciplinarians, but too often they discovered that volunteers would not accept regular army standards. Brigadier General John J. Abercrombie, a stout old smoothbore who had spent forty-six years in the military, issued a number of orders forbidding the theft of fence rails. The volunteers in his brigade found this very amusing. On one occasion he saw a group of Massachusetts men making off with a cargo of this illicit firewood, and bellowed, "*Put down those rails!*" The soldiers, however, decided that he had not been specific about *where* to put them down, so they made off through the woods to their campsite, where indeed they put them down at last. Although fretful lest a staff officer appear with orders summoning them before the general, the soldiers did not let their worry "interfere with building fires . . . and very soon the odor of boiling coffee could be distinguished."[48]

A large number of volunteer officers chose not to risk this kind of unpopularity and ridicule. In many cases, the troops they led were members of their home communities;

[46]Heg to his wife, March 23, 1862, in Theodore C. Blegen (ed.), *The Civil War Letters of Colonel Hans Christian Heg* (Northfield, MN: Norwegian-American Historical Association, 1936), 67; Marcus M. Spiegel to his wife, March 9, 1862, in Frank L. Byrne and Jean Powers (eds.), *Your True Marcus: The Civil War Letters of a Jewish Colonel* (Kent, OH: Kent State University Press, 1985), 64.

[47]Grebner, *We Were the Ninth*, 83.

[48]Davis, *Three Years in the Army*, 41, 44–45.

they could not afford the cost of imposing a disciplinary code that the men found alien or distasteful. The soldiers often regarded their thefts as a kind of prankish lark, mischievous but essentially harmless. A number of volunteer officers exhibited the same attitude.

Stories of whimsical indulgence by officers abound in the annals of Civil War soldiers. "Last Sunday the boys came to me and wanted to know 'what about getting' a pig," wrote an Ohio captain to his wife in September 1861. "I asked if it belonged to *secessia,* they said they believed so. I told them it was not necessary for a Capt. to see or know everything – they went away – the next day on the march I was presented with a piece of fresh pork finely roasted. It was very good." "Very strict orders were issued by the General against our killing hogs," wrote an Illinois soldier in the fall of 1861, "but Col. Ellis, who was ever ready to humor the boys when he could without implicating himself or violating his honor, managed to elude somewhat this order. He told the boys not to let him see them with fresh pork. The boys understood this hint and when they got fresh pork they kept it out of his sight, or, when he was around, he would persistently turn the other way, but he had fresh meat for supper nearly every night."[49]

Occasionally, officers not only turned a blind eye to unauthorized foraging, but actively participated in it. The adjutant of an Illinois regiment led an expedition against the "plantation of a noted secessionist" which yielded "six chickens, six ducks, a tub of link sausage, a pot of honey and a sack of hickory nuts, which were all bagged and sent forward to camp." An Indiana soldier wrote that his unit unearthed – and grabbed – several hundred pounds of pork from an Alabama farmer who lived along their line of march. "Col. Denby was with us," he added, "giving us 'object lessons' regarding the correct method of concealing goods acquired by discovery."[50]

Finally, a few units were led by officers whose personal convictions went beyond simply permitting their troops to rustle the occasional unauthorized ham. These commanders actively resented the conciliatory policy and deliberately ignored it as much as they possibly could. The division of Brigadier General Louis Blenker, which served in the Shenandoah Valley, had a reputation for wholesale pillage wherever it went. In western Virginia and later in middle Tennessee, Colonel Robert L. McCook's brigade took pride in its rough-and-ready behavior toward the secessionist population. As early as October 1861, it was already burning houses and public buildings in the towns along its line of march.[51]

[49]Thomas T. Taylor to his wife, September 25, 1861, Thomas T. Taylor Papers, OHS. Barber, *Army Memoirs,* 36. See also Samuel H. Putnam, *The Story of Company A, Twenty-fifth Regiment, Mass. Vols. in the War of the Rebellion* (Worcester, MA: Putnam, Davis & Co., 1886), 207–208.

[50]Clark, *Thirty-ninth Illinois,* 60–61. Horrall, *Forty-second Indiana Regiment,* 131. Colonel Denby apparently had a considerable passion for teaching his men to conceal stolen goods. In Nashville, a few months before, his troops had stumbled upon a considerable amount of pork, had artlessly carted it off in broad daylight, and had promptly been arrested. Hearing of the incident, Denby is supposed to have remarked, "I don't care a ---d---n if they steal the whole Southern Confederacy, but they must learn to hide." Ibid., 110–111.

[51]Josiah Marshall Favill, *The Diary of a Young Officer* (Chicago: R.R. Donnelly and Sons, 1909), 71; Pyne, *Ride to War,* 33; John P. Hatch to his father, June 29, 1862, John P. Hatch Papers, LC. Grebner, *We Were the*

In themselves these incidents did nothing to help defeat the Confederacy. They had scant impact on the South's economic infrastructure and contributed little toward undermining the Confederate will to resist. What they did accomplish was to make implementation of the conciliatory policy more difficult than it might otherwise have been. Southern civilians had begun the war in the firm expectation that Northern troops would conduct themselves as barbarians. The simple appearance of armed soldiers in their midst shocked and disgusted many of them, and even the mildest military occupation generated a sense of anger and mortification.[52]

The diary of Cornelia McDonald illustrates how difficult it could be to conciliate a secessionist civilian. Mrs. McDonald was a resident of Winchester, Virginia, which was captured by forces under Major General Nathaniel Banks in March 1862. Banks was an emphatic proponent of conciliation, and Mrs. McDonald confessed that the Union troops behaved well. Even so, she thought, they looked "triumphant and insolent." When a Union colonel decided to use her residence as his headquarters, she considered it outrageous, even though he proved quiet and considerate. He even discreetly removed the American flag from her porch, since it offended her, and flew it at some distance from the house. Nevertheless, she reported every minor infraction to her property rights committed by his troops, "with the intention of annoying him, and thereby disgusting him with his quarters." He invariably responded by asking her to point out the culprit. Usually she could not. On the one occasion when she did, he responded by strapping the offender over a barrel in plain sight of the house. But even this did not appease her: "[I]t was malicious in him to punish the man where I could see it."[53]

In such a climate of suspicion and hostility, most acts of kindness and generosity were lost on the Southern population. But every petty theft, every act of vandalism, every hard word on the part of Union soldiers confirmed Southerners in their resentment and vindicated their fears. In the final analysis, the success of the conciliatory policy depended on two variables: the willingness of Northern soldiers to leave civilians alone and the willingness of civilians to leave soldiers alone. From the outset, the first condition was seldom secured; and the man in the ranks soon discovered that the second was quite unlikely.

Ninth, 76–77, recounts that the regiment plundered and burned Fayetteville in western Virginia on October 19, 1861.

[52]As early as May 30, 1861, Confederate Colonel Daniel Ruggles, based at Fredericksburg, Virginia, was reporting, "Much agitation prevails along the Potomac coast from apprehension that the enemy will land, in large and small numbers, to devastate and plunder." OR 2:55.

[53]Hunter McDonald (ed.), *A Diary with Reminiscences of the War and Refugee Life in the Shenandoah Valley, 1860–1865* (Nashville, TN: Cullom and Ghertner, 1934), 40–46.

3

Early occupations

Hindsight can obscure as much as it illuminates. Knowing, as we do, that the Civil War lasted four years and cost over half a million dead, it is difficult to grasp how differently affairs appeared in early 1862. To contemporary eyes, the conflict seemed anything but stalemated; it looked as if the Union were about to gain a quick, comparatively inexpensive triumph. Within weeks, Northern forces won several glittering victories all along the military frontier: from Mill Springs in the highlands of eastern Kentucky to marshy Roanoke Island on the North Carolina coast and Pea Ridge in the Ozark Mountains of northwestern Arkansas. The important political and commercial center of Nashville capitulated without a fight in late February 1862; six weeks later, a Union fleet steamed past the guns of two Confederate forts and anchored at New Orleans, the South's largest city and chief port. Confederate morale was staggered. "[A]ccounts of our sad disasters come thick and fast," moaned a Virginia woman. ". . . We are almost in despair."[1]

Wherever Union armies marched, they perceived a white population abashed by defeat and disillusioned with secession. A Northern officer who discussed the political situation with a group of Tennesseeans discerned a recurrent theme. "[O]ne thing appears through the whole," he wrote, "that families have been divided, that brothers & neighbors have been arrayed against each other, that no one knew whom it would be safe to trust, in fact that a perfect reign of terror had been inaugurated throughout the country & that they, as a general thing, hail the Union army as deliverers rather than invaders & destroyers. . . ."[2]

As the Federal columns advanced southward, they carried with them two policies toward Southern civilians. Both were conservative, both sought to confine violence to

---

[1]Entry for February 19, 1862, Lucy (Wood) Butler diary, VHS. Similar statements during this period abound. See, for example, entry for April 28, 1862, Samuel A. Agnew diary, SHC; J. B. Jones, *A Rebel War Clerk's Diary at the Confederate States Capital,* ed. Howard Swiggett, 2 vols. (New York: Old Hickory Bookshop, 1935), vol. 1, 125, 126–127; C. Vann Woodward, ed., *Mary Chesnut's Civil War* (New Haven, CT: Yale University Press, 1981), 328–405 passim. For discussions of Confederate morale, see Bell Wiley, "The Waning of Southern Morale," in his *The Road to Appomattox* (New York: Atheneum, 1983 [1956]), 49–58; Emory M. Thomas, *The Confederate Nation, 1861–1865* (New York: Harper and Row, 1979), 138–143.

[2]Entry for March 10, 1862, Eugene Marshall diary, DUL.

the battlefield and eschewed massive destruction of property, but only one fully accorded with the spirit of Scott and McClellan. The armies that marched into Virginia, the Carolinas, and Tennessee were the main disciples of conciliation. Farther west, the policy was subtly but unmistakably different. Spawned in the internecine strife of Missouri, it extended the hand of magnanimity less easily. Unlike the conciliatory policy, which viewed practically all white Southerners as alienated brethren, the western program saw the population in terms of friends to be protected and enemies to be crushed.

THE PRAGMATIC POLICY

Among those in Missouri who found a conciliatory posture ineffectual was Brigadier General Ulysses S. Grant. Initially optimistic, in July 1861 he informed his wife that the local population seemed very responsive to the forbearance and respect for property shown by his troops. "I am fully convinced," he wrote, "that if orderly troops could be marched through this country, and none others, it would create a very different state of feeling from what exists now." Within a few weeks, however, this easy confidence had soured considerably. His brushes with Missouri bushwhackers convinced him that the locals were "great fools" who would not be satisfied "until they bring upon themselves all the horrors of war in its worst form. The people are inclined to carry on a guerilla [sic] Warfare that must eventuate in retaliation and when it does commence it will be hard to control." The attitude of the civilian population perplexed him: "Send Union troops among them and respect their rights, pay for everything you get and they become desperate and reckless because their state sovereignty is invaded. Troops of the opposite side march through and take everything they want, leaving no pay but script [sic], and they become desperate secession partisans because they have nothing to loose [sic]. Every change makes them more desperate."[3]

Missouri continued to roil. In the weeks after hurling his curt, *"This means war"* to the governor, Nathaniel Lyon pushed the state's pro-secessionist militia toward the southwestern border with Arkansas. The militia, however, united with a small Confederate army and turned to confront Lyon's forces at Wilson's Creek. In the fighting that ensued, the fiery Union leader lost both the battle and his life. By the end of August 1861, a rebel column under Sterling Price had raided far into the state's interior.

The recently appointed Union department commander, Major General John C. Frémont, could do little to retrieve the situation. As hundreds of Missourians rallied to Price or bushwhacked Northern troops, Frémont endorsed draconian measures, invoked martial law, and even attempted to free the slaves of Missouri secessionists –

---

[3]Grant to Julia Dent Grant, July 19, 1861, John Y. Simon (ed.), *The Papers of Ulysses S. Grant,* 16 vols. to date (Carbondale and Edwardsville: Southern Illinois University Press, 1967-), vol.2, pp. 72–73; Grant to Julia Dent Grant, August 3, 1861, ibid., 83; Grant to Mary Grant, August 12, 1861, ibid., 105.

though Lincoln promptly forced him to repudiate his emancipation order. Elsewhere, Kansas Senator James H. Lane, a militant Free Soiler, led his "jayhawkers" on a savage tour through the state and burned the town of Osceola, which had displayed sympathy for the rebel invaders. Frémont could not control him, nor could he retrieve the deteriorating situation in Missouri, and in November he was removed from command. Lincoln replaced him with Major General Henry W. Halleck.

Halleck was forty-six, a West Point graduate and accomplished military scholar who had left the Army in order to pursue more lucrative opportunities in law and business. When the war broke out he was in California, adding steadily to a personal estate already worth half a million dollars and supervising the publication of his legal treatise on international law. The firing on Fort Sumter and the furor it created in the North disturbed him. He wrote Senator Reverdy Johnson, a Maryland Unionist, that he worried the North "will become ultra anti-slavery, and thus add the horrors of a servile to that of a civil war." Nevertheless he resumed his military career, became a major general, and sailed for the East in October 1861. His assignment to the Department of the Missouri gave him his first direct exposure to the nature of the rebellion.[4]

Initially Halleck was quite conservative. His orders from McClellan required him "to impress upon the inhabitants of Missouri and the adjacent States, that we are fighting solely for the integrity of the Union, to uphold the power of our National Government, and to restore to the nation the blessings of peace and good order." In keeping with those instructions, one of Halleck's first acts was to issue General Order No. 3 barring fugitive slaves from his lines. Like McClellan, he wanted to avoid the Negro question as much as possible.[5]

He also thought the subordinate commanders already in Missouri had gone too far in their attempts to control the population. General Order No. 8, issued shortly after he took command, expressed severe disapproval for numerous cases of "alleged seizure and destruction of private property," which showed "an outrageous abuse of power and a violation of the rules of war." In the future, property could be seized only when absolutely necessary for the use of troops, or when the owners were actively supporting the enemy. Even then, only the highest officer in local command could give the order, and in all cases, the goods seized must be accurately itemized and receipts given. Halleck urged particular restraint in the case of property seized from active rebels: "Great caution should be used in this matter, as much injustice has been done to individuals who are not enemies, and much discredit cast upon our patriotic army by excesses committed by unauthorized persons pretending to act in the name of the United States."[6]

[4]Halleck to Reverdy Johnson, April 30, 1861, James Grant Wilson, "General Halleck, a Memoir," *Journal of the Military Service Institution of the United States* 36 (1905):553. On Halleck's early career, see Stephen E. Ambrose, *Halleck: Lincoln's Chief of Staff* (Baton Rouge: Louisiana State University Press, 1962), 3–10.

[5]McClellan to Halleck, November 11, 1861, Sears (ed.), *McClellan Papers,* 130; General Order No. 3, November 20, 1861, OR 8:370.

[6]General Order No. 8, November 26, 1861, ibid., 380–381.

Within a few weeks, however, Halleck saw enough to adopt a much harder line. The constant influx of Unionist civilians uprooted by Confederate and guerrilla depredations aroused his ire, and rebel forces in southwestern Missouri were robbing the inhabitants of food and clothing. Thousands of refugees streamed into St. Louis; their plight demanded stern measures in response. The rebels directly responsible lay beyond the reach of justice but, Halleck warned Missourians, "there are in this city and in other places within our lines numerous wealthy secessionists who render aid, assistance, and encouragement to those who commit these outrages. They do not themselves rob and plunder, but they abet and countenance these acts in others. Although less bold, they are equally guilty." He then collected $11,000 from prominent St. Louis secessionists to provide relief for uprooted Unionist civilians.[7]

Halleck clearly had little use for the conciliatory principle, with its deliberate mildness and its seemingly misguided efforts to retain full Constitutional protections for a people in the midst of an armed struggle. "Peace and war cannot exist together," Halleck instructed his command. "We cannot at the same time extend to rebels the rights of peace and enforce against them the penalties of war. They have forfeited their civil rights as civilians by making war against the Government, and upon their own heads must fall the consequences." If Union men were killed or robbed by bushwhackers, he declared, then secessionists within Federal reach could receive "the severest penalties justified by the laws of war for the crimes of their fellow rebels."[8]

At the same time, Halleck firmly rejected military actions that went beyond the scope of legitimate reprisal. When Confederate General Sterling Price wrote him an angry letter about Union depredations, Halleck replied with obvious embarrassment, "I presume you refer to a band of outlaws on the Kansas frontier. They do not belong to my command and they entered this department without my authority." He promised that no acts of wanton destruction would be tolerated and that he would deal severely with anyone who perpetrated them. Halleck already knew exactly who the guilty parties were. They were members of the 7th Kansas Cavalry – Charles R. Jennison's "Jayhawkers" of bleeding Kansas fame – and in a letter to Major General David Hunter, who commanded the neighboring Department of Kansas, he told Hunter to gain control over them: "The depredations of Jennison's men . . . are doing us immense injury in this State by making secessionists of large numbers of Union men. They do more harm than Price's whole army."[9]

Missouri formed the arena in which Federal commanders first adopted what might be called the pragmatic policy, a second way of dealing with the Southern population. The two programs had significant differences. Conciliation viewed civilian policy as

---

[7]General Order No. 13, 4 December 1861, ibid., 406; General Order No. 24, December 12, 1861, ibid., Series II, vol. 1, pp. 150–151. Barnard G. Farrar to Halleck, March 1, 1862, ibid., 170–171.

[8]General Order No. 13, 4 December 1861, OR 8:405. The section of the order in which this passage appeared dealt with Missouri guerrillas. Halleck, however, regarded the order as a fair example of his policy toward rebel civilians in general. See Halleck to Francis P. Blair, undated, quoted by Blair in a speech before the U.S. House of Representatives, *Congressional Globe,* 37th Congress, 2nd Session, part 1, p. 76.

[9]Halleck to Price, January 27, 1862, OR, Series II, vol. 1, p. 162. Halleck to Hunter, January 29, 1862, ibid., 162. See also Halleck to Lorenzo Thomas, January 18, 1862, ibid., vol. 8, p. 507.

an crucial adjunct to military strategy. It emphasized the possibility of using civilian morale to undermine the Confederacy, and therefore sought not only to tap unequivocally Unionist sentiment but also to attract Southerners whose loyalties were temporarily hostile. In contrast, adherents to the pragmatic approach thought the war had to be won militarily and so did not emphasize the role of civilian morale. Their goal was mainly to keep civilians on the sidelines. Because of this, their policy could be much more straightforward. They supported Unionists, punished active secessionists, and expected the remaining population to remain quiescent.

Halleck sought to run a taut ship in which everyone in his department, soldier and civilian alike, kept in line. Citizens who manifested support for the enemy could expect to have their property taken through confiscation or contribution. Soldiers who preyed on civilians could expect to be punished with equal severity. Such measures were designed to make the conflict between North and South a conventional military struggle as far as possible.

This did not mean that Halleck ignored the political impact of soldiers' behavior. His comments on the 7th Kansas Cavalry showed as much. So did a proclamation to his troops, issued in February 1862 as his forces embarked on active operations. Stressing the importance of good order and discipline, he appealed, "Let us show our fellow-citizens . . . that we come merely to crush out rebellion and to restore to them peace and the benefits of the Constitution and the Union. . . . They have been told that we come to oppress and to plunder. By our acts we will undeceive them."[10]

Halleck's winter offensive had two principal axes, the first from Cairo, Illinois, up the Tennessee and Cumberland Rivers, the second from Springfield, Missouri, into northwestern Arkansas. Both achieved splendid success. In mid-February 1862, a combined army-navy force led by Grant captured Forts Henry and Donelson, linchpins of the Confederate defense in Tennessee. Three weeks later, Union troops under Major General Samuel R. Curtis routed a rebel army at the Battle of Pea Ridge, Arkansas.

Grant's victory opened the Tennessee and Cumberland Rivers to rapid penetration by Union warships. Gunboats patrolling the rivers sent back word that Unionist sentiment in the region seemed strong. An Ohio colonel whose regiment went upriver by boat was impressed by the reception his men received. "All along the river our progress was greeted with cheering and waving of handkerchiefs. . . . All classes concur in their testimony that our troops treat the citizens better than the secession troops did." Similar reports came from Curtis's army as it advanced victoriously toward Little Rock. "Western Arkansas is particularly sick of the rebellion," Curtis wrote Halleck. "They never had much real affection for it."[11]

The advancing Federals left behind them a Missouri still riven by guerrilla warfare. Successive departmental commanders tried vainly to bring it under control, some-

---

[10]General Order No. 46, February 22, 1862, ibid., 563.
[11]Lieutenant William Gwin (USN), to Flag Officer Andrew Foote, March 5, 1862, ibid. 10, pt. 2:8. DeWitt Clinton Loudon to Hannah Loudon, March 13, 23, 1862, DeWitt Clinton Loudon Papers, OHS. Curtis to Halleck, April 5, 1862, OR 8:662; Curtis to W. Scott Ketchum, May 5, 1862, ibid. 13:369.

times with conciliatory tactics, sometimes by resorting to harsh measures. From mid-1862 onward, affairs in the state had scant effect on the conduct of the war as a whole. But the pragmatic policy spawned in the region remained a legacy for some time. It was the policy Halleck's forces carried with them when they marched from western Tennessee into northern Mississippi. And it remained in force when Halleck left the region in July 1862, to assume the duties of General-in-Chief.

Aside from Halleck, the other chief exemplar of the pragmatic policy was Major General Benjamin F. Butler. In many respects it seems odd to group them together. Halleck was a dull, bookish man and a West Point graduate; Butler was a flamboyant Democratic politician whose sole previous military experience had been his twenty-odd years of service with the Massachusetts militia. Where Halleck thought conventionally and systematically, Butler had a penchant for sublime improvisation. Halleck regarded the war as a contest between armies; Butler had a much stronger sense of the conflict as a struggle between polities. And yet their ways of dealing with civilians were much alike.

Until secession, Butler had been one of the strongest pro-Southern Democrats. During the 1860 election he was a Breckinridge supporter; earlier, he had even nominated Jefferson Davis for the Presidency. Like Halleck, Butler had his first view of the civil war in a border state, in his case Maryland. In April 1861, as his troops took control of the railroad lines linking Annapolis and Washington, he assured the Marylanders that his men would assist in putting down servile insurrection if one materialized. This announcement infuriated the abolitionist governor of Massachusetts, John Andrew, who thought Butler was deliberately trying to force the slavery issue with the Lincoln administration at a time when it could split Northern support for the war. At the same time, Butler warned secessionists not to use poison against his troops or he would incite the slaves against them. Similarly, when his troops occupied Baltimore he issued a proclamation announcing that while he came as a friend, he would tolerate no manifestations of sympathy toward the South. He also arrested several people and threatened to hang a wealthy secessionist.[12]

These actions made Butler a hero in the North, but they irritated the firmly conciliatory Scott and embarrassed Lincoln, who decided that Butler was a mixed asset. Butler was next sent to Fortress Monroe with orders that kept him on a short leash, but he made headlines again with his famous decision to treat runaway slaves as "contraband of war," a notion that anticipated by three months the First Confiscation Act.

Like Halleck, Butler was impatient with troops who committed depredations. "The Volunteer troops seem to have adopted the theory that all property of the inhabitants was subject to plunder," he wrote Scott shortly after assuming command at Fort Monroe. "I have taken the most energetic measures to correct this idea and

---

[12]Hans L. Trefousse, *Ben Butler: The South Called Him BEAST!* (New York: Twayne, 1957), 17–64, 72–75.

prevent plundering. There are some few flagrant instances, which can admit neither of palliation nor of justification." But he did not hesitate to retaliate against secessionists who trifled with the Union government. In July, for example, he ordered the destruction of a house from which a local Virginian had taken potshots at Northern troops. Although within months such measures would become routine, at that early stage of the war they still had the power to shock. Butler, however, thought them completely justified and indeed rather mild. He thought it better to have the house destroyed than the person or persons in it. "I thus hold the owner of the house responsible for the character of its inmates. If a mistake is made, property not life is lost."[13]

Butler's greatest opportunity to make policy toward civilians came in April 1862, when a Union fleet under Flag Officer David G. Farragut sailed past the forts guarding New Orleans and captured the Crescent City almost without a fight. Butler, who commanded the expedition's ground troops, followed the Navy into the South's greatest metropolis and immediately became its military ruler. The measures he adopted soon made him hated throughout the South. The city had a large, restive secessionist population many times the size of the Union occupation force. Butler was convinced that if he did not act promptly to overawe its residents, he would soon be forced to use wholesale violence to keep them in line. When a local gambler, William Mumford, tore down the Stars and Stripes from the U.S. Mint shortly after the city's surrender, Butler had him arrested, tried, and hanged. The act made Mumford a martyr but underscored the Union general's seriousness about maintaining order. When New Orleans women expressed their Confederate sympathies by insulting Union officers and soldiers, Butler ordered that any female who did so would be "regarded and held liable to be treated as a woman of the town plying her avocation." When a New Orleans woman laughed as a Union officer's funeral procession went by, Butler had her arrested and imprisoned for ten weeks on an island in the Gulf of Mexico. Then too, just as Halleck had done in St. Louis, he eventually imposed a contribution upon the wealthy secessionists of the city as a means to obtain funds for relief of the poor.[14]

These and similar actions, however, were not part of a campaign of large-scale repression. Butler had no vendetta against the Southern people and no desire to heap punishment on them for its own sake. His strategy was to make a few dramatic examples that would give the citizens of the occupied city pause before trifling with Federal authority. In many respects, his overall policy was temperate. He permitted

---

[13]Butler to Scott, June 4, 1861, in Benjamin F. Butler, *Private and Official Correspondence of Gen. Benjamin F. Butler During the Period of the Civil War,* comp. by Jessie Ames Marshall, 6 vols. (Norwood, MA: Plimpton Press, 1917), vol. 1, p. 123; Butler to "Mr. Cleveland," July 12, 1861, ibid., 171.

[14]General Order No. 28, May 15, 1862, OR 15:426; Special Orders No. 150, June 30, 1862, Butler, *Private and Official Correspondence* 2:36–37; General Order No. 25, May 9, 1862, OR 15:425; General Order No. 55, August 4, 1862, ibid., 538–542. There is an extensive literature on Butler's occupation of New Orleans. In particular, see Gerald M. Capers, *Occupied City: New Orleans Under the Federals, 1862–1865* (Lexington: University of Kentucky Press, 1965), 54–97; and Howard Palmer Johnson, "New Orleans Under General Butler," *Louisiana Historical Quarterly* 24 (April 1941):434–536.

most New Orleans newspapers to publish with a minimum of censorship, allowed the rabidly secessionist clergy to preach in relative freedom, and took firm steps to ensure that residents of the city received sufficient rations.

These measures might almost be termed conciliatory, except that Butler implemented his policy in such a way that the occasional draconian example overwhelmed all perception of mildness on his part. By the summer of 1862 he was easily the most hated man in the South – the dreadful "Beast" Butler who personified all that was debauched and barbaric about the Yankee cause.

CONCILIATION IN THE CAROLINAS AND VIRGINIA

Conciliation was stronger in the east. After showing early promise in western Virginia, it gained lodgments along the Atlantic coast. In August 1861, a small Union force managed to secure a small enclave at Cape Hatteras on North Carolina's Outer Banks. Although a brief rash of depredations occurred as some troops plundered the homes of local residents, the department commander, Major General John E. Wool, condemned the excesses, threatened dire punishment, and promised to indemnify the civilians thus wronged. Despite the initial unpleasantness, most inhabitants of the barrier islands warmly welcomed the National troops. A delegation urged Colonel Rush C. Hawkins, the local commander, to protect them fully, "as we have never taken up arms against your Government, nor has it been our wish to do so. We did not help by our votes to get North Carolina out of the Union." Hawkins, for his part, took great pleasure in telling Wool of the strong Unionist sentiment he encountered. It was so pronounced that he believed many local men would join the Federal army provided they could serve within North Carolina.[15]

Three months later, Major General John A. Dix dispatched a small expedition to gain control over Virginia's Eastern Shore. Militarily this expedition was a walkover; the region was strategically valueless and the Confederate government made no attempt to defend it. But as a test case for conciliation, the operation had real importance. A prominent Democratic politician, Dix believed in the policy as firmly as did McClellan. His instructions to Brigadier General Henry H. Lockwood, the officer in immediate command of the venture, were unequivocal and emphatic. One of the objectives of the expedition, Dix wrote, was to restore the Eastern Shore counties to the Union as had already been done in West Virginia. A conciliatory policy should be pursued toward everyone who was neither armed nor in the pay of the Confederate government. "No distinction should be made between the citizens of those counties in regard to the past. All who submit peaceably to the authority of the Government are

---

[15]See Wool to Colonel Rush C. Hawkins, September 10, 1861; and Wool to Winfield Scott, September 13, 1861, OR 4:607–609. Enclosure A, "Citizens of Hatteras to the Commander of the Federal Forces at Hatteras Inlet," in Hawkins to Wool, September 11, 1861, ibid., 611. At Lincoln's personal request, the War Department promptly issued General Order No. 79 (September 17, 1861), authorizing the formation of a regiment of North Carolina volunteers. Lincoln to Scott, September 16, 1861, ibid., 613.

to be regarded as loyal." Any soldier caught disturbing the person or property of a civilian, Dix insisted, was to be clapped in irons. [16]

It seemed to work. A few Union soldiers committed depredations upon touching Virginia soil, much to Lockwood's annoyance, but they were sternly dealt with. Within five days, Lockwood could report that the local population seemed "quite pleased" with Dix's conciliatory orders and were anxious to return to the Union fold.[17]

Meanwhile, yet another Union force consolidated its grip on the Sea Islands of South Carolina. In early November 1861, an amphibious expedition captured Hilton Head, Port Royal, and a number of other points in the vicinity, primarily to create a coaling station for the blockading warships that patrolled the Confederate shoreline. Like Dix and Lockwood, Brigadier General Thomas W. Sherman, the expedition commander, came ashore announcing a conciliatory policy. Unlike them, he found no Unionist sentiment among the civilians; indeed, he found almost no civilians at all. Most of the region's white inhabitants – wealthy rice and cotton planters for the most part – had fled as soon as the black outlines of the Union fleet loomed over the horizon. Sherman instead inherited a huge population of slaves, suddenly freed from their masters, confused but hopeful that their liberation might be permanent, and decidedly a major policy problem.[18]

As for the abandoned plantations in his midst, Sherman quickly discovered that with no owners around to deter them or protest, his soldiers embarked on a rampant campaign of plundering and vandalism. "The country for many miles around," wrote one Union officer apologetically, "has fallen into the hands of our armies, and, unhappily, victors are apt to be ruthless in destroying the property of conquered enemies." This excited Sherman's indignation, and on November 11 he issued a general order forbidding such conduct. "The first duty of the soldier," he lectured, "is the protection of the citizen. The political character of the citizen is not to be judged and weighed in this manner by the soldier, and there must be by him no molestation of his lawful rights. The Government alone is to decide how far the present unfortunate condition of this portion of the country is to authorize or demand a departure from the well-settled principles of American law."[19]

Then, logically enough, he asked the War Department for instructions on the extent to which he could seize private property. He noted that all the owners were disloyal and had fled, that the houses were held only by blacks, and that among his troops there was a considerable "propensity to rob and pillage the houses and plantations." In response, the War Department relayed instructions from McClellan ordering Sherman "to seize all cotton and other property which may be used to our prejudice," and have it shipped to New York, where it would be sold and the proceeds

[16]Dix to Lockwood, November 11, 1861, ibid. 5:424–425.

[17]Lockwood to Dix, November 16, 1861, ibid, 435.

[18]"Proclamation to the People of South Carolina," November 8, 1861, ibid. 6:5.

[19]William T. Lusk to his mother, November 13, 1861, in [William C. Lusk (ed.),] *War Letters of William Thompson Lusk* . . . (New York: n.p., 1911), 100; General Order No. 24, November 11, 1861, OR 6:187.

deposited in the government treasury. McClellan also thought the unattached slaves should be utilized to load the cotton and construct defensive works – apparently in order to keep them out of mischief. Beyond that, however, McClellan's orders remained firmly conciliatory:

> Private property of individuals should not be interfered with, unless it be of military utility . . . and you are justified in taking measures to prevent pillage or any outrage so far as the exigencies of the service will permit, *no matter what relations the persons or property may bear to the United States Government.*[20] (Emphasis supplied.)

Sherman, who warmly concurred with the conciliatory policy, hesitated even to go as far as McClellan directed. He was willing enough to confiscate the cotton, which was widely considered the Confederacy's major financial resource and hence essentially a public commodity, but initially he hesitated to employ the blacks within his lines. He considered them indolent by nature and hence unsuited to free labor. Besides, he wrote the War Department, they seemed too distracted by their sudden freedom to settle into any scheme of structured employment. On the whole he thought it best to encourage the coastal planters to return to their lands and promise to respect their opinions and property. The planters, however, frustrated his design by failing to return and in the meantime both soldiers and blacks continued to loot the abandoned mansions and outbuildings. Sherman soon concluded, much against his own predispositions, that the only way to preserve the planters' property was to confiscate it. The Radical Republican element heartily endorsed this measure; Salmon Chase, the staunchly antislavery Treasury Secretary, used his department to administer the acquired lands, and the stage was set for what would become the famous Port Royal experiment.[21]

The experiment was destined to produce such explosive novelties as a premature and quickly aborted emancipation attempt and the first efforts to enlist blacks as Union soldiers. But policy toward white civilians in coastal South Carolina remained conservative for many months, even after the Department of the South – as Sherman's command was designated – began to gain additional footholds along the coasts of Georgia and Florida. Faith in the shallowness of Southern support for the rebellion and in the possibility of returning them to loyalty remained high. A Union staff officer who observed the inhabitants of Beaufort, South Carolina, echoed conservative orthodoxy when he observed, "The fact is, though the people of respectability are many of them rampant, the poor whites think the war a hard thing, which they do not like to bear." A few days later, the officer succored a wounded Confederate soldier who had been captured after a minor battle. The rebel, he reported home, had seemed overwhelmed by the gentle attention he received. "Ah, there's a mistake somewhere," he quoted the man as saying, "We think you come here to murder, and burn and destroy." It would take time, the officer concluded, but by combining fierce military

---

[20]T. W. Sherman to Lorenzo Thomas, November 15, 1861, ibid., 188; Lorenzo Thomas to T. W. Sherman, November 22, 1861, ibid., 192.

[21]For the origins of the Port Royal Experiment, see Willie Lee Rose, *Rehearsal for Reconstruction: The Port Royal Experiment* (Indianapolis and New York: Bobbs-Merrill, 1964), 3–32.

vigor with kindness to all who fell within their power, "even South Carolina may learn the lesson that there is a mistake somewhere."[22]

Certainly Sherman himself agreed. At the end of February 1862, in a letter to the General-in-Chief, he wrote that McClellan's grand strategy seemed to be working. "My opinion is that you have about crushed this rebellion already. The Savannah and Charleston papers show a deeply saddened spirit among the people. . . . I know the people of the South are unable to stand this state of things long. They are quick to fight when occasion offers, but as quick to fall when misfortune occurs."[23]

Other welcome indications followed. In March 1862, a corps-sized force detached from the Army of the Potomac entered the lower Shenandoah Valley and adjoining Loudoun County. The commander of the advanced element in Loudoun County reported that "[t]he order preserved and respect for property maintained (unexpected, through misrepresentations made with regard to the Federal Army) left a favorable impression on the people, and friends to the Union came forward in every town and village and proclaimed their allegiance to the Government." A few days later, when his troops occupied Leesburg, the officer reported to his superiors, "I find considerable secession proclivity here, but we have made an impression upon them by a respect for property and proper exhibition of decorum, which they have been educated to suppose was foreign to us, as we were designated as ruthless pillagers."[24]

Inevitably, some depredations did occur as troops "liberated" fence rails, chickens, and pigs, but Major General Nathaniel P. Banks, the overall commander in the area, took pains to eliminate this. On March 13, 1862, he issued orders forbidding his troops to leave their camps without proper passes and sternly cautioned "against any injury to private or public property or any interference with rights of citizens." As for the local civilian population: "All well-disposed persons are invited to pursue their ordinary vocations. Those who enter the town for the purpose of trade or to supply its markets at reasonable prices will be assured of all proper protection by the provost-marshal. It is the object of the military authorities," Banks assured them, "to re-establish the privileges hitherto enjoyed by all classes of the American people."[25]

A Virginia native on Banks's staff worked tirelessly to convince the people of the Valley that this was indeed the case. When he received word of infractions by the soldiers – minor affairs, he thought on the whole, "no mischief done, no wanton acts of destruction" – he "interfered in every case and succeeded in giving much relief and apparent satisfaction." The problem, he thought, stemmed from a simple failure of mutual understanding: "The inhabitants believed that the army was a horde of Cossacks and vandals, whose mission was to subjugate the land, to burn, pillage, and destroy. Hence they are received with distrust and terror, and their slightest disorders

---

[22]Lusk to his mother, December 20, 1861, Lusk (ed.), *War Letters*, 110; Lusk to his mother, January 9, 1862, ibid., 114.

[23]T.W. Sherman to McClellan, February 28, 1862, OR 6:236–237.

[24]Report of Colonel John Geary, May 14, 1862, OR 5:513. The incident in question occurred on March 5. Geary's report, March 9, 1862, ibid., 549.

[25]General Order No. 26, March 13, 1862, ibid., 747.

magnified by the imagination into monsters and menacing crimes. The soldiery, on the other hand, thought they were entering a country so embittered and infuriated that every man they met was a concealed enemy and an assassin, and every woman a spitfire." Given time, he felt confident both parties would recognize their error. When that occurred, "the great majority of the people will return to their duty and loyalty, better subjects than ever before."[26]

Major General Ambrose E. Burnside's North Carolina expedition provided yet another apparent success for the conciliatory policy. Building on the earlier Hatteras enclave, in the late winter and early spring of 1862 his troops penetrated into the North Carolina coastal plain, captured Roanoke Island, New Berne, and Morehead City, and began a longterm occupation of the region. Before Burnside's departure on this venture, McClellan instructed him to use "great caution in regard to proclamations," to say as little as possible about "politics or the negro," and to "merely state that the true issue for which we are fighting is the preservation of the Union & upholding the laws of the Gen'l Govt, & stating that all who conduct themselves properly will as far as possible be protected in their persons & property."[27]

A close personal friend of McClellan, Burnside was also a firm advocate of conciliation. To the forces under his command he emphasized that they were going to North Carolina strictly "to support the Constitution and the laws, to put down rebellion, and to protect the persons and property of the loyal and peaceable citizens of the State." While on the march, he stipulated, "all unnecessary injury to houses, barns, fences and other property will be carefully avoided, and in all cases the laws of civilized warfare will be strictly observed." Burnside urged Carolinians to ignore secessionist assertions that Federal troops had come to steal slaves, destroy property, and outrage Southern womanhood. Such talk, he assured them, was ludicrously false. On the contrary, "The Government asks only that its authority may be recognized, and, we repeat, in no manner or way does it desire to interfere with your laws constitutionally established, your institutions of any kind whatever, your property of any sort, or your usages in any respect."[28]

As at Hatteras, the policy seemed to produce good results. Many of the coastal inhabitants seemed alienated from the Confederacy and anxious to return to the Union. In mid-March, Colonel Thomas G. Stevenson took the 24th Massachusetts and several gunboats to the town of Washington on the Pamlico River. There the Union troops nailed the Stars and Stripes to the courthouse, a band played gaily, and the men cheered. "I was glad to notice considerable Union sentiment expressed by the inhabitants," he reported. "From quite a number of houses we were saluted by waving handkerchiefs, and from one the national flag, with the motto, 'The Union and the

---

[26]David H. Strother, Diary, entries for March 1, 6, 1862, in Cecil D. Eby (ed.), *A Virginia Yankee in the Civil War: The Diaries of David Hunter Strother* (Chapel Hill: University of North Carolina Press, 1961), 6, 9.

[27]McClellan to Burnside, January 7, 1862, in Sears (ed.), *McClellan Papers,* 149–150.

[28]General Order No. 5, February 3, 1862, OR 9:359–360; "Proclamation Made to the People of North Carolina," February 16, 1862, ibid., 364.

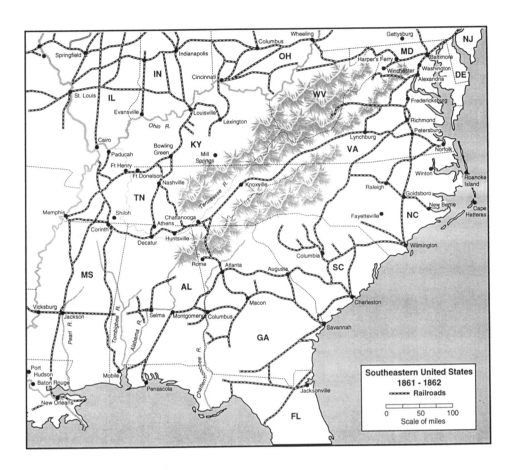

Southeastern United States
1861 - 1862
▪▪▪▪ Railroads

0   50   100
Scale of miles

Constitution,' was displayed. A large number of the inhabitants expressed a wish that sufficient force could be sent there to protect them from the rebels."[29]

By May, Burnside's force had begun to extend its control into the Albemarle Sound region, and Navy Commander S.C. Rowan issued the now standard declaration of policy toward the local population. He assured the town officials of Plymouth, North Carolina, that Union troops did not intend to "interfere with the people or to trouble private property." In exchange, he expected that the citizenry would "pursue their business and remain quiet." If they did, no harm would befall them; and as for slavery, so long as their masters did not employ their bondsmen in support of the Confederate war effort, Union forces would leave the peculiar institution alone. Rowan also left a

[29]Stevenson to Southard Hoffman, March 23, 1862, ibid., 269.

gunboat stationed at Plymouth, which helped to encourage the open manifestation of loyalist feeling among the local nonslaveholding population. Indeed, when offered the chance to enlist in a Federal militia regiment, over one hundred Washington County inhabitants did so.[30]

Yet despite Burnside's solicitude for loyal Carolinians and his determination to pursue a mild policy toward all civilians, the realities of war – the geographical expanse involved, the impossibility of rapid communications, and the resulting need for officers to exercise independent judgment – robbed him of the ability to oversee every detachment. As a result, within four days of his proclamation to the people of North Carolina, which denied any intention of fomenting widespread destruction, a Union brigade from Burnside's command burned an entire village to the ground.

On February 19, the brigade steamed aboard several gunboats up the Chowan River, intent on destroying two railroad bridges far upstream. Sometime during the morning, the flotilla was ambushed by Confederate troops – firing from the banks – after welcoming signals from a Negro woman drew them close to one shore. The next day the expedition landed and occupied the small hamlet of Winton, not far from where the ambush had occurred. The Confederate troops had disappeared, but finding that almost all the houses in the town (about twenty) had been used as storehouses and barracks, Colonel Rush C. Hawkins decided to burn the houses that had been used by the Confederate army. The resulting conflagration got out of hand and destroyed several other homes as well. In his report of the incident, Hawkins remarked – sincerely but inaccurately – that he believed it "the first instance during the war on our side where fire has accompanied the sword." He thought it therefore required explanation, and offered two of them. First, the destruction was justified as a retaliation for the ambush his troops had encountered the previous day. Second, the fact that the houses had sheltered Confederate stores and (until recently) Confederate troops rendered them legitimate military targets.[31]

Although Burnside loyally chose to support Hawkins' decision when he learned of it, it is difficult to see how he could have felt comfortable in doing so. His account of the incident to the War Department notes that just a few days prior to the incident, "it had been reported that . . . 500 loyal people at that place had raised the American flag." The report was almost certainly correct, given the widespread Unionist sentiments expressed by the inhabitants of that region. Moreover, Hawkins' narrative of the action specifies that the fusillade he received came from regular Confederate troops, not irregular partisans. Even the Negro woman who allegedly lured them into the ambush was stipulated to be the slave of a Confederate officer, not a local planter. Finally, the decision to burn the town was made, not on the spot when it was

---

[30]Wayne K. Durrill, *War of Another Kind: A Southern Community in the Great Rebellion* (New York and Oxford: Oxford University Press, 1990), 94, 102–103.

[31]Burnside to Lorenzo Thomas, February 23, 1862, ibid., p. 194. See also Commander S. C. Rowan to Flag Officer L. M. Goldsborough, February 22, 1862, *Official Records of the Union and Confederate Navies* (Washington: Government Printing Office, 1927), Series I, Vol. 6, pp. 654–655; Hawkins to Brigadier General John G. Parke, February 21, 1862; OR 9:195–196.

determined that the captured supplies could be removed in no other way, but the day previously, in the spasm of anger that followed the near-fatal ambuscade. Hawkins was explicit on that point: "[After the fusillade, t]he whole fleet came down to an anchor about 7 miles below Winton. A consultation was held, and it was agreed to return the next morning and burn the town if found to be occupied by the rebels." In the event, the town proved unoccupied, but the decision to destroy it was implemented nonetheless.[32]

What happened at Winton was clearly not in obedience to the "laws of civilized warfare," as Burnside had instructed his forces just days earlier, but was rather the product of simple frustration and rage. Hawkins' attempt at explanation was transparently unconvincing. In fact, it had not been a matter of an orderly destruction of enemy supplies that somehow got out of hand, but was accompanied by a great deal of pillaging and gratuitous destruction. A soldier in the Fourth Rhode Island wrote that while the town burned, the soldiers plundered. "[T]he boys found plenty of everything," he recalled, "and soon came flocking back to the boats loaded down with household goods, books, articles of food, and anything that suited their fancy." Another Federal informed his mother that "court houses, churches, beautifully furnished dwellings with velvet carpets, pianos, etc., all [shared] the same fate, and you may be sure that we gave it a pretty good ransacking while the flames were doing their work."[33]

The burning of Winton eloquently attested to the fragility of the conciliatory policy. Newspaper stories about it appeared in Southern papers from Petersburg, Virginia, to Wilmington, North Carolina. They did nothing to convince the population at large of the Yankees' benevolent intentions. The editor of the *North Carolina Standard* printed a letter from a Winton resident that described the burning, then asked his readers the obvious question, "After such a statement, what confidence can anyone have in the pretenses of Burnside and [Union Flag Officer Louis M.] Goldsborough, as to their designs not to disturb public property?"[34]

CONCILIATION IN KENTUCKY AND TENNESSEE

Yet another testing ground for conciliation was Kentucky. Torn between largely Southern roots and preponderantly Northern economic ties, the state was hopelessly divided between loyalty and secession. Unable to side firmly with one side or the

[32]Burnside to Thomas, February 23, 1862, ibid., 194; Hawkins to Parke, February 21, 1862, ibid., 195.

[33]George H. Allen, *Forty-six Months with the Fourth Rhode Island Volunteers, in the War of 1861–1865* (Providence, RI: J.A. and R.A. Reid, 1887), 86; John G. Barrett, *The Civil War in North Carolina* (Chapel Hill: University of North Carolina Press), 94.

[34]Item from the Wilmington (NC) *Journal*, February 27, 1862, reprinted in W. Buck Yearns and John G. Barrett (eds.), *North Carolina Civil War Documentary* (Chapel Hill: University of North Carolina Press, 1980), 38; Raleigh *North Carolina Standard,* March 12, 1862, quoted in Barrett, *Civil War in North Carolina,* 94. An episode similar to the burning of Winton, but on a smaller scale, occurred at Columbia, North Carolina, in early March. Ibid., 95.

other, its legislature finally took refuge in a desperate neutrality. Technically, of course, that was not an option – if Kentuckians would not stand for the Union then logically they stood against it – but in 1861 the Lincoln administration was hardly in a position to quibble. Whether or not the Federal government could secure the unstinting allegiance of the Bluegrass State, it must nevertheless avoid driving Kentucky into the Confederacy. "I think that to lose Kentucky is nearly the same as to lose the whole game," Lincoln confided to a friend in September 1861. "Kentucky gone, we cannot hold Missouri, nor, as I think, Maryland. These all against us, and the job is too large for us." If such a dire scenario came about it might be better simply to concede Southern independence.[35]

Even as Lincoln wrote this, however, the prospects for holding Kentucky in the Union fold had begun to improve. The border state's shaky neutrality had recently collapsed, the casualty of a witless Confederate incursion that was at once followed by the Union seizure of several important Kentucky towns along the Ohio River. Mindful of the population's delicate sensibilities, Lincoln sought to soothe their jangled nerves by sending a native son, Brigadier General Robert Anderson, to command the military Department of the Ohio that controlled the state.

Anderson promptly adopted a conciliatory posture. Although his unflinching defense of Fort Sumter the previous April had made him a national hero, the Kentuckian had been bitterly depressed by the outbreak of civil war and hoped it might be ended with little violence. In late September, he issued a proclamation to the citizens of the Bluegrass State that extended protection to anyone, regardless of political sympathy, provided he gave no active assistance to the Confederacy. A few weeks later, noting with "deep regret" that officers in his department had made a number of arrests on the "slightest and most trivial grounds," Anderson indicated that this was contrary to his wish, adding, "[M]any of those who at one time sympathized with rebellion are desirous of returning to their allegiance and wish to remain quietly at home attending to their business. A conciliatory, fair course pursued toward such persons will join them to our cause; the reverse may force them into the ranks of our enemies."[36]

Ill health forced Anderson's retirement after only a few weeks. But his second-in-command, Brigadier General William T. Sherman, continued the mild policy after taking over in early October. Although destined to become one of the most implacable advocates of hard war, at this stage of the conflict Sherman still believed in what he would later dismiss as "old West Point notions" concerning proper conduct toward noncombatants. Believing that soldiers should leave civilians scrupulously alone, he howled at troops who stole so much as a fence rail, and in general regretted the volunteers' penchant for destructive behavior. Having led a brigade at First Bull Run, he had been outraged when his men had committed a few relatively minor acts of

---

[35]Lincoln to Orville Browning, September 22, 1861, Basler (ed.), *Collected Works of Lincoln* 4:532.
[36]This proclamation does not appear in the OR, but its meaning is clear from an explanatory letter written by Anderson's assistant adjutant general. See Captain Oliver D. Greene to J.J. Anderson, Esq., September 27, 1861, OR 4:278; General Order No. 5, October 7, 1861, ibid., 296.

destruction. "No goths or vandals ever had less respect for the lives and property of friends and foes," he groused darkly, "and henceforth we ought never to hope for any friends in Virginia." When Union forces rustled cattle in central Kentucky, Sherman exploded to Anderson about "depredations that will ruin our cause." Once installed as department commander, he scrupulously paid for all property taken for Federal use and sternly punished acts of theft and vandalism. This policy, reported a correspondent of the *Cincinnati Commercial*, "has produced a marked change in favor of the Union cause."[37]

Sherman, however, seems to have followed a mild policy from the simple conviction that it was morally just and best for military discipline, not from any faith that conciliation would undermine Confederate resistance. He had already made up his mind that the war would be both long and destructive and, if anything, overestimated the extent of rebel sentiment, even in divided and nominally loyal Kentucky. His tenure in the department lasted only a few weeks before he was removed amid charges that he had suffered a nervous breakdown. The Department of the Ohio seemed to need a more phlegmatic temperament at its helm. McClellan promptly gave the job to Brigadier General Don Carlos Buell, one of his most trusted subordinates.[38]

In many respects, Buell might fairly be described as a McClellan without charisma. Like McClellan, he was a Douglas Democrat and an officer widely respected for his professionalism. Like him, he abhorred abolitionists. And like him, he was a strong advocate of conciliation. Indeed, of all Union commanders, none embraced the mild policy more firmly, nor clung to it more tenaciously, than Buell. But whereas McClellan captured his troops' devotion by dash and a winning personality, Buell elicited only a certain low-voltage respect, sometimes cordial, sometimes grudging, from those under his command. Subordinates thought him a "direct, martial-spirited man," with "an air of decision and business" about him, but in his personal style he was widely regarded as "a cold man." This coldness had considerable practical effect on his ability to impose the conciliatory policy on his subordinates. McClellan, for example, had a way of winning others to his point of view. When Southern civilians seemed unresponsive to conciliation and doubts arose about its efficacy, he could still maintain his troops' allegiance through appeals to their loyalty and sense of honor. But Buell's rigid, aloof demeanor alienated his soldiers and convinced them he was either misguided or a closet Southern sympathizer.[39]

When Buell assumed command of the Department of the Ohio, his written instructions from McClellan urged him to "bear in mind that we are fighting only to preserve the integrity of the Union and to uphold the power of the General Govern-

[37]Sherman to his wife, July 28, 1861, Sherman Family Papers, University of Notre Dame, South Bend, Indiana; Sherman to Anderson, September 29, 1861, Sherman Papers, University of Kentucky, Lexington; *Cincinnati Commercial*, October 17, 1861.

[38]For Sherman's tenure in Kentucky, see John F. Marszalek, *Sherman: A Soldier's Passion for Order* (New York: Free Press, 1993), 154–163.

[39]James A. Garfield to Harry Garfield, December 17, 1861, in Frederick D. Williams (ed.), *The Wild Life of the Army: Civil War Letters of James A. Garfield* (Lansing: Michigan State University Press, 1964), 49; Brigadier General Lovell H. Rousseau to Salmon P. Chase, April 15, 1862, Salmon P. Chase Papers, ILHS.

ment," and added that as far as military necessity would permit, he should "religiously respect the Constitutional rights of all." In general, McClellan advised, "be careful so to treat the unarmed inhabitants as to contract, not widen, the breach existing between us & the rebels. . . . It should be our constant aim to make it apparent to all that their property, their comfort, and their personal safety will be best preserved by adhering to the cause of the Union." Buell at once pursued these instructions with a fervent, one might almost say heroic, personal commitment to their fulfillment. When his troops occupied Nashville, Tennessee, late in February 1862, he issued General Order No. 13a, the foundation of his civilian policy.[40]

In it, Buell expressed his conviction that the occupation of the state capital would tap a huge reservoir of Unionist sentiment in Tennessee. He believed that "thousands of hearts . . . will swell with joy to see that honored [National] flag reinstated in a position from which it was removed in the excitement and folly of an evil hour; that the voice of her own people will soon proclaim its welcome, and that their manhood and patriotism will protect and perpetuate it." To insure this, Buell stressed the importance of a conciliatory policy: "We are in arms, not for the purpose of invading the rights of our fellow-countrymen anywhere, but to maintain the integrity of the Union and protect the Constitution under which its people have been prosperous and happy." Any overt acts that gave aid and comfort to the enemy would be halted, but only by "certain authorized persons, and is not to be assumed by individual officers or soldiers." Peaceable citizens, regardless of their sympathies, would not be "molested in their persons or property." Private property could be used for public purposes whenever military necessity required it, but only at the discretion of the highest ranking officers in the area and only with fair compensation for the owner. Soldiers could not enter the residences or grounds of citizens, for any reason, without formal authorization. Except for those who committed overt acts against the army, no civilian could be arrested without Buell's personal sanction. Finally, any soldier or officer who departed from the letter and spirit of these instructions would be severely punished.[41]

Although orders of this kind were practically standard among Federal commanders at this stage of the war, some of Buell's officers were disquieted by what they considered his excessive zeal on the subject. Buell's most influential and dangerous critic within his army was a division commander, Brigadier General Ormsby M. Mitchel, an Ohio-born West Pointer who had left the regular army to pursue a successful career as a professor of astronomy. Now back in uniform, Mitchel was obsessed with the idea that he deserved an independent command. In pursuit of this goal he began to cultivate fellow Ohioan Salmon P. Chase, and a part of his overall strategy involved taking potshots at General Buell.

Aware that Chase was already upset with Buell for having refused to undertake a campaign into Unionist east Tennessee (Buell had objected – correctly – that logistics made the move impossible), Mitchel began a letter to the Treasury Secretary by

---

[40]McClellan to Buell, November 12, 1861, Sears (ed.), *McClellan Papers,* 131–132.
[41]General Order No. 13a., February 26, 1862, OR 7:669–670.

deploring the "blunder" that had occurred when Buell had aborted this expedition. Moving on to his commander's current conduct, Mitchel launched into an extended critique of the policy exemplified by General Order No. 13a.

He had been present, Mitchel wrote, at a recent interview between Buell, the mayor of Nashville, and a delegation calling itself the "Committee of Citizens." It had distressed him to hear the commanding general assure them "in the most positive terms of full protection for themselves and their property; for which protection, no return whatever was demanded from them." Mitchel felt certain that this "extreme leniency" would "work evil and not good." In his view it did not tap Unionist sentiment, but rather insured that it would remain underground. In middle Tennessee there were thousands who, with a bit of prodding, would come out for the Union. However, "[t]hey fear the return of their military masters and they wish to have a good excuse to make for their change of sentiments, in case it is necessary." This excuse could be supplied if the Union army required citizens to take the oath of allegiance in return for military protection. If, however, everyone was protected regardless of his political loyalty, Union men had no incentive to come forth; indeed, they had good reason to remain silent, for a reversal to Northern arms would expose them to Confederate reprisals.

Therefore, if he were in charge of things, Mitchel would extend protection only to those who took the oath of allegiance, and while he would not imprison those who refused, he would certainly confiscate their property. "The poison of rebellion has penetrated deeply into the systems of our Southern people . . . ," Mitchel explained. "It needs some powerful antidote, and it can be more readily applied through the pocket than in any other way."[42]

The logic of this suggestion evidently impressed Chase, for he later suggested it to another Union commander, but it did not impress Buell. "It is not deemed advisable at present to administer the oath of allegiance or to arrest persons whose loyalty is only doubtful," Buell's adjutant replied when Mitchel raised the issue. "The general desires the protection of our forces to be extended with some liberality, and to reach a class of persons who are not hostile to us although not warmly our friends." This intention of winning over those who were lukewarm toward the Union was, of course, the very heart of the conciliatory policy.[43]

In any event, in the view of many observers, a more severe policy did not seem necessary. Another division commander, Brigadier General William Nelson, thought that the citizens of Nashville had been astonished and won over by the forbearance shown by Buell's army, particularly after the poor discipline shown by the Confederate troops during their retreat from the city. "The tide has already turned," Nelson assured Chase in a private letter of his own. "They [the population] seem to be awakening from some unpleasant dream." He felt certain that the Union men of Tennessee would soon vote the state out of the Confederacy and that "she will liberate

---

[42]Mitchel to Chase, March 2, 1862, Salmon P. Chase Papers, ILHS.

[43]Chase to Major General Irvin McDowell, June 24, 1862, ibid; Captain James B. Fry to Mitchel, March 1, 1862, OR 7:675.

the neighbours that touch her southern border." Nelson and Buell were so certain of the strength of the Union reaction in Tennessee that both counseled against the appointment of a military governor, believing instead that a freely elected governor would be just as reliable and a better emblem of conciliation.[44]

In the areas where it was attempted, the conciliatory policy in early 1862 gave every indication of proving sound. To be sure, Federal troops as yet occupied only a small portion of the Confederacy. And with hindsight it is apparent that most of these early successes occurred in regions where secession sentiment had never been strong to begin with – as in western Virginia. But contemporary Northern observers did not make that distinction. Although aware of regional variations in Southern political opinion, they believed in a generally high degree of Unionist sentiment. And for the moment, it seemed, they were correct. Many Southerners appeared to be losing heart in the war. Burnside's officers perceived it so in North Carolina, Union troops saw it that way around Port Royal, and Buell felt certain it was happening in Nashville. Even in regions where the conciliatory policy was not attempted, many officers and soldiers thought support for the Confederacy was rapidly on the wane. Butler himself believed as much, and wrote Secretary of War Edwin M. Stanton in late June that "the planters and men of property are now tired of the war, well-disposed toward the Union, only fearing lest their negroes shall not be let alone; would be quite happy to have the Union restored in all things."[45]

All eyes now turned to McClellan's great campaign against Richmond. The first six months of 1862 had brought a string of victories: Mill Springs, Forts Henry and Donelson, the seizure of the North Carolina coast, the Battle of Shiloh, and the capture of New Orleans, Island No. 10, and Memphis. The Confederacy had been bludgeoned along its entire frontier. Everyone now expected the Army of the Potomac to deliver the death blow.

---

[44]Nelson to Chase, February 28, 1862, Salmon P. Chase Papers, ILHS; Buell to McClellan, February 28, 1862, OR 7:671; Buell to McClellan, March 3, 1862, ibid., 673.

[45]Butler to Stanton, June 28, 1862, OR 15:502–503.

4

Conciliation abandoned

As spring gave way to summer, the diaries and letters of many Northerners began to fill with hopes for an early end of the war. Nearly all of them revolved around McClellan's campaign against Richmond. The Confederate capital was the heart of the rebellion, the lair of the "slave-holding aristocracy" and "military oligarchy" that had created and sustained secession. When it fell the Confederacy must surely die. "We have got New Orleans – and we are fast getting every important place," wrote a Union captain in Tennessee. "This war will soon be over. . . . When Richmond falls, the confederacy is played out." With expectations high for a victory at Richmond, Northerners could still find reason to support the conciliatory policy. It seemed to work, and it would surely ease the problems of reconstructing the Union – a task apparently now just weeks away.[1]

The great struggle for Richmond began on June 26, but not in the way Northerners expected. Instead of advancing triumphantly into the Confederate capital, McClellan's army came under a rain of hammer blows from General Robert E. Lee's Army of Northern Virginia. By the beginning of July, McClellan had abandoned his offensive and withdrawn his army into a string of hastily dug entrenchments along the banks of the James River. Despite his characterization of the retreat as a mere "change of base," most Northerners regarded it as a full-fledged defeat. The vision of an imminent end to the war vanished, replaced by anger and frustration as it became obvious that the struggle would continue indefinitely.

The first casualty of this new frustration was the conciliatory policy. Northern papers that had endorsed it at the beginning of July were publishing bitter editorials against it by month's end. The Lincoln administration also concluded that harsher measures were necessary. It issued new orders that encouraged Union armies to confiscate Southern property and live off the countryside whenever necessary. And the soldiers – always impatient with the conciliatory policy – now found that an increasing number of their generals agreed with them. Commanders who retained a magnanimous posture were derided for trying to make war "with kid gloves on."

---

[1] Hans C. Heg to Gunild Heg, May 5, 1862 and July 9, 1862, Blegen (ed.), *Civil War Letters of Colonel Hans Christian Heg*, 82, 105.

Their political backers scurried for cover. By the end of summer, support for conciliation had practically vanished.

THE CONFISCATION DEBATE AND FAILURE ON THE PENINSULA

The capture of Richmond formed the linchpin of McClellan's conservative strategy for winning the war with minimal bloodshed and bitterness. His August 1861 memorandum had called for the application of overwhelming force against the rebel capital, and the army he assembled for the purpose seemed mighty indeed. By the end of winter 1862, over 185,000 well-trained volunteers lay encamped in and around the Washington fortifications. Twenty-five miles away, a much smaller Confederate army, led by General Joseph E. Johnston, could muster barely 47,000 men. But McClellan's celebrated overcaution was already beginning to surface. Misled by inflated estimates of rebel numbers, the Union commander refused to attack Johnston's entrenched position near the old Bull Run battlefield. Instead he elected to exploit the North's superior seapower capability and ferry most of his army to Urbanna on the Rappahannock River. This scheme had two advantages: It would outflank Johnston's army and at a stroke place McClellan's army within fifty miles of Richmond.[2]

Ingenious in a purely military sense, the plan had one serious drawback. Political pressure for a prompt advance was already immense; McClellan's necessary delay while he prepared the logistical groundwork for his ambitious campaign simply swelled Northern impatience. As McClellan came increasingly under fire, his prestige dipped, and with it his ability to sustain the conciliatory policy in the face of growing opposition from the advanced Republicans. Now associated with a general who seemed reluctant to strike a blow, the policy seemed to them more flaccid than ever.

Efforts to undermine conciliation were already underway. In December 1861, Republican Senator Lyman Trumbull of Illinois had proposed a confiscation bill stronger and more encompassing than the one passed the previous summer. The debate on this new measure began ten weeks later. For the next six months – while McClellan prepared and unleashed his win-the-war offensive – Congress deliberated on whether to preserve conciliation or adopt more stringent measures.[3]

Trumbull's original bill, registered as S.151, permitted the confiscation of all property, real and personal, of anyone living where the rebellion made ordinary judicial proceedings impossible, provided the accused was in arms against the Government or was actively assisting the rebellion. It also mandated the emancipation of

---

[2]Abstract from return of the Army of the Potomac, February 1862, OR 5:732; abstract from return of the Department of Northern Virginia, February 1862, ibid., 1086.

[3]*Congressional Globe,* 37th Congress, 2nd session, part 1, p. 18. The best accounts of this debate are in Leonard P. Curry, *Blueprint for Modern America: Nonmilitary Legislation of the First Civil War Congress* (Nashville: Vanderbilt University Press, 1968), 75–100; and John Syrett, "The Confiscation Acts: Efforts at Reconstruction During the Civil War" (unpub. diss., University of Minnesota, 1971).

the convicted person's slaves and their transportation to a colony. Federal district courts would handle prosecution and deal with the confiscation in a fashion similar to prize cases or other foreign attachments. Although a clear repudiation of conciliation, the intent of the proposed bill was not, as is sometimes alleged, the inauguration of wholesale economic warfare against the South. Trumbull was after the leaders of the rebellion, not the rank-and-file. He estimated that his proposed legislation would affect barely one Southerner in ten.[4]

Conservatives, however, portrayed the bill as an indiscriminate assault on the rights of all Southerners, loyal as well as rebellious, and denounced it as unconstitutional. They also insisted that it was bad policy. Even before the debate on S.151 began, Senator Willard Saulsbury (Democrat-Delaware) sounded the keynote. Objecting to a resolution that seemed to give the military department commander in Kansas wide powers to enlist the aid of blacks and Amerindians, Saulsbury unleashed the classic argument for conciliation: "[U]nless you have or can develop what is called a Union sentiment in the South . . . you are [not] going to suppress this rebellion. Without that, I apprehend, the task of suppressing this rebellion will be too great for this Government." Senator Edgar Cowan (Republican-Pennsylvania) concurred. So, in major speeches against the bill, did Senators John C. Ten Eyck (Republican-New York), Orville Browning (Republican-Illinois), John S. Carlile (Union-Virginia), and John B. Henderson (Democrat-Missouri). Carlile pointedly quoted a number of conciliatory proclamations by Lincoln and Union military commanders and added, "Let us march steadily on observing the line of policy laid down by ourselves." Consistency demanded it, and recent events seemed to vindicate it. "Think you . . . if General Halleck and Commodore Foote had announced to the people of Tennessee that their purpose was to confiscate their property and turn them houseless and homeless upon the world, Nashville and Clarksville would have been ours? Would they not have been reduced to ashes, and would not their people have rushed with eagerness to the field and arrayed themselves under the standard of rebellion?"[5]

The Radical wing of the Republican party, however, not only insisted on pursuing a confiscation bill, but considered the Trumbull version too weak. They sought to make it more sweeping in its operation. Their reasons had less to do with the war effort as such than with their long held desire to secure freedom for Southern bondsmen. One senator favoring confiscation – Henry Wilson (Republican-Massachusetts) – candidly announced that emancipation was indeed his primary concern. "I care something for the confiscation of the property of the leading rebels," he went on; "but I do not wish to touch the property of the masses of the people. I think the distinction is a just one – that the leaders should be punished, and that the masses of the people should feel that they will be forgiven and protected if they return to their loyalty." The Radicals, in short, did not seriously regard confiscation as a war measure.[6]

The War Democrats, however, did, and Senator Joseph A. Wright (Democrat-

---

[4]*Congressional Globe,* 37th Congress, 2nd Session, 942–943, 1557.
[5]Ibid., 334; ibid., pt. 2, p. 1049, 1052, 1137, 1139, 1157–1161.
[6]Ibid., 1895.

Indiana) spoke for many when he urged confiscation as an act "essential to put down this rebellion." He thought it would enable Union forces to supply themselves from the countryside around them. Even so, close examination of Wright's speech suggests that he saw S.151 as directed primarily against "landed proprietors," not the Southern commoner. Like Trumbull, he saw the proposed act as one that would operate against the leading rebels. Moreover, Wright endorsed the strict orders in effect against pillaging. "The armies of the Government should be subsisted by the rebels only under regulations prescribed by the Government, and not by the liberty of indiscriminate pillage." Such a measure satisfied Wright's idea of a "vigorous prosecution of the war."[7]

Moderate Republicans also supported S.151, but voiced considerable doubts about its constitutionality and introduced a number of amendments intended to remove the constitutional difficulties. With conservatives hoping to kill the bill outright, Radicals hoping to sharpen its bite, and moderates fretting about its legality, the Senate in early May referred the matter to a select committee. Its membership favored the moderates, and soon they reported out a modified bill modeled after one proposed by Senator Jacob Collamer (Republican-Vermont). Before any property could be taken, the new bill (S.310) required individual conviction of rebels on charges of inciting or engaging in an insurrection. It permitted the property of certain classes of rebels to be seized, but only to be held pending judicial proceedings against them. It mandated the emancipation of the convicted defendant's slaves, permitted the President to emancipate the slaves of rebels in places still in rebellion six months after the bill's passage, and – as a major concession to the Radicals – authorized the President to enlist blacks as soldiers.[8]

Meanwhile, confiscation legislation in the House of Representatives had a rockier time of it. The judicial committee reported out several confiscation measures with the recommendation that they not be passed, and it required more than a month for the first of these bills even to be debated before the full House. Conservatives fought these proposals vigorously, and a caucus of House moderates announced its opposition to both confiscation and emancipation. As in the Senate, a select committee was formed to hammer out a compromise bill, and in mid-May the committee offered two of them: H.R. 471, which dealt with confiscation, and H.R. 472, which concerned emancipation. Despite their difficult birth, however, both measures went beyond what the Senate seemed willing to accept. When they were presented before the upper house, that body rejected H.R. 471. Instead it passed a milder version more in accord with the mood of the North, which was less enamored with punitive measures now that Federal victories augured an early end to the war. Even the mainstream Republican *New York Times*, after an early endorsement of confiscation, backed away and derided "these premature, ill-considered and sweeping manifestations of resentment."[9]

[7]Ibid., 1877.
[8]Ibid., 2112, 2165.
[9]*New York Times*, April 24, 1862. See also *Boston Post*, March 17, 25, 1862, and April 1, 1862.

While Congress debated confiscation, McClellan's Army of the Potomac embarked on its great expedition against Richmond. His original idea of disembarking at Urbanna was spoiled when the outnumbered Confederate army prudently withdrew behind the Rappahannock River. With the rebels now in a position from which they could rapidly counter an Urbanna landing, McClellan instead took his gigantic army to Fort Monroe, at the tip of the peninsula between the York and James Rivers. An armada of over 400 ships ferried nearly 100,000 Union soldiers to that point; Mc-Clellan put his columns in motion on April 4. "I shall carry this thing on *en grand,*" the young commander had told his wife, "& crush the rebels in a single campaign." But he still sought to avoid excessive bloodshed. Confronted by 15,000 Confederate troops entrenched at Yorktown, McClellan elected not to assault the works but resorted to a siege instead.[10]

This decision, militarily questionable, proved to be politically expensive at a time when McClellan could not afford it. Complaints about his caution had surfaced as early as the previous autumn; they had grown worse in March when Union troops, sent to occupy the abandoned Confederate lines at Manassas, realized that the position could not have contained an army larger than McClellan's own. A scattering of logs disguised to resemble cannon – derisively labeled "Quaker guns" – became a byword for the North's humiliation, and critics blamed McClellan.

Lincoln, already under pressure to remove McClellan outright, relieved him of his responsibilities as General-in-Chief, on the pretext that McClellan would have his hands full managing the Army of the Potomac in the field. Strain between general and administration increased when it became clear that McClellan had not left enough troops to protect Washington during his absence. To make up the deficit, Lincoln removed an entire corps – 40,000 men – from McClellan's control. The frustrated general felt certain the administration was out to get him. Lincoln felt equally certain that McClellan did not appreciate his quite genuine efforts to protect the general from political enemies. "[I]t is indispensable to *you* that you strike a blow," he told Mc-Clellan as the Yorktown siege began. "The country will not fail to note – is now noting – that the present hesitation to move upon an entrenched enemy, is but the story of Manassas repeated."[11]

With olympian contempt, McClellan refused to change either his politics or his tactics. For a month he kept his army stalled before Yorktown while sweating artillerists emplaced heavy guns to bombard the rebels into submission. When the Confederates withdrew instead, McClellan was not disappointed. "It would have been easy for me to have sacrificed 10,000 lives in taking Yorktown," he told his wife Ellen, "& I presume the world would have thought me brilliant. I am content with what I have done. . . ." Although this statement was less than candid – he had earlier promised Ellen that he did not want the rebels to "get away from me without a sound

[10]McClellan to Mary Ellen McClellan, August 2, 1861, Sears (ed.), *McClellan Papers,* 75; McClellan's report, August 4, 1863, OR 11, pt. 1:7–11.
[11]Lincoln to McClellan, April 9, 1862, Basler (ed.), *Collected Works of Lincoln* 5:185.

drubbing" – his pleasure in obtaining a bloodless victory accorded with his faith in the conciliatory policy.[12]

As his army crept toward Richmond during May, McClellan began preparations to capture the Confederate capital by siege, not assault. Indeed, as it became clear that the rebels would defend a line close to the city limits, McClellan worried about the impact a battle would have on civilian lives and property. The city might be severely damaged, perhaps even destroyed. Worse, he confessed that "I do not know that I can control fully this army of volunteers if they enter the city on the heels of the enemy after an assault. I will do my best to prevent outrage & pillage, but there are bad men in all armies & I hope I shall not be forced to witness the sack of Richmond."[13]

McClellan had reason to worry. Despite his attempts to imbue the men with his own views about protecting civilian property, the Army of the Potomac possessed its full quotient of thieves, freelance foragers, and officers willing to look the other way. During the march to Manassas, one soldier noted a variety of misdeeds, "such as robbing hen roosts, killing hogs, slaughtering beef cattle, cows, the burning of a house or two and plundering of others left alone or in the care of some old darkey. . . ." The officers, for their part, "seemed to have no control over their men. We have never seen anything like this before," wrote one indignant officer, "and it reminds me forcibly of the Spanish and Portuguese troops during Wellington's campaign in the [Iberian] peninsula."[14]

More incidents occurred on the Virginia peninsula. "McClellan's orders for the protection of property are very strict," wrote Union Major Charles S. Wainwright, "even to forbidding the burning of rails; but it is very hard to enforce them." Boisterous soldiers rustled livestock and looted abandoned houses, he reported, although they usually left occupied dwellings alone. Wainwright added that while McClellan was doing his best to keep the men in line, "he is not well supported in it by all his subordinate commanders, many of them allowing their feelings of hatred to the rebels to interfere with their obedience of orders, and some even condemning him for too great leniency towards them." But Wainwright himself endorsed McClellan's policy, partly on grounds of good military discipline and simple justice, but also because he thought it politically wise. The South, after all, was part of the United States, and its populace were alienated Americans. "Our object is to put down the rebellion, not to open wider the breach of estrangement, or to impoverish our own country. It appears very strange to me that so many men, sensible ones too in most matters, should be so shortsighted, and allow their feelings so entirely to get the better of their judgment."[15]

[12]McClellan to Mary Ellen McClellan, [May 8, 1862], Sears (ed.), *McClellan Papers,* 260; McClellan to Mary Ellen McClellan, May 3, [1862], ibid., 252.

[13]McClellan to Mary Ellen McClellan, [May] 22, 1862, ibid., 274.

[14]William H. Walling to his sister, March 13, 1862, William Henry Walling Letters, CWMC, USAMHI; entry for March 25, 1862, Favill, *The Diary of a Young Officer,* 71.

[15]Entries for May 11, 14, 1862, Allan Nevins (ed.), *A Diary of Battle: The Personal Journals of Colonel Charles S. Wainwright, 1861–1865* (New York: Harcourt, Brace & World, 1962), 60–62.

McClellan's orders applied to the protection of all private property, regardless of the owner's political sympathies or even his degree of complicity in the rebellion. At the close of May, Wainwright's unit found itself camped on the farm of a wealthy doctor who owned over a hundred slaves and was, moreover, a member of the convention that had voted to remove Virginia from the Union. "Our provost-marshal grumbles a great deal at having to furnish a guard to his house," Wainwright wrote, "and says the men ought to hang him." A no-nonsense man but a conservative one, the major commented, "I agree with him as to the hanging, but not that our men should be allowed to turn into common thieves and murderers."[16]

The palpable tension, even in McClellan's army, that existed between those who wanted to punish "rebels" and those who sought to protect "errant brothers," underscored the larger strains that beset the conciliatory policy everywhere. Northerners understood that they were fighting to make the Southerners their countrymen again, which dictated one course of action; but they were also absorbing bitter blows in the process, which tempted them to lash out in unrestrained violence. Time for a conciliatory approach was running out. Fortunately, the war seemed nearly over.

Hundreds of miles from the Peninsula, in western Tennessee, Colonel Manning F. Force waited for McClellan to end the struggle. Halleck had recently captured the strategic rail town of Corinth, adding yet another victory to the string of Northern successes. The civilians Force saw around him seemed, by every word and act, to confess that they were beaten. "You see it," he wrote a friend, "in the little uneasiness of manner, the unconscious and unintentional deference of the chief men, when they come to see us." A day later, he dashed off another letter filled with the excitement of imminent triumph. "The great point looked to is Richmond. Every paper is snatched, and every person who has been near Corinth, or any other place in communication with America, is assaulted for news from Richmond."[17]

Senator Charles Sumner also viewed a Northern victory as imminent. In early June, as McClellan recovered from a desperate but thwarted Confederate counterattack, the devoted abolitionist informed the Duchess of Argyll that "[i]t seems pretty certain that the *military power* of the rebellion will be soon broken. . . . [Secretary of State William H.] Seward assured me yesterday that it would 'all be over in 90 days.'" The possibility actually troubled Sumner. He worried that it would quench the incipient movement toward emancipation, already underway with tentative Congressional measures that affected only federal territories, and at the moment trembling on the brink of a confiscation bill that would free the slaves of disloyal owners and even permit them to carry arms in battle. Earlier he had complained of the victories at Fort Donelson and elsewhere that they "will help us abroad, but hurt *the* cause at home." In

---

[16]Entry for May 30, 1862, ibid., 67.

[17]Manning F. Force to "Mr. Kebler," June 16, 17, 1862, Manning F. Force Papers, UW. For similar expressions of confidence in the war's imminent close, see Garfield to his mother, June 12, 1862, Williams (ed.), *Wild Life of the Army*, 113; and G.W. Whitman to his mother, June 1 and June 9, 1862, in Jerome M. Loving (ed.), *Civil War Letters of George Washington Whitman* (Durham, NC: Duke University Press, 1975), 54, 55; Salmon P. Chase to Irvin McDowell, June 6, 1862, Salmon P. Chase Papers, ILHS.

his letter to the duchess, Sumner thought – one might almost say hoped – that victory would not come so easily. "Thus far we have no sign of such surrender. There are some who expect it. . . . But it seems hard to believe that men, who have made such professions & declarations, & whose pride is terribly enlisted, will submit." Yet the longer Southerners fought, the more endangered the institution of slavery would become, and "unless the slave states submit, Slavery will be directly abolished by military decree."[18]

On June 25, the long-awaited offensive against Richmond finally began. One Union division probed the outer belt of Confederate defenses. More attacks would soon have followed, but the Southern commander, General Robert E. Lee, struck first – and fiercely. The following afternoon, in a daring assault against the most exposed part of McClellan's army, Lee made an all-or-nothing bid to drive the Federals back. The initial attacks were repulsed, but Lee revised his arrangements and continued his counterstroke the next day. McClellan began a fighting retreat, hoping to reach the protective shield of the Union gunboats that patrolled the James River estuary. He fired off a bitter dispatch that blamed the administration for his predicament, then cut his telegraph lines and headed south.

For six days the two armies grappled among the swamps, woodlots, and farms east of Richmond, with Lee determined to destroy McClellan's army and McClellan equally determined to get it safely away. The Northern people and soldiers in other theaters, aware only that a desperate battle was underway, strained for any word about the outcome. "We are all in the dark about Richmond," wrote Colonel Force. "The news of his advance on the 25th came in detail. But nothing but rumors of his subsequent repulse, accompanied by rumors of his regaining ground, have reached us."[19]

The optimistic rumors proved false. After the initial defeat, the Army of the Potomac won every encounter but kept retreating. On July 2, it reached the James River intact. The Confederate government trumpeted that Richmond was saved. McClellan announced that he had effected a successful "change of base." His enemies whooped derisively at that, and even his friends had trouble explaining it.

Shaken by the sharp reversal but glad that McClellan had not lost his army, President Lincoln boarded a steamer for Harrison's Landing, Virginia, where the army was licking its wounds. McClellan, aware that a confiscation bill was being considered in Congress, aware too that many Northerners were beginning to express exasperation with forbearance toward rebels, urged the President not to abandon conciliation. On July 8, he presented Lincoln with his famous "Harrison's Landing letter."[20]

---

[18]Sumner to Francis W. Bird, February 19, 1862, Beverly Wilson Palmer (ed.), *The Selected Letters of Charles Sumner,* 2 vols. (Boston: Northeastern University Press, 1990), vol. 2, p. 101. See also Sumner to Francis Lieber, March 29, 1862, ibid., 107. Sumner to the Duchess of Argyll, June 9, 1862, ibid., 119–120. I have reversed the order of the quoted passages for the sake of clarity.

[19]Force to Kebler, July 2, 1862, Manning F. Force Papers, UW.

[20]McClellan had probably been considering such a letter even prior to the Seven Days' Battles just ended. This may be inferred from a dispatch sent to Lincoln on June 20, offering to lay before the President "my views as to the present state of military affairs throughout the whole country." McClellan to Lincoln,

It was perhaps the most powerful expression of the conciliatory policy crafted during the war. In it, he urged that the government treat the conflict as one to be conducted "upon the highest principles known to Christian Civilization." It should be directed solely against "armed forces and political organizations," not the Southern population. Private property and noncombatants "should be strictly protected; subject only to the necessities of military operations." Any private property taken for military use should be paid for; "pillage and waste should be treated as high crimes; all unnecessary trespass sternly prohibited; and offensive demeanor by the military towards citizens promptly rebuked."

Military arrests, he continued, should not be tolerated, nor oaths of allegiance imposed. Except for slaves actively involved in the Confederate war effort and those who might be appropriated by the government for its own use, the army should have nothing to do with slavery, "either by supporting or impairing the authority of the master." Rather cautiously, he added that the government might extend the principle of appropriation so as to manumit slaves on a state by state basis – he mentioned Missouri, western Virginia, and Maryland as possibilities – "and the expediency of such a military measure is only a matter of time." If done in a "constitutional and conservative" manner, a limited emancipation might thus be possible. But, he warned, "A declaration of radical views, especially upon slavery, will rapidly disintegrate our present Armies."[21]

Lincoln, characteristically, accepted the letter politely and turned at once to military matters. A consummate politician, he knew that the time for the limited struggle envisioned by McClellan had run out and that whatever the technical propriety or impropriety of McClellan's having broached such matters, only successful generals could impose policy.[22]

The war, in any case, had moved beyond conciliation. The confiscation bill, still under consideration in Congress, continued its grueling metamorphosis into a viable bill. A joint conference committee hacked out a compromise bill that cut about two thirds of the Senate version, incorporated a weakened version of the House bill, and added a new section that would emancipate the slaves of persons who continued to aid the rebellion after the act became law. On July 16, the compromise bill passed both houses. Once satisfied that the bill was constitutional, Lincoln signed it into law the

June 20, 1862, Sears (ed.), *McClellan Papers*, 304. Traditionally called "the Seven Days," Lee's counterstroke actually lasted only six. The seventh day is sometimes considered June 25, when McClellan launched his first tentative attack on Richmond, and sometimes July 2, the day he completed his retreat.

[21]McClellan to Lincoln, July 7, 1862, ibid., 344–345.

[22]McClellan to S.L.M. Barlow, July 23, 1862, ibid., 370; "Memorandum of Interviews Between Lincoln and Officers of the Army of the Potomac," Basler (ed.), *Collected Works of Lincoln* 5:309–312. Lincoln's thoughts on the prospects for conciliation may easily be inferred from the actions he took in the next few weeks. His views on generals imposing policy is plain enough from a letter he wrote to Major General Joseph Hooker in early 1863: "I have heard, in such a way as to believe it, of your recently saying that both the Army and the Government needed a Dictator. Of course it was not *for* this, but in spite of it, that I have given you the command. Only those generals who gain successes, can set up Dictators. What I ask of you now is military success, and I will risk the dictatorship." Lincoln to Hooker, January 26, 1863, ibid. 6:78–79.

The Death of Conciliation

The repulse of McClellan's army from Richmond in June 1862 ended all prospect for an early Union victory and led to Northern cries for an end to "kid glove" treatment of Southern civilians. (Courtesy, Civil War Times Illustrated Collection)

Lincoln's Emancipation Proclamation dismayed many Northerners and enraged most white Southerners, who considered it an incitement to slave insurrection. In this savage drawing by pro-Southern cartoonist Adalbert Volck, Lincoln composes the proclamation with his foot on the Constitution. Images of John Brown and the Saint-Domingue massacre festoon the background. (M. and M. Karolik Collection, courtesy, Museum of Fine Arts, Boston)

following day. Like many advanced Republicans, Senator Sumner bitterly regretted that this Second Confiscation Act had been so watered down by repeated wrangling. Still, he informed a London acquaintance, "the Bill of Confiscation & Liberation, which was at last passed, under pressure from our reverses at Richmond, is a practical Act of Emancipation."[23]

As an actual blow to rebel property, the act amounted to little. Because of its requirement that confiscation cases be tried in court, it was unworkable as a means by which to visit severe damage on Southern resources. One historian has estimated that as of December 27, 1867, the total proceeds from enforcement of the act amounted to a paltry $129,680. Other Civil War historians have interpreted it as an endorsement of military confiscation. But that sort of action, as conservatives opposed to the measure tirelessly pointed out, was already legitimate under the laws of war. The bill was not intended to cripple the South's ability to make war. Rather, its proponents were interested in punishing the rebellion's ringleaders – Trumbull's "one Southerner in ten." In short, it was another blow at the slaveholding aristocracy.[24]

And it was a blow against slavery, which in any event was already collapsing as Union armies trampled the delicate order in the South. But that was intended less as an attack on Southern resources than a way to do what antislavery men had wanted to do for years. Wilson had already said as much, and Sumner remarked that the emancipation provision was the only part of the bill that interested him. "It was only in this respect that I valued it. The Western men were earnest for reaching the property of the rebels. To this I was indifferent except so far as it was necessary to break up the strongholds of slavery."[25]

Ultimately, what mattered about the Second Confiscation Act was the signal it sent, both to Southerners and to Union officers. Confederates perceived it, quite rightly, as a repudiation of the conciliatory policy. Union officers so inclined could see it as a green light to go after Southern property. Certainly it widened the parameters of the measures the Federal government was willing to accept. And it left the conciliatory field commanders without a sufficient base of political support. Among the first to feel the effects of this was Major General Don Carlos Buell.

MITCHEL AND BUELL IN NORTHERN ALABAMA

"In one thing I fear we have been mistaken," wrote James Garfield to his brother in May 1862. "We have believed in a suppressed Union sentiment in the South. It is my opinion, formed against my will, that there is not enough Union (unconditional) feeling south of Kentucky to plant the seeds of public faith in." Garfield scrawled this letter from an encampment near the Tennessee-Mississippi state line. The deeper the

---

[23]Sumner to John Bright, August 5, 1862, Palmer (ed.), *Selected Letters of Charles Sumner* 2:122.

[24]James Garfield Randall, *The Confiscation of Property During the Civil War* (Indianapolis: Mutual Printing and Lithographing, 1913), 15.

[25]Sumner to John Bright, August 5, 1862, Palmer (ed.), *Selected Letters of Charles Sumner* 2:122.

western armies advanced into the South, the more soldiers began to make similar complaints. Early observations and reports had indicated a substantial outpouring of Unionist sentiment. But while pockets of such sentiment did exist, Federal troops mainly noticed the hostility etched in Southern faces, underscored by the shameless price-gouging of local farmers and merchants. Overheated camp gossip magnified the threat posed by wicked secessionists. "They say the citizens are all secesh here and nearly [every night] they sho[o]t one of the picket guards," wrote a recently enlisted Ohio private, adding manfully, "but I doubt that."[26]

In general, the Ohioan was right, but attacks by individual Southerners, partisan bands, and irregular cavalry did occur. They picked off sentries, murdered weary stragglers, swooped down on wagon trains and isolated outposts, burned critical railroad bridges, and sniped at steamers chugging up and down the broad western rivers. These menaces, seemingly ubiquitous, inflamed the fears and fed the resentments of Northern men. They placed further strain on the conciliatory policy, nowhere more noticeably than in southeastern Tennessee and northern Alabama.

Rolling hills, tidy farms, and limestone caverns filled this region, which lay on the fringe of the Appalachian massif. Most counties in the area had returned majorities against disunion when they voted for delegates to the secession conventions, and as in most areas with divided loyalties, neighbor suspected neighbor. Nocturnal violence among them was not rare. The first Union troops – one division, 8,000 men – appeared in the region as early as April, just after the bloody but victorious battle at Shiloh two hundred miles to the west. They were led by Brigadier General Ormsby M. Mitchel, who had already registered his impatience with conciliation in private letters to Secretary Chase. Mitchel established his headquarters at Huntsville, Alabama, astride the Memphis and Charleston Railroad. He threw out regiments to garrison the rail line, and with regular supply uncertain, augmented his troops' rations with orderly but fairly extensive foraging.

Mitchel's soldiers had mixed feelings about the Huntsville area. Some thought "a decided Union sentiment" prevailed; others viewed the inhabitants as "full of prejudice against Yankees." A great deal depended on the treatment the Federals received. Bad experiences could trigger prompt reprisals. A company of the 21st Ohio, passing through the region by rail, received sniper fire from bushwhackers. The captain ordered the train halted at the next station, satisfied himself that the men who had committed the deed lived in a certain house, and went there at once. The women who answered the door said the men in question were away "on business." The captain's manner relaxed and he grew garrulous, chatting away with the nervous women while one of his sergeants disappeared. After a while the women noticed the smell of smoke,

---

[26]Garfield to his brother, May 1, 1862, Williams (ed.), *Wild Life of the Army*, 89. Christian Zook to "kind, loveing friends at home," February 22, 1862, typescript copy of manuscript letter in the collection of Todd D. Miller, Jeromesville, Ohio. Another man recalled that even in Kentucky, the soldiers of his regiment feared that secessionists would poison their water supply, and guards were posted to prevent it. F.W. Keil, *The Thirty-fifth Ohio, A Narrative of Service from August, 1861 to 1864* (Fort Wayne, IN: Archer, Housh & Co., 1894), 11.

but the captain assured them it was nothing. Finally, when the thickening fumes could no longer be dismissed, the captain remarked nonchalantly, "I guess the house is on fire," and walked away. The sergeant had been upstairs, torching the curtains and mattress in one of the bedrooms.[27]

Such summary acts of retaliation soon escalated. At Paint Rock, Alabama, a train carrying troops under Colonel John Beatty also received a fusillade from local bushwhackers. Beatty stopped the train, went back to the village with a file of soldiers, and peremptorily summoned the residents for a meeting. "I told them that this bushwhacking must cease," Beatty recorded in his diary that night. "Hereafter every time the telegraph wire was cut we would burn a house; every time a train was fired upon we would hang a man; and we would continue to do this until every house was burned and every man hanged between Decatur and Bridgeport. . . . We proposed to hold the citizens responsible for these cowardly assaults, and if they did not drive these bushwhackers from amongst them, we should make them more uncomfortable than they would be in hell." So saying, Beatty's men burned the town, seized three citizens as hostages, and continued their journey to Huntsville.[28]

Mitchel fully approved of Beatty's action. He wrote the War Department complaining of "small bands of armed citizens, who still continue their outrages along the railway line and elsewhere," and added that he had arrested a few active secessionists when they refused to condemn the guerrillas. Mitchel viewed himself as acting on behalf of the local Unionist population quite as much as for the benefit of his own troops. Some of the arrested secessionists should go to Northern prisons, he continued, "and in this the best citizens have agreed with me." Assistant Secretary of War P.H. Watson responded by authorizing the general to send the worst offenders to Fort Warren, the military prison in Boston harbor.[29]

Like the pragmatic policies of Halleck and Butler, Mitchel's program tried to punish civilians who actively helped the enemy while attempting to remain on good terms with those who behaved themselves. And although he personally had little use for conciliation, in theory at least the antiguerrilla program was not incompatible with conciliation. No one seriously expected Union forces to ignore partisan attacks, and summary execution for men who fought outside regular military formations was a long-established tradition. Besides, the bushwhackers sometimes preyed on local civilians as well, extorting supplies from them and then terrorizing them into silence.

The real problem arose from the perception of most Union troops that the civilians both knew the identities of the guerrillas and willingly assisted them. The 42nd Indiana, for example, blamed the population of Wartrace, Tennessee, for a surprise incursion by rebel cavalry. Their suspicions were based on nothing more substantial

[27] Alex Cope, *The Fifteenth Ohio Volunteers and Its Campaigns* (Columbus, n.p., 1916), 170; S. S. Canfield, *History of the 21st Regiment Ohio Volunteer Infantry, in the War of the Rebellion* (Toledo: Vrooman, Anderson & Bateman, 1893), 45.
[28] Entry for May 2, 1862, John Beatty, *Memoirs of a Volunteer, 1861–1863*, ed. Harvey S. Ford (New York: W.W. Norton, 1946 [1879]), 108. See also J.W. Keifer to his wife, May 3, 1862, J.W. Keifer Papers, LC.
[29] Entry for May 5, 1862, Beatty, *Memoirs of a Volunteer, 1861–1863*, 109; Mitchel to Edwin M. Stanton, May 8, 1862, OR 10, pt. 2:174; Watson to Mitchel, May 8, 1862, ibid., 175.

than the fact that local citizens had visited their camp "and professed in earnest manner friendship for the Union cause." The subsequent attack, however, made such professions seem duplicitous. The Hoosiers were certain the civilians had really come to spy on them, and that they had given the enemy precise information concerning the camp's layout.[30]

Occasional insults from area residents made Northern tempers flare. A Huntsville woman allegedly spit on an Ohio soldier, and was slapped for it. Another Buckeye promised to kill one obnoxious townsman if he ever again called him an "Abolitionist." The Ninth Ohio, already known for rough dealings with civilians, continued its career of mayhem in Huntsville. "Fires sometimes broke out in local Rebels' houses," wrote the unit historian. "Of course we, in our innocence, never knew how they started. In our honest way we helped with rescue and salvage; and the 35th Ohio was our staunch ally in this work of mercy. We carried beds out-of-doors, for example, and threw glasses and porcelain out of windows."[31]

That sort of conduct officially infuriated Mitchel, who wired Secretary of War Edwin M. Stanton of "the most terrible outrages" perpetrated by "lawless brigands and vandals" connected with the army; he even requested permission to hang soldiers found guilty of such crimes. Stanton granted it. But observers noticed that nothing much seemed to happen. In particular, Mitchel did little to address the shocking sack of Athens, Alabama, on May 2, 1862.[32]

On that date, a brigade of midwestern troops under Colonel John B. Turchin entered the town in an ugly mood. Accounts vary, but apparently one regiment had just suffered a cavalry attack in Athens; some believed they had seen a few of the townspeople assist the rebel horsemen by taking potshots of their own. Turchin, a Russian immigrant and a former Czarist officer, informed his troops that he would turn his back for two hours – an announcement that implied, as he surely meant it to imply, that they should use the time to ransack the town. They did. One group of soldiers entered the home of one woman, vandalized her belongings, insulted her, threatened to shoot her, then attempted to rape her black servant. Other bands spread out into other homes, offices and stores, stole cash and valuables, smashed goods, fired shots into residences, and made sexual advances on female slaves.[33]

The incident quickly became notorious to both troops and civilians in the area. Yet despite common knowledge of the incident, no immediate action was taken to investigate the incident or bring the culprits up on charges. The outraged citizens of Athens petitioned Mitchel for redress, but he coolly responded that their charges were nonspecific: They indicated the names of no individual soldiers, only that the

[30]Horrall, *Forty-second Indiana Volunteer Infantry*, 119–121.

[31]Canfield, *Twenty-first Ohio*, 47; Grebner, *We Were the Ninth*, 106.

[32]Mitchel to Stanton, May 19, 1862, OR 10, pt. 2:204; Stanton to Mitchel, May 22, 1862, ibid., 209.

[33]Summary of court-martial proceedings against Col. John B. Turchin, embodied in General Orders No. 39, August 6, 1862, OR 16, pt. 2:273–278. See also MS. Recollections, James Fenton Papers, Regimental Papers of the Civil War, WRHS; George H. Puntenney, *History of the Thirty-Seventh Regiment of Indiana Infantry Volunteers.* . . . (Rushville, IN: Jacksonian Book & Job Department, 1896), 24–25; and Roy Morris, Jr., "The Sack of Athens," *Civil War Times Illustrated* 24 (February 1986):26–32.

depredations had been perpetrated by Turchin's men. Surely no one could expect him to arrest an entire brigade.[34]

Colonel Jesse S. Norton, commander of the 21st Ohio Infantry, did investigate the issue – perhaps at Mitchel's request, but more probably on his own initiative. Despite the mattress-burning episode by one of the company captains, Norton's regiment was known at the time for its relative mildness toward the local population; 900 citizens of the town of Huntsville, for example, petitioned Mitchel to have the 21st Ohio retained as Huntsville's provost guard. The 21st also spent a week during this period in Athens where Norton became acquainted with the people there. In any event, Norton concluded that not only had Turchin's men been guilty of pillaging, but that Mitchel had known about it and done nothing. He later claimed to have submitted reports to Mitchel on the subject, only to see Mitchel decline to take any action.[35]

It is possible that Norton reported his suspicions to the War Department outside normal channels. Certainly by July, Mitchel was in hot water with Stanton and preparing a lengthy defense of his alleged failure to repress Union depredations. At about the same time, that fervent conciliator Don Carlos Buell arrived at Huntsville and began looking into the allegations himself. On July 5, Buell's headquarters preferred charges against Colonel Turchin and ordered a court martial board to assemble at Athens immediately.[36]

Norton, meanwhile, left his regiment and went to Washington to press charges against Mitchel. En route he stopped long enough to lay two accusations before the editor of the *Louisville Courier*: First, that Mitchel was using his position to speculate illegally in the cotton trade; and second, that he had acquiesced in Turchin's sack of Athens. The newspaper published the story, and it was soon picked up by the national press. Around July 23, Norton submitted a deposition on the matter to the Joint Committee on the Conduct of the War.[37]

What happened next formed one of the strongest indications of the rapidly shifting mood of the government, the army, and public opinion. The Joint Committee took no action concerning Norton's information. Secretary of War Stanton did, but not the kind Norton desired. Hearing that the colonel was in the capital without proper leave and that his attempt to press charges against Mitchel violated normal military channels, he issued an order for Norton's arrest. Norton quickly left town, but was soon relieved of his command and sent home in disgrace. Mitchel then visited Washington to answer the charges, received a clean bill of health, and in due course gained a larger command.

Turchin, meanwhile, underwent trial in Athens. The president of the board, Brig-

[34]Mitchel to George S. Hunter and Others, Committee, Athens, [Alabama], May 24, 1862, OR 10, pt. 2:212–213.

[35]Canfield, *Twenty-first Ohio*, 48.

[36]Mitchel to Stanton, July 19, 1862, OR 10, pt. 2:290–295; Special Orders No. 93, July 5, 1862, ibid., 16, pt. 2:99.

[37]Norton's testimony was not published in the printed reports of the Joint Committee on the Conduct of the War and the original committee notes apparently have not survived. But an abstract of Norton's testimony before the committee was printed in the *Cincinnati Gazette*, July 24, 1862.

adier General James A. Garfield, was initially inclined to condemn both Turchin and Mitchel. In a private letter written on July 5, he told a friend, "General Mitchel has accomplished a good deal [in the area], but his men have committed the most shameful outrages here that the history of war has shown." Four days later he wrote another acquaintance, "There has not been found in American history so black a page as that which will bear the record of General Mitchel's campaign in Northern Alabama. . . . I fear his reputation will not be enhanced by the incidental revelations of this trial. The town, which contains some of the finest village residences I have ever seen, was, by Colonel Turchin, given up to pillage and in the presence of the Russian (Colonel Turchin) was sacked according to the Muscovite custom."[38]

By July 17, however, Garfield had substantially modified his opinion, at least of Turchin. Before their first meeting, he had expected to find "as fierce and brutal a Muscovite as the dominions of the Czar could produce." Instead he saw "a fine manly figure with expansive forehead, mild blue eye[s] with an unusual depth of piercing intelligence which at once won respect." Garfield's sympathy for Turchin only increased in the days that followed. Learning that Confederate Brigadier General John H. Morgan had begun a cavalry raid into Kentucky, Garfield wrote that he was almost delighted. "It will do us good to have a few score towns in Kentucky, Indiana and Ohio plundered. It is particularly pertinent that these things should happen . . . while General Mitchel is being persecuted and Colonel Turchin is in his third week of trial for not dealing quietly enough with rebels and their property." It was a remarkable comment. Before the trial, Garfield had spoken of "shameful outrages," "ravages," and "pillage." But after ten days of hearings in which witness after witness testified in detail about the crimes committed in Athens, Garfield essentially shrugged off the matter with the frivolous statement that Turchin was being tried "for not dealing quietly enough" with Southern persons and property.[39]

What had changed? Garfield's stated sympathy for Turchin may explain some of it, but it is surely not insignificant that his transformation in sentiment coincided with the first confirmed reports that McClellan had been defeated near Richmond. Northern newspapers displayed the same shift in opinion. On July 7, the *Cincinnati Gazette* gave front-page coverage to a long letter from "Zeke," a Union soldier correspondent who reported the incident at Athens. "No indignity could have been offered our troops, justifying the outrages. No act of the people guaranteed such wanton vandalism. The matter demands an investigation. . . . For the sake of the reputation of the Union cause and the Union arms, I hope so." Zeke concluded with adulatory comments about General Buell. "The people of Tennessee and Alabama regard him most favorably. . . . [He] is just the man to restore peace and tranquility to the rebel-ridden department under his charge." The letter was dated July 2; it appeared alongside the first early reports of McClellan's repulse. Two weeks later, the *Gazette* published another report by a correspondent covering the Turchin trial. Referring to the charges

---

[38]Garfield to his wife, July 5, 1862, Williams (ed.), *Wild Life of the Army,* 119; Garfield to his brother, July 9, 1862, ibid., 121.
[39]Ibid., 123; Garfield to his brother, July 24, 1862, ibid., 125.

against Mitchel printed in the *Louisville Courier*, the reporter wrote, "I have heard much of this, and General Mitchell's [sic] acts, individual and as a General commanding, have been much criticized as wanton and disgraceful." Turchin's actions, he observed, logically reflected on Mitchel. "He took no heed of the matter . . . but left it for the secretary of Gen. Buell."[40]

Just two days later, however, the *Gazette* ran an article headlined "The Truth About the Charges Against Gen. Mitchell [sic]." The truth, apparently, was that there was no truth to them. Mitchel's alleged cotton speculation was a lie, and Mitchel had actually ordered Colonel Norton to investigate the incident at Athens. Norton, the paper went on, had brought back "improbable stories" that implicated Mitchel. As for the sacking of Athens itself, "we suspect that [the incident] has been vastly magnified, if not a great part manufactured, by those who, in the same district, are now conciliating the rebels and demoralizing the army." Other articles in the same issue accused Buell of turning Union services "in a new channel, that of catching negroes and returning them to their masters." The next day the *Gazette* commented editorially that Buell should be relieved of command.[41]

Turchin's court martial board ultimately found him guilty of failing to restrain his men and of violating General Order No. 13a, Buell's standing order forbidding depredations. It sentenced him to be cashiered from the service. But having done so, all but one member of the board urged clemency. Turchin's offense, they argued, "was committed under exciting circumstances, and was one of omission rather than commission." Buell angrily insisted that the sentence be carried out. He noted that similar disorders had marked the progress of Turchin's command wherever it had gone (albeit not to the same degree), and that the real issue was not one of taking rebel property for military use. That, he said, was proper "whenever the public interest demands it." The real issue was "[t]he wanton and lawless indulgence of individuals in acts of plunder and outrage," which undermined morale and good military discipline. "Such conduct does not mean vigorous war; it means disgrace and disaster. . . ."[42]

Buell's opinion, however, was suddenly in the minority. A member of the court martial board, Colonel Beatty, had already reached a different conclusion, and by midsummer 1862 most Union soldiers had come to share it. "Turchin's brigade," he admitted candidly, "has stolen a hundred thousand dollars' worth of watches, plate, and jewelry in northern Alabama." Acts of that nature were extreme, "for war cannot justify the gutting of private houses and the robbery of peaceable citizens for the

---

[40]*Cincinnati Gazette*, July 7, 22, 1862.

[41]Ibid., July 24, 25, 1862. The *Cincinnati Daily Commercial*, a War Democrat journal, displayed an even more striking shift in editorial policy. At the beginning of July, it defended McClellan's practice of guarding Southern property (July 3, 1862), and subsequently condemned the sacking of Athens as "the most shameful affair of the war" (July 17, 1862). Eleven days later, Turchin had become "a great General" (July 28, 1862) and the paper printed with approval a long letter that commented, "Never, never will this Rebellion be closed, until they are made to dread the power of our army, and taught the terrible lesson that men who dare to rebel against good government and wise political rule, must meet with severe punishment" (July 29, 1862).

[42]General Order No. 39, August 6, 1862, OR 16, pt. 2:277.

benefit of individual officers or soldiers." But, Beatty continued, "there is another extreme, more amiable and pleasant to look upon, but not less fatal to the cause. Buell is likely to go to that. . . .

He is inaugurating the dancing-master policy: "By your leave, my dear sir, we will have a fight, that is, if you are sufficiently fortified; no hurry; take your own time." To the bushwhacker: "Am sorry you gentlemen fire at our trains from behind stumps, logs, and ditches. Had you not better cease this sort of warfare? Now do, my good fellows, stop, I beg of you." To the citizen rebel: "You are a chivalrous people; you have been aggravated by the abolitionists into subscribing cotton to the Southern Confederacy; you had, of course, a right to dispose of your own property to suit yourselves, but we prefer that you would, in future, make no more subscriptions of that kind, and in the meantime we propose to protect your property and guard your negroes."

Turchin's policy was bad enough, Beatty went on, but Buell's policy "is that of the amiable idiot." He thought there was a better policy than either, a policy that countenanced no plunder but at the same time, extended no special protection to rebels, a policy that would "march boldly, defiantly" through the Confederacy, crushing anyone, soldier or civilian, who aided and abetted the rebellion. "In short," Beatty concluded, "we want an iron policy that will not tolerate treason, that will demand immediate and unconditional obedience as the price of protection."[43]

The Lincoln administration agreed. Although Buell, a major general and department commander, had insisted that Colonel Turchin, having been found guilty, should be dismissed from the service, the War Department declined to sustain him. Instead, under pressure from Turchin's powerful friends in Illinois, including its governor, Stanton not only retained Turchin in the service, but actually promoted him to brigadier general. The promotion technically invalidated the court martial verdict; a new trial was never convened. And although Turchin was relieved of his command, he went without assignment only until September. Then President Lincoln personally asked Stanton to place him at the head of a new brigade. Short of actually removing Buell, it is hard to imagine what more devastating insult the administration could have offered him. Soldiers, public opinion, and government had all had a bellyful of conciliation.[44]

AN END TO THE KID GLOVES: POPE'S ORDERS

The new climate was illustrated by the reception given a series of draconian orders issued by Major General John Pope in mid-July. In the wake of Federal reverses in the Shenandoah Valley and amid concerns about the progress of McClellan's operations against Richmond, the Lincoln administration had brought Pope east to help improve

[43]Entry for July 14, 1862, Beatty, *Memoirs of a Volunteer,* 117–118.
[44]James Robert Chumney, "Don Carlos Buell: Gentleman General," (unpub. Ph.D diss., Rice University, 1964), 143; Lincoln to Stanton, September 5, 1862, Basler (ed.), *Collected Works of Lincoln* 5:406.

the situation. On June 26, Pope received command of a number of previously independent formations, now assembled into a single "Army of Virginia."

Pope, a forty-year old career officer, had won an important victory at Island No. 10 in April 1862, and enjoyed a reputation for aggressiveness. He also had great ambition and a finely honed sense of the value of good political contacts. For several weeks before taking the field with his newly formed command, Pope haunted the ballrooms and salons of Washington. He announced himself, in testimony before the Joint Committee on the Conduct of the War, as an emancipationist and a strong critic of both McClellan's strategic decisions and his conservative policies toward enemy civilians. Within a short time he became the darling of the Radical Republicans.[45]

While still in Washington, Pope issued a series of orders to his newly created Army of Virginia that created a considerable furor, not only within his command but also throughout North and South at large. The first got him off to a bad start. Many of Pope's new soldiers had suffered repeated defeat at the hands of Confederate General Thomas J. "Stonewall" Jackson. Deciding that this had made them excessively cautious, he published an address designed to improve their fighting spirit.

"I have come to you from the West," it read in part, "where we have always seen the backs of our enemies. . . . I hear constantly of taking strong positions and holding them – of lines of retreat and bases of supplies. Let us discard such ideas. . . . Let us look before and not behind. Success and glory are in the advance. Disaster and shame lurk in the rear." Clumsily bombastic, the address irritated Pope's soldiers, angered McClellan's cronies (who assumed it was meant to reflect on McClellan), amused the Confederates, and embarrassed much of the North. In succeeding days, however, Pope began distributing a number of orders dealing with the Virginia civilians in the territories occupied by his army. If the address seemed to mark him as a lout, the new orders won widespread respect.[46]

The first of these, General Order No. 5, was issued on July 18. It directed that as far as practicable, the Army of Virginia should live off the land, and that only loyal citizens would be paid for goods requisitioned. General Order No. 6, published the same day, stated that two days' cooked rations would be carried by his troops at all times, and that "all villages and neighborhoods through which they pass will be laid under contribution." In this way, Pope expected to decrease the transportation needs of his command and thus increase its mobility and speed.[47]

Sometime between July 18 and 23 – probably July 20 – Pope issued General Order No. 7. It made the local population responsible for curbing sabotage and guerrilla activity, on the grounds that "[e]vil-disposed persons in rear of our armies who do not themselves engage directly in these lawless acts encourage them by refusing to

[45]See, for example, his testimony before the Joint Committee on the Conduct of the War (July 8, 1862); U.S. Congress, *Report of the Joint Committee on the Conduct of the War*, 3 vols. (Washington: Government Printing Office, 1863) vol. 1, pp. 276–82; and his remarks at a dinner with Secretary of the Treasury Salmon P. Chase, in David Donald (ed.), *Inside Lincoln's Cabinet: The Civil War Diaries of Salmon P. Chase* (New York: Charles Scribners Sons, 1954), 96–97.

[46]Pope to Officers and Soldiers of the Army of Virginia, July 14, 1862, OR 12, pt. 3:473–74.

[47]General Order No. 5, July 18, 1862, ibid., pt. 2:50; General Order No. 6, July 18, 1862, ibid.

interfere or to give any information by which such acts can be prevented or the perpetrators punished." If a railroad, wagon road, or telegraph line were damaged, all inhabitants within five miles of the occurrence would be turned out to repair the damage and pay an indemnity. If a Union soldier were fired upon, the house from which the shot had been fired would be destroyed, or if the offense occurred in open countryside, the inhabitants within five miles would pay an indemnity. Any persons detected in acts of sabotage or bushwhacking would be shot without trial.[48]

General Orders No. 5, 6, and 7 lay within the bounds of the law of war as it then existed and were, as Pope later pointed out, "common in the history of warfare." In fact, they resembled the sort of occupation orders that were quickly becoming the norm in the western theater. But it is curious that Pope issued them before he left Washington and thus before he could assess for himself whether conditions in his new area of responsibility made the orders necessary. He later claimed that Secretary of War Edwin Stanton had drafted these two orders as well as the bombastic address. And, to be sure, on July 22 the War Department published an executive order authorizing military commanders in Virginia and elsewhere to "seize and use any property, real or personal, which may be necessary or convenient . . . for supplies or other military purposes." The pattern suggests that the Lincoln administration not only knew and approved of Pope's orders, but also intended them as a kind of signal.[49]

Lincoln himself had already made clear his own grudging support for a harder policy against the South. To a Treasury official in occupied New Orleans who complained that Union policy seemed headed toward emancipation and that this would alienate Southern Unionists, Lincoln responded witheringly, "What would you do in my position? Would you drop the war where it is? Or would you prosecute it in future with elderstalk squirts charged with rosewater? Would you deal lighter blows rather than heavier ones? Would you give up the contest leaving any available means unapplied?" The reaction of Lincoln's Cabinet to a less restrictive policy was also positive. Secretary of the Treasury Chase reported that at a Cabinet meeting on July 21, the President "had been profoundly concerned at the present aspect of affairs, and had determined to take some definitive steps in respect to military action and slavery." He read off a series of orders, the first of which was the executive order encouraging military commanders to live off the countryside. The assembled secretaries, Chase wrote, unanimously approved it.[50]

Additional instructions from Pope's headquarters went out a few days later. On

[48]General Order No. 7, July [10?], 1862, ibid., 51. This date, as it appears in the OR, is surely incorrect. John C. Ropes, in his study *The Army Under Pope* (New York: Charles Scribner's Sons, 1881), 175–176, reprints the order under date of "July 20."

[49]Pope's report, January 27, 1863, ibid., 23. Jacob D. Cox, *Military Reminiscences of the Civil War,* 2 vols. (New York: Charles Scribner's Sons, 1900), vol. 1, pp. 222–223. Executive Order, July 22, 1862, OR 11, pt. 3:362. For an interpretation of Pope's orders that differs from this one, but which shares the opinion that the Lincoln administration intended them as a new statement of policy, see Daniel E. Sutherland, "Abraham Lincoln, John Pope, and the Origins of Total War," *Journal of Military History* 56 (1992):567–586.

[50]Lincoln to Cuthbert Bullitt, July 28, 1862, Basler (ed.), *Collected Works of Lincoln* 5:346; entry for July 21, 1862, Donald (ed.), *Inside Lincoln's Cabinet,* 95.

July 23, Pope issued General Order No. 11, which specified that unit commanders of the Army of Virginia "will proceed immediately to arrest all disloyal male citizens within their lines or within their reach in rear of their respective stations." Only those willing to swear an oath of allegiance and to furnish sufficient security for its observance would be permitted to remain within Union lines. The remainder would be escorted South beyond the pickets of the army and if found again would be considered spies. Anyone who took the oath and subsequently violated it would be shot and his property would be seized. The order also forbade communication of any sort whatever between persons living within Union lines and those residing beyond. Finally, on July 25, Pope issued the last of his draconian directives, General Order No. 13, which stated that no guards would thereafter be placed over private homes and property of any description whatever: "Soldiers were called into the field to do battle against the enemy," the order ran, "and it is not expected that their force and energy should be wasted in protecting private property of those most hostile to the Government."[51]

Pope's soldiers largely applauded the new orders. "His last order, relating to guarding the private property of rebels, and the abolishment of it, is the best thing that has been done yet, I think," wrote one Ohioan. ". . . We have been exposing ourselves to all kinds of weather protecting [Southern] property while at the same time they have their sons in the rebel service fighting against us." The historian of the Tenth Maine Volunteer Infantry Regiment noted that General Order No. 11 "gratified us exceedingly for a while." General Order No 13, for its part, "called out a hearty amen in all our corps."[52]

But others were less enthusiastic. Brigadier General Marsena R. Patrick considered them "the Orders of a Demagogue!" "Anyone who has had experience," wrote a disapproving New Jersey cavalryman, "knows too well that the best disciplined army is like a swarm of destructive locusts, the passage of a conflagration, and the ravages of an earthquake; and to stimulate it to unnecessary excesses is an outrage upon humanity." An officer recently transferred from the South Carolina coast was even less restrained in his indignation: "Pope's orders are the last unabatable nuisance. . . . We are henceforth to live on the enemy's country, and to this as a stern military necessity, I say 'Amen!' But mother, do you know what the much-applauded practice means? . . . It means that the poor, and the weak, and the helpless are at the mercy of the strong – and God help them!"[53]

Recently appointed General-in-Chief Henry W. Halleck was also less than happy about Pope's new policy. Although not averse to dealing sternly with guerrillas and active secessionists – his tenure in Missouri demonstrated that – some of Pope's orders struck Halleck as "injudicious," and his grasp of international law led him to question

[51]General Order No. 11, July 23, 1862, OR 12, pt. 2:52; General Order No. 13, July 25, 1862, ibid., 52.

[52]John F. Sosman to his sister, July 28, 1862, Sosman Family Papers, WRHS; Gould, *First-Tenth-Twenty-ninth Maine Regiment,* 162.

[53]Entry for July 18, 1862, David S. Sparks (ed.), *Inside Lincoln's Army: The Diary of Marsena Rudolph Patrick, Provost Marshal General, Army of the Potomac* (New York: Thomas Yoseloff, 1964), 108; Pyne, *Ride to War,* 50; William T. Lusk to his mother, August 19, 1862, Lusk (ed.), *War Letters,* 177.

General Order No. 11. But he felt unwilling to countermand them, he wrote Mc-Clellan, since he understood they had the President's approval. Still, he had misgivings: "An oath of allegiance taken through force is not binding, and to put over the lines those who do not take it is only adding numbers to the rebel army. What he has made the general rule should be only the exception, and I have so advised him."[54]

If Halleck seemed nonplussed by Pope's directives, McClellan greeted them with outright contempt, doubtless increased by the fact that he perceived Pope as a direct rival. He wrote his wife on August 8 that he would issue an order that would "strike square in the teeth of all [Pope's] infamous orders & give directly the reverse instructions to my army – forbid all pillaging & stealing & take the highest Christian ground for the conduct of the war – let the Govt gainsay it if they dare." The following day McClellan issued General Order No. 154, which was in effect a lengthy comment on the Lincoln administration's recent executive order that also spoke obliquely about Pope's new policy. McClellan authorized seizure of personal property if necessary for military purposes, but specified that detailed records would be kept and receipts issued *in all cases,* regardless of a given civilian's loyalty. He continued, "The idea that private property may be plundered with impunity is perhaps the very worst that can pervade an army," and added, "The general commanding takes this occasion to remind the officers and soldiers of this army that we are engaged in supporting the Constitution and laws of the United States and in suppressing rebellion against their authority; that we are not engaged in a war of rapine, revenge, or subjugation; that this is not a contest against populations, but against armed forces and political organizations; that it is a struggle carried on within the United States, and should be conducted by us upon the highest principles known to Christian civilization."[55]

McClellan's directive, intended as a major policy statement, struck little responsive chord among Northern opinion-makers. A number of newspapers reprinted it, but mostly without comment. Pope's orders, however, received warm endorsements, particularly among the Republican press. The *Chicago Tribune,* for example, exulted, "THE KID GLOVE POLICY ABANDONED" and editorialized: "We are to have no more of this watching and guarding the homes and farms and niggers of rebels in the confederate service. . . . The Federal armies will make a clean sweep. For just this have the people sent them." The *New York Times* concurred, "It now seems as though we [are] to wage war in downright, deadly earnest. The recent orders of Gen. Pope are the key-note of this new policy."[56]

War Democrat newspapers also greeted Pope's orders with praise. "[They] have the right ring about them," said the *Cincinnati Daily Commercial.* "They are the best emanations we have had from Washington in many weeks." By contrast, it editorialized, McClellan's operations had seemed "more like a magnificent piece of diplomacy than a war." Conservative journals seemed more troubled. The *Chicago*

---

[54]Halleck to McClellan, August 7, 1862, OR 11, pt. 3:359.

[55]McClellan to Mary Ellen McClellan, August 8, 1862, Sears (ed.), *McClellan Papers,* 388; General Order No. 154, August 9, 1862, OR 11, pt. 3:362–64.

[56]*Chicago Tribune,* July 24, 26, 1862; *New York Times,* July 27, 1862.

Times, not yet the "Copperhead" organ it would eventually become but disturbed by the impending passage of the Second Confiscation Act, had already urged that "whatever the policy to which the party in power may attempt to commit the country," Democrats should not withdraw their support for the war. It agreed that "the egregious fallacy of an available Union sentiment in the South is exploded," and it endorsed Lincoln's executive order as moderate: "[T]he President directs that no property shall be destroyed in wantonness or malice, and that sufficiently accurate accounts shall be kept, both as to negroes and ordinary property seized, as will enable the government to make compensation in proper cases."[57]

Carried out in that spirit, the President's order would command "the approbation of Christendom," the *Times* believed. It still hoped for a continuation of the conciliatory policy, however ("They are rebels, but brothers"), and the savage glee with which the Republican press greeted Pope's orders gave its editors pause. In mid-August, the newspaper published an editorial applauding McClellan's General Order No. 154 – one of the few Northern papers to discuss, much less endorse, the directive – and like McClellan himself, the *Times* affected to believe that it was "explanatory" of the real intent behind the President's executive order. It was hardly that.[58]

Yet for all their approval of a harsher line against Southern civilians, even the "vigorous war policy" newspapers noted with satisfaction that Union troops were actually continuing to behave with restraint. On July 24, the *New York Tribune,* which had endorsed Pope's orders as warmly as any Northern journal, carried this account of a road march made by a division in Pope's army: "There was little straggling or plundering along the way, and regiments came in at night with ranks as full as when they started out in the morning. Gen. Schurz rightly held his brigade and regimental commanders to a strict accountability for the presence and order of their men." Four days afterward, the *Tribune* reported that "[a] large number of our soldiers have an idea that Gen. Pope's orders give them permission to help themselves to anything they can find, and consequently they have been roaming through the country killing chicken, sheep, etc., extensively. Some of them having been punished severely by their officers, such practices have nearly ceased."[59]

What is one to make of the contradiction between the enthusiasm voiced by the Northern press for a hard line against the Southerners and its obvious satisfaction that Union troops were still being obliged to behave with restraint? It seems apparent that at this stage of the conflict, Northern sentiment was satisfied with the rhetoric of a hard war; it did not yet demand the reality. Indeed, one of the most striking things about Pope's orders is their lack of real impact. General Order No. 11, for example, seems not to have been enforced at all. Brigadier General Jacob D. Cox, an officer in Pope's army during this period and one of the more discerning participants to write about the war, believed that it "was probably intended more to terrify citizens from playing the part of spies than to be literally enforced, which would, indeed, have been

---

[57]*Cincinnati Daily Commercial,* July 19, 29, 1862; *Chicago Times,* July 16, 23, 24, 1862.
[58]Ibid., July 26, August 9, 18, 1862.
[59]*New York Tribune,* July 24, 28, 1862.

hardly possible. No real severity was used under it. . . ." No record exists of civilians being shot or incarcerated as a result of the order. The Confederate government, alarmed by Pope's orders, stipulated that officers captured from Pope's army should be held without parole. But all were exchanged by October 1862, an indication that even Southerners did not regard the actual implementation of the policy as very harsh.[60]

The one order that did have substantial impact was General Order No. 5, which, as the New York *Tribune* reported, produced a brief wave of pillaging. "Our men . . . now believe they have a perfect right to rob, tyrannize, threaten & maltreat any one they please, under the Orders of Gen. Pope," wrote a disgruntled brigade commander. "Satan has been let loose." Pope's army, reported another officer, "has completely desolated the country . . . vegetables, fruit, corn, and everything that could be used, are swept as clean as if a swarm of Pharo[ah]'s locusts had been here."[61]

Indeed, even soldiers who initially welcomed Pope's orders were dismayed by their consequences. Lieutenant James Gillette thought the directive to live off the countryside would "do more than victories of armies" to win the war. "A lenient course has ruined us," he wrote his father. "Nothing can save us now but rigid enforcement of rules which will encourage the loyal while the disloyal are terrified." Soon, however, he noted that straggling soldiers had begun to rob indiscriminately from wealthy secessionists and poor whites alike. "The lawless acts of many of our soldiers are worthy of worse than death," he fumed. "The villains urge as authority – 'Gen Pope's order.'" Within weeks, Gillette found that the situation had degenerated into anarchy, and he hoped that arriving units from McClellan's army would "infuse some honesty" into his own. "It is becoming sadly demoralized," he wrote. "From Pilfering secessionists [Pope's troops] have come to indiscriminate marauding & from that to stealing from each other so that it is not safe to leave anything out of sight five minutes. . . . Indiscriminate thieving seems the order of the day." Abuses of General Order No. 5 grew so rampant that on August 14, Pope found it necessary to issue a clarifying directive. "It is to be distinctly understood that neither officer nor soldier has any right whatever, under the provisions of that order, to enter the house, molest the persons, or disturb the property of any citizen whatsoever."[62]

Whether Pope would have modified, abandoned, or perhaps even redoubled his other draconian orders must remain a matter of speculation, for Confederate generals Robert E. Lee and Stonewall Jackson saw to it that he did not get the chance. In

[60]Cox, *Reminiscences* 1:223; Jefferson Davis to R. E. Lee, July 31, 1862, OR, Series II, vol. 4, pp. 830–31; 836–37; Robert Ould to Brigadier General Lorenzo Thomas, September 25, 1862, ibid., 913.

[61]Entries for July 20 and 21, 1862, Sparks (ed.), *Inside Lincoln's Army*, 110; entry for August 14, 1862, William Penn Lloyd diary, SHC. See also Edmund Randolph Brown, *The Twenty-seventh Indiana Volunteer Infantry in the War of the Rebellion* (Monticello, IN: n.p., 1899), 186. For more on the impact of Pope's orders on Virginia civilians, see Daniel E. Sutherland, "Introduction to War: The Civilians of Culpeper County, Virginia," *Civil War History* 37 (1991):120–137.

[62]Gillette to his father, July 22, 1862, James J. Gillette Papers, LC; Gillette to his mother, July 31, 1862, ibid; Gillette to his father, August 7, 1862, ibid; General Order No. 19, August 14, 1862, OR 12, pt. 3:573.

August, as the Lincoln administration forced McClellan to abandon his Peninsula Campaign and return to the Washington area, Lee's Army of Northern Virginia outmaneuvered and thrashed Pope's minions in the campaign of Second Manassas. Lee followed up his victory with an immediate advance into Maryland, hoping to persuade that border state to enter the Confederacy, and in any event to forage on Northern soil while battered Virginia recovered from eighteen months of warfare. McClellan, reluctantly retained in command of the Army of the Potomac, followed in pursuit. On September 17, he brought Lee to bay at Sharpsburg, Maryland, and in a frightful slugfest – the bloodiest single day of the entire war – fought him to a draw. Although McClellan should have done much better, the fact remained that Lee's army still withdrew sullenly into Virginia. The battle thus looked enough like a victory that Lincoln felt able to issue his preliminary Emancipation Proclamation, a measure he had decided on in mid-July.[63]

CONCILIATION: A POSTMORTEM

If there had been any remaining doubt about the death of conciliation, the Emancipation Proclamation ended it. Lincoln warned that unless the South abandoned the war by the first of January 1863, the slaves residing in the rebellious areas would become forever free. To no one's surprise, the proclamation outraged Southern opinion, the more so since it conjured fears of the race war white Southerners had always feared. It intensified Southern resistance, alienated potential Unionists, and in short, did exactly the things the conciliatory policy tried to avoid. Lincoln, however, had decided he could no longer afford to be conciliatory. Continued deference to a possibly illusory and certainly impotent Southern Union sentiment exasperated him. Why did they not assert themselves, he wondered, when the Federal armies came down to support them? "The paralysis – the dead palsy – of the government in this whole struggle is, that this class of men will do nothing for the government, nothing for themselves, except demanding that the government shall not strike its open enemies, lest they be struck by accident!" At the close of July he wrote August Belmont, a New York financier and prominent McClellan ally, that "[t]his government cannot much longer play a game in which it stakes all, and its enemies stake nothing. Those enemies must understand that they cannot experiment for ten years trying to destroy the government, and if they fail still come back into the Union unhurt."[64]

Historians of the Civil War have attributed a variety of reasons for the failure of the conciliatory policy. Some have argued that from the beginning, its proponents failed to understand the true nature of the conflict and that a hard war was somehow inevitable. That seems unreasonable. Prior to 1861, the United States had a well-

---

[63]See Chapter 6.

[64]Lincoln to Cuthbert Bullitt, July 28, 1862, Basler (ed.), *Collected Works of Lincoln* 5:344–345; Lincoln to Belmont, July 31, 1862, ibid., 350–351.

established tradition of restraint in war and an equally established tradition of political compromise. Further, modern scholarship partially vindicates the notion that a minority of Southerners led the South into secession, although it is probably true that Northerners underestimated the common Southerner's enthusiasm for disunion once it had become a reality. Certainly a conciliatory policy served the Union well in the war's early months, when the retention of the border states was a touch-and-go affair, and it scored some notable successes along the fringe of the Confederacy, which seemed to confirm the policy's effectiveness. Then, too, while no one has made a careful examination of Southern morale during the spring of 1862 – admittedly a difficult subject on which to reach convincing conclusions – considerable anecdotal evidence suggests that it may indeed have been on the verge of collapse, as many Union soldiers suspected. In short, conciliation just might have worked.[65]

Others, taking their cue from Ulysses S. Grant, have argued that conciliation failed because Northerners changed their minds about the tenacity of Southern resistance. In his memoirs, the Union war hero offered the famous statement that until the spring of 1862, he had supposed the Southern people were not in earnest and that one or two decisive Federal successes would make them quit the war. "[Forts] Donelson and Henry," he continued, "were such victories." But when they led only to the furious Confederate counterattack at Shiloh, "then, indeed, I gave up all idea of saving the Union except by complete conquest." He added that until that time he had ordered his troops to protect all private property, regardless of the owner's loyalty. But afterward, "I regarded it as humane to both sides to protect the persons of those found at their homes, but to consume everything that could be used to support or supply armies."[66]

Historians who rely on Grant's postwar recollections make two mistakes. First, they err by assuming that Grant's statement reflected the common opinion among Northern commanders and policymakers in the spring of 1862. In fact, most Union commanders regarded the war as being close to over. Second, they assume that it represents Grant's actual thinking during the period. It does not. Two months after Shiloh, for example, Grant still considered Southern civilians to be lukewarm about the war. He wrote his wife that he thought the conflict could be ended at once "if the whole Southern people could express their unbiased feeling untramelled [sic] by by [sic] leaders." He thought two things might help, and both of them accorded closely with the classic tenets of the conciliatory policy. It would be useful if Southerners stopped mistakenly thinking of the Union war effort as "Abolitionest" in character. Then, too, "There has been instances of negro stealing, [Northern] persons going to

---

[65]On the possibility that a relatively small political elite led the South into secession, see Eugene D. Genovese, *The Political Economy of Slavery: Studies in the Economy and Society of the Slave South* (New York: Vintage Books, 1965); Michael P. Johnson, *Toward a Patriarchal Republic: The Secession of Georgia* (Baton Rouge: Louisiana State University Press, 1977); and George C. Rable, *The Confederate Republic: A Revolution Against Politics* (Chapel Hill: University of North Carolina Press, 1994).

[66]Grant, *Memoirs* 1:368–369.

the houses of farmers who have remained at home, being inclined to Union sentiments, and before their eyes perswaid [sic] their blacks to mount up behind them and
go off." Grant's thinking hardened during the course of the summer, but even just
prior to the issuance of the Emancipation Proclamation, he thought the South could
not sustain the war much longer. "You will see the greatest fall in a few weeks of rebel
hopes that was ever known," Grant wrote while four Confederate armies launched
separate offensives. "They have made a bold effort, but it is a spasmodic effort without
anything behind to fall back on. When they do begin to fall all resources are at an end
and rebellion will soon show a rapid decline."[67]

Yet another theory about the failure of conciliation – a variant of Grant's idea –
ascribes its demise to the strength of guerrilla resistance encountered by Union troops
once they entered Southern territory, which is taken as evidence of Southern tenacity.
The trouble with this explanation is that the Federals met that sort of resistance
almost from the war's beginning. Certainly it placed a strain on the conciliatory
policy, yet until the summer of 1862 that strain seemed manageable. Some Northerners even saw partisan resistance as evidence that the Confederacy was on its last
legs. From northern Alabama, a Union colonel confided to his diary in June 1862,
"Rebels destroyed R.R. behind us last night. Small parties of from twenty-five to fifty
and one hundred mounted guerrillas are all through the country. Poor C.S.A. fast
giving up the ghost." Irregular warfare did not impress Union Brigadier General John
P. Hatch, either. "I believe the resources of the south are about played out," he wrote
his father from Virginia. "[T]heir guerrilla warfare will in the end hurt themselves
more than us."[68]

A fourth explanation, not well-accepted by historians but asserted with considerable force by McClellan, Buell, and various Democratic politicians, was that the
Radical Republican element deliberately scuttled conciliation in favor of a war aimed
at destroying slavery and transforming the South's socioeconomic structure. This
argument has a few features in its favor. The radical wing of the Republican party did
indeed desire such ends, and its constant machinations toward confiscation and
emancipation were designed as means to attain them. But for many months this wing
of the party was kept in check. Most Union military commanders, even those who
were "pragmatists," not "conciliators," did not want to get embroiled with the slavery
issue, and the bulk of Northern public opinion considered secessionists and abolitionists as tugging at two ends of the same rope around the country's neck. What enabled
them to capture the support of Lincoln, a Congressional majority, and many Union
officers for their program?

A fifth possibility seems to best fit the facts. More than anything else, McClellan's

---

[67]Grant to Julia Dent Grant, June 12, 1862, Simon (ed.), *Grant Papers* 5:143; Grant to Julia Dent Grant,
September 14, 1862, ibid. 6:44.

[68]Entry for June 20, 1862, typescript diary of Lieutenant Colonel William A. Robinson, 77th Pennsylvania Volunteer Infantry, Regimental Papers of the Civil War Collection, WHRS; Hatch to his father,
August 13, 1862, John P. Hatch Papers, LC.

failure on the Peninsula triggered the collapse of conciliation, because it dramatically increased the other pressures already at work: the Radicals who wanted to expand the war's goals, the troops who had never embraced the policy, and most importantly, the average Northern civilian, who now saw a seemingly imminent triumph disappear into a stalemate whose duration no one could predict.

5

War in earnest

Amid howls of merriment, the soldiers arrived in camp atop a carriage drawn by four horses stolen from some hapless local farmer. They were "cutting a grand splash" through the middle of their regiment when an unfamiliar officer suddenly shouted for them to dismount. One of the soldiers hooted that he would obey no orders but those of his company commander. Enraged, the officer seized a musket from one of the men; "had it been loaded," an observer swore, "he would have shot the fellow." It quickly developed that the officer was none other than Major General William T. Sherman. The merriment abruptly ceased. Sherman thereupon ordered the soldiers to unhitch the horses, remove their harnesses, and drape them across their own shoulders. He then forced the men to draw the carriage back to its owner, a distance of over two miles.[1]

The soldiers in question were new to the army, recruited after the reversals of mid-summer 1862 had led the Lincoln administration to call another 300,000 volunteers to the colors. When the new cadres arrived, veterans everywhere noticed that they exhibited a streak of vandalism greater than anything most had yet seen. Many attributed the greenhorns' demeanor to the strident cries throughout the North for an end to "kid glove" warfare. A New York officer blamed "the accursed conduct of the press with its clamor for a vigorous prosecution of the war" and "the savage appeals of our journals at home." And, indeed, a private in the recently recruited 155th Pennsylvania recalled that many of his comrades were convinced that "it was their bounden duty to forage upon all inhabitants of the enemy's country."[2]

With conciliation discredited, emancipation proclaimed, and new orders from the War Department that encouraged the military seizure of rebel property, it might be thought that Federal commanders would have welcomed such zeal. Many, however, did not. Brigadier General James W. Denver deplored the marauding of the new

[1][James W. Denver] to his wife, November 29, 1862, James W. Denver Letter, HCRWTC, USAMHI. The letter is unsigned. Richard J. Sommers, the archivist-historian at the U.S. Army Military History Institute, deduced the author's identity based on internal evidence. I am indebted to Dr. Sommers both for his research on the letter and for bringing it to my attention.

[2]Lusk to his mother, November 22, 1862, Lusk (ed.), *War Letters of William Thompson Lusk*, 231–232; John H. Kerr, *Under the Maltese Cross: Antietam to Appomattox: Campaigns of the 155th Pennsylvania Regiment* (Pittsburgh, Regimental Association, 1910), 87–88.

troops. "I do not see how men claiming to be enlightened and educated can do such things," he wrote his wife, adding that he and his fellow officers were trying to stop "these lawless acts." His discomfort stemmed from more than mere ethical concern. "If allowed to go on it will not be long before the soldier will be sunk in the cowardly plunderer – for men loaded with plunder are always cowards, – and instead of an army we will have an undisciplined mob. Selfpreservation to say nothing of humanity requires that discipline be maintained. . . ."[3]

Denver's comment helps to explain why Union commanders did not immediately embrace a hard war policy once conciliation had been repudiated. Military men have long been great sentimentalists, largely because sentiment – duty, patriotism, honor, courage – helps them to master the arduous tasks that befall them. As C.S. Lewis has acutely observed, "In battle it is not syllogisms that will keep the reluctant nerves and muscles at their post in the third hour of the bombardment. The crudest sentimentalism . . . about a flag or a country or a regiment will be of more use." And as General Denver realized, it was at best an uncertain business to extinguish certain kinds of sentiment and expect the rest to function. The rectitude that made soldiers spare the property of civilians might appear unrelated to the discipline that sustained men in battle. But many Civil War officers believed the moral fabric of soldiers was all of a piece; it could not be casually rent.[4]

On a less metaphysical level, freelance pillaging jeopardized the efficacy of authorized foraging should such an expedient become necessary. Denver noted that the old regiments stole very little except a few chickens and pigs. "But the new ones want to sweep the country as with a besom of destruction, leaving nothing behind on the road for any troops that may come after us." They seemed to have "a particular grudge at the corn and fodder, the very thing it is most important to us to preserve for our own purposes."[5]

Finally, like other forms of human endeavor, military operations carried opportunity costs. Troops being used to perform one function – say, to spread out across the countryside to destroy crops and seize livestock – could not readily be used to perform another. As long as commanders believed that the road to victory lay principally upon the battlefield, and as long as they could supply their armies through conventional means, they were understandably reluctant to divert large numbers of their forces to the destruction of Southern property.

Thus, for a variable but significant period of time, an intermediate step separated the demise of the conciliatory policy from the rise of hard war measures. Unlike conciliation, this step had no definite contemporary label. Some called it "a vigorous war policy" or "making war in earnest," but essentially it was an extension of the

---

[3]Denver to his wife, November 29, 1862, James W. Denver Letter, HCWRTC, USAMHI.

[4]C.S. Lewis, *The Abolition of Man, or Reflections on Education with Special Reference to the Teaching of English in the Upper Forms of Schools* (paperback edition; New York: MacMillan, 1955 [1947], 34. For a detailed analysis of the perceived connection between moral and soldierly virtues, see Gerald F. Linderman, *Embattled Courage: The Experience of Combat During the Civil War* (New York: Free Press, 1987).

[5]Denver to his wife, November 29, 1862, James W. Denver Letter, HCWRTC, USAMHI.

pragmatic policy, a program of relative mildness or severity depending on civilian behavior and the army's military needs.

THE WESTERN THEATER, JUNE–DECEMBER, 1862

The first departure from the conciliatory policy was an upsurge in authorized foraging – a phenomenon much more widespread in the western theater than the east, and attributable to the divergent logistical problems faced by eastern and western commanders. In Virginia and along the Atlantic coast, Union generals were almost always able to rely upon regular lines of supply. Although due in part to the region's abundance of rail and water communications, the main explanation was the bald fact that Union forces in the east were less fortunate than their western counterparts in capturing Southern territory. As a result, their supply lines simply never lengthened. In addition, the intensive operations in northern Virginia virtually denuded that region of crops and forage. The Confederate army had stripped it of much of its foodstuffs in the early months of the war, and the subsequent military campaigns never permitted the area to recover. Hence the region in which the Army of the Potomac operated was too barren to permit successful foraging.

Union generals in the west, in contrast, found that the region's railroads and river systems usually could not supply their armies' complete needs. Shortfalls occurred even when western forces operated close to rail and water communications. Railroads were vulnerable to interdiction: More than one offensive collapsed because of a timely cavalry raid against its rear. Most critically, western armies often had to operate in areas where suitable rail and water communications were unavailable. To overcome such a disadvantage, it became essential to take supplies directly from the countryside.

Among the first to encounter this reality was Major General Samuel R. Curtis, whose Army of the Southwest operated in the barren Ozark plateau along the Missouri-Arkansas border, over 200 miles beyond the nearest railhead at Rolla, Missouri. Wagon trains could not meet the supply needs of the army over such an extended distance; indeed, they had difficulty even keeping up with Curtis's infantry. Although reluctant to have his troops resort to foraging – during the Mexican War he had seen how easily it could degenerate into wanton pillaging – he had little choice. As Curtis anticipated, such expedients led to some thievery, but the authorized foraging was bad enough: In the sparsely populated region his troops had to strip the countryside almost bare. "I leave nothing for man or brute in the country passed over by my army," Curtis reported, "except a little saving to feed the poor." Curtis tried to turn the situation to political advantage. He ordered that all foraging officers should distinguish between loyal and disloyal civilians. The former would receive certificates for the amount and value of property seized, so that they could later receive compensation; the latter would receive nothing. In this way, foraging became a way to punish rebellion.[6]

East of the Mississippi River, armies took a bit longer to resort to foraging, partly because the suspension of offensive operations in early June 1862 made such expedients less necessary. Although the victories at Fort Donelson, Shiloh, and Corinth had given Union forces control over most of western and central Tennessee, Halleck did not press his advantage. Instead, he parceled out his immense army across the huge expanse of conquered territory. Designed to consolidate the Federals' grip on the region, his decision had the unintended effect of paralyzing further advances for several months. Halleck, however, did not have to deal with the consequences. In July, the Lincoln administration summoned him to Washington to assume the mantle of General-in-Chief, and his successor, Ulysses S. Grant, inherited the unfortunate strategic position. Over the next four months, Grant slowly revised Halleck's flawed arrangement so as to concentrate a force strong enough to regain the offensive.[7]

It was during Grant's tenure that resort to foraging mainly began, and then for three reasons. First, regular supplies occasionally proved inadequate even despite the army's relatively passive posture, and officers permitted their quartermasters to supplement rations directly from neighborhood farms. (They also confiscated horses, mules, and other livestock to meet the army's transportation needs.) Second, the Federals were impressed by the Confederates' own practice of liberally stripping goods from the countryside. Seeking permission to confiscate forage and horses from a certain neighborhood, one Union general pointed out that everything in that section was already being carried South, "and unless we react promptly will be used against us by the rebels." Finally, western commanders foraged in response to War Department orders issued in August 1862 that encouraged all Federal armies to do so as a means of punishing the rebellion. Halleck was not long in Washington before he heard the drumbeat for an end to the kid gloves. "As soon as the corn gets fit for forage," he wrote his successor, "get all the supplies you can from the rebels in Mississippi. It is time they should feel the presence of war on our side."[8]

Some of Grant's subordinates were initially uncomfortable with the idea. Brigadier General John A. Logan reminded officers to "use your utmost endeavors to protect the rights of private property, suffering nothing to be taken except what is absolutely necessary for your command, and then only by paying or agreeing to pay the owner a just compensation for the same." Major General William T. Sherman thought that

---

[6]William L. Shea and Earl J. Hess, *Pea Ridge: Civil War Campaign in the West* (Chapel Hill: University of North Carolina Press, 1992), 11; Curtis to J. C. Kelton, April 19, 1862, OR 13:364; Curtis to Carr, December 28, 1861, ibid. 8:473.

[7]Grant took formal command of the District of West Tennessee on July 17. It embraced the entire region between the Tennessee and Mississippi Rivers and also included the Union base at Cairo, Illinois. See Special Field Orders No. 164, July 16, 1862, OR 17, pt. 2:101; and General Order No. 62, July 17, 1862, ibid., 102.

[8]L.F. Ross to Major General John McClernand, August 22, 1862, ibid., vol. 17, pt. 2:183–184; General Order No. 107, August 15, 1862, ibid., Series III, vol. 2, p. 388; General Order No. 109, August 16, 1862, ibid., 397; Halleck to Grant, August 2, 1862, ibid., Series I, vol. 17, pt. 2:150.

"[t]oo much looseness exists on the subject of foraging." While the rules of war entitled an army to take "certain articles of forage and provisions" from the country "within limits," it was "a delicate right" that must be exercised by only a few authorized parties, and then under specific guidelines. Quartermasters requisitioning fodder from local inhabitants, he instructed, were to use "all possible forbearance," explain the necessity for their action, and leave vouchers to be redeemed upon proof of loyalty.[9]

The worst aspect of foraging, as Sherman well understood, was the temptation it offered troops to steal private property for their own use. Their appetite for plunder thus whetted, some men began to actively seek out opportunities for theft by straggling from their units, and soon lost sight of their duty altogether. Sherman authorized summary punishment for stragglers who committed depredations upon private property, and ordered mounted patrols to shoot anyone who robbed or vandalized. "This demoralizing and disgraceful practice of pillage must cease," he insisted, "else the country will rise on us and justly shoot us down like dogs and wild beasts."[10]

Grant too deplored the fact that Union troops sometimes preyed on Southern civilians, and in one instance cut off the pay of two offending regiments until they reimbursed a Tennessee village for damages committed. His policy was not based on any lingering faith in conciliation – he considered Southern women and children "wors[e] rebels than the soldiers who fight against us" – but rather on common sense and simple justice. He harbored no vindictiveness against civilians, writing his wife, "Soldiers who fight battles do not suffer half their horrors." Punishment should be reserved for those who actively supported the rebellion. As for less offensive civilians, Grant insisted that his troops should leave them alone, even threatening death to soldiers who pilfered, marauded, or destroyed private property. Such "gross acts of vandalism" were calculated, he said, "to destroy the efficiency of an army and to make open enemies of those who were before, if not friends, then at least non-combatants."[11]

In general, Grant sought to create a passive civilian population, not a demoralized one, and he by no means assumed that they were all implacably hostile. His foraging orders emphasized the need to give receipts for *all* goods taken, which "should set forth as far as possible the [political] status of the parties who are deprived of their property." In mid-December, he even made arrangements to help needy families by selling supplies or giving them away free, possibly offsetting the cost by forced contributions from disloyal persons. Indeed, when practicable, Grant preferred to have known secessionists bear the burden of the army's requisitions. And his orders

[9]Logan to Major M.R.M. Wallace, July 7, 1862, ibid., 80. See also Captain Stewart R. Tresilian [Logan's aide de camp] to Colonel L. Osburn, July 7, 1862, ibid. Logan repeated the same language in the instructions subsequently issued to an Illinois regiment. Logan to Colonel Garrett Nevins, July 24, 1862, ibid., 115; General Order No. 44, June 18, 1862, ibid., 16.

[10]Ibid; General Order No. 45, June 21, 1862, ibid., 23; General Order No. 49, July 7, 1862, ibid., 89.

[11]Grant to Rosecrans, August 2, 1862, *Grant Papers* 5:260; Grant to Julia Dent Grant, June 3, 1862, ibid., 138; General Order No. 56, June 24, 1862; ibid., 151; Special Field Orders No. 1, November 7, 1862, OR 17, pt. 2:326–327. See also Special Field Orders No. 2, November 9, 1862, ibid., 331–332.

required that foraging parties leave families a sixty-day supply of provisions. This standard, however, was "not to be construed to deprive the soldier of his rations whilst the country affords it. If suffering must fall on one or the other, the citizen must bear it."[12]

Originally, Grant, in common with most commanders on both sides, regarded foraging as an ancillary logistical expedient. It gave troops a bit of fresh food and eased the burden on regular supply lines, but that was all. A near-disaster to his army, however, opened his eyes to the wider potentialities of living off the land. In early November, Grant, intent on the capture of the river fortress of Vicksburg, embarked his army on an overland march through Mississippi. By mid-December he had reached the town of Oxford, about sixty miles from his starting point and about twice that distance from his objective. Then, on December 20, Confederate cavalry under Major General Earl Van Dorn captured and destroyed his forward supply depot at Holly Springs. Simultaneously, Brigadier General Nathan Bedford Forrest's raiders successfully interdicted his rail communications in western Tennessee. Grant, his army suddenly cut off from regular supply, abruptly abandoned his offensive, gave orders for his troops to live off the land, and hoped he could reconstruct a viable supply line before his army starved in the field.

To his astonishment, however, the army not only survived but actually feasted during its retreat. It turned out that northern Mississippi contained a huge food surplus. "I was amazed at the quantity of supplies the country afforded," he later remembered. "It showed me that we could have subsisted off the country for two months instead of two weeks without going beyond the limits designated." It was a lesson Grant did not forget, and one he credited with helping to inspire his decisive march against Vicksburg the following May.[13]

Regularized foraging expanded into middle Tennessee when, in November 1862, Major General William S. Rosecrans replaced Don Carlos Buell as commander of the Department of the Cumberland. The troops in the region welcomed the change, for Buell had stolidly maintained his conciliatory policy to the bitter end. Having previously served in western Tennessee, Rosecrans at once encouraged his troops to forage, and indeed considered the expedient vital. Although based at Nashville with good railroad and river communications, Rosecrans nevertheless found it difficult to keep his army properly fed, and without amassing an enormous stockpile of supplies he despaired of ever taking the offensive across the barren Cumberland plateau to his front. To create such a stockpile, foraging parties routinely swept the countryside. Confederate parties did the same, and frequent skirmishes occurred as both sides struggled to obtain supplies from the land between the rival armies. By February

---

[12]Grant to Sherman, November 10, 1862, ibid., 336; Special Field Orders No. 21, December 12, 1862, ibid., 405; Grant to Jeremiah C. Sullivan, December 23, 1862, ibid., 465; Grant to Sullivan, December 26, 1862, ibid., 490; Special Field Orders No. 35, December 29, 1862, ibid., 550–506.

[13]Grant, *Memoirs* 1:435. Colonel Manning F. Force commented, "We gathered great stores of corn, fodder, beans, rye, and salt, cattle, sheep and hogs, with a little sugar, and were delighted at 'short rations.'" Force to "Mr. Kebler," January 13, 1863, Manning F. Force Papers, UW.

1863, Rosecrans was clamoring for more cavalry, not so much for service on the battlefield as to enable his foraging trains to gain hegemony over disputed districts.[14]

As soon as Rosecrans instituted his foraging policy, he gave his men clear guidelines to follow. Unionist citizens were to be paid in cash or offered a voucher for reimbursement; citizens known to be disloyal would receive only a receipt inscribed, "To be settled hereafter as the Government may direct." To prevent abuses, authorization for foraging parties must come from division level or higher. Officers using foraging permits were strictly charged to follow Rosecrans' procedures. Those who let soldiers pillage or enter private homes without permission would be cashiered from the service.[15]

Using a formula that was rapidly becoming standard among Union officials, Rosecrans distinguished between three classes of Southern civilians: Unionists, outright secessionists, and "peaceable inhabitants, who honestly and truly abstain from any interference . . . with military matters." This latter class, he ordered, were entitled to protection from violence or plunder and would be allowed to "enjoy their local rights, subject only to needful surveillance to prevent them from being used as tools for mischief." Unionists, of course, would be treated as full-fledged United States citizens. But those "who are hostile to our Government, repudiating its Constitution and laws, have no rights [except under] the laws of war and the dictates of humanity." Where possible, Rosecrans' officers preferred to forage from known secessionists, especially wealthy ones.[16]

Both War Department directives and those of senior western commanders emphasized that foraging should be done "in an orderly manner" and under the supervision of "officers who can be relied upon to maintain order."[17] In practice, of course, it further exacerbated the private soldier's already chronic habit of taking food for personal use. Occasionally, senior officers found such exploits amusing. Rosecrans, for example, whimsically described how a Union brigade had "attacked the pigs of Danville, deploying skirmishers for that purpose" and killed "eight of the hairy rascals" before the brigade commander could be told that "these natives were non-combatants, as loyal as possible considering their limited information." More often, however, generals regarded such episodes with distaste. Orders against unauthorized foraging liberally sprinkle the pages of the *Official Records,* as do complaints about the units most notorious for their marauding proclivities. But once the door was opened,

[14]Richard C. Watson to his sister, December 8, 1862, Richard C. Watson Letters, CWMC, USAMHI; Rosecrans to Halleck, January 30, 1863, OR 23, pt. 2:23; Rosecrans to Halleck, February 2, 1863, ibid., 34. For Rosecrans' logistical situation, see Edward Hagerman, *The American Civil War and the Origins of Modern Warfare* (Bloomington: Indiana University Press, 1988), 197–198, 209–213.

[15]General Order No. 17, November 17, 1862, OR 20, pt. 2:61–62.

[16]General Order No. 19, November 19, 1862, ibid., 72; Thomas to Rosecrans, November 18, 1862, ibid., 65.

[17]The language quoted is Grant's. See Grant to Brigadier General Charles S. Hamilton, November 4, 1862, ibid., 320.

it became well-nigh impossible to police the soldiers closely, and indeed, the line between authorized and unauthorized foraging often seemed to blur.[18]

The ease with which even official expeditions could produce abuses is indicated by a letter from Colonel Manning F. Force to a friend back in Ohio. Force recorded that he had recently taken a foraging party to secure corn and fodder and had personally supervised the detail. When it became apparent that some troops were also stealing turnips, Force posted guards to prevent it. A bit later, he noted with satisfaction that one of the guards was "apparently keeping off with his bayonet, a group who wished to push through the fence." But as Force drew closer, it became obvious that the guard was actually digging up turnips with his bayonet, and thrusting them through the fence under the pretence of a vigorous performance of his duty. Completely baffled, Force wrote, "I turned away and did not see it."[19]

With officers unable to control the foraging, the only hope was for soldiers to control themselves. This, in one sense, they completely failed to do, for their letters, diaries, and reminiscences universally attest that restrictions on foraging were observed mainly in the breach. The same accounts, however, abundantly demonstrate that the civilians in their midst were anything but a faceless, Manichean "other." When George Landrum's sister expressed dismay that he had seized an Alabama farmer's wheat to feed his horse, Landrum's justification was specific. "The old fellow voted for secession twice, and is now getting his rights, and I would rather have him starve than the horse. My horse is doing all in his power for the Nation and the old man all he can against it." While encamped near Iuka, Mississippi, Edward A. Webb reported,

Some of the Boys went to a Secesh house and asked where they could get some good water to drink Says he there is a frog pond good enough for you Northern thieves we come back and told the Major – he told us to go and get what we wanted so of course we went and took Corn Sweet Potatoes Water Mellon Chickens Turkey Geese Sheep Pigs Calves and every thing else we could find So you See that he did not make much out of us. . . .

Such accounts illustrate how soldiers became acquainted with the Southerners; they knew who was "secesh" and, more rarely, who was Unionist. Above all – as Webb's list of foraged items attests – they knew who was rich, and since they generally equated wealth with membership in the planter aristocracy, they often found a happy correlation between "secesh property" and the property most likely to provide an abundance of food.[20]

[18]Rosecrans to Grant, August 17, 1862, ibid., 177. See, for example, Captain B.P. Chenowith to Halleck, June 30, 1862, ibid., 53–54; Halleck to Stanton, July 7, 1862, with enclosures, ibid., 34–66; Halleck to Stanton, July 12, 1862, with enclosures, ibid., 91–94; Sherman to Hurlbut, July 10, 1862, ibid., 88–89; General Order No. 54, July 19, 1862, ibid., 106; Philip H. Sheridan to Gordon Granger, July 29, 1862, ibid., 132; Lieutenant C. Goddard to "Commanding Officer of the Town of Ripley, Mississippi," October 9, 1862, ibid., 271–272; and General Order No. 2, November 5, 1862, ibid., 321.

[19]Force to "Mr. Kebler," October 11, 1862, Manning F. Force Papers, UW.

[20]George W. Landrum to his sister, August 12, 1863, George W. Landrum Letters, WRHS; Edward A. Webb to his sister, August 24, 1862, Edward A. Webb Papers, WRHS.

Even soldiers ardent for a confiscatory policy wanted it applied to "Rebel property." Some letters and diaries are quite explicit on this point. "There was an old Secesh [who] lived close by. The boys found it out and they went and took his Fowls, potatoes, Honey and every thing they can get their eyes on. . . . We went out a forageing. Found plenty of fodder at a rich man's house. . . . We captured a mule from a hard Secesh. . . . We stopt at a large farm and after talking a while we found out that her Husband was in the Rebel army. She is rich but the soldiers took nearly all she had." A soldier in Rosecrans' army wrote home that "when some of the boys gets holt of any property belon[g]ing to the rebels they distroy it as fast as they can and then say dam him he is the coss of bringing us here." A few men, the writer added, would seize foodstuffs from any family with men in the rebel army. He personally would not: "i canot halve the hart to take from the helplis famlies when i see a nice looking house and plenty around it i will halve a chicken if i can ketch it."[21]

It is quite likely that the zest with which soldiers embraced foraging pulled the generals along farther than they might otherwise have gone. Certainly it forced them to become more philosophical. Captain William McCarty noted how generals who had formerly condemned assaults on Southern property now looked on "rather approvingly" as their soldiers took fence rails and burned cotton gins and barns. He thought they could scarcely do otherwise. "[I]t would have been almost impossible to have kept down rebelion and mutany in the army had our men been compelled much longer to guard & protect the families and property of those in the regular army who [we are] fighting against."[22]

The most hardened foragers were often white Southerners – Unionists who had seen their own families humiliated and despoiled by secessionists and held vengeance in their hearts. "They know more than we do, what will cure the South," Captain McCarty wrote of cavalrymen from Tennessee and Mississippi, "and they go for laying everything wast[e] before us." On a recent march, he had seen the Southerners set fire to nearly everything along their route except people's actual residences.[23]

As McCarty's letter suggests, even such destructive behavior had limits. While never absolute, boundaries on acceptable behavior clearly existed. Soldiers took mainly foodstuffs; the stealing of jewelry and other property was more rare. They often showed reluctance about entering houses or, if they did, would not venture beyond the common areas. If they burned anything, it was generally cotton gins or other outbuildings associated with the economic life of a plantation or farm. Most

[21]Entry for November 30, 1862, Alva C. Griest diary, HCWRTC, USAMHI. Entries for November 28, 1862, January 18, 24, 25, 1863, diary, George P. Metz Papers, DUL. Elias Brady to his wife, November 24, 1862, Elias Brady Papers, SHC. For other examples, see Charles Harding Cox to his sister, December 20, 1862, Lorna Lutes Sylvester (ed.), "The Civil War Letters of Charles Harding Cox," *Indiana Magazine of History* 68 (1972):42; entries for July 15-October 17, 1863 passim., Alva C. Griest diary, HCWRTC, USAMHI.

[22]William W. McCarty to his mother, November 8, 1862, William W. McCarty Letters, CWMC, USAMHI.

[23]McCarty to his mother, November 8, 1862, William W. McCarty Letters, CWMC, USAMHI. See also George W. Landrum to his sister, May 6, 1863, George W. Landrum Letters, WRHS.

interestingly, the physical presence of civilians tended to inhibit extreme behavior. Fearing just the opposite, white Southerners sometimes fled, but this was a mistake. "When the inhabitants have remained at home and behaved themselves their property has not been much injured," a surgeon in the 92nd Ohio told his wife. He was certain enough of the dynamic to advise her, "Should the rebels ever succeed in making a raid into Ohio, you must not run away. It will be better for you and your house to remain at home."[24]

It would be wrong, however, to suggest that foraging activity was a benign affair. Even under ideal circumstances it was psychologically stressful for civilians. Economically it could be devastating, particularly in regions where armies operated for extended periods. "Southern & Northern soldiers take our property," wailed a Tennessee planter, "Each pretending to fear it may fall into the hands of the other & be turned against them So between the men with bayonets all will finally be lost and opulent families brought to ruin." Ironically, the "opulent families," though milked the heaviest by foragers, were often the ones best able to withstand it. Poor people were much more vulnerable, and in well-foraged districts the long-term effect was to drive thousands of them to depend on the Federal government for rations.[25]

By the spring of 1863, western generals had initiated a routine foraging system, grasped the concept of area denial, and embraced the destruction of railroads and such quasipublic property as grist mills. They had even begun to accept, although not to condone, the fact that their troops were chronically commiting acts of pillage and vandalism. "Our armies," Sherman wrote his brother in January 1863, "are devastating the land, and it is sad to see the destruction that attends our progress – we cannot help it. Farms disappear, houses are burned and plundered, and every living animal killed and eaten. General officers make feeble efforts to stay the disorder, but it is idle. . . ."[26] Such destructive energies, however, remained simply cause for regret. Neither Sherman nor his commander had yet harnessed those energies in major operations against Southern infrastructure and society.

THE EASTERN THEATER, SEPTEMBER 1862 – DECEMBER 1863

In sharp contrast to affairs in the west, the Army of the Potomac was far more slow to adopt a program of foraging and area denial. Its predominant conduct in late 1862 and throughout 1863 continued to emphasize a conservative brand of warfare little changed from that of McClellan. McClellan himself had departed. Hard on the heels of the North's off-year elections in the autumn of 1862, Lincoln finally got rid of the

[24]J. Dexter Cotton to his wife, June 21, 1863, J. Dexter Cotton Papers, LC.

[25]Entry for October 19, 1863, John Houston Bills diary, SHC.

[26]Sherman to John Sherman, January 25, 1863, in Rachel Thorndike Sherman (ed.), *The Sherman Letters: Correspondence Between General and Senator Sherman from 1837 to 1891* (New York: Charles Scribner's Sons, 1894), 185.

troublesome general. On the evening of November 7, a special War Department courier delivered a message to McClellan at his headquarters, ordering him to turn over command of the Army of the Potomac to Major General Ambrose E. Burnside. Two days later, the former "Young Napoleon" reviewed his troops for the last time, bade them an emotional farewell, and retired north to await new instructions that never came. With his removal, the most visible military advocate of conciliation disappeared from the war. Don Carlos Buell, another commander known for his mild policy toward Southern civilians, had been relieved from command of the Army of the Ohio twelve days before.

The conciliatory spirit of McClellan and Buell did not in itself account for their removal. Lincoln dispensed with them primarily because neither general showed sufficient energy and aggressiveness against the enemy. Buell had permitted a Confederate army under General Braxton Bragg to raid deep into Kentucky and then return to Tennessee unscathed. McClellan, after fighting Lee's Army of Northern Virginia to a stand-off at Antietam, had permitted the Confederates to withdraw unmolested into Virginia and had refused even to cross the Potomac in pursuit for over a month thereafter. The President was more interested in prompt action by a fully reliable army commander than with that commander's views on civilian policy. His selection of Burnside to replace McClellan attests to this. During his expedition to the North Carolina coast, Burnside's policy toward the local inhabitants had been notably conciliatory in character. And although he had since become disillusioned with the mild policy, his instincts concerning conduct toward Southern civilians remained conservative. The new commander was also known to be friends with McClellan and was, like McClellan, a Democrat.

Burnside remained in command of the Army of the Potomac for less than three months. During that period, he fought and lost the Battle of Fredericksburg, then began an abortive second campaign that bogged down in an unexpected Virginia rainstorm and became known derisively as the "Mud March." His brief tenure brought no changes in McClellan's basic policy toward Southern civilians. Indeed, General Order No. 154 – which McClellan had written explicitly as an attack on the sterner policies adopted by Pope, Lincoln and Stanton – remained the official guideline for the eastern army's foraging and confiscation activities at least through February 1863, while authorization for foraging remained at corps level or higher as late as November 1863.[27]

The one change that did occur was a noticeable upsurge in the frequency of soldiers' depredations against Southern property. Significantly, it began not in late October, when the Army of the Potomac returned to Virginia soil, but rather in early September, at a time when the army was operating in loyal Maryland – and a predominantly

---

[27]General Order No. 8 [Hooker], February 6, 1863, OR 25, pt. 2:55; General Order No. 100 [Meade], November 5, 1863, ibid., 422. Interestingly, this conservative style continued in the teeth of repeated demands from Halleck to take supplies from the countryside. (See, for example, Halleck to Major General George G. Meade, August 5, 1863, ibid. 29, pt. 2:8; and Halleck to Meade, September 15, 1863, ibid., 186–187.) A key problem was that the countryside was practically denuded.

Unionist part of Maryland at that. Most of the problem could be traced to stragglers, a class of soldiers whose motivation and sense of identification with the Federal cause tended to be weaker than among those who stayed with the colors. On September 9, McClellan had found it necessary to threaten the death penalty for soldiers found guilty of marauding and trespassing on the property of Maryland civilians.[28]

Yet while officers frequently blamed the depredations on stragglers, some of it appears to have stemmed from the coarsening of values characteristic of veteran soldiers. An Indiana cavalryman, noting that his regiment had begun to lean heavily on the countryside for supplies, was astonished by the brazenness of his comrades. "They will take a man's meal and demand his sack to carry it in, or kill the sheep or hogs in his door yards, and ask his assistance in dressing them. Women's tears are nothing, and their talk of starvation unheeded." As in the western theater, they gravitated toward the property of secessionists. "One farmer here lost nearly three hundred sheep the first night our boys encamped," a soldier wrote home. "If he had not been a rebel, his property would have been guarded from pillage. Our officers say nothing if we take a rebel's turkeys, hens, or sheep to eat; they like their share. But if we find a Union man, a provost guard is detailed to protect his property."[29]

Even so, the Army of the Potomac remained far short of the destructive standard then common among western troops. Brigadier General Alpheus S. Williams, a division commander in the Twelfth Corps, wrote home that the late-November destruction of three haystacks by "[s]ome rascally fellows" marked "the first of this kind of wanton destruction I have seen." He blamed it not on ideological fury against Southerners but rather on a Union brigade commander's unwise refusal to let the troops use the hay for bedding. Sheer hunger often motivated acts of petty theft, but even then Union troops often found little to sustain them. Much of northern Virginia had been stripped by the Confederate army during its long encampment in the region during the winter of 1861–1862; the near-constant campaigns in the region since then had prevented its recovery. Even fodder for horses could not be gotten locally. "With us not a thing is to be had in the country," wrote Colonel Charles S. Wainwright. "On the contrary, hosts of the half-starved inhabitants look to our commissary for food and to keep them alive." And although Burnside established regular procedures for foraging and confiscation of livestock, the essential conservatism of the policy was indicated by the fact that such activities had to be authorized at corps-level or above – as opposed to division-level or even brigade-level in the west.[30]

---

[28]General Order No. 155, September 9, 1862, ibid. 19, pt. 2:227. McClellan found it necessary to follow up this directive with another one some three weeks later. See General Order No. 159, October 1, 1862, ibid., 376.

[29]Entry for October 31, 1862, Samuel J. B. V. Gilpin Diary, E. N. Gilpin Papers, LC. See also William H. Walling to his sister, November 6, 1862, CWMC, USAMHI. Edwin Oberlin Wentworth to his wife, November 8, 1862, Edwin Oberlin Wentworth Papers, LC.

[30]Alpheus S. Williams to his daughter, December 14, 1862, in Milo M. Quaife (ed.), *From The Cannon's Mouth: The Civil War Letters of General Alpheus S. Williams* (Detroit: Wayne State University Press, 1959), 152; entry for December 7, 1862, in Nevins (ed.), *A Diary of Battle*, 133; General Order No. 188, November 29, 1862, OR 21:810–811.

The bombardment and looting of Fredericksburg formed the chief incident of destructive behavior during Burnside's tenure. The shelling itself fully accorded with contemporary laws and usages of war: The Federals informed the Confederates of their intentions well ahead of time, and gave ample opportunity for the town's residents to find safety elsewhere. Moreover, it had a direct military purpose, for it sought to neutralize Confederate sharpshooters who were contesting the passage of the Rappahannock. But the extensive vandalism to the town that occurred before, during, and after the battle obviously had no such efficacy, although some officers afterward insisted that since Fredericksburg had refused to surrender and had been taken by storm, under the laws and usages of war it could legitimately be sacked.[31]

Although technically correct, such ex post facto justifications did nothing to explain the motivations behind the looting spree. One historian has suggested that it began in response to "the frustrations of battle, especially defeat." Another has argued that the plundering reflected a new ideological fierceness aimed at Southerners in general. Of the two explanations, the second best fits the evidence, but with one important qualification. Most eyewitnesses recalled that the vandalism was directed primarily at the wealthiest homes in town, which suggests that the target was the local "aristocracy" and hence, presumably, the most virulent secessionists.[32]

Time and again, these eyewitness accounts emphasize the expense and quality of the goods destroyed. This one is typical of many:

Boys came in . . . *loaded* with *silver* pitchers, silver spoons, silver lamps and castors, etc. Great three-story houses furnished magnificently were broken into and their contents scattered over the floors and trampled on by the muddy feet of the soldiers. Splendid alabaster vases and pieces of statuary were thrown at 6 and 700 dollar mirrors. Closets of the very finest china were broken into and their contents smashed onto the floor and stamped to pieces. Finest cut glass ware goblets were hurled at nice plate glass windows, beautifully embroidered window curtains torn down, rosewood pianos piled in the street and burned or soldiers would get on top of them and kick the key-board and internal machinery all to pieces.[33]

But although the presumed secessionist aristocracy formed the chief target of the looting, some troops nevertheless refused to participate. A Union general occupied a fine house belonging to his brother-in-law, "a damned rebel," and invited a Minnesota regiment to remove from the residence anything it wished. The Minnesotans not only

[31]Edwin V. Sumner to Mayor and Common Council of Fredericksburg, Virginia, November 21, 1862, ibid., 783; Sumner to Mayor, etc., November 22, 1862, ibid., 788 (the actual shelling of Fredericksburg did not begin until December 11); Francis A. Walker, *A History of the Second Army Corps in the Army of the Potomac* (New York: Charles Scribners, 1886), 153.

[32]Linderman, *Embattled Courage*, 193; Bruce Catton, *Glory Road: The Bloody Route From Fredericksburg to Gettysburg* (Garden City, NY: Doubleday, 1952), 67.

[33]Major F.E. Pierce (108th New York) to "Ed," December 17, 1862, in the Dorsey Pender Papers; quoted in Douglas Southall Freeman, *Lee's Lieutenants: A Study in Command,* 3 vols. (New York: Charles Scribner's Sons, 1942–1944), vol. 2, p. 344. For similar accounts, see entry for December 12, 1862, Thomas F. Galwey diary, LC; Abraham Welch to his sister, December 27, 1862, Abraham Welch Letter, SHC; Curtis C. Pollack to his mother, December 18, 1862, Curtis C. Pollack Letters, CWMC, USAMHI; John S. Weiser to his parents, January 1, 1863, John S. Weiser Letters, CWMC, USAMHI; and Allen, *Forty-six Months With the Fourth R.I. Volunteers,* 175.

declined, but spontaneously established a protective guard around the house and saved it from destruction by other troops.[34]

The high command also condemned the looting and took measures to curtail it. Major General Darius N. Couch, chief of the Second Corps, placed a provost marshal at the Rappahannock bridges with orders that nobody should recross to the Union encampment with plunder. Sentries, dutifully collecting stolen goods as the looters attempted to return, soon gathered an "enormous pile of booty." Even if the looting of Fredericksburg did reflect a new ideological severity against Southerners, wealthy or otherwise, it had little sequel. And almost none of this new severity seems to have infected the senior commanders, most of whom continued to wage war in a fashion not much different from the days of McClellan.[35]

Their conservatism was particularly evident in their failure to take effective action against Confederate sources of supply. Although Lee's army drew much of its victuals from the railroads that came up from Richmond and the Deep South, a significant portion of its food and forage came from Virginia itself, often from areas within easy reach of Union forces. In contrast to western forces, who had inaugurated a consistent policy of taking potential rebel supplies directly from the farms that produced them, units in the Army of the Potomac usually acted only after the goods belonged to the Confederate army. Even in the Northern Neck, a prosperous, easily accessible peninsula between the Potomac and Rappahannock estuaries, the eastern army consistently neglected its opportunity to forage. On the contrary, it permitted Confederate cavalry to draw beef and fodder from the area.[36]

The head of the Union Quartermaster Department, Major General Montgomery C. Meigs, repeatedly urged Colonel Rufus Ingalls, the Army of the Potomac's quartermaster general, to exploit the Northern Neck's resources. Ingalls replied diffidently that this had been done to some extent, but that it was not altogether safe because of guerrillas, armed inhabitants, and raiding Confederates. With some exasperation, Meigs urged Burnside to consider the logistical possibilities, writing that he had been impressed with the fact that the Northern Neck contained over 800 square miles of fertile, well-cultivated territory. European armies, Meigs continued, had waged entire wars for the possession of smaller provinces than that:

[34]R.I. Holcombe, *History of the First Regiment Minnesota Volunteer Infantry* (Stillwater, MN: Eastern and Masterman, 1916), 266–268.

[35]Darius N. Couch, "Sumner's 'Right Grand Division,'" in Clarence C. Buel and Robert U. Johnson (eds.), *Battles and Leaders of the Civil War*, 4 vols. (Reprint ed., New York: Thomas Yoseloff, 1956 [1887]), vol. 3, p. 108. Couch's indignation was apparently a postwar phenomenon. His battle report is positively misleading in its attempt to soft pedal the vandalism. "[S]carcely an inhabitant was found remaining in the city; very little property was maliciously destroyed, the troops taking tobacco, flour, and other eatables, wherever found; order and discipline reigned." Couch's report, January [?], 1863, OR 21:222.

[36]For example, in late December the 8th Pennsylvania Cavalry seized 150 cattle belonging to Lee's army. Pleasonton to J.H. Taylor, December 28, 1862, OR 21:893. On the Confederates' drawing of supplies from the Northern Neck, see Lee to James A. Seddon, April 4, 1863, ibid. 25, pt. 2:703. On Lee's supply difficulties in general, see Douglas Southall Freeman, *R.E. Lee: A Biography*, 4 vols. (New York: Charles Scribners Sons, 1935), vol. 3, pp. 491–495.

Is it not worthwhile to occupy it, to deprive the rebels of its resources, in produce, in taxes, in conscripts, in recruits, in information? Could not a small column have restored the authority of the Union over this land; enabled the Government to give effect to its confiscation and sequestration acts; cut off from the rebels valuable sources, and draw from loyal owners by payment, and from rebels by seizure, and receipts payable after the war, on proof of loyal conduct from their date, large supplies of grain, of forage, of tobacco, of cattle, and of horses, for the support of our army?

The war, Meigs concluded, was "gradually assuming the aspect of a long one, to be settled by exhaustion." In such circumstances, "every pressure we can put upon a rebel is so much toward the end."[37]

Burnside paid no attention, nor did his successor, Major General Joseph Hooker. Their failure to act on Meigs's suggestion cannot be explained by the persistence of a conciliatory spirit. Although Burnside remained a rather conservative commander, he nevertheless believed that if the Union troops expected success, they must learn to match the earnestness of their opponents – a perspective that surely would have seen little problem in putting additional pressure on rebels. Hooker, for his part, was an anti-McClellan partisan with strong Radical Republican ties. The more likely explanation is that a western-style exploitation of local resources simply did not accord with their Virginia-influenced experiences with war.[38]

Ironically, the closest approach to hard war in late 1862 and early 1863 came from southeastern Virginia, a military backwater whose operations exerted scant effect on the war as a whole. Indeed, the very marginality of the area was itself a spur to the adoption of such measures. With only slender forces at their disposal, Federal generals in that district believed that major offensives were out of the question. If they were to hurt the enemy at all, it must be through raids against his crops and war resources.

During the autumn of 1862 and well into 1863 the department commander in southeastern Virginia was Major General John A. Dix. Formerly one of the strongest conciliatory generals, Dix had enough political savvy to realize that the mild policy was no longer viable. Nevertheless he retained a great deal of sympathy for the civilians within his jurisdiction, and often leaped to their defense. But a few of Dix's subordinates sought to strike a blow at the enemy, among them Brigadier General Henry M. Naglee. On his own initiative, Naglee in mid-December 1862 decided to conduct a reconnaissance into Matthews, King and Queen, and Middlesex Counties. Two cavalry squadrons destroyed a large tannery producing leather for the Confederate army. Other soldiers came upon "several large herds of hogs and sheep on the road to the commissariat," and Naglee did not hesitate "to turn their direction toward our

---

[37]Meigs to Burnside, January 12, 1863; ibid., 966–967. Ingalls had earlier written that "The country in which this army has operated is exhausted of all kinds of forage. The country between the Potomac and the Rappahannock [the Northern Neck] for 20 miles below here has been stripped. Had we succeeded in our attempt to move on, we might then have procured much fodder from the Peninsulas." Ingalls to Meigs, December 17, 1862, ibid., 863.

[38]George W. Julian, *Political Recollections, 1840 to 1872* (Chicago: Jansen, McClurg and Company, 1884), 235.

lines." He also ordered his quartermaster to seize horses, cattle, and other livestock from those who had an abundance, keeping careful record of everything they took.[39]

Similar actions continued, albeit sporadically, into the spring of 1863. In January, a detachment of cavalry from Yorktown burned a ferry and railroad depot near West Point, Virginia. They also confiscated horses and goods presumed to have been brought in through the blockade. Three months later, Major General Erasmus D. Keyes organized an expedition to raid Matthews County and "destroy or bring in a lot of grain collected for the rebels." A few days afterward, he explained to Halleck that he was doing all in his power to thwart rebel efforts to draw provisions from the region. "Eight hundred of my men came in last night after destroying a large amount of grain and bringing in many sheep and cattle and mules . . ." he reported. "We have certainly destroyed about 30,000 bushels of grain within a week past."[40]

This of course was precisely the sort of action Meigs had fruitlessly urged upon Burnside in January. But the Department of Virginia had limited ability to carry out such operations, and besides, Dix was a cautious commander. He showed as much during the Confederate invasion of Pennsylvania, when Halleck asked him to take advantage of Lee's absence to make raids against the vulnerable tidewater region. Dix quietly resisted the idea, leading Keyes, his chief subordinate, to write in some perplexity, "Am I to understand your telegram to forbid my making more raids anywhere?" Raids, he continued, "have a wonderful effect by producing discontent among the people against the Confederate Government. They demand protection, and, if the raids are repeated, the old and sick will call home their sons and brothers to protect their homesteads, and in that way the rebel army will be melted away."[41]

Keyes's argument is intriguing, for in many respects it anticipated the logic of Sherman's eventual Savannah and Carolinas campaigns. And as early as the summer of 1862, in fact, Keyes had begun to talk about defeating the Confederacy by attacking its crops and the rail network that distributed foodstuffs throughout the South. But Keyes's poor performance in the battles around Richmond, coupled with rumors about his physical cowardice, had discredited him; when the Army of the Potomac left the James River region, he had been quietly shelved at Yorktown. Thus he had neither the stature nor the resources to implement his own views on the war. And Dix was hardly the superior to lend much support.[42]

THE GUERRILLA MENACE

A final aspect of the pragmatic policy was its role in the guerrilla struggle, which is today one of the relatively forgotten dimensions of the Civil War. In popular memory,

[39]Naglee's report, December 16, 1862, ibid., 50–51.

[40]Report of Major General Erasmus D. Keyes, January 10, 1863, ibid., 124; Keyes to Halleck, April 6, 1863, ibid., 585; Keyes to Halleck, April 8, 1863, ibid., 588.

[41]Keyes to Dix, June 16, 1863, ibid. 27:168–169.

[42]Keyes to Meigs, July 21, 1862, ibid. 11, pt. 3:332.

it mainly recalls the glamorous partisan exploits of a Major John S. Mosby or Brigadier General John H. Morgan – regularly commissioned Confederate officers who fought in unorthodox but mostly above-board fashion. Even those aware of its more sinister incarnation tend to think of the guerrilla struggle as something confined to the wilds of Missouri. In fact, guerrillas sprang up literally everywhere, from the Unionist "Buffalos" who bedeviled coastal North Carolina to the secessionist "bushwhackers" who haunted the banks of the Mississippi River. And their brand of warfare was neither chivalrous nor romantic but simply murderous.

While both sides had to contend with irregular forces, their role as invaders forced Union soldiers to deal with guerrillas far more often; indeed, in most districts they were simply a fact of life, unwelcome but pervasive. Secessionist guerrilla fighters were of four kinds. The first category, guerrillas only by extension of the word, were regularly organized Confederate cavalry who happened on occasion to adopt irregular tactics. The second were partisan rangers of the sort authorized by the Confederate Congress in April 1862, with Mosby's 43rd Virginia Battalion being the preeminent example. Because they responded to higher authority and wore distinctive uniforms, the laws of war accorded these two varieties full belligerent rights. The remaining two categories enjoyed no such rights. These were politicized civilians who fought covertly, masquerading as noncombatants, and simple outlaws for whom the war was mainly an excuse to indulge in mayhem. Theoretically all four groups were distinct, but in practice Union authorities did not always distinguish carefully between them. The confusion was not exclusively in the minds of Federal soldiers, for it was not uncommon for individual guerrillas to gravitate from one group to another.

Guerrilla fighters posed two kinds of threat. On the one hand they derailed trains carrying military supplies, attacked foraging parties, waylaid soldiers who became separated from their units, and in general threatened the effective conduct of military operations. But they also enforced the secessionist political order in occupied regions where the Confederate government could exert no direct influence. Guerrillas preyed on Southern Unionists from the war's outset, and undermined efforts to restore Union political control at every opportunity. By March 1864, for example, the town of Bolivar, Tennessee, had been under Union occupation for two full years, yet the mere threat of guerrilla retaliation derailed an election called by the state's military governor, Andrew Johnson. "The people are warned by a poster from 'Willey Hags Capt of Forrests Scouts' not to hold such Election under pain of being Arrested & Carried South for trial," recorded a local planter. "[A] goodly number of Country Voters came to town to Vote, but all feared the Guerillas & no Election was held. Great God what will be the end. Law & order forbidden."[43]

In their efforts to curb this menace, Northern commanders adopted measures that had heavy impact upon Southern civilians. The policies that arose in western Tennessee in mid-1862 are typical of those elsewhere, and illuminate an important phase

[43]Entry for March 5, 1864, John Houston Bills diary, SHC.

in the military education of the two generals most associated with the eventual hard war of 1864–1865: Grant and Sherman.

During the early summer of 1862, Grant and Sherman found themselves beset by the same bushwhacking and guerrilla raids that already plagued Union forces in Missouri and Buell's army in southeastern Tennessee and northern Alabama. Grant's solution, in common with most Northern commanders, was to hold local residents accountable for guerrilla depredations. He was not so clumsy as to do so indiscriminately, however. His orders on the subject specified that reparations would come solely from the property of persons "sympathizing with the rebellion," and then only enough to "remunerate the Government all loss and expense of collection." They reflected the same discriminate, proportional severity that characterized Grant's general policy toward Southern civilians.[44]

The discriminatory aspect was well-expressed by Rosecrans, who served for a time under Grant's command. Unionist civilians would receive the army's protection, provided they performed certain "active duties" to demonstrate their loyalty. Civilians who did not possessed no rights "save those which the laws of war and humanity accord. . . ." And those found making war against Union troops outside regular Confederate formations would be regarded as "enemies of mankind" with "the rights due to pirates and robbers" – in other words, no rights at all. Rosecrans' instructions thus sustained the rough-and-ready division of the Southern population into three categories: Unionists, who would receive active protection; inactive Confederate sympathizers, who, under the laws of war, would be protected in their persons but might be liable for contributions to support the occupying army; and active Confederate partisans who would be dealt with sternly.[45]

By early July, Grant had begun flirting with the idea of removing the worst secessionist sympathizers from his rear areas. Shortly before Halleck's selection as general-in-chief, Grant wired him, "There are a great many families of officers in the rebel army here who are very violent. Will you approve of sending them south of our lines?" Halleck replied that he would, but Grant does not seem to have applied the policy.[46] Still, he raised it again a few weeks later. On July 28, Grant informed

[44]General Order No. 60, July 3, 1862, *Grant Papers* 5:190. See also OR 17, pt. 2:69. For the implementation of this policy, see, for example, W.T. Sherman's Special Order No. 130, July 12, 1862, ibid., 96.

[45]General Order No. 92, July 12, 1862, ibid., 97. See also Brigadier General W.L. Elliott [of Rosecrans' headquarters] to Brigadier General George Morgan, August 6, 1862, ibid., 154–155. Elliott instructed Morgan to seize all cotton, keeping careful records. When bridges and other public property required repair, he should use slaves belonging to secessionists to do the work and return them when the work was completed. "Notify the inhabitants within reach of your lines that any words or actions hostile to the Government will oblige you to treat the parties as enemies, who can receive only the rights of belligerents, whose property belongs to the United States. The women and children will be ordered beyond our lines, their property seized for the benefit of the United States, and their houses burned."

[46]Grant to Halleck, July 10, 1862, ibid. 17, pt. 2:88; Halleck to Grant, July 10, 1862, ibid. No record of the order's implementation exists. To be sure, Grant on July 10 issued Special Orders No. 14, which ordered certain specified persons to leave Union lines within five days. But when Confederate Brigadier General M. Jeff Thompson complained to Union Brigadier General Alvin P. Hovey about the order, Hovey sent him a copy of Special Orders No. 15, which "considerably modifie[d]" the previous directive. See

Halleck: "There is an evident disposition on the part of many of the citizens to join the Guerillas [sic] on their approach. I am decidedly in favor of turning all discontented citizens within our lines out South." Halleck vigorously endorsed the idea. "It is very desirable that you should clean out West Tennessee and North Mississippi of all organized enemies," he told Grant. "If necessary, take up all active sympathizers, and either hold them as prisoners or put them beyond our lines. Handle that class without gloves, and take their property for public use."[47]

This time, Grant enforced the policy, and informed Rosecrans to give no protection to three known secessionists. "If they don't like [it]," he wrote, "advise them to quit[.] I favor turning out of our lines all suspicious persons, and the use of their property for public purposes. This is in accordance with instructions just received from Washington." The next day he ordered Rosecrans to send troops to counter a Confederate detachment known to be in the vicinity of Ripley, Mississippi. "Let them impress all the teams they want, and bring in all the cotton they can lay their hands on[,] Union men being permitted to come along and sell theirs. Oppressive secessionists may be arrested, and their horses, and mules, & whatever else they may have of service to the Government taken."[48]

Meanwhile in Memphis, Sherman applied himself to the task of controlling that large, restive metropolis and the region surrounding it. Understandably, the red-haired general's status as the "Inventor of Total Warfare" has made the evolution of his views the object of special scrutiny. But it has often led commentators to overemphasize features in Sherman's earlier thought that point toward his eventual emergence as the preeminent practitioner of hard war, while understating elements that contradict or modify the classic portrayal. John Bennett Walters, the historian perhaps most responsible for creating this image of Sherman, traced the origins of his hard war thinking back to the early autumn of 1862, when Sherman, frustrated by the constant guerrilla activity in his sector, burned the village of Randolph, Tennessee, in reprisal. Walters strongly implied that this action was unique for the time period, and explicitly maintained that with it, Sherman abandoned "all restraints" in making war upon civilians. In fact, however, Sherman's words and actions suggest a somewhat different picture, especially when placed in the context of other episodes during the same period.[49]

Hovey to Grant, July 15, 1862, with enclosures, OR 17, pt. 2:98–99. Neither Special Orders No. 14 nor 15 appear in the OR, but Hovey's concluding sentence to Thompson implies that Special Orders No. 15 suspended the evacuation provision. "Should any families embraced within the orders above alluded to be obstinate and refuse to comply with Orders, No. 15, *they shall be escorted* to the distance of 10 miles from this city [Memphis.]" (Emphasis supplied.) Ibid., 99.

[47]Grant to Halleck, July 28, 1862, Simon (ed.), *Grant Papers* 5:243; Halleck to Grant, August 2, 1862, OR 17, pt. 2:150.

[48]Grant to William S. Rosecrans, August 10, 1862, Simon (ed.), *Grant Papers* 5:283; Grant to Rosecrans, August 11, 1862, ibid., 285–286.

[49]For the characterization of Sherman, see John F. Marszalek, "The Inventor of Total Warfare," *Notre Dame Magazine* 18 (Summer 1989): 28–31. Studies emphasizing Sherman as the author of the hard war policy include John W. Brinsfield, "The Military Ethics of General William T. Sherman: A Reassessment," *Parameters* 12 (1983):36–48; and John B. Walters, *Merchant of Terror: General Sherman and Total War* (New

Like most other commanders, Sherman reacted to guerrilla activity by holding prominent secessionists responsible for it. In July 1862, he arrested twenty-five local residents after bushwhackers fired on a foraging train. "I am satisfied," he wrote Halleck, "we have no other remedy for this ambush firing than to hold the neighborhood fully responsible, though the punishment may fall on the wrong places." In so doing he pursued a policy quite in keeping with that of other Union commanders from Missouri to Virginia – and, for that matter, many Confederate commanders as well.[50]

The background to the Randolph incident itself begins with a letter written by Sherman to Grant's chief of staff on September 4. In it he recounted excellent progress in the construction of Fort Pickering, a river bastion just south of Memphis designed to protect the city against recapture. He also noted the sometimes questionable fervor exhibited by Colonel Josiah W. Bissell of Sherman's engineering regiment. Bissell had just destroyed some houses at Hochelrode's Landing below Memphis and brought in black women and children. "He is so energetic and full of zeal that I have not checked him," Sherman wrote, "though I fear he may cause the very thing we endeavor to prevent, viz, the firing on boats." There had already been several instances in which Union steamers on the Mississippi River had received fusillades from small Confederate parties along the shore. Sometimes the culprits were rebel cavalry; often they were locally organized bands of Southern guerrillas. In recent weeks, however, such actions had been few, and although Sherman favored "the condign punishment of any one committing such outrage," he nevertheless believed "we must be careful not to render ourselves too harsh, or they will naturally seek revenge."[51]

Three weeks later, however, bushwhackers peppered the packet vessel *Eugene* as it plied the river near the village of Randolph, about twenty-five miles above Memphis. Sherman immediately issued orders for the 46th Ohio regiment and a section of guns to board two steamers, disembark at Randolph, and retaliate. His instructions to the officer in charge, Colonel C.C. Walcutt, were as specific as he could make them. He explained in detail both what he wanted done and why it was necessary. "Acts of this kind must be promptly punished," Sherman wrote, and even though the chance of reaching the actual perpetrators was remote, "the interest and well-being of the country demands that all such attacks should be followed by a punishment that will tend to prevent a repetition."

For that reason, Walcutt was to strike Randolph at daybreak the next morning. Unless he should happen upon the offending guerrilla band itself, the colonel was to destroy the town, "leaving one house to mark the place." Sherman stipulated that Walcutt should make sure the inhabitants understood exactly what had prompted the

York: Bobbs-Merrill, 1973). John Bennett Walters, "General William T. Sherman and Total War," *Journal of Southern History* 14 (1948), 448, 462. John F. Marszalek follows Walters' basic interpretation in *Sherman: A Soldier's Passion for Order*, 194–196.

[50]Sherman to Halleck, July 14, 1862, OR 17, pt. 1:23.

[51]Sherman to Major John A. Rawlins, September 4, 1862, ibid., 201. For the sake of clarity, I have modified the order of the sentences in these passages.

reprisal: "Let the people know and feel that we deeply deplore the necessity of such destruction, but we must protect ourselves and the boats which are really carrying stores and merchandise for the benefit of secession families, whose fathers and brothers are in arms against us." He added that if an extraordinary case arose, Walcutt had discretionary authority to spare more than one house. "[B]ut let the place feel that all such acts of cowardly firing upon boats filled with women and children and merchandise must be severely punished." The general concluded by saying that everything must be done in good order. "Keep your men within reach of your voice," he enjoined, "and do your work systematically. Let your quartermaster take a minute account of every house or piece of property destroyed by this order, with the names of owners if possible."[52]

Although the severity of Sherman's order cannot be gainsaid, the most striking feature was its almost surgical precision. This was not the ranting of a general savagely determined to cast aside all restraint. On the contrary, the order reflected a sound grasp of the principles of military reprisal and the conditions that must be present if the reprisal is to succeed, most notably its emphasis on systematic destruction, with no pillaging of property or assaults on the townspeople of Randolph, and its insistence that the inhabitants understand exactly why their houses were being burned. Vattel himself had agreed that such acts might be justified by "the necessity of chastizing an unjust and barbarous nation, of checking her brutality, and preserving ourselves from her depredations." And Sherman's intent, after all, was to force the enemy to observe the laws of war.[53]

It is possible to question the wisdom, and even the justice, of burning Randolph. Sherman was all but certain that no one from the town had actually participated in the sniping incident. He thought the likely culprits were "a small force of guerrillas from Loosahatchie." Thus his retaliatory blow would almost certainly land on the innocent. Even so, it is difficult to deny that Sherman could make a reasonable case for his action. In the eyes of international law, the "innocence" of an enemy population has never been absolute. In Sherman's day, the right of noncombatants to their lives had largely been secured, but their right to property remained more tenuous, and most commentators viewed the protection normally accorded it as enlightened forbearance, not absolute principle. Furthermore, the Randolph episode appears less condign when one compares it with other similar incidents that had occurred almost since the war began. For example, it had none of the vengeful pillaging that had accompanied the destruction of Winton, North Carolina, in February 1862 – an act occasioned, in any

---

[52]Sherman to Walcutt, September 24, 1862, ibid., 235–236. See also Sherman to Rawlins, September 26, 1862, ibid., pt. 1:144–145.

[53]Vattel, *Law of Nations,* 367. Book III, Ch. ix, para. 167. This justification for reprisal appears in all studies of the concept. For a contemporary citation, see H.L. Scott, *Military Dictionary* (New York: D. Van Nostrand, 1861), 658. A good discussion of reprisal, as the idea had evolved by the mid-19th century, appears in Geoffrey Best, *Humanity in Warfare: The Modern History of the International Law of Armed Conflicts* (London: Methuen, 1983), 166–179.

case, not by irregular guerrillas but by regular Confederate infantry who had merely opened fire from ambush.[54]

Three days after the burning of Randolph, Sherman publicly announced his intention to punish further attacks on riverboats by expelling ten Memphis families whenever an attack occurred. He informed Grant's chief of staff of his decision, and added that he would "visit on the neighborhood summary punishment" for attacks in their vicinity. "It may sometimes fall on the wrong head," he wrote, "but it would be folly to send parties of infantry to chase these wanton guerrillas." Grant forwarded a copy of Sherman's letter to Halleck with the endorsement that it embodied a policy "which I approve but have given no order for."[55]

The burning and the threat curtailed further ambuscades upon river steamers, but only for a few weeks. In mid-October, the *Catahoula* suffered two killed and several wounded from a guerrilla fusillade. Sherman promptly made good his threat. Evidently pleased with its handling of the Randolph mission, he tapped the 46th Ohio for another retaliatory assignment, ordering it to march down the west bank of the Mississippi and destroy all houses and crops along the fifteen-mile stretch of river in which the attacks had occurred. Here again, Sherman gave Walcutt discretionary authority to "except from the execution of this order all parties that he may have reason to believe have not been rendezvousing with the guerrillas." But at the point where the *Catahoula* received fire, Walcutt "found much complicity with the guerrillas, and he burned their places."[56]

In addition, following three other attacks, a total of forty secessionist families received orders to leave the city and move beyond Union lines. A petition from several Memphis residents implored him to suspend his directive long enough for them to send representatives to ask the area Confederate authorities to cease attacks on unarmed boats. Sherman granted a fifteen-day reprieve for them to make the attempt, but warned that the rebel commanders "must know and feel that not only will we meet them in arms, but that their people shall experience the full measure of the necessary consequences of such barbarity." Even so, Sherman ultimately suspended the expulsion order in all but a few cases. His tactics evidently worked: The attacks ceased for several months.[57]

In his correspondence with his family and with Grant during this period, Sherman often used melodramatic language that has since become well-known through frequent (one is tempted to say inevitable) quotation. The most famous such passage occurs in a letter to Grant dated October 4, 1862:

[54]Sherman to Walcutt, September 24, 1862, OR 17, pt. 2:236. For the Winton episode, see Chapter 3.
[55]Special Orders No. 254, September 27, 1862, ibid., 240; Sherman to Rawlins, October 18, 1862, ibid., 280.
[56]Special Orders No. 283, October 18, 1862, ibid., 280–281; Sherman to Rawlins, October 21, 1862, ibid., 285.
[57]Sherman to Miss P.A. Fraser, Memphis, October 22, 1862, ibid., 287–288. The petition is not preserved in the OR but its contents can be inferred from Sherman's reply. Sherman to Edwin M. Stanton, December 16, 1862, War 1861–1865 Papers, NYHS.

[The local] people begin to realize that the Northwest intends to fight to the death for the Mississippi River. This is my hobby, and I know you will pardon me when I say that I am daily more and more convinced that we should hold the river absolutely and leave the interior alone. Detachments inland can always be overcome and are at great hazard, and they do not convert the people. They cannot be made to love us, but they can be made to fear us, and dread the passage of our troops through their country. . . . We cannot change the hearts of those people in the South, but we can make war so terrible that they will realize the fact that, however brave and gallant and devoted to their country, still they are mortal and should exhaust all peaceful remedies before they fly to war.

In this excerpt, one can readily see the kernel of Sherman's eventual hard war philosophy, particularly in its reference to making Southerners dread the passage of Union forces through their territory. But it would be misleading to suggest that in the fall of 1862 it was anything more than that. His orders to a Union cavalry commander, issued less than three weeks after this desolating letter to Grant, retained a conservative flavor. Deciding that it was time to strike the guerrillas directly, he ordered Colonel Benjamin H. Grierson to take his Sixth Illinois Cavalry regiment and raid Shelby Depot, Tennessee. There he would "clean out effectually such buildings as have been used for a rendezvous to guerrillas operating thereabouts. . . ." All armed men in the vicinity were to be killed or captured; their houses and property should be burned or brought away. But, Sherman stipulated, the soldiers must know that a Union "reaction" had already begun to occur among Tennessee civilians, "of which we should take advantage." He wanted the people to see a strong Federal government, not a vindictive one; a government that could protect as well as destroy and whose destructive energies were unleashed judiciously, not wantonly. "Subordinates and privates must not pillage, but commanders may do anything to impress upon the people that guerrillas must be driven from their midst, else they must necessarily share the consequences." By mid-November Sherman believed that his policy had aroused Union sentiment in the area and that "a conversion of the people to our cause has begun."[58]

Sherman was mistaken. Neither retaliation nor a liberal attitude toward the general population did much to curtail the irregular warfare, which continued for the balance of the conflict. And although senior commanders usually sought to punish communities in a firm but controlled fashion, the situation was inherently so volatile that it created an upward spiral of violence. Some groups of soldiers reacted to sniping incidents on the spot and began to destroy civilian property without higher authorization. When guerrillas fired at Union vessels along the western rivers, it became common practice to go ashore and burn the nearest dwellings. Sometimes yet more drastic measures were attempted. In August 1863, for example, the sack of Lawrence, Kansas, by Confederate guerrillas under William C. Quantrill provoked an unusual response from the Federal district commander, Brigadier General Thomas C. Ewing, Jr. Fed up with continued irregular warfare in northern Missouri, Ewing banished all

---

[58]Sherman to Grant, October 4, 1862, OR 17, pt. 2:261; Special Orders No. 285, October 22, 1862, ibid., 289–290; Sherman to Halleck, November 17, 1862, ibid., 351.

civilians – some 10,000 people – within most of a four-county area. The action, he hoped, would deny the guerrillas the supplies and support on which their efforts depended.[59]

Such actions were of course fully as harsh as anything the war would see. But essentially they remained expressions of the pragmatic policy. Unlike the eventual hard war efforts of 1864–1865, their purpose was not to undermine the Confederacy's political and economic ability to resist, but rather to curb civilians so that the conventional military contest could proceed. Yet by accustoming soldiers to regard Southern civilians as enemies, and by making the destruction of private property a normal practice, the antiguerrilla campaign helped lay the groundwork for the greater hard war measures still to come.

[59]See, for example, "Memorandum," [1863], Edward Paul Reichhelm Papers, LC, p. 2; D.P. Chapman to his sister, April 11, 1863, D.P. Chapman Papers, HEHL; entry for April 5, 1863, John Q.A. Campbell diary, WRHS; Bela T. Saint John to his father, May 17, 1863, Bela T. Saint John Papers, LC. Ewing to Major General John M. Scofield, August 25, 1863, OR 22, pt. 2:472–473; General Order No. 11, August 25, 1863, ibid., 473. See also entries for August 26-September 8, 1863, "Diary of Events in Dept. of the Missouri, 1863," John M. Schofield Papers, Library of Congress; and Michael Fellman, *Inside War: The Guerrilla Conflict in Missouri During the American Civil War* (New York and Oxford: Oxford University Press, 1989), 95–96. The estimate of 10,000 affected civilians is in McPherson, *Battle Cry of Freedom,* 786.

6

Emancipation: Touchstone of hard war

No Union foray against Southern property was more far-reaching in its effects than the decision to attack slavery. A factory wrecked by soldiers could be repaired in a few months. A field stripped of corn by a foraging party could be replaced in a year. Even a town, burned in reprisal or through sheer vindictiveness, could in time be restored and made to thrive. Emancipation, however, carried implications that went well beyond the immediate task of subduing the rebellion. Americans would have to live with its results forever.

For that reason, the destruction of slavery was never so simple as the seizure of crops and livestock or the dismantling of Southern railroads. It was different too in that a significant number of Americans insisted on it quite apart from any military efficacy. For years, abolitionists had argued that immediate, uncompensated emancipation was a moral imperative. When the Civil War began, they were the first to deem it a military necessity as well, but everyone understood that such pronouncements buttressed a preexisting agenda. Yet the abolitionists' moral commitment to the eradication of slavery made their practical arguments no less cogent. (Indeed, their relative freedom from the racial prejudices of the day enabled them to see the military wisdom of emancipation more quickly than most.) And in any event, it proved impossible for most Americans to contemplate an attack on slavery on narrowly military grounds. Like the abolitionists, once awakened to the issue of emancipation, their appraisals often fused political, military, and moral logic.

Typical were the views of Colonel Hugh B. Ewing, a kinsman of William T. Sherman and a staunch Catholic. In August 1862, he wrote his wife a disapproving letter from his brigade's encampment in western Virginia. It bothered him, he told her, that she differed with him on the wisdom of emancipation. The Church, he wrote, had always taught him that slavery was wrong and should be tolerated only because its sudden abolition would lead to "convulsion." But history told Ewing that every country that deferred emancipation eventually succumbed to complete ruin. Knowing this, Ewing continued, he had long opposed the abolitionists for insisting upon immediate emancipation. So drastic a solution would be convulsive; he had believed it better to let the Southern people dismantle slavery gradually. But instead of laying the foundation for a gradual future emancipation, the Southerners were in fact laying the foundation for its perpetuation and extension – and intended to do so "on the smoking ruins of the U S Government – that great gift of God to oppressed humanity. . . ." In so doing, Ewing wrote, "They have convulsed the entire Nation," thereby removing the only reason for tolerating slavery in the first place. And, he warned, "This convulsion, the child of Slavery, threatens, every day it lasts, to make you a widow and our children orphans – If emancipation would end it, would I be true to my wife & children to spare it?" He thought not, and he told his wife pointedly that she would not "at the end of the war see preserved both the Slave system & your husband. If Slavery is not broken, the war will last long supported & fed by it – and the loss of life on both sides will be frightful."[1]

By the summer of 1862, many Northerners agreed with him. "[I]t is a delusion in the North to suppose that there are any means of pacification short of utterly subduing the aristocracy of Slavery," wrote one Pennsylvania cavalryman. An Ohioan about to enlist maintained that until the North adopted an emancipation policy, and began using the slaves of rebels in every capacity, "nothing but disaster and defeat awaits us." Abraham Lincoln concurred. His visit to McClellan's army in early July convinced him that "the war must be prosecuted with more vigor, and that some decisive measures were necessary on the slavery question." Even as Ewing scolded his wife, a draft of the preliminary Emancipation Proclamation reposed in the President's writing desk, awaiting only a significant Federal victory for its publication.[2]

MILITARY ATTITUDES TOWARD SLAVERY

Such a step remained enormously controversial, however. Slavery, it was true, had dogged American political and social life since its founding. Despite repeated compromises and accommodations, despite the heartfelt wishes of most Americans, the problem had never gone away for long. Yet it was so thorny a conundrum, so filled with other headaches – Constitutional questions, economic concerns, racial worries – that even after it sundered the Union, many people convinced themselves that the cost of destroying slavery would be disastrously high.

The Federal government had therefore begun the war with a political commitment to defeat the South without touching slavery. Most Northerners considered that prudent. They did not wish to vindicate Southern fears about an "Abolitionist" Republican administration and thus legitimize their decision to secede. They also wanted to hold the border states, and of course hoped to tap latent Unionist sentiment

---

[1] Ewing to Henrietta Ewing, August 10, 1862, Hugh B. Ewing Papers, OHS.

[2] James M. McPherson, who has conducted an extensive study of soldiers' diaries and letters on this subject, estimates that almost 30 percent of Union troops were pro-emancipation by the summer of 1862. (He adds that many more were converted to it later.) See his *What They Fought For, 1861–1865* (Baton Rouge: Louisiana State University Press, 1994), 57. Entry for July 12, 1862, William Penn Lloyd Diaries, SHC; entry for July 23, 1862, Joseph J. Scroggs Diary, CWTIC, USAMHI; Gideon Welles, "A History of Emancipation," *Galaxy* 14 (December 1872):840.

in the South. An antislavery course would jeopardize all these aims. In October 1861, the conservative Republican *Boston Daily Advertiser* summarized the prevailing view when it railed against the "insane folly" of the abolitionists, whose dogmatic demands for an immediate, uncompensated end to slavery had long ago destroyed the emancipation movement in Virginia and had actually increased Southern intransigence on the slave issue. "The same folly," it warned, "is now repeated by those who urge the conversion of this war into a war for emancipation."[3]

Domestic political considerations also made it desirable to avoid the slave issue. While Lincoln personally believed that slavery formed the heart of the rebellion, and a substantial minority of other Northerners agreed, the majority did not. Most thought the free and slave states might have coexisted indefinitely but for abolitionist agitation; some feared that emancipation would lead at once to an influx into the North of African Americans who would compete for jobs. Sheer racism exerted a powerful influence: Many Northerners considered enslavement an appropriate status for blacks. To them, emancipation meant the first step on the road to black equality, which seemed nothing worth fighting for. The constitutional difficulties involved with emancipation concerned many conservatives and moderates. So did fears that emancipation might touch off a mammoth, continent-wide version of the revolt that had annihilated the slaveholding class on the Caribbean island of Saint-Domingue in 1791.[4]

For all these reasons, in the war's early months the Lincoln administration tried hard to keep the Negro out of the conflict. "Certain it is that the Republicans . . . are 'no friends of slavery;'" Secretary Chase assured a prominent Kentuckian, "but it is just as certain that they have never proposed to interfere . . . with slavery in any State." The insistence on keeping it a "white man's war" extended even to the refusal to enlist free Northern blacks as soldiers, and on a trip to Washington, the abolitionist clergyman Moncure D. Conway discovered that "the mere mention of a Negro made the President nervous, and frightened some others of his cabinet much more." In keeping with this policy, Union forces routinely promised Southerners not to interfere with slavery, and vowed to deal sternly with servile insurrections should any occur.[5]

Yet it was obvious that the South gained a military advantage from its nearly four million slaves. The *Montgomery Advertiser* called them "a tower of strength to the Confederacy," pointing out that their labor meant that a higher percentage of Southern white men could serve in the army without jeopardizing the South's economy. Some slaves also assisted the Confederate war effort more directly, by constructing

---

[3]*Boston Daily Advertiser,* October 4, 7, 1861.

[4]For a detailed account of this revolt, see C.L.R. James, *The Black Jacobins: Toussaint L'Ouverture and the San Domingo Revolution* (new edition; London: Allison and Busby, 1980).

[5]Chase to Dr. T.S. Bell, May 16, 1861, Civil War Miscellany, William P. Palmer Collection, Western Reserve Historical Society. The Conway quote is from Benjamin Quarles, *The Negro in the Civil War* (Boston: Little, Brown, 1953), 30. On the refusal to enlist black volunteers, see ibid., 24–29, Dudley Cornish, *The Sable Arm: Black Troops in the Union Army, 1861–1865* (Reprint ed., Lawrence: University of Kansas Press, 1987 [1956]), 1–78 passim., and Joseph T. Glatthaar, *Forged in Battle: The Civil War Alliance of Black Soldiers and White Officers* (New York: Free Press, 1990), 1–10 passim.

fortifications, unloading supplies, and so on. But if slaves were an important Southern resource, they were also an unwilling resource, and they could be turned. The radical wing of the Republican Party thought it should be done at once. Nothing, wrote Joshua Giddings in May 1861, would strike "such terror to the whole south" as an emancipation proclamation. It would "compel every fighting man to remain at home and look to their negroes instead of going into the army to kill our friends." Senator Charles Sumner of Massachusetts agreed. "It is often said that the war will make an end of Slavery," he told a Republican state convention in October 1861. "This is probable. But it is surer still that the overthrow of Slavery will make an end of the war." As the months went on, the drumbeat of emancipation sounded ever more insistently from the ranks of the Radical Republicans.[6]

The Lincoln administration resisted such appeals. Yet it soon became apparent that whatever Union officials and generals might proclaim, the millions held in bondage viewed the conflict as a chance for liberation. The Union army might not be interested in the slave, but the slave was fervently interested in the army. Fugitive slaves trickled into Union lines even before the firing on Fort Sumter. The first were returned, but in May 1861 a group of runaways sought refuge at Fort Monroe, Virginia. The commander, Major General Benjamin F. Butler, decided to grant it. The slaves in question, he said, had been helping to construct Confederate fieldworks. As such, he was justified in holding them as "contraband of war." Butler's use of the term was loose but his argument made excellent practical sense. When Butler explained his decision to the War Department, Lincoln found it unobjectionable, and permitted it to stand. In early August, the U.S. Congress codified the general principle into its First Confiscation Act, which declared the forfeiture of any slaves used in direct support of the Confederate war effort. The military necessity of such a policy was obvious.[7]

Yet Lincoln took care to keep the plea of military necessity tightly defined. His resolve was tested at the end of August 1861, when another commander in far-away Missouri issued an order that Lincoln found impermissible. Major General John C. Frémont, who commanded the Western Department, considered stern measures necessary to suppress the considerable guerrilla activity in that region. On August 30, therefore, he declared martial law throughout Missouri and mandated the court-martial and execution of all persons taken with arms in their hands within Union lines. Then, as a way to punish those who aided and abetted the partisans, he ordered that the property of active rebels might be confiscated and their slaves declared free.[8]

---

[6]*Montgomery Advertiser,* November 6, 1861, quoted in James M. McPherson, *The Struggle for Equality: Abolitionists and the Negro in the Civil War and Reconstruction* (Princeton, NJ: Princeton University Press, 1964), 62. Giddings to Chase, May 4, 1861, in Salmon P. Chase Papers, ILHS. The Sumner quote is in Hans L. Trefousse, *The Radical Republicans: Lincoln's Vanguard for Racial Justice* (New York: Alfred A. Knopf, 1969), 204.

[7]A.J. Slemmer to Lorenzo Thomas, March 18, 1861, OR, Series II, vol. 1, p. 750. For the origin of the "contraband" order, see John B. Cary to Butler, March 9, 1891, in Butler, *Private and Official Correspondence* 1:102–103.

[8]Proclamation, Western Department, August 30, 1861, OR 3:466–467.

Many Northerners, including a surprising number of conservatives, applauded Frémont's proclamation as an appropriate expression of military necessity. But others suspected that it was motivated chiefly by politics. Frémont, after all, had been the Republican presidential candidate in 1856 and enjoyed cordial ties with the abolitionist wing of that party. Ethan Allen Hitchcock, a retired army general living in St. Louis, considered him "an instrument in the hands of abolitionists" and thought he had probably been "duped" into issuing his proclamation. Lincoln regarded the order as politically motivated and instructed the general to rescind its emancipation provision.[9]

Although he did not say so publicly, in a private letter to his friend Senator Orville Browning (Republican-Illinois), the President emphatically rejected the argument that emancipation might derive from military necessity. It was one thing, Lincoln argued, to seize someone's farm for temporary military use. "But to say that the farm shall no longer belong to the owner, or his heirs forever; and this as well when the farm is not needed for military purposes as when it is, is purely political, without the savor of military law about it. And the same is true of slaves." While Lincoln particularly objected to the idea that a general might issue an emancipation order, his logic applied equally to emancipation by executive order under the war power – as the letter went on to acknowledge. In any event, he wrote Browning that the permanent future condition of slavery "must be settled according to laws made by law-makers, and not by military proclamations."[10]

These two episodes – Butler's "contraband" order and Frémont's abortive proclamation – established the limits of acceptable military interference with slavery during the war's first year. After Frémont's failed effort, no Union general moved overtly against the "peculiar institution" for several months. A few, like Brigadier General James H. Lane (an ex-U.S. Senator of strong antislavery views), opined privately that "[c]onfiscation of slaves and other property which can be made useful to the Army should follow treason as the thunder peal follows the lightning flash." But most found it militarily expedient and politically congenial to have nothing to do with slavery. Soldiers, ran a common refrain, should be neither "negro stealers nor negro catchers."[11]

Some, like Major General John A. Dix, thought an antislavery policy would seriously complicate the Northern war effort. Once it became generally known that Union forces would receive and harbor fugitive slaves, he wrote, their numbers would increase rapidly and Federal armies would soon be "oppressed by a useless burden." Not only would the liberated slaves be a military encumbrance, it would seem as if the government were meddling in something "entirely foreign to the great questions of

---

[9]For Northern reaction, see McPherson, *Struggle for Equality,* 72–74; Nevins, *War for the Union* 1:334–335. Ethan Allen Hitchcock to Henry Hitchcock, November 1, 1861, Hitchcock Collection, MOHS; Lincoln to Browning, September 22, 1861, Basler (ed.), *Collected Works of Lincoln* 4:531; and Lincoln to Frémont, September 2, 1861, ibid., 506.

[10]Lincoln to Browning, September 22, 1861, Basler (ed.), *Collected Works of Lincoln* 4:531–532.

[11]J.H. Lane to S.D. Sturgis, October 3, 1861, OR 3:516; John A. Dix to Simon Cameron, August 8, 1861, ibid., Series II, vol. 1, p. 673.

political right and duty in the civil strife which has been brought upon us by disloyal and unscrupulous men." The Northern cause, he concluded, was "a holy one and should be kept free from all taint."[12]

Dix wrote those words to McClellan, who needed no urging on the matter. Shortly after taking command of the Army of the Potomac, McClellan had met individually with a number of Washington abolitionists, including the formidable Massachusetts senator Charles Sumner, and warned each that "I was fighting for my country & the Union, not for abolition and the Republican party." Such comments, when addressed to members of Congress, bordered on insubordination and may have seemed gratuitous. But McClellan believed that "[t]he Radicals had only the negro in view, & not the Union. . . . They cared not for the results, knew little or nothing of the subject to be dealt with, & merely wished to accomplish a political move for party profit, or from sentimental motives."[13]

McClellan's opposition to emancipation stemmed heavily from his political convictions, but even commanders without partisan agendas were reluctant to press for an antislavery policy. The military utility of such a policy seemed questionable at best; the political complications were enough to deter most officers from dealing with slavery more than necessary. Shortly after taking command of the Department of Missouri in November 1861, for example, Major General Henry W. Halleck issued General Order No. 3, which forbade fugitive slaves to enter the army's lines. Officially he reasoned that if slaves could freely enter and leave Union encampments, they would pose a security risk. Privately one gathers that he simply wished to avoid the embarrassment of having to deal with slavery at all.

The order provoked an outcry from the Radical Republicans, who assumed that it indicated a proslavery conviction on Halleck's part, but Halleck insisted that military necessity alone had dictated his stance, and mused that abolitionists could be more dangerous than the enemy. Representative Francis P. Blair, Jr., who defended Halleck on the floor of Congress, read a letter from Halleck that emphasized Halleck's willingness to follow the lead of his civilian superiors. "I am ready to carry out any lawful instructions in regard to fugitive slaves, which my superiors may give me," Halleck wrote, "and to enforce any law which Congress may pass. But I cannot make law, and I will not violate it." In a veiled reference to his willingness to take stronger measures against slavery if the government desired it, he added, "You know my private opinion on the policy of confiscating the slave property of rebels in arms. If Congress shall pass it, I shall enforce it."[14]

[12]Dix to McClellan, August 21, 1861, ibid., Series II, vol. 1, p. 765.

[13]George B. McClellan, *McClellan's Own Story* (New York: Charles Webster, 1884), 33, 35. McClellan's complaint about the Radical Republicans appeared in his manuscript memoirs but was deleted prior to publication by his editor and literary executor, William Prime. See Stephen W. Sears, *George B. McClellan: The Young Napoleon* (New York: Ticknor and Fields, 1988), 116–118.

[14]Halleck to Dix, November 25, 29, December 6, 1861, John A. Dix Papers, LC. Halleck to Blair, undated letter read by Blair on the floor of the U.S. House of Representatives, December 12, 1861, *Congressional Globe,* 37th Cong., 2d sess., 76.

Major General Ulysses S. Grant, Halleck's chief subordinate, had a similar attitude on the subject of slavery. Like Lincoln, Grant recognized from the outset that the mere fact of war profoundly jeopardized the peculiar institution. "In all this I can but see the doom of Slavery," he wrote his Missouri father-in-law a week after the firing on Fort Sumter. "The North do not want, nor will they want, to interfere with this institution. But they will refuse for all time to give it protection unless the South shall return soon to their allegiance." In the meantime, however, he studiously followed the policy established by his superiors. When Frémont issued his proclamation freeing the slaves of Missouri secessionists, Grant instructed his officers to enforce it. When the Lincoln administration subsequently forced Frémont to back down, Grant read it as a message not to touch slavery, and returned at least one fugitive slave to his master. He also enforced Halleck's General Order No. 3, warning a balky subordinate that orders must be obeyed regardless of one's private views. Grant revealed his own personal perspective in a letter to his father: "My inclination is to whip the rebellion into submission preserving all constitutional rights. If it cannot be whipped in any other way than through a war against slavery, let it come to that legitimately. If it is necessary that slavery should fall that the Republic may continue its existence, let slavery go." The decision concerning that necessity rested in the hands of his superiors; Grant was content to leave it that way. As late as August 1862 he insisted, "I have no hobby of my own with regard to the negro, either to effect his freedom or to continue his bondage. If Congress pass any law and the President approves, I am willing to execute it."[15]

William T. Sherman saw clearly the complications that accompanied the use of fugitive slaves, and considered Halleck's policy much the best. "The well-settled policy of the whole army now," he told his command in mid-June 1862, "is to have nothing to do with the negro. 'Exclude them from camp' is General Halleck's reiterated order. We cannot have our trains encumbered by them, nor can we afford to feed them, and it is deceiving the poor fellow to allow him to start and have him forcibly driven away afterward." Sherman departed from Halleck's noninvolvement policy with reluctance. In September he wrote his brother, Republican Senator John Sherman, that if the army tried to protect and feed the hordes of black refugees that came its way, the attempt would soon hamstring military operations. From a soldier's

---

[15]Grant to Frederick Dent, April 19, 1861, in Simon (ed.), *Grant Papers* 2:3–4; Grant to John Cook, September 12, 1861, ibid., 2:243–244; Grant to Jesse R. Grant, November 27, 1861, ibid., 3:227; Grant to Jesse R. Grant, August 3, 1862, ibid., 5:264. A useful summary of Grant's evolving attitudes toward the issue is Brooks D. Simpson, "'The Doom of Slavery': Ulysses S. Grant, War Aims, and Emancipation, 1861–1863," *Civil War History* 36 (1990):36–56. Grant's actual words form a sharp contrast to David Donald's offhand statement that "military leaders like General Grant demanded more men and pointed to the large numbers of Negroes who would willingly serve for their freedom." (Donald, *Lincoln Reconsidered*, 138.) Demands of that sort, indeed, are the sort of thing one would expect had emancipation derived primarily from military necessity. But few military men made them, and Grant, with his careful subordination to civilian authority, was not among those who did.

perspective, it seemed, emancipation was less a potential military advantage to be exploited than a political reality to be accommodated.[16]

The few officers who did support emancipation were clearly animated by politics. Frémont's proclamation, although possibly influenced by a genuine sense of its military necessity, seemed politically motivated after he refused to modify it without a direct presidential order. When John Pope appeared before the Joint Committee on the Conduct of the War in early July 1862 and endorsed the elimination of slavery, it was as an officer openly courting the Radical Republicans. An even more blatant example was Major General David Hunter, a vocal antislavery officer who actively sought a berth from which he could free blacks. Late in January 1862, he wrote Secretary of War Stanton, "Please let me have my own way on the subject of slavery. The administration will not be responsible. I alone will bear the blame; you can censure me, arrest me, dismiss me, hang me if you will, but permit me to make my mark in such a way as to be remembered by friend and foe." Shortly afterward, the War Department placed him in command of the Department of the South. Perhaps understandably, Hunter interpreted the assignment as a green light to pursue his program of military emancipation.[17]

Officially the Department of the South consisted of the states of South Carolina, Georgia, and Florida. In reality it was confined to a number of small enclaves along the Atlantic coast. Nowhere else did local conditions yield such possibilities for military emancipation. Most of the coastal planters had fled months before at the approach of Union troops, leaving behind thousands of unsupervised slaves who were free in all but name. The Federal government had naturally assumed the task of caring for these abandoned slaves. Treasury Department agents put them to work harvesting cotton for sale to Northern mills, and Treasury Secretary Salmon P. Chase lent his office and personal support to dozens of Northern missionaries and teachers who sought to educate the Sea Island blacks. In this hospitable environment, Hunter moved almost at once to emancipate the slaves in his department. On April 13, he clarified the standing of certain contrabands in the district by simply declaring them free men. Then, interpreting his orders to organize the blacks within his lines into "squads, companies, or otherwise" as actual authorization to raise black troops, Hunter began active recruiting – an astonishing measure in its own right, but not so astounding as the one to come. Late in April, he declared martial law throughout the region. Finally, on May 9 Hunter announced flatly, "Slavery and martial law in a free country are altogether incompatible," and therefore he declared all slaves in Georgia, Florida and South Carolina "forever free."[18]

Nothing in Hunter's official correspondence indicated a military rationale for the decision, and his statement about the incompatibility of slavery and martial law was

---

[16]General Order No. 43, June 18, 1862, OR 17, pt. 2:14–15; Sherman to John Sherman, September 3, 1862, William T. Sherman Papers, LC.

[17]Hunter to Stanton, January 29, 1862, Edwin M. Stanton Papers, LC.

[18]General Order No. 11, May 9, 1862, OR 14:341.

illogical on its face. On the contrary, no condition was more ideal for slavery, with its strong need for imposed order, than martial law. The closest thing to a military rationale that Hunter offered occurred in a letter to Republican Senator William P. Fessenden, whose son was one of his aides. The Union armies, Hunter wrote, could not continue to serve "as a police force for the protection of property" of rebels. "Liberate the slaves by proclamation," Hunter reasoned, "and the props of the Southern Confederacy are knocked away."[19]

Hunter did not inform the Lincoln administration of his intentions ahead of time, an omission that strongly suggested his political motivation. The President only learned of the emancipation directive weeks later, and then through the newspapers. Once it became general knowledge, however, several Cabinet officers and a number of other prominent Republicans urged Lincoln to sustain the order, which is almost certainly the outcome Hunter had in mind. But Lincoln refused to let a general prod him along. On May 22, he ordered Hunter to rescind the proclamation.[20]

Hunter's transparent attempt to influence policy in Washington may have been done by a military man, but the motivations were political. Much the same situation obtained in Louisiana, where Brigadier General John W. Phelps embarked upon his own antislavery program. Oddly enough, Phelps's policy brought him into conflict with his immediate superior, Ben Butler, the same Butler who had earlier created the "contraband" concept.

Butler began his rule in Louisiana with a policy rather different from the one he pursued in Virginia. Although tough-minded toward those who openly supported the rebel cause, he sought to reassure Louisiana whites at large. "All persons well-disposed toward the Government will receive the safeguard and protection of the armies." "[A]ll rights of property of whatever kind will be held inviolate," subject to the "laws of the federal Union." According to some reports, he even handed several fugitive slaves back to their owners despite Congressional passage of a new article of war, issued in March, which forbade the military to return slaves.[21]

Phelps, who commanded Camp Parapet just west of New Orleans, was a confirmed abolitionist. Not only did he protect the slaves who entered his lines, he also permitted his troops, in the words of a Butler aide-de-camp, to "range the country, insult the Planters and entice negroes away from their plantations." Since this had the effect of undermining slave discipline in the area, the local planters complained vocally. Butler was embarrassed, but Phelps refused to modify his policy. By mid-June, nearly 300 fugitives were at Camp Parapet. Unable to deal with the problem locally, Butler referred the matter to Lincoln and Stanton. "I respect his [Phelps's] honest sincerity of

[19]Francis Fessenden, *Life and Public Services of William Pitt Fessenden,* 2 vols. (reprint edition; New York: Da Capo Press, 1971 [1907]), vol. 1, pp. 255–56.

[20]"Proclamation Revoking General Hunter's Order of Military Emancipation of May 9, 1862," May 19, 1862, Basler (ed.), *Collected Works of Lincoln* 5:223.

[21]Butler to Stanton, May 25, 1862, OR 15:439–440; *New Orleans Daily Picayune,* May 2, 1862, quoted in Bell Irvin Wiley, *Southern Negroes, 1861–1865* (reprint edition; New Haven: Yale University Press, 1965 [1938]), 187; Louis S. Gerteis, *From Contraband to Freedman: Federal Policy Toward Southern Blacks, 1861–1865* (Contributions in American History No. 29; Westport, CT: Greenwood Press, 1973), 67.

opinion," Butler wrote, "but I am a soldier, bound to carry out the wishes of my Government so long as I hold this commission, and I understand that policy to be the one I am pursuing. I do not feel at liberty to pursue any other."[22]

Butler then enclosed a lengthy manifesto from Phelps that set forth Phelps's views on the slave question. Arguments concerning the military advantages that might accrue from emancipation were conspicuous by their absence. Instead, Phelps pushed three major points: first, that slavery was unjust and out of keeping with the principles on which the republic had been founded; second, that "the slave system of labor is giving shape to the government of the society where it exists, and that government is not republican in form or in spirit" – a restatement of the Slave Power concept; and third, that the United States government could successfully carry out a policy of emancipation.[23]

At the end of July, Phelps sought to create three regiments of African Americans for local defense, arguing that he needed reinforcements and that, in any case, black troops were better acclimated than whites for duty in the miasmic lowlands. The practical utility of such a force was obvious, but even here Phelps's rationale went beyond military considerations. Southern society, he argued, was on the verge of dissolution. It was better to enlist former slaves in the Union cause for, left to their own devices, they might take up "robbery and plunder." Butler referred the matter to Washington. Privately, he wrote his wife, "Phelps has gone crazy."[24]

The Lincoln administration did little to resolve the problem. Stanton merely advised Butler to use his "accustomed skill and discretion" to avoid a rift with Phelps, and reminded Butler that Congress had forbidden the army to return fugitive slaves. He also noted that as a matter of simple humanity, slaves should not be permitted to suffer. Even so, Stanton carefully concluded, his instructions were not intended to establish any new policy with respect to slavery.[25]

Behind the scenes, the Lincoln administration was moving precisely toward a new policy, but not because its generals were clamoring for it. No commanders urged emancipation on the ground of the military advantages that would presumably flow from it. The few who did exert pressure, directly or indirectly, on the Lincoln administration – Frémont, Hunter, and Phelps – did so because of their preexisting opposition to slavery. Other generals, like Dix, McClellan, and Buell, had equally entrenched political reasons for opposing emancipation. The balance – senior officers who were truly impelled by military considerations – viewed the prospect of emancipation primarily as a military inconvenience, albeit a policy decision that the civilian administration might eventually adopt. They were quite willing to wait for Lincoln to act.

---

[22]Captain Edward Page to Butler, May 27, 1862, Benjamin F. Butler Papers, LC; Butler to Stanton, June 18, 1862, OR 15:486.

[23]Phelps to Captain R.S. Davis, June 16, 1862, OR 15:486–490.

[24]Phelps to Butler, July 30, 1862, in Butler, *Private and Official Correspondence* 2:125–126; Butler to his wife, August 2, 1862, ibid., 148.

[25]Stanton to Butler, July 3, 1862, OR, Series III, vol. 3, p. 200.

THE PUSH FOR EMANCIPATION

The pressures on the Lincoln administration to free the slaves came mainly from outside the army, usually in inverse proportion to Northern military success. The Bull Run defeat, for example, strengthened the hand of abolitionists and advanced Republicans. The *New York Tribune* edged cautiously toward an emancipation policy. Even the more moderate *New York Times* acknowledged that the Negro lay "at the bottom of this fight." In December 1861, Senator Lyman Trumbull introduced his stronger confiscation bill, calling in part for the emancipation of secessionists' slaves. Meanwhile Representative Thaddeus Stevens (Republican-Pennsylvania) urged the President to free the slaves under his war powers as commander-in-chief. And Representative Owen Lovejoy (Republican-Illinois) introduced a bill that would make it a crime for soldiers or sailors to capture or return fugitive slaves.[26]

By the end of 1861, the Lincoln administration itself began to flirt with emancipation proposals. To be sure, the first move in that direction qualified more as an unwelcome attempt to exert pressure on the President than a true administration measure. In December, Lincoln's first Secretary of War, Simon Cameron, found himself in deep trouble with the President amid damning reports of inefficiency and corruption in the letting of military contracts. Fearing that Lincoln might remove him, Cameron sought to gain radical support in a bid to keep his Cabinet post. To do so, he prepared, without Lincoln's knowledge, an annual report to Congress calling for both the emancipation of slaves as a war measure and the enlistment of blacks into the army. Knowing that the President would defuse this political bombshell as soon as he learned of it, Cameron leaked it to the press to make sure the radicals would discover and reward his efforts.[27] The gambit did not work. Lincoln promptly ordered the radical passages deleted from the report; a month or so later, he deleted Cameron from his Cabinet, replacing him with Edwin M. Stanton.

Lincoln resisted a premature emancipation order because he sought to maintain the broadest possible base of support for the Union war effort. He hoped to alienate neither the border state congressmen, whose slaveholding constituencies would surely scream at the first sign of an assault on their "peculiar institution"; nor conservative Republicans, whose misgivings about slavery were generally offset by grave constitutional doubts about the legality of emancipation; nor the Democrats, most of whom combined the same legal doubts with a hearty loathing for anything that might raise the political and social status of blacks. Nevertheless, on the subject of slaves Lincoln was far from indifferent. "I have always hated slavery, I think, as much as any Abolitionist," he had told an Illinois crowd in 1858. And although reluctant to embrace the abolitionist dogma of both immediate, uncompensated emancipation

[26]*New York Tribune,* August 6, 12, 1861; *New York Times,* July 25, 29, 1861; *Congressional Globe,* 37th Cong., 2nd sess., part 1, pp. 18–19; ibid., p. 6; ibid., pp. 33–34.

[27]Erwin Stanley Bradley, *Simon Cameron, Lincoln's Secretary of War: A Political Biography* (Philadelphia: University of Pennsylvania Press, 1966), 202–203. See also T. Harry Williams, *Lincoln and the Radicals* (Madison: University of Wisconsin Press, 1941), 59.

and full equality for blacks, Lincoln nevertheless believed that slavery lay very much at the heart of the political crisis that had plagued the nation since 1848 and had now erupted in bitter civil war. Even as he resisted Radical Republican pressures in favor of immediate, uncompensated emancipation, Lincoln initiated a more moderate emancipation program of his own.[28]

On March 6, 1862, he recommended passage of a joint resolution promising federal compensation to any state "which may adopt gradual emancipation of slavery." Although he offered it as a war measure, his proposal came at a time not of Union reversals but of major successes on the Carolina coast and in Tennessee. Moreover, the advantages he saw resulting from it were largely political; the relationship of the measure to the war effort was tenuous indeed. Asserting that the Confederate leadership "entertain the hope that this government will ultimately be forced to acknowledge the independence of some part of the disaffected region," and that the loyal slave states would then join the Confederacy, Lincoln went on to aver vaguely that this hope alone sustained the rebellion: "To deprive them of this hope, substantially ends the rebellion; and the initiation of emancipation completely deprives them of it." It would be hard to imagine a less convincing piece of reasoning than that.[29]

Lincoln's proposal had little to do with the three legitimate military advantages that could be expected to flow from emancipation. It would not affect the use of African Americans in support of the Confederate military – an issue satisfactorily addressed, in any event, by the "contraband" doctrine and the First Confiscation Act. It would not deprive the South of the slaves engaged in propping up the Confederacy's war economy. It said nothing about the use of blacks in support of the Union war effort, either as laborers or soldiers. It was not, in short, a measure of "military necessity" in any meaningful sense of the term. Rather, it was a clear extension of the Republican Party's longstanding antipathy toward slavery, shaped by the need to retain the support of the border states and to avoid the constitutional difficulties in the path of federally sponsored emancipation. Lincoln hoped that the border states, by initiating a state sponsored program of compensated emancipation, would begin a movement that the Southern states might later adopt after the war's conclusion. A state sponsored program would avoid the constitutional obstacles, allay conservative fears of a strong central government, and place slavery firmly on the road to ultimate extinction. As an added incentive to the border states, Lincoln warned that if the war continued, "it is impossible to foresee all the incidents, which may attend and all the ruin which may follow it. Such as may seem indispensable, or may obviously promise great efficiency towards ending the struggle, must and will come." This could be read as a veiled threat of future, uncompensated emancipation.[30]

In the months that followed, the executive and legislative branches worked amicably for the overthrow of slavery wherever the federal government had clear authority to act. On March 10, Congress passed a new article of war that forbade Union troops

---

[28]Speech at Chicago, Illinois, July 10, 1858, Basler (ed.), *Collected Works of Lincoln* 2:492.
[29]"Message to Congress," March 6, 1862, ibid., 5:144–46.
[30]Ibid.

to enforce the Fugitive Slave Act (although the act itself remained on the books until 1864). A few weeks later the President signed into law a bill for the compensated emancipation of slaves in the District of Columbia. Subsequent legislation ended slavery in the territories without compensation, provided for a more vigorous suppression of the African slave trade, and made provision for the education of black children in the District of Columbia. Clearly the President had an antislavery agenda that existed separately from the conduct of the war.

In the meantime, Lincoln eagerly waited for the border states to take up his call for compensated emancipation. Their failure to do so profoundly disappointed him. His order revoking Hunter's proclamation of military emancipation contained a warning for them to act on his moderate proposition while they still could. Directing attention to the joint resolution of March 6, he wrote pointedly that it had been adopted by large majorities in both houses of Congress, and stood as "an authentic, definite, and solemn proposal of the nation to the States and people most directly interested in the subject matter," slavery. "The change it contemplates," he urged, "would come gently as the dews of heaven, not rending or wrecking anything. Will you not embrace it?"[31]

The border states did not. In the meantime, the Peninsula campaign collapsed and Congress moved toward a harder line. On July 12 (the same day Congress passed the Second Confiscation Act), Lincoln met with twenty-seven border state Congressmen and Senators and urged them again to support a program of compensated emancipation. "If the war continue long . . . ," he pointed out, "the institution in your states will be extinguished by mere friction and abrasion – by the mere incidents of war."[32] The border state men refused, and with their refusal Lincoln realized he must risk losing their support. He needed that of the antislavery faction more. A course of emancipation also accorded with his personal wishes and with the growing spirit in the North that demanded that the South be hurt. Even so, nothing in Lincoln's appeal to the border state men touched upon the military advantages of emancipation. Instead, he emphasized that the war itself was palpably eroding the foundation on which slavery rested.

Hard on the heels of his unsuccessful interview with the border state congressmen, Lincoln made his fateful decision to emancipate the slaves by executive order. In a private conversation with Navy Secretary Gideon Welles and Secretary of State Seward on July 13, he told them of his intention. Welles's account of the conversation, written in 1872, comes closer than any other to suggesting a true military rationale for the decision:

Further efforts with the border States would, he thought, be useless [Welles wrote]. That was not the road to lead us out of this difficulty. We wanted the army to strike more vigorous blows. The Administration must set the army an example, and strike at the heart of the rebellion. The

---

[31]"Proclamation Revoking General Hunter's Order of Military Emancipation of May 9, 1862," May 19, 1862, ibid., 223. The military irrelevance of a change that could come as "gently as the dews of heaven" scarcely needs to be underscored.

[32]"Appeal to Border State Representatives to Favor Compensated Emancipation," July 12, 1862, ibid., 317–319.

country, he thought, was prepared for it. The army would be with us. . . . If the rebels did not cease their war, they must take the consequences of war. . . . [Emancipation] was a military necessity, absolutely essential to the preservation of the Union. We must free the slaves or be ourselves subdued. The slaves were undeniably an element of strength to those who had their service, and we must decide whether that element should be with us or against us.[33]

Welles's account dwells heavily on slavery's status as "the heart of the rebellion" and emphasizes the symbolic value of an attack upon it as a signal to the army to "strike more vigorous blows." Emancipation, in this light, appears as a measure inspired by a political appraisal of the rebellion's ultimate source, and a propaganda device to underscore the repudiation of a conciliatory policy.

From a purely military standpoint, the chief significance of Lincoln's rationale, as Welles recorded it, lay in the concluding line. Slaves were an element of strength to the South; the Union must seize that element and use it to its own advantage. Thousands of fugitive slaves were already laboring on behalf of the North both in military encampments and cotton fields supervised by federal officials. An emancipation policy might encourage more slaves to desert their masters. Yet the military efficacy of the Emancipation Proclamation, in this respect, was questioned as soon as Lincoln issued it, a step he took on September 22, 1862, five days after McClellan's victory at Antietam. Critics called it a "brutem fulmen." Lincoln himself wondered whether it would have any more practical effect than the Pope's bull against the comet. In its preliminary form, the proclamation liberated no slaves at all. It merely stipulated that unless the rebellious states returned to the Union by New Year's Day, 1863, the slaves residing within them would be free. And, obviously, until Federal armies subsequently conquered those states, the bondsmen would in fact remain enslaved.[34]

Searching for some tangible military significance in the logic behind the Emancipation Proclamation, both Southern sympathizers and neutral observers concluded that Lincoln intended it as an incitement for blacks to rise up in a gigantic slave revolt. Baltimore caricaturist Adalbert Volck, a secessionist sympathizer, crafted a savage cartoon in which he portrayed Lincoln dipping his pen in the devil's inkwell to write the proclamation, a picture of the Saint-Domingue slave insurrection festooned on the wall behind him. Confederate President Jefferson Davis exploded that Lincoln's directive was "the most execrable measure recorded in the history of guilty man." Some Southerners, outraged by what seemed the inauguration of a war of extermination, even urged "the raising of the *black flag*, asking and giving no quarter thereafter." The British government, according to one recent assessment, also viewed the proclamation as a desperate incitement to race war, and briefly considered inter-

---

[33]Welles, "A History of Emancipation," 843.

[34]Thomas Barnett to Samuel L. M. Barlow, September 27, 1862, S. L. M. Barlow Papers, HEHL; "Reply to Emancipation Memorial Presented by Chicago Christians of All Denominations," September 13, 1862, Basler (ed.), *Collected Works of Lincoln* 5:420. Although offered even as Lincoln was preparing to issue the preliminary Emancipation Proclamation, this lengthy document (pp. 419–425) contains a very full argument *against* the military and political wisdom of emancipation; Preliminary Emancipation Proclamation, ibid., 433–436.

vention to prevent so atrocious an occurrence. Even some Union soldiers, although willing to see the coming of emancipation, had made up their minds that it would trigger a bloody Negro uprising. The slaves, wrote an Ohio colonel in July 1862, "hate their masters & would rejoice at the opportunity of being allowed to avenge in blood the oppressions which their race has endured for centuries. . . . Should the fortunes of war make it necessary for the North to make this a war of selfpreservation the bloodiest page of human history remains yet to be written." And if arms were actually placed in the hands of the slaves, he warned, "much of this country will be left but a desert."[35]

Lincoln, in fact, entertained no hopes for a mammoth revival of the Saint-Domingue revolt or Nat Turner's rebellion. Indeed, his final Emancipation Proclamation, issued in January 1863, explicitly enjoined the liberated bondsmen "to abstain from all violence, except in necessary self-defense." The conduct of fugitive slaves prior to September 1862, in any case, gave every indication that they were little interested in wreaking bloody vengeance on their erstwhile masters. Aside from isolated acts of violence, frequently after substantial provocation, most slaves exercised impressive forbearance. Most remained on their owners' farms and plantations until Union forces entered the immediate neighborhood, and many stayed on afterward.[36]

More significant was the reinforcement that the proclamation gave to the decision, made in July 1862, to begin recruitment of black soldiers. The Militia Act of 1862 authorized the president to organize blacks and utilize them "for any military or naval service for which they may be found competent." Clandestine experiments with black soldiers had already begun in Louisiana and South Carolina. But many within the army sharply doubted the military wisdom of using African American troops. Most of their objections revolved around simple racism. Lieutenant Colonel Charles Francis Adams thought that making soldiers of former slaves would do more harm than good. He thought it would take five years to train them into effective fighting men. Others simply detested the idea of black men in uniform. It seemed not so much to elevate the black as to degrade the white. "We don't want to fight side by side with the nigger," wrote a New York corporal. "We think we are a too superior race for that." "[N]one of our soldiers seem to like the idea of arming the Negroes," noted a Union officer in March 1863. "Our boys say this is a white man's war and the Negro has no business in it." Offered a promotion if he would serve in a black regiment himself, the officer refused: "Not any Niggers for me!" It took time and observation for Union

[35]Dunbar Rowland (ed.), *Jefferson Davis, Constitutionalist: His Letters, Papers and Speeches* 10 vols. (Jackson: Mississippi Department of Archives and History, 1923) vol. 5, pp. 409–11; Jones, *A Rebel War Clerk's Diary at the Confederate States Capital* 1:159; Howard Jones, *Union in Peril: The Crisis Over British Intervention in the Civil War* (Chapel Hill and London: University of North Carolina Press, 1992), 138–230; DeWitt Clinton Loudon to his wife, July 9, 1862, DeWitt Clinton Loudon Papers, OHS.

[36]Emancipation Proclamation, January 1, 1863, Basler (ed.), *Collected Works of Lincoln* 6:30; Leon F. Litwack, *Been in the Storm So Long: The Aftermath of Slavery* (New York: Vintage Books, 1980 [1979]), passim., esp. 180–186.

soldiers to appreciate the fighting qualities of black troops. As late as April 1863, W.T. Sherman continued to express skepticism on the subject. "With my opinions of negroes and my experience," he wrote, "I cannot trust them yet."[37]

In short, the wisdom of employing blacks in the army, although later vindicated by the courage and élan of men of color in uniform, seemed in September 1862 very much open to question. The pervasive racist assumptions of the period suggested that Negro troops might prove ineffective and that white troops would be demoralized by their presence. The drawbacks of an emancipation policy, on the other hand, were obvious and well-described at the time. By attacking the political, social, and economic foundations of the South, it would only intensify Confederate resistance. It would alienate the border states. It would undermine Northern support for the war effort by transforming a war to preserve the Union, which most Northerners embraced, into a war to free the black, which many in the North – perhaps a majority – found violently repugnant.

Why then did Lincoln go forward with his decision to emancipate the slaves? An interpretation based on narrow "military necessity" fails to satisfy; the evidence in favor of it leaves much to be desired. The army did not press for it. The military advantages to be gained from it were seldom articulated and were, in any event, open to serious query. It is more persuasive to recognize the strength of the antislavery movement, to acknowledge Lincoln's personal antipathy toward the holding of human beings in bondage, and to note that by the autumn of 1862 the political climate for emancipation was much more favorable than had previously been the case.

From the war's outset, according to Gideon Welles, Lincoln regarded chattel slavery as lying at the heart of the rebellion, but initially hoped the border states would take the lead in actually placing it on the road to extinction. Such a move by the border states would eliminate two of the obstacles that prevented Lincoln from moving against slavery at once. Obviously, it would prevent the defection of the border states. It would also avoid the constitutional difficulties involved. By the summer of 1862, however, both of these obstacles had greatly diminished in size.[38]

As a practical matter, the border states could no longer leave the Union: Thousands of Federal troops in Missouri and Maryland forcibly held both states, while additional Union forces garrisoned the major strategic points in Kentucky. Moreover, it seems apparent that Lincoln had acquired a certain contempt for Southern Unionists. They

[37]Militia Act of 1862, embodied in General Orders No. 91, July 19, 1862, OR, Series II, vol. 2:281; Worthington Chauncey Ford (ed.), *A Cycle of Adams Letters, 1861–1865*, 2 vols. (Boston: Houghton, Mifflin, 1920), vol. 1, p. 171; Oscar O. Winther (ed.), *With Sherman to the Sea: Civil War Reminiscences of Theodore F. Upson* (Bloomington: Indiana University Press, 1958), 55–56, 69, 101; Sherman to his wife, April 17, 1863, in M.A. DeWolfe Howe (ed.), *Home Letters of General Sherman* (New York: Charles Scribner's Sons, 1909), 252–253. For surveys of sentiment among Union soldiers regarding the use of blacks as combat troops, see Robertson, *Soldiers Blue and Gray*, 30–32; Wiley, *The Life of Billy Yank*, 119–120. Wiley believed that when the issue first surfaced in the summer of 1862, "the overwhelming majority of Union soldiers appear to have been against the proposal" (Ibid., 119).

[38]Welles, "History of Emancipation," 841.

struck him as a timid lot. As they had done little to support the Union cause, Lincoln may have become convinced that they would also do little to support the Confederacy. In any event, so unconcerned was he with the sentiments of Kentuckians that he issued his preliminary Emancipation Proclamation while an army of 50,000 Confederates stood on Bluegrass soil.

Similarly, the constitutional obstacle also seemed less troublesome. By the summer of 1862, Lincoln had already bent the constitution in a variety of unprecedented ways; he had survived the experiment every time. Then, too, more Northerners were becoming comfortable with the idea of emancipation as a legitimate exercise of the president's war powers as commander-in-chief. As long ago as 1837, John Quincy Adams had suggested the legality of such a step. And after the Richmond fizzle, the strengthening desire to punish the South helped to dissolve misgivings about what increasingly seemed an arcane constitutional quibble.[39]

This introduces a third improvement in the situation. When the war broke out, most Northerners had viewed an assault on slavery as unnecessary and counterproductive. The presumably small hornet's nest of secessionist traitors at Richmond could be destroyed without it; no need to dignify their revolution by vindicating their talk of an abolitionist conspiracy up north. By the summer of 1862, although still short of a majority, a much larger number of Northerners agreed that slavery was central to the struggle. No one saw this more clearly than the Union soldiers who entered the South and observed the "peculiar institution" at first hand. The corrosion of slavery as a result of the war forced the military either to prop up the institution or hasten its doom, and few soldiers considered it worth preserving. The military grew to see blacks as virtually their only certain allies in the South, and relied on them for intelligence and as guides. More than anything else, however, direct exposure to slavery convinced many that it lay at the root of the rebellion and thus, in an ultimate sense, its destruction should form a Union war aim. "Men are beginning to see things in quite a different light from what they did six months ago," an Iowa soldier wrote his wife; "and we believe that the *Hydra Headed Monster Slavery* (which has cost the lives of hundreds, yea thousands of our fellow men) will soon be crushed into oblivion. . . ." A Minnesota colonel took satisfaction in the pained expressions on slaveholders' faces when Union soldiers carried off their bondsmen. "Crippling the institution of slavery," he exulted, "is . . . striking a blow at the heart of the rebellion, and inflicting upon our enemies the greatest possible injury, which latter I conceive to be the policy of war."[40]

Even so, the soldiers' response to the Emancipation Proclamation fell short of regarding it as a measure from which extensive military results could be expected. Many rejected it outright. McClellan, predictably, found the President's decision

[39]John Hope Franklin, *The Emancipation Proclamation* (Garden City, NY: Doubleday, 1963), 15.
[40]Ormsby M. Mitchel to Edwin M. Stanton, May 4, 1862, OR 10, pt. 2:162; George Lowe to his wife, July 22, 1862, George Lowe Papers, HEHL; Lucius Hubbard to Mary Hubbard, September 8, 1862, Lucius Hubbard Papers, MNHS.

repellant, and in a letter to a Democratic friend he wrote that he viewed it as a signal for the inauguration of "servile war." He briefly considered public repudiation of the Emancipation Proclamation until several friends within the Army of the Potomac persuaded him that this would be quite unwise. Ultimately he issued a lukewarm general order informing his troops of the proclamation, adding suggestively, "The remedy for political error if any are committed is to be found only in the action of the people at the polls." As for the proclamation's implicit message for "more vigorous blows," McClellan underscored that the army would continue to be guided "by the same rules of mercy that have ever controlled its conduct toward the defenceless."[41]

A large number of his soldiers found the emancipation decision disturbing. "I am getting daily disgusted with the way the war is conducted," growled a New Hampshire captain. "There is already too much nigger in the matter and if it comes to be an abolition war . . . I will have nothing to do with it." An artillery officer wrote that the Emancipation Proclamation, "after opening with a very short reassertion that the object of the war is the restoration of the Union, goes on to change it into an abolition one virtually." He added dourly, "I do not hear much said here in the army on the subject, but all think it unadvised at this time; even those most anti-slavery. It has been evident that this was what the radicals have been driving at for some time past, but I had hoped that Mr. Lincoln would have had force enough to resist."[42]

Other uniformed Federals were pleased by Lincoln's course of action. "My hopes are somewhat revived since Old Abe has come out with his proclamation . . . ," wrote one soldier. "[E]vry boddy knows that slavery was the cuase [sic] of this war and slavery stands in the way of puting down this rebelion and now let us put it out of the way." Said another: "I am like the fellow that got his house burned by the guerillas he was in for emancipation subjugation extermination and hell and damnation. We are in war and anything to beat the south."[43]

Perhaps the most common reaction was one of wait-and-see. Even the young abolitionist Robert Gould Shaw — soon to achieve fame as the colonel of the African American 54th Massachusetts — received the news of Lincoln's proclamation with restraint. "I suppose you are all very much excited about it," he wrote his mother. "For my part I can't see what *practical* good it can do now. Wherever our army has been, there remain no slaves, and the proclamation won't free them where we don't go."[44]

---

[41]McClellan to William H. Aspinwall, September 26, 1862, Sears (ed.), *McClellan Papers*, 482; McClellan to his wife, September 25, [1862], ibid., 481; Cox, *Military Reminiscences* 1:359–361; McClellan to Lincoln, [October 7, 1862], transmitting text of General Order No. 163, Sears (ed.), *McClellan Papers*, 494.

[42]James B. Post to his wife, October 16, 1862, James B. Post Letters, CWMC, USAMHI; entry for September 30, 1862, in Nevins (ed.), *A Diary of Battle*, 108–109.

[43]J. V. Boucher to his wife, September 29, 1862, Boucher Family Papers, CWMC, USAMHI; Amory K. Allen to his wife, January 8, 1863, "The Civil War Letters of Amory K. Allen," *Indiana Magazine of History* 31 (1935):361.

[44]Shaw to his mother, September 25, 1862, Robert Gould Shaw Letters, HLHU. See also G.W. Whitman to his mother, September 30, 1862, Loving (ed.), *Civil War Letters of George Washington Whitman*, 71; Brigadier General Alpheus S. Williams to his daughter, October 28, 1862, in Quaife (ed.), *From the Cannon's Mouth*, 142.

THE MILITARY SEQUEL TO EMANCIPATION

A hundred days separated Lincoln's issuance of the preliminary Emancipation Proclamation, which threatened the death of slavery if the rebellion continued, and his signing of the final document making it the Union's actual policy. New Year's Day 1863 brought celebrations in black communities all across the North, as well as areas occupied by Federal troops. The churches were packed in Boston and thousands joined a torchlight procession through Norfolk, Virginia. At Parris Island, South Carolina, a minister presented the regimental colors to Colonel Thomas W. Higginson, commander of the all-black First South Carolina Infantry. He made a short speech. When he had finished, a congregation of African Americans spontaneously broke into "My country, 'tis of thee." To Colonel Higginson it seemed like "the choked voice of a race at last unloosed."[45]

Lincoln's act was widely applauded. An assemblage of New Orleans Unionists, for example, congratulated the President for at once doing justice to the slaves and inflicting on the rebels "the blow best calculated to reduce them to obedience of the laws." But it was just as widely denounced. The Democratic *New York World* called the Emancipation Proclamation "clearly unconstitutional and wholly void unless sustainable as a war measure. A war measure it clearly is not, inasmuch as the previous success of the war is the only thing that can give it validity."[46]

Which view was more nearly correct? The answer depended on what aspect of the proclamation one chose to emphasize. The document signed by Lincoln on January 1, 1863, not only freed the slaves in most of the Confederate South, but also stipulated that former slaves would be received into the armed services. Although experiments in raising African American troops had begun as early as August 1862 – the First South Carolina was one result – the final Emancipation Proclamation unequivocally embraced the recruitment of black troops. Ultimately 186,000 African Americans would wear the Union blue. Of these, more than half had been slaves when the war broke out. By 1865, they accounted for nearly ten percent of the total Federals in uniform, and played a significant role in the rebellion's overthrow.

As an instrument of economic warfare against the South, however, the proclamation contributed little. Here the critics were exactly right: Only when Union troops were on the spot did large numbers of slaves leave their masters. This did not mean that the war produced little strain on slavery. Across the South, bondsmen grew more insubordinate, and might threaten to leave unless their owners made concessions. Worried masters withdrew their slaves from areas threatened by Northern troops and took them deep into the interior, resulting in significant stress to the normal economy. But such disruptions had begun well prior to the issuance of the Emancipation Proclamation, and would have continued regardless.

The proclamation's military utility could be criticized in one further respect. From a soldier's perspective, given the half-million slaves who escaped or fell into Union

[45]Thomas Wentworth Higginson, *Army Life in a Black Regiment* (Boston: Beacon Press, 1962), 40–41.
[46]*New York Times*, January 4, 1863; *New York World*, January 3, 1863.

hands during the course of the war, the one thing the government could helpfully provide was a consistent policy toward such refugees, and this the Lincoln administration deliberately did not do. A number of areas in the South were excluded from the proclamation and theoretically left "precisely" as if it had not been issued. The forty-eight counties of western Virginia were exempted, as were several counties in the southeastern part of the state. Much of southern Louisiana was also spared, as was the entire state of Tennessee, to say nothing of the border states which, although nominally loyal, were also the scene of active hostilities. Yet these were often the areas most thoroughly under Union control. As a result, department commanders in these regions had to sift between African Americans who were free – either through operation of the Confiscation Acts, or because they had fled from affected areas, or because they had always been free – and those who remained enslaved. The position was doubly awkward because loyal slaveowners demanded the Army's assistance in preserving their property, yet by Congressional order the Army was forbidden to return fugitive slaves.

Without a uniform, consistent, well-considered government policy, commanders were forced to improvise. In southeastern Virginia, General John A. Dix found himself responsible for 5,000 "contrabands," with another 10,000 African Americans outside direct federal control. Dix considered them an "embarrassment" to his operations. Small wonder. At the time of the preliminary Emancipation Proclamation, his entire military force numbered only about 23,000. He tried without success to interest Northern governors in bringing the contrabands to free states, but they considered such a step political suicide. Yet the contrabands not only represented an additional administrative and logistical burden, their presence also destabilized the slavery that still legally existed in this portion of Virginia. In the winter of 1862–63, Dix removed the contrabands to Craney Island in the James River estuary, hoping to ease his problem that way. He ordered it done humanely, but Union soldiers nevertheless chased the refugees down like so many rabbits, and in some instances, left women and children to shiver on wharves for two days before receiving transport to the island. Conditions on the island were terrible; disease and overcrowding contributed to a dreadful mortality rate. In the spring of 1863, Dix, hoping both to make the contrabands self-sufficient and isolate them from the Union troops who alternately detested and exploited them, finally approved efforts to place them on abandoned lands.[47]

A similar predicament confronted Major General Nathaniel P. Banks, the Union department commander in Louisiana. The Emancipation Proclamation applied in some parts of the state but not in others, yet slavery was in its death throes even where the proclamation did not obtain. Banks captured the problem succinctly: "The masters had rights in law . . . which they could not execute. The negroes enjoyed a freedom which they could not justify in law." He solved the problem through a system of contract labor. Devised by his predecessor, Ben Butler, the contract system as refined by Banks worked as follows: Blacks were "induced" to return to the

[47]Gerteis, *From Contraband to Freedman,* 26–28.

plantations "where they belong." (The alternative was arrest for vagrancy and forced service in public works projects.) Once on the plantations they were deemed to have acquiesced in a labor contract with the owner obligating them to a year of "diligent and faithful labor" and "subordinate deportment." Employers were to provide food, clothing, proper treatment (no whipping), and were to give the laborers either a monthly wage or one-twentieth of the crop, to be divided among all hands.[48]

This was far from a flawless solution. Because it amounted to forced labor, blacks constantly chafed at its restrictions and gave Union authorities no end of headaches. It soon developed that the employers refused to use old and invalid persons, so these had to be placed on "home farms" run by the Army. It also transpired that the planters insisted on the military's aid in enforcing control over their labor force. Banks tended to side with the planters, in large measure because the planters' interest coincided with the Army's own need for order. Provost marshals and guards sometimes intervened directly against "insubordinate" freedpeople. More frequently, they simply sided with planters when laborers complained of rough treatment. Either way, the task of organizing and maintaining the labor contract system absorbed an enormous amount of the Army's attention.

In relatively quiet sectors like tidewater Virginia and southern Louisiana, commanders might be able to afford such a drain on their time and resources. Where active operations were in prospect, however, such distractions seemed unacceptable. Intent on subduing Vicksburg, Ulysses S. Grant discovered that he was rapidly becoming swamped with refugees. He had put hundreds to work on military projects, but thousands more kept appearing, and in mid-February 1863 he tried to staunch the flood. Henceforth, Grant directed, "the enticing of Negroes to leave their homes to come into the lines of our army is positively forbidden." Those already within Union camps would not be turned out, but no more refugees would be accepted, and if the army should want additional military laborers it would acquire them as needed.[49]

Grant promptly informed General-in-Chief Halleck of his decision. For six weeks Halleck said nothing, suggesting by implication that he considered Grant's decision acceptable. But on the last day of March 1863, apparently under pressure from Secretary of War Stanton, he told Grant to rescind his exclusion order. The government's policy, he reminded his subordinate, was to "withdraw from the enemy as much productive labor as possible. . . . Every slave withdrawn from the enemy is equivalent to a white man put *hors de combat*." The Union would use the ex-slaves as military laborers. It would use them as soldiers. Such measures might be mistaken, Halleck conceded, but "[t]heir good or bad policy is a matter of opinion before they are tried; their real character can only be determined by a fair trial." It was the duty of every officer to give them such a trial.[50]

---

[48]Ibid., 65–82.

[49]Special Field Orders No. 2, February 12, 1863, OR 24, pt. 3:46–47.

[50]Grant to Halleck, February 18, 1863, ibid., pt. 1:18; Halleck to Grant, March 31, 1863, ibid., pt. 3:157.

Halleck concluded with a broader comment on the direction the conflict had taken:

The character of the war has now very much changed within the last year. There is now no possible hope of reconciliation with the rebels. The Union party in the South is virtually destroyed. There can be no peace but what is forced by the sword. We must conquer the rebels or be conquered by them. The North must conquer the slave oligarchy or become slaves themselves – the manufacturers mere "hewers of wood and drawers of water" to Southern aristocrats.

Here was the nub of the matter. The complexities of emancipation might sometimes be burdensome. As an economic weapon it might be flawed. Even as a device to tap new reservoirs of military manpower it might ultimately prove misguided. But as a symbol of Northern resolve, a touchstone of its intention to smash the slaveholding aristocracy that had spawned secession, emancipation was indispensable. It meant that the Lincoln administration would crush the rebellion by any means necessary.[51]

[51] Ibid. The quoted phrase refers to Joshua 9:21.

From pragmatism to hard war

Grant's postwar narrative of his campaign against Vicksburg includes a famous vignette that vividly conjures up the advent of hard war. In May 1863, just after defeating a rebel detachment, Grant's army entered Jackson, Mississippi. At Grant's order, Union soldiers went to work, wrecking the town's railroad connections and destroying its war factories. Accompanied by Sherman, Grant then paid a personal visit to one textile mill, which, he remarked dryly, "had not ceased work on account of the battle nor for the entrance of Union troops." The operatives – most of them women – continued to work oblivious of their visitors. In imagination, one can see the two travel-stained generals laconically chewing their ubiquitous cigars amid the din and bustle of production. Yard upon yard of tent cloth spews forth from the looms, the initials "C.S.A." woven prominently into each bolt. Outside the factory, a small mountain of cotton is stacked and baled and waiting for the looms. Finally Grant turns to his trusted lieutenant. "I told Sherman I thought they had done work enough. The operatives were told they could leave and take with them what cloth they could carry." His narrative concludes with one brief, matter-of-fact sentence: "In a few minutes cotton and factory were in a blaze."[1]

As Grant's account suggests, his operations during the spring and summer of 1863 saw the application of recognizably hard war measures. Indeed, they inaugurated the new strategy. To be sure, the conflict had already generated considerable destruction, and some of it was quite as bad as anything the struggle would ever produce. The war was not yet a year old before at least seven villages were destroyed or heavily damaged by Union troops. German-American troops had set fire to Fayetteville, Virginia, on October 19, 1861; two days later, other Federals did the same to Fredericktown, Missouri. Ohio home guardsmen, enraged by guerrilla activity just across the Ohio River from their homes, crossed into Guyandotte, Virginia, and burned much of that town on November 10. Three communities – the Missouri villages of Dayton and Columbus and Logan Court House, Virginia – were heavily damaged by fire in January 1862, while Winton, North Carolina, went up in flames

---

[1] Grant, *Memoirs* 1:507.

in mid-February. Since then Union forces had similarly damaged a dozen or more Southern towns.[2]

Some of this destruction had been sheer vandalism, but most had occurred in retaliation, deserved or otherwise, for bushwhacking and other partisan incidents. In that sense it might be considered, like Sherman's burning of Randolph, Tennessee, simply a rigorous application of the pragmatic policy. Railroads and canals had also been attacked, but such actions were solidly in the time-honored tradition of interdicting enemy lines of supply. From the outset of the conflict, both sides regarded the capture or destruction of railroad property as legitimate. The Confederates seized or wrecked a large amount of rolling stock at Harpers Ferry in May 1861; they also burned railroad bridges in that vicinity. When Union forces knifed into western and middle Tennessee, rebel cavalry and guerrillas inaugurated a campaign against Union trains and Union-occupied railroads that persisted until the end of the war. During the Maryland Campaign, Lee's Army of Northern Virginia unsuccessfully attempted to wreck key sections of the Chesapeake and Ohio Canal. Had he succeeded in his bid to carry the war into Pennsylvania, one of Lee's objectives was the destruction of a key railroad bridge across the Susquehanna River at Harrisburg – which was indeed destroyed during the Gettysburg Campaign the following June. Union detachments in North Carolina and elsewhere also mounted raids to destroy segments of the Confederate rail grid. In short, when Sherman's men began to dismantle the railroads, water towers, engine houses and switching stations in and around Jackson in May 1863, they were doing nothing new. The same was true of their demolition of warehouses and factories in the town, for that had been the fate of foundries and mills, when obviously engaged in support of the enemy war effort, since the early months of the war.[3]

Nevertheless, the year 1863 marked a significant watershed, because during that year one can see the emergence of large-scale destruction carried out, in fairly routine fashion, by large bodies of troops. The difference was less qualitative than quantitative. What mattered was not the novelty of such actions, but rather their dramatic expansion in scale. Even so, a combination of strategic insight and practical circumstances meant that the first resort to hard war was largely confined to Grant's army. As has been seen, the Army of the Potomac abstained from anything similar, while units along the coast conducted such operations on only the most modest scale. Yet Grant

---

[2] Grebner, *We Were the Ninth,* 76–77; report of Colonel J.B. Plummer, October 31, 1861, *Official Records* 3:209; report of Adjutant J.C. Wheeler, November 13, 1861, ibid. 5:412; report of Lieutenant Colonel D.R. Anthony, January 4, 1862, ibid. 8:45–46; and Anthony's report, January 13, 1862, ibid., 46–47; report of Colonel E. Siber, January 23, 1862, ibid. 5:502. On Winton, North Carolina, see Chapter 3.

[3] John D. Imboden, "Jackson at Harper's Ferry in 1861," in Buel and Johnson (eds.), *Battles and Leaders of the Civil War* 1:122–123; Frank E. Vandiver, *Mighty Stonewall* (New York: McGraw-Hill, 1957), 147, 148; and reports of a Union action near Vienna, June 16, 1861, *Official Records* 2:128–129. Freeman, *Lee's Lieutenants* 2:160n; ibid., 3:33; and Barrett, *Civil War in North Carolina,* 131–148 passim. Report of Colonel John W. Geary, October 18, 1861, *Official Records* 5:242; report of Major General Nathaniel Banks, December 20, [1861], ibid., 398; and report of Colonel Samuel H. Dunning, January 9, 1862, ibid., 405.

did not inaugurate the new policy in isolation. He merely applied a program already being espoused in the highest policy-making circles of Washington.

THE VIEW FROM THE TOP

In the period after the Emancipation Proclamation, Northern policymakers increasingly came to grips with the fact that the nature of the war had decisively changed. The year-end report of Quartermaster General Montgomery C. Meigs, for example, stressed the virtues of living off the enemy, and lamented that the army had long been slow to "learn the inevitable necessities of success;" it had been too tender about enemy property. "The horses, hay, and grain of the rebellious States were spared by our troops, though freely at the service of the insurgents." Fortunately, Meigs reported with satisfaction, Union forces had recently learned to depend on the country for part of their supplies, which, "though not making war support war entirely," nevertheless helped relieve the burden on the Federal treasury. "Our people are being slowly schooled to arms, and the war, thus far singularly free from the outrage which in other countries has attended civil commotions, begins at length, by its inevitable destruction of property and life, to bear upon the territory we occupy with a portion of the fearful weight necessary to crush rebellion."[4]

Halleck played a key role in explaining this change to western commanders, particularly in an important policy statement first issued to Rosecrans on March 5, 1863, and subsequently distributed to several other department commanders as well. The statement was occasioned by a letter from Major General J.J. Reynolds, a division commander in the Army of the Cumberland. Disgusted by rebel depredations upon Unionists living in middle Tennessee, Reynolds urged Federal armies to "[d]espoil the rebels as the rebel army has despoiled the Union men. Send the rebels out of the country, and make safe room for the return of loyal men. Let these loyal men feel that the country is once more in their possession instead of being possessed by their oppressors. Aid them in its possession for awhile, and they will soon acquire confidence sufficient to hold it." His superiors had liked the idea and sent it to Halleck for his consideration.[5]

In a response addressed to Rosecrans, Halleck approved Reynolds' suggestion regarding "a more rigid treatment of all disloyal persons within the lines of your army." He declined to issue further orders on the subject, since Rosecrans, like other Federal commanders, had already been "urged to procure your subsistence, forage, and means of transportation, so far as possible, in the country occupied." Furthermore, unless he received orders to the contrary, Rosecrans as an army commander had full power to "enforce all laws and usages of war, however severe they may be. . . ." It was up to him, the commander on the spot, to determine when it was best to apply these

---

[4]Quartermaster General's Annual Report, November 18, 1862, ibid., Series II, vol. 2:806, 809.
[5]Reynolds to Major George E. Flynt, February 10, 1863, ibid. 23, pt. 2:55–57.

laws rigidly, or when "a more lenient course is of greater advantage to our cause."[6] Even so, Halleck continued, Rosecrans should always make distinctions among the inhabitants of areas in which his army operated, and he went on to outline the trinary division that had become common among Federal commanders. "The people of the country in which you are likely to operate may be divided into three classes," Halleck wrote. The first class embraced the "truly loyal, who neither aid nor assist the rebels, except under compulsion, but who favor or assist the Union forces." Halleck advised that unless absolutely necessary, Union forces should refrain from requisitioning supplies from such people, who should receive active protection. If it became necessary to take their property, for whatever reason, they should either be paid in cash or else fully indemnified, with receipts given.

The second class encompassed those "who take no active part in the war, but belong to the class known in military law as noncombatants." Strictly speaking, to be sure, they were noncombatants by courtesy only, since in a civil war there was no such thing as neutrality – one was either a loyal citizen or an enemy sympathizer. Even so, "so long as they commit no hostile act, and confine themselves to their private avocations," they should be left alone as much as possible – "nor is their property to be seized, except as a military necessity." However, they remained subject to forced loans, military requisitions, and to have their houses used as soldiers' billets. If they remained passive, they would be accorded protection. But if after receiving protection they took up arms against the occupiers, or aided and abetted the enemy, then they would become "war rebels, or military traitors" – the penalty for which was death, and/or the seizure of their property.

The third class consisted of those who did not bear arms for the enemy but who remained "openly and obviously hostile to the occupying army." For such people Halleck authorized severe measures:

Such persons not only incur all the obligations imposed upon other non-combatant inhabitants of the same territory, and are liable to the same punishment for offenses committed, but they may be treated as prisoners of war, and be subjected to the rigors of confinement or to expulsion as combatant enemies. I am of the opinion that such persons should not, as a general rule, be permitted to go at large within our lines. To force those capable of bearing arms to go within the lines of the enemy adds to his effective forces; to place them in confinement will require guards for their safekeeping, and this necessarily diminishes our active forces in the field. You must determine in each particular case which course will be most advantageous. We have suffered very severely from this class, and it is time that the laws of war should be more rigorously enforced against them. A broad line of distinction must be drawn between friends and enemies, between the loyal and the disloyal.[7]

In preparing this letter, Halleck was almost certainly guided by his inside knowledge of a major War Department policy statement then in the works. A committee of five officers and one civilian had begun to prepare a set of general instructions for the

[6]Halleck to Rosecrans, March 5, 1863, ibid., 107.
[7]Ibid., 107–108.

Maj. Gen. Henry W. Halleck, author of a respected treatise on international law, began the war with a conservative mindset but never embraced conciliation. He fully concurred in the Lincoln administration's repudiation of it. "There can be no peace but what is forced by the sword," he wrote in March 1863. "The North must conquer the slave oligarchy or become slaves themselves." (Courtesy, Civil War Times Illustrated Collection)

Lieut. Gen. Ulysses S. Grant made the first experiments with "hard war" in mid-1863. As commander of the Union armies in 1864–1865, he presided over its adoption as a major instrument of Northern victory. "This policy," he maintained after the war, "exercised a material influence in hastening the end." (Courtesy, National Archives, Washington)

conduct of Union armies in the field. Six weeks after Halleck's letter to Rosecrans, the War Department published the committee's handiwork. Known officially as General Order No. 100, the instructions were more commonly called "Lieber's Code," after Francis Lieber, the civilian committeeman who wrote practically the entire document.

Lieber was a German-born jurist and author of a number of learned legal treatises, most notably two books entitled *Political Ethics* (published in 1838) and *Civil Liberty and Self Government* (1853). An antislavery activist, he had admired John Brown's 1859 Harpers Ferry raid, and had written the following year that Americans stood sorely in need of "a daily spanking like a naughty boy." A devastating crisis, like the one Napoleon had visited on Lieber's native Prussia in 1806, might benefit the United States and lead to "regeneration"; and while it might be wicked to pray for such a calamity, he had maintained stoutly that "as a historian I have a right to say that when nations go on recklessly as we do – dancing, drinking, laughing, defying right, morality and justice, money-making and murdering – God in his mercy has sometimes condescended to smite them, and smite them hard, in order to bring them to their senses, and make them recover themselves. . . ." Such was the austere vision that created "Lieber's Code."[8]

When the war broke out, Lieber vigorously supported the North's war effort. Tragically, his youngest son entered the Confederate forces and died in May 1862. His other two boys enlisted in the Union army. When one of them lost an arm at Fort Donelson, Lieber traveled to Tennessee to succor him, and there met Halleck. With a mutual interest in international law, both men knew each other's work and began a cordial personal relationship. In August 1862, Halleck asked Lieber for his views on guerrilla warfare. "The rebel authorities," he wrote, "claim the right to send men, in the garb of peaceful citizens, to waylay and attack our troops, to burn bridges and houses and to destroy property and persons within our lines. They demand that such persons be treated as ordinary belligerents." Lieber, already at work on the question independently, responded with a thick essay that landed on Halleck's desk before the month was out. It basically drew a distinction between "partisans" – officially authorized troops who merely adopted irregular tactics – and "self-constituted guerrillas." The first class, provided they wore uniforms or some distinguishing identification, were indeed entitled to treatment as ordinary belligerents. The second, however, were simply "freebooters," "brigands," or "assassins," and entitled to nothing but summary execution. Halleck thanked him for the effort and ordered 5,000 copies for distribution to the army.[9]

[8]Francis Lieber, *Manual of Political Ethics,* 2 vols. (Philadelphia: J.B. Lippincott, 1890 [1837]); and idem., *On Civil Liberty and Self Government* (Philadelphia: J.B. Lippincott, 1859 [1853]). For background on Lieber, see Frank Freidel, *Francis Lieber, Nineteenth Century Liberal* (Baton Rouge: Louisiana State University Press, 1947). Quoted in George M. Fredrickson, *The Inner Civil War: Northern Intellectuals and the Crisis of the Union* (paperback ed., New York: Harper Torchbooks, 1968 [1965]), 48.

[9]Richard Shelly Hartigan, *Lieber's Code and the Law of War* (Chicago: Precedent, 1983), 6–7. Halleck to Lieber, August 6, 1862, *Official Records,* Series III, vol. 2, p. 301. See Francis Lieber, "Guerrilla Parties Considered with Reference to the Laws and Usages of War," reprinted in Hartigan, *Lieber's Code,* 31–44. Halleck to Lieber, August 20, 1862, ibid., 78.

But Lieber had a larger project in mind. In November 1862, he wrote Halleck that "since the beginning of our present War, it has appeared clearer and clearer to me, that the President ought to issue a set of rules and definitions providing for the most urgent issues occurring under the Law and usages of War, and on which our Articles of War are silent." Halleck brushed him off – "I have no time at present to consider the subject" – but Lieber persisted, and in December Halleck created a committee to explore the issue.[10]

The resulting code had propaganda as well as legal purpose. Even as he labored on the new military guidelines, Lieber also played a dominant role in the creation of the Loyal Publication Society, whose mission was to oppose the Peace Democrats and rally support for a vigorous prosecution of the war. Like many good Republicans, Lieber had felt frustration during the conciliatory phase of the struggle, and in August had written Halleck that "loyal men . . . have longed for vigour and decision, [but] they have felt as though the government was not sufficiently in earnest. They have longed for concentrated blows, physical and moral, and the government has directed a scattered pelting." Unformulated but redolent within Lieber's thought was the awareness that the end of conciliation, the military confiscation order, and the issuance of the Emancipation Proclamation all indicated that the time for war in earnest had arrived. But how to conduct this new contest in a manner that would reflect well on the Union cause?[11]

General Order No. 100 offered Lieber's response. As one commentator has remarked, it was "less a rigid legal code than a persuasively written essay on the ethics of conducting war." It was also the western world's first formal set of guidelines for the conduct of armies in the field. As such, it had a profound impact on subsequent international law. Lieber anticipated this, and wrote Halleck that General Order No. 100 "will do honor to our country. It will be adopted as a basis for similar works by the English, French and Germans. It is a contribution by the U.S. to the stock of common civilization."[12]

But although often touted as a humanitarian milestone, Lieber's Code was thoroughly dedicated to providing the ethical justification for a war aimed at the destruction of the Confederacy. The orders asserted the laudable conviction that "[m]en who take up arms against one another in public war do not cease on this account to be moral beings, responsible to one another and to God." Yet they also insisted: "The more vigorously wars are pursued the better it is for humanity. Sharp wars are brief."[13]

---

[10]Lieber to Halleck, November 13, 1862, ibid., 79; Halleck to Lieber, November 15, 1862, ibid., 80; Special Orders No. 399, December 17, 1862, *Official Records,* Series III, vol. 2, p. 951. The committee membership included Lieber, Major Generals Ethan A. Hitchcock, George Cadwallader, George L. Hartsuff, and Brigadier General J. H. Martindale.

[11]Fredrickson, *Inner Civil War,* 131; Lieber to Halleck, August 1, 1862, Hartigan, *Lieber's Code,* 76.

[12]Frank Freidel, "General Orders 100 and Military Government," *Mississippi Valley Historical Review* 32 (March 1946):549. Lieber to Halleck, May 20, 1863, Hartigan, *Lieber's Code,* 108. For the long-term significance of Lieber's Code, see Hartigan, *Lieber's Code,* passim., and Best, *Humanity in Warfare,* 155–259 passim.

[13]Hartigan, *Lieber's Code,* reprints General Order No. 100 in full. For the quoted material, see pp. 48, 50 – paragraphs 15 and 29, respectively. See also General Order No. 100, April 24, 1863, *Official Records,* Series III, vol. 3:148–164.

Much of General Order No. 100 dealt with conduct toward enemy combatants – treatment of wounded, prisoners of war, flags of truce, and similar matters. It also incorporated Lieber's earlier conclusions about guerrilla warfare. But significant portions discussed the status of enemy civilians and property. At the core of this discussion lay Lieber's definition of military necessity: "those measures which are indispensable for securing the ends of the war, and which are lawful according to the modern law and usages of war." In theory, its potential was sweeping; it "allows of all destruction of property, and obstruction of the ways and channels of traffic, travel, or communication, and of all withholding of subsistence or means of life from the enemy; of the appropriation of whatever an enemy's country affords necessary for the subsistence and safety of the Army. . . ."[14]

However, Lieber wrote, "it does *not* permit the wanton devastation of a district . . . and, in general, military necessity does not include any act of hostility which makes the return to peace unnecessarily difficult." Although most forms of public property should be appropriated by the occupying army as a matter of course, churches, hospitals, and educational establishments were to be protected. And "[p]rivate property, unless forfeited by crimes or by offenses of the owner, can be seized only by way of military necessity, for the support or other benefit of the Army or of the United States." Lieber's Code also prohibited "wanton violence," pillaging, unauthorized destruction, and so on – "even after taking a place by main force." It even stipulated that officers might lawfully kill soldiers who committed such acts on the spot.[15]

Lieber himself was disturbed by persistent reports of malicious or unnecessary destruction by Union troops. Shortly after his code was issued, he wrote Halleck privately asking him to issue "a strong order, directing attention to those paragraphs in the Code which prohibit devastations, demolition of private property, etc." Lieber had received reports of wanton destruction of property by Union troops, and found them alarming. "It does incalculable injury," he wrote. "It demoralizes our troops, it annihilates wealth irrevocably and makes a return to a state of peace and peaceful minds more and more difficult." Yet Lieber's Code included little that dealt explicitly with a belligerent's obligations toward civilians. Thus it erected few strong barriers against severe treatment.[16]

Indeed, several paragraphs of the Code argued that protection to enemy civilians was the exception, not the rule. The Code also endorsed the age-old principle of military retaliation – which kept the door open for further Randolph-style reprisals – and its section on hostages did not address the taking of hostages to deter guerrilla action, a dubious but not-uncommon practice among some Union commanders. It did repeat the trinary division of enemy noncombatants into the loyal, who merited protection, and two classes of the disloyal – "those citizens known to sympathize with the rebellion without positively aiding it, and those who, without taking arms, give positive aid and comfort to the rebellious enemy without being bodily forced

[14]Hartigan, *Lieber's Code*, 48.
[15]Ibid.
[16]Lieber to Halleck, May 20, 1863, Hartigan, *Lieber's Code*, 109.

thereto." But the Code merely stated that "[t]he commander will throw the burden of the war, as much as lies within his power, on the disloyal citizens," without differentiating between the two classes of disloyal citizens and without setting concrete limits to what might be done provided it was a "military necessity." The range of permissible actions was thus made, in large degree, a matter of the motivations of Union commanders.[17]

Lieber's Code, then, was ambiguous. On the one hand, it enjoined Union forces to behave with humanity. On the other, it declined to set specific limits on what those forces might do to achieve victory, and largely prohibited only unauthorized destruction. It also included that pregnant sentence, "The more vigorously wars are pursued the better it is for humanity." The line between wanton destruction and vigorous prosecution, in Lieber's formulation, was hazy at best. He left discernment of its exact location to the judgment – sound or otherwise – of the commander on the scene. In itself, General Order No. 100 codified the pragmatic conception of policy toward Southern civilians. But taken together with other War Department statements from the same period, it opened the door to the hard war measures of the conflict's final years.

GRANT AND SHERMAN IN MISSISSIPPI: JANUARY– AUGUST 1863

After the failure of his initial overland campaign against Vicksburg, Grant took most of his army down to Milliken's Bend, a few miles up the Mississippi River from the Confederate fortress. While in this region, Federal troops routinely augmented their rations locally. They also practiced area denial, making efforts not only to supply themselves from the countryside, but also to prevent the Confederates from doing so. They achieved this sometimes by confiscating crops and livestock and sometimes by destroying them. In early April, for example, Brigadier General Frederick Steele took his division to Deer Creek, Mississippi, gathered about a thousand horses, mules, and cattle, as well as many wagons and buggies, and burned about 500,000 bushels of corn. Part of the severity stemmed from incidents of bushwhacking near Greenville on the Mississippi River. His orders from Sherman specified that "one object of your expedition is to let the planters and inhabitants on Deer Creek see and feel that they will be held accountable for acts of guerrillas and Confederate soldiers who sojourn in their country for the purpose of firing on our boats passing Greenville. . . ." Yet Steele was not to inflict indiscriminate punishment. Planters who stayed at home and remained passive were to be molested as little as possible. Those who fled would be considered disloyal, "and you can take their hogs, corn, or anything you need." Similarly, cotton that was clearly private property should be left alone, but cotton

---

[17]Ibid., 49–50, 71. For a more extended discussion of the limitations of Lieber's Code as it applied to noncombatant immunity, see Johnson, *Just War Tradition*, 312–316.

marked "C.S.A." was to be brought away and burned. Sherman's instructions went on to authorize Steele's men to seize or destroy all provisions required by the army or which might be used by the Confederate army in Vicksburg. But he was to leave what the "peaceful inhabitants" needed to survive. Significantly, Sherman's orders referred only to the planter class, not non-slaveholding whites. Thus, what Sherman had in mind was indeed severity, but it was a directed severity aimed primarily at the disloyal planter class.[18]

Steele's troops, however, exceeded instructions, and destroyed "everything there was to eat on the plantations," not just the surplus that would have gone to the Confederate army. An Iowa soldier wrote home that "We burnt every thing & took all the Horses Mules & Niggars that we came acrost our train resembled a Fantastic Company on general Traning [sic] day." He estimated that the division had destroyed over a million bushels of grain and at least fifty cotton gins and grist mills.[19]

Steele regretted the overzealousness, and proposed to return the carriages, buggies, and farming tools that had been seized from Deer Creek families, so that the civilians would be able to plant a crop. Sherman concurred. "War at best is barbarism, but to involve all – children, women, old and helpless – is more than can be justified. Our men will become absolutely lawless unless this can be checked. . . . We surely have [a right to take] corn, cotton, fodder, &c., used to sustain armies in war. Still, I always feel that the store necessary for a family should be spared, and I think it injures our men to allow them to plunder indiscriminately the inhabitants of the country."[20]

The army command remained concerned with abuses and vandalism. The worst of these were occasions when Northern troops committed acts of arson, as in mid-January 1863 when some anonymous Federals set fire to the town of Napoleon, Arkansas. Sherman gave instructions to save as many buildings as possible, and told his brother-in-law that he "would throw the man who started the fire into the flames if he caught him." In his official report of the episode, he wrote that since it would be impossible to fix blame on the perpetrators, the only way to apply a remedy will be to assess the damages upon the whole army, officers included. "No man in the army," Sherman added, "has labored harder than I have to check this spirit in our soldiers,

---

[18]Sherman to Steele, March 31, 1863, *Official Records* 24, pt. 3:158. See also the report of Brigadier General Stephen G. Burbridge, December 27, 1862, ibid. 17, pt. 1:629–630. Shortly before the Battle of Chickasaw Bluffs, Sherman detached Burbridge's brigade with orders to destroy the line of the Lake Providence and Tallulah Telegraph, which he did. His brigade also took 196 head of cattle, which may or may not have been in the hands of rebel forces, and wrecked the Vicksburg, Shreveport and Texas Railroad for a distance of about half a mile. The brigade also burned a great deal of cotton and other supplies, most of which seemed destined for the Confederate government.

[19]Report of Brigadier General Frederick Steele, April 10, 1863, ibid. 17, pt. 1:502. Robert Bruce Hoadley to his cousin, May 29, 1863, Robert Bruce Hoadley Papers, DUL. "General training day" was an annual slave holiday common on Southern plantations. See also "Galway" [a Union cavalry major and soldier-journalist] in the *New York Times,* April 24, 1863: "It may be said here that the cotton-gins, mills, &c., of the only Union family on the route [of Steele's march], were given to the flames, the same as those of others. In this case, as in nearly all the others, the ardor of our soldiers carried them away so much that they never waited for orders to set fire to a corn-mill or haystack, but did it at once as a matter of course."

[20]Sherman to Steele, April 19, 1863, *Official Records* 24, pt. 3:209. See also Sherman to Rawlins, April 19, 1863, ibid., 208.

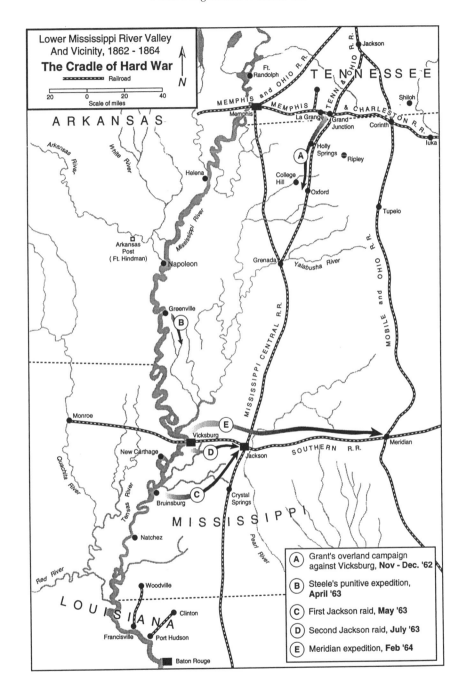

Lower Mississippi River Valley
And Vicinity, 1862 - 1864
The Cradle of Hard War
Railroad
20   0   20   40
Scale of miles
N

A Grant's overland campaign
   against Vicksburg, **Nov - Dec. '62**

B Steele's punitive expedition,
   April '63

C First Jackson raid, **May '63**

D Second Jackson raid, **July '63**

E Meridian expedition, **Feb '64**

and I am free to admit we all deserve to be killed unless we can produce a state of discipline when such disgraceful acts cannot be committed unpunished."[21]

In March, a Union colonel was outraged to see troops aboard steamers taking potshots at cattle, or landing at a plantation to chase after poultry and pigs. Notifying his immediate superior of the incident, the colonel wrote that he had issued a stern order on the subject, and vowed that "with the grace of God sustaining me, I will enforce it if I have to shoot men both in and out of shoulder straps. We cannot make good soldiers out of thieves and robbers, neither can we expect success to follow us if thus we outrage every principle of truth and justice. I am ashamed to see our good cause thus prejudiced."[22]

Grant meanwhile pondered the capture of Vicksburg. Although geographically he was now much closer to the river fortress, his major strategic problem remained unsolved: how to get into a position from which the city could be attacked successfully? From January through April 1863, he tried a number of options, none of which succeeded. The common element in each of the foiled plans was that all were intended to establish a secure line of supply by which he might march against the city. Eventually, however, he decided against further attempts, and instead took one of the most daring gambles of the entire war.

On the night of April 16, 1863, Admiral David Dixon Porter, the naval officer in charge of the riverine flotilla cooperating with Grant's army, led part of his force on a midnight run directly under the guns along the Vicksburg bluffs. Darkness shielded Porter's vessels part of the way; even after the Confederates spotted them and opened fire, the Union squadron escaped with the loss of only one transport. More steamers made the dash five nights later. Once below the Vicksburg batteries, Porter's fleet awaited the arrival of Grant's army, which now took barges and shallow-draft steamers through a series of bayous that wound past Vicksburg on the Louisiana side of the river.

Forty miles east of Vicksburg lay Jackson, the state capital and a point at which four railroads converged. One of these led to Vicksburg. If Grant meant to seize Vicksburg, he would first need to choke off that crucial supply artery; for that reason, Jackson became his first big objective. Yet to march upon Jackson necessarily meant exposing his own line of supply to ruinous interdiction by the Confederate army at Vicksburg. Consequently Grant decided to maintain almost no supply line at all. Just as his troops had done after the disastrous raid upon Holly Springs, they would live mainly off the country. This time, however, the choice was deliberate.

The orders went out on April 20, and included a paragraph authorizing commanders to collect cattle, corn and other supplies along the line of march. But they

---

[21]Entry for January 18, 1863, Ms. diary, Hugh B. Ewing Papers, OHS; Sherman to Lieutenant Colonel Walter B. Scates, January 17, 1863, OR 17, pt. 2, 572. For the ongoing concern to prevent abuses, see, for example, Sherman's General Order No. 3, January 12, 1863, ordering officers to locate and punish anyone with stolen private property (ibid., 556–557); and Grant to Hamilton, January 20, 1863, complaining of "outrageous conduct" by the notorious Seventh Kansas Cavalry – "Jennison's Jayhawkers." (ibid., 575).

[22]Colonel Clinton B. Fisk to Brigadier General Leonard F. Ross, March 6, 1863, ibid. 24, pt. 3:87.

also prohibited "wanton destruction of property, taking of articles, unless for military purposes, insulting citizens, [and] going into and searching houses without proper orders from division commanders. . . . All such irregularities will be summarily punished." Grant's troops began crossing the Mississippi at Bruinsburg ten days later. At the beginning of May, his three army corps headed inland, hugging the south bank of the Big Black River and guarding the ferries against any attempted crossings by Confederate troops. With them rattled along several hundred wagons loaded with ammunition and a few staples like salt and coffee. For the balance of their rations the troops depended on local plantations and farms. It worked. "We have fine times now," one of Grant's soldiers wrote home in early May. "We live fat. Plenty of the best beef and mutton. This is a great mutton country." The only thing lacking was coffee, but the men substituted "good sassifras tea." Since the army brought only a limited number of wagons along when it crossed the river, detachments also fanned out over the countryside to confiscate wagons and draft animals.[23]

As Grant's instructions made clear, the extensive foraging was intended simply to keep the army adequately supplied during its campaign. Inevitably, however, some soldiers abused the latitude implicit in such a system and vandalized local property. An Iowa soldier noted that abandoned plantations were particularly hard hit, with furniture broken up and scattered. Alarmed at such behavior, Major General James B. McPherson issued an order that forbade foraging except by authorized parties. He required it to be read every evening after evening roll call; sergeants memorized it so that they could recite it when adequate lighting was unavailable.[24]

The army fought two minor preliminary battles with detachments from the main Confederate army, and by the evening of May 13 had reached the vicinity of Jackson. Ahead of them, a small Confederate force under General Joseph E. Johnston barred entrance to the town. The next day, two Union corps attacked the rebels, forced them back, and entered the town. Since Grant did not intend to hold Jackson, he decided instead to destroy its war-related factories and wreck the railroad net in the area so as to hamstring Johnston if he returned to the town. He gave Sherman explicit instructions on May 14:

Designate a brigade from your command to guard the city. Collect stores and forage, and collect all public property of the enemy. . . . [Direct troops] to commence immediately the effectual destruction of the river railroad bridge and the road as far east as possible, as well as north and south. . . . Troops going east of the river should destroy all C.S.A. cotton and stores they find.

Sherman promptly complied and gave specific instructions for the destruction of the railroads. It must be "extended out as far as possible," he wrote, "and must be

[23]Special Orders No. 110, April 20, 1863, ibid. 24, pt. 3:213; Isaac Jackson to Moses Jackson, [May] 8, 1863, Joseph O. Jackson (ed.), *"Some of the Boys . . . ": The Civil War Letters of Isaac Jackson, 1862–1865* (Carbondale: Southern Illinois University Press, 1960), 90; Grant, *Memoirs* 1:493; Grant to Sherman, May 9, 1863, *Official Records* 24, pt. 2:285; U.S. Grant, "The Vicksburg Campaign," Buel and Johnson (eds.), *Battles and Leaders* 3:499.

[24]Entry for April 30, 1863, John Q. A. Campbell Diary, J.Q.A. Campbell Diaries, WRHS (see also Charles Brown Tompkins to his wife, May 6, 1863, Charles Brown Tompkins Papers, DUL; Brown, *History of the Fourth Minnesota*, 190.

complete. The rails and ties will be taken up and placed in stacks, and the ties set on fire, in order to warp the rails and so render them unfit for use." The brigade assigned to guard the town was instructed to destroy "everything public not needed by us," including types, printing presses, and sugar. The town arsenals, Confederate government foundry, and a factory for making gun carriages went up in smoke. (So did the state penitentiary, although in this case the inmates were probably responsible.) Sherman also elected to destroy "a very valuable cotton factory," but not without some hesitation. Its owners appealed for him to spare it, "based on the fact that it gave employment to very many females and poor families, and that, although it had woven cloth for the enemy, its principal use was in weaving cloth for the people." But Sherman decided that regardless of its primary current use, it could easily be converted to war production. He concluded that it was better for the Federal government to compensate the owners (who were apparently Unionists) and feed the poor families whose livelihood was destroyed, rather than leave the factory standing.[25]

At the same time, it irked him that some officers were treating the authorized destruction as an excuse to indulge simple thievery. Reports reached him that the provost marshal in Jackson was permitting soldiers to steal the contents of stores. "That, if true, is wrong," he told the commander of the brigade guarding the city. "Only such articles should be taken as necessary to the subsistence of troops, and the private rights of citizens should be respected. . . . The feeling of pillage and booty will injure the morals of the troops, and bring disgrace on our cause. Take every possible precaution against fires at the time of our leaving to-morrow."[26]

Despite Sherman's warning, at least two unauthorized fires occurred. Just as he was leaving Jackson, he later wrote, a "very fat man" came to see him and inquired if his hotel was going to be burned. "I told him we had no intention to burn it, or any other house, except the machine-shops, and such buildings as could easily be converted to hostile uses." The man professed to be a Unionist; Sherman replied, with heavy sarcasm, that this was obvious from the name of his lodge, the "Confederate Hotel." Even so, he insisted that he intended to leave it standing. But Union soldiers – reportedly bearing a personal grudge against the hotel keeper – burned the establishment anyway. A Catholic church also went up in flames, although Sherman concluded that its destruction was probably an accident. On the whole, he thought that as good discipline had been maintained as was possible in the circumstances, and he blamed much of the pillaging on "bad rum found concealed in the stores of the town."[27]

After burning Jackson's war manufactories, the Army of the Tennessee swung sharply west and headed for Vicksburg. Following two sharp fights at Champion's Hill on May 16 and at Big Black River the next day, Grant's army reached the outskirts of the river city on May 18. There it resumed contact with Porter's gunboats,

---

[25]Grant to Sherman, May 14, 1863, *Official Records* 24, pt. 3:312; Special Order No. 105, May 14, 1863, ibid.; Sherman to Mower, May 15, 1863, ibid., 314, and General Order No. 35, May 15, 1863, ibid., 315; Sherman's Report, May 24, 1863, ibid., pt 1:754.

[26]Sherman to Mower, May 15, 1863, ibid., pt. 3:315.

[27]Sherman, *Memoirs* 1:322; Report of William T. Sherman, May 24, 1863, *Official Records* 24, pt. 1:755.

reestablished a solid line of supply, and began the siege operations that would end with Vicksburg's surrender on July 4.

In the meantime, Grant sent out strong detachments with orders to strip the region of provisions and forage, as well as to destroy railroad bridges. "All negroes, teams, and cattle should be brought in," he explained to one subordinate, "and everything done to prevent an army coming this way supplying itself." Johnston still hovered with his relief force to the northeast of Grant's army, gathering additional troops and looking for a way to help the garrison trapped in Vicksburg to defeat Grant. Grant's policy of systematically stripping the countryside was designed to deny Johnston an opening.[28]

Such operations during the Vicksburg campaign illustrate the strong linkage between actions taken against the Southern economic infrastructure and those against Confederate forces on the battlefield. In most respects they formed clear examples of the emergent hard war strategy. But they were not yet intended to achieve results independently of the traditional battlefield orientation. And while they surely placed substantial hardship on Southern civilians, neither Grant nor anyone else saw this destruction as more than an unfortunate byproduct of military necessity. His orders at the outset of the spring campaign against Vicksburg illustrate this point. So do his instructions to Lieutenant Colonel Samuel J. Nasmith, when he ordered Nasmith to capture an enemy artillery battery reportedly near Greenville, Mississippi. "On your return, in case of pursuit, destroy all bridges and corn-cribs, bring away all negroes disposed to follow you, and teams of [horses] to haul them and their plunder," Grant wrote, but "[k]eep your men out of the houses as much as possible, and prevent plundering." Grant also wanted Nasmith to pin the blame for any harshness on the Confederate army. "Give the people to understand if their troops make raids necessary, all their crops and means of raising crops will be destroyed." In short, Grant's main objective was simply to deny the enemy supplies that might support a bid to relieve besieged Vicksburg.[29]

The same directed severity was evident in his instructions to Major General Stephen Hurlbut, the commander in charge of his primary supply base at Memphis. As his campaign against Vicksburg swung into action, he ordered Hurlbut to use his cavalry to divert attention from his own movements. They were to seize livestock and destroy corn, wheat, and "everything that can be made use of by the enemy in prolonging the war." But they were not to enter private homes or destroy anything without military purpose. "In other words, cripple the rebellion in every way, without insulting women and children or taking their clothing, jewelry, &c."[30]

Some soldiers found this brand of warfare unobjectionable. "Had the Feds always done as they are now doing – fight with sword in one hand, and the torch in the other! – I believe the war would have been over long ago. No man in his sober sense,

---

[28]Grant to Brigadier General Peter J. Osterhaus, May 26, 1863, *Official Records* 24, pt. 3:351. See also Grant to Mower, June 2, 1863, ibid., 375.

[29]Grant to Nasmith, June 25, 1863, ibid., 437.

[30]Grant to Hurlbut, May 5, 1863, ibid., 274–275.

would leave a club in [the] enemies' [sic] hand to have his own head broken with." Others were more troubled. When Hurlbut began making raids as Grant had ordered, a participant reflected that the whole thing was somewhat disturbing. "While I cant but agree that [it] is doing a great deal toward weakening the enemy," he wrote home, "I can't but feel a kind of a sense of injustice connected with it. It appears too much like rob[b]ing, indiscriminately, the *innocent* with the *guilty,* the *poor* with the *rich,* and causing to suffer alike, the *just* with the *unjust,* the [illegible] poor with the aristocratical rich. . . . But then, in war you know we are not able to make those nice distinctions as one observed in civil life."[31]

Even so, some distinctions were in fact observed. Hurlbut evidently required his troops to confine their authorized severities to Mississippians only – Federal authorities tended to regard Tennessee as already in the process of Reconstruction. In mid-June, for example, Major John Henry received orders to leave Memphis with 500 cavalry and raid northern Mississippi: "Suffer no property to be disturbed in Tennessee, but in Mississippi you will seize all the horses and mules and able-bodied male negroes that you can find, and destroy all crops and implements of agriculture that you find below Hernando, where you can do so without delaying your movements." Henry's instructions also warned, "Suffer no pillage of houses or insult to defenseless people."[32]

Hard on the heels of Vicksburg's surrender, Grant dispatched Sherman with orders to return to Jackson, drive Joseph Johnston's army once more from the town (which it had reoccupied), and "do the enemy all the harm possible." Implicit in these orders was the intention to obviate the need to occupy Jackson permanently by completing the job of destruction begun in May. Sherman's orders for the movement contained the usual stern words about depredations – "Private pillage and plunder must cease; our supplies are now ample, and there is no use or sense in wanton pillage." Brigade quartermasters and commissaries could collect such forage and provisions as might be required, but they must do so through supervised foraging parties and "the people of the country should be protected as far as possible against the cruel and wanton acts of irresponsible parties. Stragglers and camp-followers found out of place should be dealt with summarily."[33]

Sherman's corps reached Jackson on July 9. Rather than attacking Johnston's army head on, Union artillery blasted the Confederate defenders while Northern infantry dug lines of contravallation around the western end of the town. On the evening of the 16th, Johnston evacuated Jackson and headed east. It was, all in all, a creditable exhibition of conventional battlefield tactics. What was already happening away from

[31]George Hovey Cadman to his wife, May 9, 1863, George Hovey Cadman Letters, SHC (I have slightly altered the punctuation of this passage in order to clarify its meaning); Davis Halderman to David Clark, June 4, 1863, Todd D. Miller Collection, Jeromesville, Ohio.

[32]Brigadier General James C. Veatch [District of Memphis] to Major John Henry, June 17, 1863, OR 24, pt. 3:416–417. Lincoln's executive order of July 22, 1862 (General Order No. 109, August 19, 1862) specifically excluded Tennessee from the list of states in which military confiscation was encouraged.

[33]Grant to Sherman, July 3, 1863, OR 24, pt. 3:461; Grant, *Memoirs* 2:576; Special Orders No. 53, July 6, 1863, OR 24, pt. 3:482.

the battlefield, however – and what would happen to Jackson once Federal troops occupied the town – was something new. On July 13, Grant had sent further instructions for Sherman "to break up Johnston's army and divert it from our rear, and, if possible, to destroy the rolling stock and everything valuable for carrying on war, or placing it beyond the reach of the rebel army. . . ." With Vicksburg in Union hands and Johnston's army beaten and in full retreat – it would "perish by heat, thirst, and disappointment," Sherman crowed – little more, by the usual rules, remained to be done. Yet during the following days, Sherman divided his corps into working parties and they set to work. Infantry meticulously dismantled the railroads for ten miles on every side of the city. Cavalry departed with orders to break the critical Mississippi Central Railroad at many places – it was, Sherman informed Grant, "to be so effectually destroyed that the enemy will not even attempt its reconstruction." Other troops wrecked Jackson's remaining factories and burned the massive, heaped-up cotton bales that rebel infantry had used for breastworks. Meanwhile foraging parties swarmed over the countryside.[34]

Superficially it resembled the previous raid against Jackson two months before. Yet the military situation was now quite different. There was no delicate siege underway against a formidable enemy army and no relief force hovering in the area. There was, in short, little need for such destruction if the objective were the "pragmatic" one of preventing an enemy force from operating against Union troops in the area. Similarly, the Union supply lines were now restored and providing troops with ample food. Thus there was no pressing necessity to live off the land. What happened around Jackson during mid-July 1863 was unmistakably different from what had gone before. It was a clear attempt to destroy the region's economic value to the Confederacy, without significant other factors at work. And it was done with a thoroughness unusual, if not altogether unprecedented.

"Our foraging parties now go out about fifteen miles, but are invariably guarded by a regiment of infantry," Sherman reported to Grant on July 14. "We are absolutely stripping the country of corn, hogs, sheep, poultry, everything, and the new-growing corn is being thrown open as pasture fields or hauled for the use of our animals." *Absolutely stripping* was a new note and a sharp contrast with previous policy, which had stressed the need to leave local inhabitants with enough food to get by. The self-justifying tone in Sherman's dispatch was also new, for such extensive destruction had previously been visited on a district only in retaliation for guerrilla activity. Sherman made no mention of such specifics, however. The rationale he gave – and it is curious, although characteristic, that he felt the need to offer one – emphasized a sort of loose but sweeping "war guilt":

The wholesale destruction to which this country is now being subjected is terrible to contemplate, but it is the scourge of war, to which ambitious men have appealed, rather than the judgment of the learned and pure tribunals which our forefathers had provided for supposed

---

[34]Grant to Sherman, July 13, 1863, ibid., 507; Sherman to Grant, July 17, 1863, ibid., pt. 1:528.

wrongs and injuries. Therefore, so much of my instructions as contemplated destroying and weakening the resources of our enemy are being executed with rigor. . . .

It sounds exactly like the theory of "collective responsibility" that John Bennett Walters insisted animated Sherman's policy toward Southern civilians by autumn 1862. More likely, however, the explanation for this outburst was a bit different.[35]

Sherman's orders for the movement against Jackson laid the usual stress on good troop conduct, and his instructions for the occupation of the town emphasized the repression of "all pillage, plundering, and rowdyism." The same directive enjoined the chief commissary to retain a supply of provisions, in part, "to relieve starving people." Nothing in the instructions contemplated anything like the wholesale severity Sherman described in his letter to Grant. By all rights, what happened in and around Jackson in July should have simply been a repeat of what had happened in May. Something had changed, but it was not Sherman's policy.[36]

It was instead the attitude of the rank and file. When the Northern soldiers entered the town they discovered a number of "torpedoes" – land mines – left by the departing Confederates, which wounded several men. The following day, a Union brigade commander described the vandalism that occurred to a library in the capitol building. "The torpedo trap had angered the troops," he explained, "& disinclined them to strict ward[ship] over the enemy's books, & they rapidly disappeared." So did many other items: A soldier who remained in camp outside Jackson noted that some of his comrades brought back "a good deal of plunder" when they returned from town. Then too, about this time Indiana and Ohio soldiers began to learn that rebel cavalry under Major General John Hunt Morgan had raided across the southern parts of their home states, burning barns and dwellings as they went. Several days after the Jackson raid, a midwestern soldier responded to a report that Morgan's men had stolen his father's horse and inflicted modest damage on his family's property. Writing home about it, he offered this comment on the army's reaction to Morgan's raid: "Some of the boys swear they will fire every house until they get satisfaction. Some of the Indiana troops say they intend to carry matches from now until the end of war." Moreover, the Confederates in leaving Jackson had themselves set fire to part of the town, and it is not difficult to understand how soldiers who might be reluctant to initiate an unauthorized act of arson could find it easy to help an existing blaze along. As Sherman noted, "The enemy burned nearly all the handsome dwellings round about the town because they gave us shelter or to light up the ground to prevent night attacks. He also set fire to a chief block of stores in which were commissary supplies, and our men, in spite of guards, have widened the circle of fire, so that Jackson, once the pride and boast of Mississippi, is now a ruined town."[37]

[35]Sherman to Grant, July 14, 1863, ibid., 526.

[36]General Order No. 54, July 17, 1863, ibid., pt. 3:524–525.

[37]Entries for July 17, 18, 1863, Ms. Diary, Hugh Boyd Ewing Papers, OHS; entry for July 17, 1863, diary of Bela T. Saint John, Bela T. Saint John Papers, LC; Jackson to Ethan A. Jackson, July 26, 1863, Jackson (ed.), *Some of the Boys,* 116–117; Sherman to Admiral David Dixon Porter, July 19, 1863, OR 24, pt. 3:531.

The assistant provost marshal in charge of keeping order in the town wrote despairingly of his futile efforts to do so. The rebels had set "very large fires" as they left Jackson, wrote Major Thomas T. Taylor of the 47th Ohio, and as word of the Confederate evacuation spread, Union soldiers from all units in Sherman's army "came straggling in, huzzaing, shouting and plundering." Taylor deployed an entire brigade to control the disorder but it was no use:

[T]he brigade was absorbed and still I had need of more men, then new [fires] broke out – Ammunition had to be moved, fire engines worked. I was directed to do it. So down I went and I worked alone[,] sometimes I could not see the men in the intense heat, whole blocks would thus be consumed in [a] very short space of time. The citizens were perfectly stupefied and appeared indifferent. . . . [T]he fire raged until night, extinguish it in one section and it would burst out in another – It reminded me of the burning of Rome. Many of the houses I regret to say were set on fire by our men and many excesses were committed by them in pillaging & plundering. The army acted more as a mob, than as disciplined soldiers.

Taylor remarked that only "twenty or thirty" soldiers from each regiment actually committed these acts. But "out of so large an army [that] made quite an extensive crowd and this number disgraced our entire army."[38]

Even so, the destruction was hardly complete. Sherman noted that the "State house, Governor's mansion, and some fine dwellings, well within the lines of entrenchments, remain untouched." And the senior Union commanders took steps to restore to the region's population some of what had been taken from them during the Vicksburg and Jackson campaigns. A large amount of rations was issued to families that stayed in Jackson and also to the citizens of Raymond (this in addition to food and medicine for Confederate wounded there). To Sherman, Grant wrote, "Impress upon the men the importance of going through the State in an orderly manner, abstaining from taking anything not absolutely necessary for their subsistence while travelling. They should try to create as favorable an impression as possible upon the people." Provisions and forage, when requested, were issued to all persons in the area from Bruinsburg to Jackson to Vicksburg – i.e., the arc of the recent overland march – "whose resources had been taken for the supply of our army."[39]

Indeed, in the weeks that followed, Grant, Sherman and a number of other officers believed that a Union reaction was possible in central Mississippi, and might even already be underway. "In this part of Mississippi," Grant wrote Hurlbut in early August, "the people acknowledge themselves subjugated, the Southern cause lost, and are holding meetings to devise plans for coming back into the Union." To encourage this welcome development, a new policy seemed desirable. Grant's army, which had only recently taken the first steps in hard war, now reverted to something approaching the conciliatory policy of old.[40]

Grant's orders for military conduct in the state, issued on August 1, offered Mississippians the opportunity to "pursue their peaceful avocations" without molesta-

---

[38]Taylor to his wife, July 19, 1863, Thomas T. Taylor Papers, OHS.
[39]Sherman to Admiral David Dixon Porter, July 19, 1863, OR 24, pt. 3:531; Grant, *Memoirs* 1:577.
[40]Grant to Hurlbut, August 4, 1863, OR 24, pt. 3:575.

tion from Union authorities, provided only that they did not aid or abet guerrilla activity in their midst. His policy on foraging, until recently among the most non-restrictive of any senior Union commander, grew quite conservative. Use of private property was now to be exceptional, and required the authorization and supervision of a corps commander – a policy almost identical to the one followed by the Army of the Potomac, where McClellan's old views remained a strong legacy. Finally, the new directive condemned conduct "disgraceful to the American name," and ordained that from then on, commanders of regiments and detachments would be held personally responsible for depredations committed by their men. "[T]hose who prove themselves unequal to the task of preserving discipline . . . will be promptly reported to the War Department for muster-out. Summary punishment must be inflicted upon all officers and soldiers apprehended in acts of violence or lawlessness."[41]

The August order underscores the fact that Grant, although willing to inflict destruction on a large scale if necessary to defeat the enemy, was far from embracing a policy of indiscriminate devastation. Nor was Sherman, who in early August courtmartialed several soldiers who had burned a cotton gin without authorization during the return march to Vicksburg from Jackson. They should have been shot out of hand, he wrote. "The amount of burning, stealing, and plundering done by our army makes me ashamed of it. I would quit the service if I could, because I fear that we are drifting to the worst sort of vandalism." Sherman's comment pointed up a salient problem in the evolving policy of directed severity. The operations of Grant's army in Mississippi had conditioned soldiers to acts of destruction. The hard war measures of 1864–1865 had made their appearance, however briefly, in the second Jackson raid. The compelling question from here on would be how to inflict necessary destruction without releasing a wave of depredations in its train.[42]

THE STRATEGY OF RAIDS, 1864–1865

In the months that followed the second raid on Jackson, hard war became the dominant Federal policy, thanks primarily to Grant's accession to command of all the Union armies. This probably owed less to Grant's views – for Halleck, his predecessor, also shared the vision of a war to the knife – than Grant's greater prestige and ability to make things happen. The measures that Halleck had pressed upon subordinates for more than a year began under Grant to characterize the Union war effort as a whole.

The framework in which these measures operated has been well-explained by Herman Hattaway and Archer Jones. In *How the North Won,* a military history of the Civil War, they argue that by early 1864, Grant had adopted what they term a "strategy of raids." According to their interpretation, the strategy came about because of the North's failure to win through a strategy of annihilation, which emphasized the destruction of Southern armies in decisive battle, or by a strategy of "exhaustion by

---

[41]General Order No. 50, August 1, 1863, ibid., 570–571.
[42]Sherman to Rawlins, August 4, 1863, ibid., 574.

territorial acquisition," which emphasized the permanent conquest of rebellious areas. The first failed because mid-nineteenth century armies had proven almost invulnerable to outright destruction, the second because it required too many troops to hold captured territory.[43]

The raiding strategy became an alternative way to implement the strategy of exhaustion. Northern forces would not seek to capture vast stretches of the Confederacy, since such a task would fatally diminish the Federal army with endless garrison detachments. Instead they would hold certain key points from which to launch expeditions against Southern croplands, railroads, and war resources. The Union strategy of 1864–1865 aimed at both the destruction of rebel armies and the destruction of rebel war-making capability.

The two-pronged strategy was not a new idea. Almost a year earlier, Rosecrans had written Halleck, "This war must be conducted to annihilate the military power and exhaust the resources of the rebels." He had even attempted a major cavalry raid against Southern railroads in pursuit of the second objective. But "Streight's raid" – named for Colonel Abel D. Streight, the expedition's luckless commander – ended with the loss of the entire force to the Confederates and no compensatory damage to the enemy rail net. The experiment was not repeated. In large measure, Rosecrans's tenure as army commander was characterized only by large-scale foraging not much different from late 1862.[44]

Sherman, however, successfully carried out a prototype of the raiding strategy in his July 1863 descent on Jackson. In February 1864, he conducted a second such operation by leading 21,000 troops against the town of Meridian in east central Mississippi. Meridian stood at the intersection of two railroads, one of which connected Vicksburg with Selma, Alabama, and the other, Corinth and Mobile. Destruction of this rail net would, in Sherman's words, "close the door of rapid travel and conveyance of stores from Mississippi and the Confederacy east." It would also make it far more difficult for the rebels to attempt major incursions against the Federally controlled Mississippi River. Moreover, the town itself contained a stockpile of Confederate supplies as well as several important war factories that Sherman wanted to eliminate.[45]

Starting out from Vicksburg on February 3, 1864, Sherman's forces swept rapidly across the state. They lived off the countryside, partly so as not to be encumbered by a regular supply train and partly in order to strip the region of surplus corn, meat, and

---

[43]A good discussion of the "strategy of raids" is in Herman Hattaway and Archer Jones, *How the North Won: A Military History of the Civil War* (Urbana: University of Illinois Press, 1983), 487–496. See also Sherman to Halleck, December 26, 1863, OR 31, pt. 3:498.

[44]Rosecrans to Halleck, January 29, 1863, OR 23, pt. 2:20–21; Brigadier General A. D. Streight to Brigadier General James A. Garfield, April 9, 1863, ibid. 224; Rosecrans to Halleck, February 22, 1863, ibid., 81; and Rosecrans to Halleck, February 27, 1863, ibid., 90. During Rosecrans' mid-summer Tullahoma Campaign, his army relied heavily on foraging. See William M. Lamers, *The Edge of Glory: A Biography of General William S. Rosecrans, U.S.A.* (New York: Harcourt, Brace and World, 1961), 275–291 passim.

[45]Sherman to Nathaniel P. Banks, January 16, 1864, OR 32, pt. 2:114.

forage. Such a movement would have been impossible had the Confederates been able to offer serious opposition, but they had no major units in the region, and were in any event too taken aback by the raid to mount a sustained defense. To Sherman's chagrin, however, the Southerners did manage to remove most of the military stockpiles and rolling stock before his troops entered Meridian. But they could not remove the warehouses, arsenal, and other military facilities. Sherman's troops did that for them – permanently. In eleven days they marched the 150 miles between Vicksburg and Meridian, then spent the next five days meticulously dismantling the area's railroads and factories. When it was over, about 115 miles of railroad, 61 bridges, and 20 locomotives had been destroyed. Sherman pronounced the work "well done," and added: "Meridian, with its depots, store-houses, arsenal, hospitals, offices, hotels, and cantonments no longer exists."[46]

Grant had approved the Meridian expedition, and it formed a good example of the sort of war he expected to conduct against the South. Indeed, his early planning for an 1864 campaign suggests an emphasis on logistical warfare even greater than the actual effort. Unimpressed by the seemingly endless "On to Richmond" offensives that had characterized the war in Virginia, Grant suggested that this hoary strategy should be discarded in favor of operations against the rail net that supplied the Confederate capital and Lee's army. A mobile force of 60,000 men should be sent to New Bern, North Carolina, or Suffolk, Virginia, and then "move out, destroying the [Weldon] railroad as far as possible." He also suggested the occupation of Raleigh, North Carolina, less because of its intrinsic importance than because it would serve as a base from which to menace a second line, the Piedmont Railroad, connecting Richmond with the lower Confederacy. This was similar to Sherman's concept of launching raids from the Mississippi River but not holding the interior. In a letter to Halleck on this subject, Grant offered four reasons to make such an effort against Raleigh and the Weldon Railroad, all of which highlighted logistics. First, it would disrupt Confederate communications with Richmond and Lee. Second, in carrying out the operation, Union forces could "live upon the country and . . . reduce the stores of the enemy." Third, the movement would gain "possession of many negroes who are now indirectly aiding the rebellion." And fourth, it would "effectually blockade Wilmington, the port now of more value to the enemy than all the balance of their sea coast."[47]

Halleck, however, poured cold water on the plan as soon as he learned of it. Although conceding the idea "has much to recommend it," he worried (with good

---

[46]This damage estimate is drawn from E.B. Long, *The Civil War Day by Day: An Almanac, 1861–1865*, reprint ed. (New York: Da Capo Press, 1985 [1971]), 464; Sherman's official report, March 7, 1864, OR 32, pt. 1:176. For a detailed account of the raid, see Margie Riddle Bearss, *Sherman's Forgotten Campaign: The Meridian Expedition* (Baltimore: Gateway Press, 1987).

[47]Grant to Halleck, January 19, 1864, OR 33, pt. 1:394–395. See also Grant to Thomas, January 19, 1864, ibid. 32, pt. 2:142–143; Thomas to Grant, January 30, 1864, ibid., 264; John G. Foster to Halleck, February 24, 1864, ibid. 31, pt. 1:286; Foster to Halleck, February 24, 1864, ibid. 33, 602–604; Sherman to Grant, January 19, 1864, ibid. 32, pt. 2:147. Foster had already conceived a plan similar to Grant's, for which see Foster to Halleck, October 8, 1863, ibid. 29, pt. 2:267.

reason) about what Lee might do if substantial portions of the Army of the Potomac were detached to operate from Suffolk or New Bern. "[I]t may be said that by operating in North Carolina we would compel Lee to move his army there. I do not think so. Uncover Washington and the Potomac River, and all the forces which Lee can collect will be moved north, and the popular sentiment will compel the Government to bring back the army in North Carolina. . . ." Halleck therefore urged a direct attack on Lee via the shortest line of supply.[48]

Halleck wrote in his capacity as General-in-Chief, but with the full awareness that he would soon be replaced by Grant. The change came on March 9, 1864. (Halleck stayed on as Chief of Staff, a job he rather preferred anyway.) Once installed in his new post, with the newly revived rank of Lieutenant General, Grant began planning at once for the 1864 campaigns. The hard war policy as it was implemented in 1864–1865 cannot be understood without knowing something of Grant's overall design.

First, Grant saw the war as a whole. Until that time, most Union generals had persistently viewed the conflict in terms of separate theaters and so placed little premium on cooperative effort. The various Union armies had behaved, in Grant's opinion, "like a balky team, no two pulling together." As a result, the outnumbered Confederate forces had been able to shift troops from one place to another, shoring up each threatened point by diverting strength from quiet sectors. In this way, Johnston had gathered over 30,000 soldiers for a vain but bothersome effort to relieve Vicksburg. In this way as well, troops from all over the Confederacy had gathered to administer a near-crippling blow to Rosecrans at Chickamauga. To prevent a recurrence, Grant wanted a simultaneous advance along the entire front.[49]

Second, Grant was less interested in occupying strategic points than with destroying the enemy's main forces, on the theory that when no armies remained to defend them, the strategic points would fall as a matter of course. Important cities like Richmond and Atlanta were useful chiefly because the main Confederate armies would fight for them, and in the course of fighting they could be destroyed. Grant put this concept succinctly in a letter to Major General George Gordon Meade, commander of the Army of the Potomac: "Lee's army is your objective point. Wherever Lee goes, there you will go also."[50]

Third, Grant wanted the 1864 spring offensive to be as strong as possible, and he regretted the detachment of so many Union troops on passive occupation duty. Some of this could not be helped – by this period of the war, the Federal armies had to contend with well over 100,000 square miles of captured hostile territory – but it struck Grant that all too often the passive stance was unnecessary. At an April conference with Lincoln, Grant suggested that these detachments could do their jobs "just as well by advancing by remaining still; and by advancing they would compel the enemy to keep detachments to hold them back, or else lay his own territory open

---

[48]Halleck to Grant, February 17, 1864, ibid. 32, pt. 2:411–413.
[49]Grant's report, July 22, 1865, ibid. 46, pt. 1:11.
[50]Grant to Meade, April 9, 1864, ibid. 33:828.

to invasion." Lincoln grasped the point at once. "Oh, yes!" he said. "I see that. As we say out West, if a man can't skin he must hold a leg while somebody else does."[51]

Finally, Grant expected to combine destruction of Southern armies with destruction of Southern war resources. Although Sherman would become the general most identified with this policy, Grant had a profound understanding of the fact that Civil War armies had become too large and too powerful to destroy in open combat. Their annihilation required not only military defeat but also the elimination of the food-stuffs, forage, ammunition, and equipage necessary to maintain them in the field. His instructions to Sherman reflected this: "You I propose to move against [Joseph E.] Johnston's army, to break it up, and to get into the interior of the enemy's country as far as you can, inflicting all the damage you can against their war resources."[52]

Grant's final plan for the great 1864 campaign called for offensive operations along the entire military frontier. In the eastern theater, the Army of the Potomac would advance against General Robert E. Lee's Army of Northern Virginia. Two smaller forces would "hold a leg": Major General Franz Sigel would advance up the Shenandoah Valley while Major General Benjamin F. Butler would conduct an amphibious operation against the Richmond-Petersburg area. Out west, Sherman's three armies would move upon Johnston's Army of Tennessee. Grant had hoped that yet another force, under General Banks, might advance from Louisiana against Mobile, Alabama, but for political reasons Banks marched up the cotton-rich but strategically irrelevant Red River valley. Except for Banks, who had already made – and lost – his campaign, all these armies jumped off in early May.

While the main armies grappled with one another in Virginia and northern Georgia, smaller Union detachments chipped away at Confederate war resources. Federal troops under Major Generals George Crook and William Averell attacked targets in southwest Virginia, including the Virginia and Tennessee Railroad, the large salt works at Saltville, and the lead mines near Wytheville. Butler's offensive quickly fizzled, while the simultaneous advance by Franz Sigel came to grief at the Battle of New Market. In the latter case, however, Grant simply relieved Sigel, substituted Major General David Hunter, and tried again.

Hunter, as might be expected from a general who had earlier sought permission to ravage the homes of Southern slaveholders, believed in hard war. His campaign of "fire and vandalism" in the Shenandoah Valley quickly became notorious. After a victorious battle at Piedmont on June 5, his forces entered the important Confederate supply depot of Staunton and destroyed the city's railroad property, steam mill, foundry, and carriage and woolens factories. Three days later they occupied Lexington, home of the Virginia Military Institute, which they promptly torched. The chief advocate of the burning was apparently Hunter's chief of staff, Virginia-born Colonel David H. Strother, who termed V.M.I. "a most dangerous institution, where treason

---

[51]Grant, *Memoirs* 2:142–43.
[52]Grant to Sherman, April 4, 1864, OR 32, pt. 3:246.

was systematically taught." At Hunter's direction, they also destroyed the home of former Virginia governor John Letcher, an act made in retaliation for Letcher's issuance of a proclamation inciting the populace to wage guerrilla warfare upon the Union invaders. At least one Federal soldier applauded. "Father," he wrote home, "Hunter is just the man for the [job] of putting down this rebellion he is a fierce and savage looking man he has no mercy on the Rebels."[53]

Hunter soon ran into trouble, however. As his army pressed on toward Lynchburg, a town of great importance to the Confederate war effort, Lee detached troops from his own beleaguered army to confront Hunter. Fourteen thousand veteran infantry left the Army of Northern Virginia and were redeployed into the Shenandoah Valley. Within a week, Lieutenant General Jubal A. Early succeeded in repulsing the Federal raiders from Lynchburg, and Hunter withdrew into the Allegheny Mountains – thereby leaving Washington and the North exposed.[54]

Hunter's foolhardy movement opened the way for Early to march down the Shenandoah Valley, cross the Potomac, raid western Maryland, and briefly threaten Washington itself. During this operation, his troops also burned Chambersburg, Pennsylvania, in reprisal for the perceived excesses of Hunter's raid. As Early noted, "A number of towns in the South, as well as private country homes, had been burned by Federal troops," adding, "I came to the conclusion that it was time to open the eyes of the North to this enormity, by an example in the way of retaliation." In July he instructed his cavalry to demand $100,000 from the people of Chambersburg. When the townsmen could not or would not meet the requisition, Confederate troopers burned the community to the ground.[55]

Rebuffed in his daring attempt to enter Washington, Early still managed to hold onto the Shenandoah Valley. In early August, Grant dispatched Major General Philip H. Sheridan to take command in that region. True to the new Union strategy, Sheridan received orders not only to defeat Early but also to end the Valley's days as the "Breadbasket of the Confederacy." Once Early's force had been beaten, Grant wrote, the pursuing troops should "eat out Virginia clear and clean as far as they go, so that crows flying over it for the balance of the season will have to carry their provender with them." Nothing, Grant stipulated, "should be left to invite the enemy to return. Take all provisions, forage and stock wanted for the use of your command. Such as cannot be consumed, destroy." The rationale was partially to deprive Lee's army of food and forage, but since Lee drew most of his supplies from the Deep South, the

[53]Entry for June 12, 1864, Eby (ed.), *A Virginia Yankee in the Civil War*, 255-256; Seibert to his parents, June 13, 1864, Benjamin Franklin Seibert Papers, HCWRTC, USAMHI.

[54]For Hunter's raid, see Marshall Moore Brice, *Conquest of a Valley* (Charlottesville: University Press of Virginia, 1965). See also Henry A. DuPont, *The Campaign of 1864 in the Valley of Virginia and the Expedition to Lynchburg* (New York: National Americana Society, 1925), and George E. Pond, *The Shenandoah Valley in 1864* (New York: Charles Scribners Sons, 1883).

[55]Jubal A. Early, *War Memoirs: Autobiographical Sketch and Narrative of the War Between the States* (Bloomington: Indiana University Press, 1960), 401. For a discussion of this incident, see Everard H. Smith, "Chambersburg: Anatomy of a Confederate Reprisal," *American Historical Review* 96 (1991):432-455.

main purpose was to undermine the Valley's continued potential as a corridor of invasion (as Lee had done in 1863 and as Early had recently done only weeks previously). The burning of crops and forage would also make it more difficult for guerrillas to operate in the region.[56]

The destruction began on August 17, when Sheridan's cavalry burned "evry [sic] barn & stack as far as we went" in the lower Valley. It went into high gear a month later, after Early's badly outnumbered Confederates suffered defeat in two sharp battles that forced them to yield the entire valley to Union domination. Having chased Early as far as Staunton, Sheridan considered further pursuit useless. He began a withdrawal back into the lower Shenandoah Valley. As he did, he turned his efforts against the regions's crops and livestock. Union cavalry stretched a cordon across the Valley floor and systematically fired barns and herded away animals. One trooper counted 167 barns ablaze at one time. By mid-October, Sheridan could report, "I have destroyed over 2,000 barns filled with wheat, hay and farming implements; over 70 mills, filled with flour and wheat; have driven in front of the army over 4,000 head of stock, and have killed and issued to the troops not less than 3,000 sheep."[57]

Sheridan's operations in the Valley produced not only an economic effect on Confederate supply, but also a psychological effect on Virginia civilians. "They have tasted the bitter fruit of secession, and have had enough of it. . . ." wrote a Vermont soldier." "They see the grim determination of the North, and they begin to feel that to hold out longer is to fight against inevitable destiny." Sheridan put it more succinctly. "The people here," he informed Grant, "are getting sick of the war."[58]

Even before Sheridan defeated Early's army, Sherman, after a prolonged four-month campaign, had succeeded in capturing Atlanta. Having seized it, he faced some serious choices about what to do with it. Conceivably he might have converted the city into a major base for further operations, but logistical considerations militated against such a course. His current base, Nashville, was some 150 miles distant and linked to Atlanta only by a single railroad, which remained vulnerable to interdiction by the opposing Army of Tennessee (now commanded by General John B. Hood).[59] Sherman could not afford to remain idle – he still had Hood's army to defeat – and the maintenance of a large garrison in Atlanta would divert needed forces from active campaigning. Accordingly, he hit upon an unusual expedient: He ordered the forced

---

[56]Grant to Halleck, July 14, 1864, OR 40, pt. 3:223; Grant to Sheridan, August 26, 1864, ibid. 37, pt. 2:202.

[57]Entry for August 17, 1864, diary of William G. Mills, Miscellaneous Manuscript Collection, LC; J. R. Bowen, *Regimental History of the First New York Dragoons . . .* (n.p.: by the author, 1900), 243; Sheridan to Grant, October 7, 1864, OR 43, pt. 2:307–308. See also "Report of Property Captured, Destroyed and Lost By the Middle Military Division, Major General P. H. Sheridan Commanding, During the Campaign Commencing August 10, 1864 and Ending November 16, 1864," November 23, 1864, Record Group 393, Part 1, Entry 2414, Box 2, NA.

[58]"Anti-Rebel" [pseudonym for Wilbur Fisk] to Editor, *Freeman,* October 4, 1864, Fisk Papers, LC; Sheridan to Grant, October 7, 1864, OR 43, pt. 2:307–308.

[59]Hood's predecessor, Joseph Johnston, had been relieved of command in mid-July, because of President Jefferson Davis's belief that he was not resisting Sherman's advance aggressively enough.

evacuation of the city's population. Sherman's forces continued to occupy Atlanta until mid-November, when they embarked upon their famous March to the Sea.[60]

Before leaving, Federal engineers destroyed the main railroad depot, roundhouse, and machine shops of the Georgia Railroad, and also a foundry, oil refinery, freight warehouse, various dry goods stores, theaters, fire stations, hotels, and slave markets. At some point, the set fires got out of hand and spread to other areas, resulting in the devastation of about two hundred acres of the city. Although most of the work was carried out by the engineers, a large number of off-duty Federals contributed gratuitous acts of arson and vandalism.

On November 15, Sherman's army left the smoldering city and began its famous March to the Sea. Of all the operations of the American Civil War, this one was perhaps the most remarkable – and certainly the most famous example of hard war. The initial impetus for the move came from the same predicament that had led him to order the city's evacuation. Because his forces dangled at the end of a tenuous supply line stretching back well into Tennessee, further advances seemed impossible if he continued to rely upon it. Sherman solved the problem by electing to change his base. He would abandon the present line, leave an adequate force to defend Tennessee against rebel incursions, and establish a new base at Savannah on the Atlantic coast. To do so, however, would require a 220-mile trek across Georgia that could only be accomplished by living off the country. The movement took a leaf from Grant's maneuver during the Vicksburg Campaign, albeit with such audacity and on such a scale that even Grant hesitated before authorizing it.

Indeed, Hood did as predicted and took advantage of Sherman's decision to mount an equally audacious invasion of Tennessee. But Sherman left Major General George H. Thomas with an ample force to deal with the threat, and although Thomas behaved with exasperating slowness he eventually crushed Hood's army in the Battles of Franklin and Nashville (fought on November 30 and December 15–16, respectively). The Army of Tennessee practically went out of existence, leaving Lee's army as the Confederacy's only substantial remaining military force.

Meanwhile, Sherman's forces, advancing against little or no opposition, carved a swath across Georgia sixty miles wide . "[W]e had a gay old campaign," declared one of his men. "Destroyed all we could not eat, stole their niggers, burned their cotton & gins, spilled their sorghum, burned & twisted their R. Roads and raised Hell generally as you know an army can when 'turned loose.'" By Christmas Eve 1864, Sherman had entered the city of Savannah on the Atlantic coast. In February 1865, he headed northward into the Carolinas, repeating on an even grander scale the pattern of his March to the Sea. Ultimately these marches, more than anything else, destroyed the Confederacy. They smashed the remainder of the Confederate rail network, eliminated

---

[60]A detailed discussion of the evacuation, as well as the subsequent Savannah and Carolinas campaigns, appears in Chapter 8.

foodstuffs and war resources, completed the ruin of Southern morale, and caused the desertion of thousands of Confederate soldiers who had resisted valiantly for years.[61]

The Federals continued the strategy of raids right up to the end of the war. In December 1864, troops under Major General George Stoneman left Knoxville, Tennessee, on a lengthy expedition against Confederate salt works, lead mines, and supply depots in southwestern Virginia. They subsequently pierced into North Carolina, destroyed railroads, foundries, and other war resources, and ultimately joined Sherman's army as it came up through the Carolinas. In March-April 1864, cavalry under Major General James Harrison Wilson knifed through Alabama and western Georgia on similar business; their most important contribution was the demolition of the arsenals, factories, warehouses, and rail facilities in Selma. Wilson continued to destroy Confederate war resources even after Lee surrendered his army to Grant. These extensive Federal raids not only characterized the closing days of the conflict, they formed a central element in Southern folk memories of the war for a century to come.[62]

[61]"Divine" to Captain J. H. Everett, December 19, 1864, J. H. Everett Papers, Georgia Historical Society, in Doubleday and Company Collection: Research Notes for Bruce Catton's Centennial History of the Civil War, LC. The literature on Sherman's Savannah and Carolinas Campaigns is voluminous, but see especially John G. Barrett, *Sherman's March Through the Carolinas* (Chapel Hill: University of North Carolina Press, 1956); Davis, *Sherman's March;* Jacob D. Cox, *The March to the Sea – Franklin and Nashville* (New York: Charles Scribner's Sons, 1883); John M. Gibson, *Those 163 Days: A Southern Account of Sherman's March from Atlanta to Raleigh* (New York: Coward-McCann, 1961); Joseph T. Glatthaar, *The March to the Sea and Beyond: Sherman's Troops in the Savannah and Carolinas Campaigns* (New York: New York University Press, 1986); Katherine M. Jones, *When Sherman Came: Southern Women and the "Great March"* (Indianapolis: Bobbs-Merrill, 1964); Walters, *Merchant of Terror,* 127–210; and Richard Wheeler, *Sherman's March* (New York: Thomas Y. Crowell, 1978).

[62]See Ina Woestemeyer Van Noppen, *Stoneman's Last Raid* (Raleigh: North Carolina State College Print Shop, 1961), and James Pickett Jones, *Yankee Blitzkrieg: Wilson's Raid through Alabama and Georgia* (Athens: University of Georgia Press, 1976).

8

The limits of hard war

For a variety of reasons, the shift to hard war occasioned little public debate among Northern policy- and opinion-makers. This was partly because it came gradually, and partly because the press continued to emphasize developments on the battlefield, so that many Northerners never confronted the full implications of the hard war measures. Then too the Democratic Party proved unable or unwilling to capitalize on the issue, despite strong reservations about a "war of subjugation" and the fact that their presidential standard bearer in 1864 had been one of the most fervent defenders of the old conciliatory policy.

But if debate were lacking, comment was not. Some Federal commanders – preeminently Sherman – felt compelled to explain the military necessity and moral legitimacy of their actions. So did other officers, including some who resisted the new policy. Northern newspapers also offered opinions on the issue. And of course the soldier in the ranks, whose job it was to execute the new policy, had ideas of his own. It is thus possible to reconstruct some of the moral calculus that influenced hard war operations.

THE MORAL CALCULUS

Although the raids of 1864–1865 played a critical role in the military defeat of the Confederacy, interest in the raids for modern readers lies mainly in the effect they had on the civilians in their path. In the literature, one repeatedly finds the suggestion – and often the explicit argument – that in these operations may be seen the first stirrings of twentieth century "total war," with its radical erosion of traditionally held values of noncombatant immunity. Sometimes the raids are regarded as either having been atrocities or, at a minimum, as pushing the American way of war down a slippery slope that eventually led to atrocities. At least two writers, for example, have drawn direct connections between Sherman's march and the 1968 My Lai massacre.[1]

---

[1]See Walters, *Merchant of Terror,* xiii; and James Reston, Jr., *Sherman's March and Vietnam* (New York: MacMillan, 1984).

One cannot therefore discuss these operations without leaping into the cataract of moral judgment. For the historian that is a dangerous place to be, yet to avoid this challenge, when dealing with the events of 1864–1865, would be to shun precisely their dimension of greatest significance. Even so, the best way to approach the issue – at least for the historian – is not to apply some external ethical theory, however sophisticated and persuasive, to the actions of Hunter, Sheridan, Sherman and others, but rather to discover their own justifications, and to ask what response their conduct evoked among informed Northern opinion.

The most rewarding subject for such an inquiry, as many writers have already discovered, is William Tecumseh Sherman. That is not so much because Sherman's soldiers conducted the most memorable hard war operations. Rather those operations are memorable in large measure because of the ways in which Sherman attempted to explain and justify them. Several other generals presided over actions similar in type, if not always in scale, to the Savannah and Carolinas Campaigns. And always looming above Sherman were Halleck, Grant, and Lincoln – men who counseled and approved, at least tacitly and often directly, the sort of war for which Sherman became notorious. But Sherman stands alone in his vigorous, consistent, almost obsessive efforts to come to grips with the morality of what he and others were doing.

One of the best windows into his thought, as he stood poised on the brink of his great campaigns of 1864–1865, is a letter he wrote in January 1864 to Major Roswell M. Sawyer, his assistant adjutant general in Huntsville, Alabama. During the coming campaign, Sawyer's responsibility would be to help administer the vast rear area of the Department of the Tennessee while Sherman took the field. Sherman intended the letter as a major policy statement, not only to provide official guidance to his subordinate, but also with a view toward publication in the Northern press. The letter is often quoted as his definitive pronouncement against all Southern civilians ("A people who will persevere in war beyond a certain limit ought to know the consequences. Many, many people with less pertinacity have been wiped out of national existence.") Closer inspection, however, plainly shows that Sherman's actual views – although certainly flinty enough – were less sweeping and more complex.[2]

Sherman wrote in order to acquaint Sawyer with his personal views on "the treatment of inhabitants known or suspected to be hostile or 'secesh.'" This formulation of course implicitly recognized the existence of inhabitants who were *not* hostile, and Sherman had long endorsed the existing Union policy of distinguishing between Unionist, neutral, and actively hostile Southern civilians. And the organization of his letter, far from vowing "eternal war" against all Southerners, was instead carefully crafted to emphasize the Federal policy of substantial forbearance.

He began by pointing out that European practice, "whence we derive our principles of war," contained two strands of tradition. The first tradition viewed war as a matter between "kings or rulers, through hired armies, and not between people." Violence

---

[2] Sherman to Sawyer, January 31, 1864, OR 32, pt. 2:281. For Sherman's eye to publication, see Sherman to John Sherman, April 17, 1864, Thorndike (ed.), *The Sherman Letters,* 228.

under such circumstances was confined to the armies "and should not visit the homes of families or private interests." But there was a second tradition that in his view was more applicable to the Civil War. Although he did not call it by name, Sherman clearly meant what Vattel and other jurists termed the "insurrectionary principle" – the law governing internal revolt, whereby the insurgents were not belligerents but traitors and outlaws. The example he offered Sawyer formed a classic illustration of the insurrectionary principle:

I will only instance that when in the reign of William and Mary the English army occupied Ireland, then in a state of revolt, the inhabitants were actually driven into foreign lands and were dispossessed of their property and a new population introduced. To this day a large part of the north of Ireland is held by the descendants of the Scottish emigrants sent there by William's order and an act of Parliament.

This then was the sort of policy that the Federal government might by rights apply – and, as he made clear a bit further on, that it might indeed eventually apply if the war continued long enough.[3]

In the meantime, however, "the question arises, should we treat as absolute enemies all in the South who differ from us in opinion or prejudice, kill or banish them, or give them time to think and gradually change their conduct so as to conform to the new order of things which is slowly and gradually creeping into the country?" – by which he meant the end of slavery and the introduction into the South of a free labor system. His answer to this question was that the Southerners should be given time. "So long as non-combatants remain in their houses and keep to their accustomed business their [secessionist] opinions and prejudices can in nowise influence the war, and should not be noticed." This was not of course the same thing as saying that they should be completely shielded from the realities of war. Union forces had a clear duty to take provisions and livestock that might be used against them by the enemy. In the same way they had a right to punish, banish, or restrain "any one [who] comes out into the public streets and creates disorder," just as they could punish civilians who acted as spies. These, he accurately noted, were "well-established principles of war."[4]

Sherman then went on to make his point about the possibility of someday adopting King William's Irish policy. "When the inhabitants persist too long in hostility it may be both politic and right [that] we should banish them and appropriate their lands to a more loyal and useful population." Interestingly, Sherman did not suggest that this policy should apply across the board. Rather he had in mind a single class – the same class that, from the outset, Northerners had blamed for the war. "No man," he wrote, "will deny that the United States would be benefited by dispossessing a *rich, prejudiced, hard-headed, and disloyal planter,* and substituting in his place a dozen or more patient, industrious, good families, even if they be of foreign birth." (emphasis supplied) Sherman added pointedly that it might be a good idea to sit some of these "Southern gentlemen" down and explain to them a few home truths; for example, that

[3]Sherman to Sawyer, January 31, 1864, OR 32, pt. 2:279.
[4]Ibid.

"they did not create the land; that the only title to its use and usufruct is the deed of the United States, and if they appeal to war they hold their all by a very insecure tenure."[5]

To be sure, the planters might be so "prejudiced" that they would never recant, but Sherman had greater expectations for the Southern commoner:

[I] hope, as the poorer and industrial classes of the South realize their relative weakness and their dependence upon the fruits of the earth and good will of their fellow-men, they will not only discover the error of their ways and repent of their hasty action but bless those who persistently maintained a constitutional Government strong enough to sustain itself, protect its citizens, and promise peaceful homes to millions yet unborn.

In fact, he thought that the "non-slaveholding classes" might already be alienating themselves from those who wished to continue the struggle. "Already I hear crimination." And, returning to the planters, he added, "Those who have property should take warning in time."[6]

The bottom line, as Sherman expressed it, was this: "Whilst I would not remit one jot or tittle of our nation's right in peace or war, I do make allowances for past political errors or prejudices. . . . To those who submit to the rightful law and authority all gentleness and forbearance; but to the petulant and persistent secessionists, why, death is mercy . . ."[7] In short, Sherman's letter was squarely in line with previous Federal policy: a trinary division of the Southern population, with differing codes of conduct for each, and a directed severity to be visited upon surplus crops and live-stock, but not private homes, and against open, avowed secessionists, not those who were neutral or loyal. And, again in line with Northern opinion, there was a greater presumption of guilt concerning the slaveholding aristocracy than among Southern yeomen or mechanics. A prescription for indiscriminate, all-annihilating total war this emphatically was not.[8]

Sherman carried this policy with him when his armies marched into Georgia. His orders for the March to the Sea, for example, authorized foraging only by regularly designated parties commanded by "discrete officers" who would gather provisions but "endeavor to leave with each family a due portion for their maintenance." Soldiers could neither enter dwellings nor trespass, and while horses, wagons, and mules could be appropriated "freely," soldiers should "discriminate between the rich, who are usually hostile, and the poor and industrious, usually neutral or friendly." Corps commanders alone possessed authority to destroy houses, cotton gins, and grist mills, and while it had become customary to regard the latter two as military targets,

[5]Ibid., 280. "Usufruct" refers to the legal right of using and enjoying the fruits or profits of something belonging to another.

[6]Ibid.

[7]Ibid., 281.

[8]Ibid. Interestingly, a Union soldier posted in Sawyer's area of responsibility noted in the wake of Sherman's letter that " . . . I believe the people are getting more reconciled to Federal rule[.] [T]hey find themselves properly protected, and our boys are getting very friendly with them. I have heard several of the ladies say here that we are the civillest [sic] soldiers that have ever been in Athens [Alabama] . . . . " George Hovey Cadman to his wife, April 2, 1864, George Hovey Cadman Letters, SHC.

Sherman specified during the Savannah Campaign that their destruction should be punitive only:

In districts and neighborhoods where the army is unmolested, no destruction of such property should be permitted; but should guerrillas or bushwhackers molest our march, or should the inhabitants burn bridges, obstruct roads, or otherwise manifest local hostility, then army commanders should order and enforce a devastation more or less relentless, according to the measure of such hostility.

Here again was directed severity, and in this case the reason behind it went beyond the simple right of retaliation. The Savannah Campaign required Sherman's armies to abandon one supply line completely and march to a new base over 200 miles distant, like a trapeze artist flying from one bar to another. To do this successfully required the troops to make consistent and fairly rapid progress, otherwise they would soon strip a given area completely, and if delayed in their movement to new croplands, would begin to starve in the field.[9]

Subordinate commanders tried to prevent excesses. Major General Joseph Osterhaus, commanding the Fifteenth Corps, specified that a strong provost guard would precede each of his divisions to prevent "willful vandalism . . . by worthless characters." He also mandated the placement of guards at all occupied dwellings and forbade foraging parties to enter homes without written permission from division commanders. Other corps and division commanders issued similar instructions. Brigadier General Giles A. Smith urged his division to "keep constantly in mind that we are not warring on women and children. Foraging parties will take such articles as are needed for the health or subsistence of the men, but no houses will be entered by them, and all officers, guards, or soldiers are ordered to shoot on the spot any person caught firing a building, or any other property, without orders." Fourteenth Corps commander Jefferson C. Davis insisted that "no good can result to the cause of their country from indiscriminate destruction or burning of the homes of women and children." The most effective way to prevent this, he went on, was for division commanders to hold brigade, regimental, and company officers directly answerable for the conduct of their troops.[10]

Among commanders in other theaters, a similar policy prevailed. Told by Grant to render the Shenandoah Valley "a barren waste," Philip Sheridan did exactly as instructed. But his orders for the operation specified that "no villages or private houses will be burned," and in general those instructions were complied with. Some efforts were also made to leave the inhabitants with enough food for personal use. An exception to the rule against destroying homes occurred around Harrisonburg, when one of Sheridan's staff officers, Lieutenant John Meigs, was waylaid and killed by

[9]Special Field Orders No. 120, November 9, 1864, OR 39, pt. 3:713.

[10]Special Orders No. 171, November 14, 1864, OR 44:455. See, for example, General Order No. 92 [Third Division, Fifteenth Corps], November 14, 1864, ibid., 457; Special Orders No. 281 [Seventeenth Corps], November 14, 1864, ibid., 458; General Order No. 21 [Twentieth Corps], November 14, 1864, ibid. 44:463; General Order No. 25, November 17, 1864, ibid., 482; Circular, Fourteenth Army Corps, November 18, 1864, ibid., 489–490.

Two Practitioners of Hard War

Maj. Gen. Philip H. Sheridan and his cavalry rendered the Shenandoah Valley –
"breadbasket of the Confederacy" – useless as a source of food for Southern armies. His
operations produced not only an effect on Confederate logistics, but also exerted a
psychological effect on Virginia civilians. "They have tasted the bitter fruit of secession,
and have had enough of it. . . ." wrote a Vermont soldier. "They see the grim determination of the North, and they begin to feel that to hold out longer is to fight against
inevitable destiny." (Courtesy, Civil War Times Illustrated Collection)

Maj. Gen. William T. Sherman became synonymous with "hard war." His Marches to the Sea and through the Carolinas starkly displayed the Confederate government's inability to protect its citizens. "This may not be war but rather statesmanship," he wrote; "nevertheless it is overwhelming to my mind that there are thousands of people abroad and in the South who reason thus: If the North can march an army right through the South, it is proof positive that the North can prevail. . . ." (Courtesy, Civil War Times Illustrated Collection)

guerrillas. In response, Sheridan ordered the burning of all houses within a five-mile radius of the incident – a draconian measure but scarcely unique, especially at that stage of the war. Indeed, Sheridan's razing of the Valley, for an operation of its scale, was probably one of the more controlled acts of destruction during the war's final year.[11]

Even the orders of David Hunter, whose raid up the Shenandoah Valley in June 1864 provoked far more outrage than Sheridan's, show a consistent – almost finicky – insistence upon a directed severity. Like Sherman's Savannah Campaign, Hunter's conception for the raid required his troops to live largely off the countryside, receiving only resupplies of ammunition. He clung to this idea so tenaciously that when thirty wagon loads of forage happened to materialize from the rear, a staff officer fired off a letter in complaint. Livestock and crops were to be taken as necessary, and only loyal civilians would receive compensation, but "[b]rigade and other commanders will be held responsible that there is no waste." Hunter meant this to apply not only to the distribution of foodstuffs once taken but also to foodstuffs and other property left behind. Informed that stragglers from the division of Brigadier General Julius Stahel had entered houses and carried off "dresses, ornaments, books, [and] money," while doing "wanton injury to furniture," Hunter was outraged. This, his adjutant informed Stahel, was "in gross violation of the spirit of the order for levying supplies upon the country." He pointed out that many area residents "have been very kind to our wounded, and it is neither just nor politic to allow wanton outrages and injuries to be inflicted upon any people." In one case, he continued, one of Stahel's foraging parties had located several barrels of flour, appropriated what they needed or could carry, then "emptied the other barrels over the fields." The officer pointed out that such an action was "a devastation, and not a recognized levying of subsistence upon the country."[12]

In addition to widespread foraging, Hunter's troops also destroyed railroads, factories, and public stores at Staunton, Lexington, and elsewhere. That of course was unexceptional. The burning of the Virginia Military Institute, however, violated a prohibition in General Order No. 100 against damaging educational institutions

---

[11]Grant to Sheridan, August 26, 1864, ibid. 37, pt. 2:202. For the implementation of the order, see James W. Forsyth [Sheridan's chief of staff] to Brigadier General Wesley Merritt, September 28, 1864, ibid. 43, pt. 2:202; Orders [Sixth Corps], October 5, 1864, ibid., 292; William M. Russell to Merritt, October 5, 1864, ibid., 293; and Brigadier General George A. Custer to Captain Amasa E. Dana, September 30, 1864, ibid., 220: "I have the honor to report that my command destroyed 9 large mills and about 100 barns yesterday – the mills were filled with flour and wheat; the barns were filled with threshed wheat and hay. I also destroyed a large number of stacks and hay found standing in the fields. I brought away about 150 head of beef-cattle, or perhaps nearly 200 head; also about 500 head of sheep. No dwelling houses were destroyed or interfered with." This is corroborated in Aldace F. Walker, *The Vermont Brigade in the Shenandoah Valley, 1864* (Burlington, VT: Free Press Association, 1869), 128. George T. Stevens, *Three Years in the Sixth Corps* (2nd ed., New York: D. Van Nostrand, 1870), 414–415. Brigadier General W.H. Seward to Brigadier General John D. Stevenson, October 6, 1864, OR 43, pt. 2:305–306; Sheridan to Grant, October 7, 1864, ibid., 308.

[12]General Order No. 29, May 22, 1864, ibid. 37, pt. 1:517–518; General Order No. 29, 22 May 1864, ibid., 517–518; Major Charles G. Halpine to Major General Franz Sigel, June 9, 1964, ibid., 619, 628; Halpine to Stahel, May 30, 1864, ibid., 556–557.

(although in fairness to Hunter, most of the Institute's corps of cadets had recently fought Union forces at the Battle of New Market). And he issued instructions that applied the torch to a number of private residences in retaliation for guerrilla activity.[13]

Early in Hunter's raid, for example, his adjutant issued the following order to a major of New York cavalry:

Proceed at once to Newtown, ascertain the house from which our [wagon] train was fired upon last night, and burn the same with all the outbuildings thereto. Notify the inhabitants of the town and along the pike if our trains or escorts are fired upon in that way again, that the commanding general will cause to be burned every rebel house within five miles of the place at which the firing occurred.

When the incident was repeated, Hunter made good his threat. A few days later the same New York major received these instructions:

You will detail from your command 200 men, with the proper complement of commissioned officers, to proceed to Newtown to-morrow morning at 3 o'clock, for the purpose of burning every house, store, and out-building in that place, except the churches and the houses and out-buildings of those who are known to be loyal citizens of the United States. You will also burn the houses, &c., of all rebels between Newtown and Middletown. You will spare the house and premises of Dr. Owens, of Newtown, he having been very kind to our wounded soldiers. . . .

This second order, however, went unfulfilled. The affected citizens pleaded for clemency and also presented a letter from the local guerrilla chieftain, who threatened to shoot over forty Federal prisoners if the major carried out Hunter's instructions.[14]

When his troops entered Lexington, Hunter discovered a "violent and inflammatory" proclamation from the pen of former Virginia Governor John Letcher, "inciting the population of the country to rise and wage a guerrilla warfare on my troops." Hunter had earlier published a warning against anyone aiding and abetting irregular warfare. Since Letcher had fled and was beyond the reach of punishment, Hunter ordered his residence burned instead. Mrs. Letcher reportedly received only five minutes' grace to remove valuables from the home before it was destroyed.[15]

The burning of Letcher's home, coupled with the destruction of VMI and other buildings, made Hunter's raid an epitome of the Federal hard war policy out of all proportion to its intrinsic significance. Hunter's "campaign of fire and vandalism"

[13]Hunter's preliminary report, June 8, 1864, ibid., 95–96. See also his final report, August 8, 1864, ibid., 96–97.

[14]P.G. Bier to Major Timothy Quinn, May 24, 1864, ibid., 528; Bier to Quinn, May 30, 1864, ibid., 557; Virgil I. Carrington, *Gray Ghosts and Rebel Raiders* (paperback ed., New York: Ballantine Books, 1973), 247–248.

[15]Hunter's report, August 8, 1864, ibid., pt. 1:97.Charles W. Turner (ed.), "General David Hunter's Sack of Lexington, Virginia, June 10–14, 1864: An Account by Rose Page Pendleton," *Virginia Magazine of History and Biography* 83 (1975):178. See also Henry Kyd Douglas, *I Rode With Stonewall* (Chapel Hill: University of North Carolina Press, 1940), 288. The former reprints a letter from a Lexington resident dated June 18, 1864; the latter reprints excerpts from an undated letter by Samuel H. Letcher, Governor Letcher's son.

aroused fury among Confederates and created misgivings even in the North. This notoriety owed mainly to two factors. First, Hunter's eventual retreat into the wilds of West Virginia not only opened the way for Jubal Early to embark on his famous raid against Washington, it also meant that for many weeks the only news of Hunter's exploits came from exaggerated Southern reports of his raid. Second, Hunter's burning of VMI, Letcher's home, and other property formed the Confederate justification for the retaliatory burning of Chambersburg, Pennsylvania, on July 30. The incident made headlines throughout the North, and inspired much introspection about the military destruction of civilian property.[16]

Two months later, for example, Halleck expressed to Sherman his disapproval of "General Hunter's course in burning private houses or uselessly destroying private property. That is barbarous." He used it to illustrate an abuse of the hard war policy, contrasting it with Sherman's appropriate actions – for example, the stripping of crops, burning of mills, and evacuation of Atlanta's civilian population. A number of Northern newspapers condemned both the burning of Chambersburg and the alleged Union excesses that had provoked it. The conservative *Washington Daily National Intelligencer* editorialized that it had always opposed "all barbarism and vandalism in the prosecution of the present unhappy war." Conceding the probable truth of Early's charges that Hunter's raid "caused widespread ruin wherever he passed," the newspaper noted caustically that destruction of civilian property and military incompetence often went hand in hand. Ineffective generals such as Hunter "seem to be aware that they *must do something to satisfy the public,* and, not being able to win battles and make conquests in the military sense of these words, they betake themselves to the cheap resorts of license and violence against defenceless 'sympathizers with the rebellion.'" (emphasis in the original)[17]

This was somewhat unfair. Whatever Hunter's eventual mistakes, his destruction of civilian property had occurred hard on the heels of several impressive victories that carried Union forces farther up the Valley than ever before. But the *Intelligencer's* comment well-illustrated the widespread belief, particularly among conservatives and Democrats, that the war could and should be won without resort to such measures. The paper concluded by calling upon Lincoln to enforce the prohibition, made in his July 1862 executive order, against "wanton and malicious" destruction of Southern property. "[I]t is a source of profound regret to us that the President, animated as we know him to be by humane impulses, does not take some measures to vindicate his authority on this subject, and rescue his orders from the contempt into which they have fallen."[18]

Republican newspapers, by contrast, endorsed the hard war policy and defended it by emphasizing its appropriate discrimination. In early August, the *New York Times*

---

[16]The quoted phrase is that of Henry Kyd Douglas, a Confederate staff officer who witnessed the raid's aftermath. See *I Rode With Stonewall,* 287.

[17]Halleck to Sherman, September 28, 1864, OR 39, pt. 2:503; *Washington Daily National Intelligencer,* August 25, 1864.

[18]Ibid.

published a lengthy editorial that drew a sharp distinction between the Confederate burning of Chambersburg – which had involved "turning half-naked women and babies out from their flaming houses" – and a recent raid by Major General Lovell H. Rousseau in Alabama, which had been characterized by laudable restraint:

[Rousseau] found in a certain village, named Loachapoka, a depot of rebel stores and a factory. These were very properly burnt, but the adjacent houses of the citizens were saved by the personal exertions of the General and his soldiers – the latter putting their own wet blankets on the roofs. In Talladega, a Confederate gun-factory was broken up rather than burned, for fear that private houses might also suffer.

Here was hard war as Northerners liked to imagine it: orderly, surgical, and easy to justify. Few were comfortable defending the destruction of private homes, and the *New York Times* was not among them: "If General Hunter did burn the residence of the Governor of Virginia, we hold it an act unworthy of a Federal officer . . ."[19]

The Republican press was accurate enough in its representation of the Union army as employing a policy of directed severity, but naive – or more probably, disingenuous – in its obtuseness about the frequency of abuses. Even so, the Democratic Party largely chose not to capitalize on this aspect of the Lincoln administration's handling of the war. It preferred instead to emphasize the military stalemate, the administration's constitutional abuses, and above all its emancipation policy. Criticism of property destruction surfaced primarily in vague, sweeping remarks about a "war of subjugation" or "extermination."[20]

There were good reasons for this. The war had divided the Democratic Party into three basic constituencies: the War Democrats, composed of members who believed that partisan politics should be suspended for the duration; the Peace Democrats (often derisively labeled "Copperheads"), who sought an immediate armistice and a negotiated settlement; and the "legitimist" Democrats, who generally endorsed a war for the Union but insisted that their party should play the role of a loyal opposition. Excessive criticism of Federal hard war measures would alienate the War Democrats. The peace faction, for its part, would find such carping beside the point, since it viewed the entire military effort as wrong. Thus the legitimist Democrats, despite clear misgivings, could not convert the Union conduct of the war into an effective political issue.

Even so, legitimist Democrats occasionally did fault the Lincoln administration for its acquiescence in military destruction of Southern private property. McClellan, the party's presidential nominee, was well-known for his refusal to make war on civilians. "Contrast the career of McClellan," urged a supporter, "with that of some others, of a Hunter . . . for instance, in their fell spirit of fanaticism, emulating the example of Attila, alienating more friends than conquering foes, embittering their enemy with a burning sense of wrongs in violation of civilized warfare. . . ." August Belmont

---

[19]*New York Times,* August 8, 1864.
[20]Joel H. Silbey, *A Respectable Minority: The Democratic Party in the Civil War Era, 1860–1868* (New York: W.W. Norton, 1977), 63–88 passim.

asked, "[W]ho can doubt that the South will fight to the last extremity, if the fatal policy of confiscation and forcible emancipation is to be persisted in[?]" Reverdy Johnson, the respected Unionist senator from Maryland, composed an open letter that supported McClellan and repudiated Lincoln, in part because of "[Lincoln's] having not only not punished, but, as far as the public know, left unrebuked the vandal excesses of military officers of his special selection." And Robert C. Winthrop informed a Democratic rally in New York that "the all-important end of re-establishing the Union has been almost shut out of sight; so mixed up and complicated has it been with schemes of philanthropy on one side [a reference to the Peace Democrats], and with schemes of confiscation, subjugation and extermination on the other." The policy of the Lincoln administration, Winthrop continued, had inspired a "spirit of desperation and hatred" among Southerners and made battlefield victories harder to achieve. "For never, my friends, do victories cost us so much, and come to so little, as when they are wrung from a foe who has been goaded and maddened to despair. . . ."[21]

A sharp query against the hard war policy also surfaced from Major General Don Carlos Buell, the discredited conciliatory commander who had been shelved by the Lincoln administration nearly two years previously. In early August 1864, Buell resigned from the army. He probably did so in a fit of pique after being offered only opportunities to serve under commanders less senior than himself. But he chose to post his reasons on higher ground, and revealed them in an open letter that was widely reprinted. "I believed that the policy and means with which the war was being prosecuted were discreditable to the nation and a stain upon civilization," Buell wrote. He recalled the conciliatory policy "wisely declared by Congress in the beginning of the war" but undermined "by the intrusion of sectional rancor, and the injudicious or unfaithful acts of agents of the Government." With its eventual demise came "a system of spoliation and disfranchisement[;] the cause was robbed of its sanctity, and success rendered more difficult of attainment."[22]

For Buell, the trouble with Federal hard war policy was that it treated Southern civilians as implacable enemies, not as alienated Americans, and so intensified a resistance than might otherwise have softened. The *Washington Daily National Intelligencer* agreed. "Do you really hate the people against whom you are now making war?" it editorialized "TO OUR CITIZEN SOLDIERS" a few weeks before the election: "When you have seen old men and women and children – the infirm, the sick, and the innocent – driven from their blazing homes, gathering in hopeless misery around some dying camp fire, shivering, starving, shelterless, did you feel an impulse prompting you to aid in carrying anguish and desolation and extermination throughout . . . the South, merely to give immediate emancipation to a race who were a

---

[21]Speech of Richard S. Spofford, Newburyport, Massachusetts, September 29, 1864, reprinted in *Washington Daily National Intelligencer,* October 18, 1864; *New York World,* November 3, 1864; *Speech by Hon. Robert C. Winthrop at the Great New York Ratification Meeting* [September 17, 1864] (Boston: J. E. Farwell and Co., 1864), 7, 9.

[22]Quoted in *Washington Daily National Intelligencer,* September 6, 1864. See, also, Buell to Almon P. Rockwell [Buell's former aide-de-camp], July 10, 1864, Almon P. Rockwell Papers, LC.

thousand times happier as you found them than as you would leave them?" If not, the paper urged, they should cast their ballots for McClellan.[23]

Some soldiers never got used to the destruction. During the Red River Campaign, an Illinois captain noted that whenever the troops were allowed to disembark from their river transports, a few of them invariably turned into firebugs. These few, he continued, made it necessary to enforce "the most rigid rules." Such "reprobates" were the very ones that most bitterly objected to restraint, "calling it protecting rebel property and all that, claiming a great deal of principle and Patriotism in commit[t]ing their depredations. Fudge and fudge to a large mass of the same kind of talk in northern newspapers and perhaps all of it. It is all gammon. Such ravages and destruction even when done under orders, tends more to demoralize and injure our troops than all the injury it does the Rebel cause."[24]

Another captain – this one in Sheridan's cavalry – was asked by a Peace Democrat if he were "one of those of those dreadful men we read of." She recorded his rueful answer: "Yes . . . I am one of the 'barnburners,' destroyers of homes, etc. I don't like such work. . . . It is not civilized war. Although much is military necessity, much could be avoided. Harshness is never of any use. We lose by this." He thought it turned every Southern civilian into an enemy.[25]

Feeling as they did, it would not be surprising if both captains did vote for McClellan. Most soldiers, however, wound up voting *against* McClellan, and by impressive margins. They did so for a variety of reasons, not simply so that they could go on wrecking railroads and burning mills. But they understood the necessity for such destruction. A Rhode Island chaplain who served with Sheridan recalled the day when Union cavalry began seizing the livestock of the Shenandoah Valley and the first great columns of smoke and flame rose from "doomed secession barns, stacks, cribs, and mills." The time, he wrote, "had fully come to peel this land and put an end to the long strife for its possession. . . . The flames here shortened the work of the war, and so were a mercy."[26]

The Confederate burning of Chambersburg, Pennsylvania, made such severities more palatable to many Northern soldiers. As they passed through Winchester, Virginia, some of Sheridan's men tried to set it afire in retaliation for Chambersburg, but the flames were extinguished before they could do any damage. Another soldier who witnessed the razing of the Shenandoah Valley confessed that his unit had burned some sixty houses as well as grain-laden barns. "[I]t was a hard looking sight to see the women and children turned out of doors at this season of the year," he wrote home, "but no worse than for those of chambersburg."[27]

---

[23] *Washington Daily National Intelligencer,* October 18, 1864.

[24] Entry for March 19, 1864, typescript diary, William H. Stewart Papers, SHC.

[25] Entry for December 3, 1864, Harold E. Hammond (ed.), *Diary of a Union Lady, 1861–1865* (New York: Funk & Wagnalls Co., 1962), 320.

[26] Frederic Denison, *Sabres and Spurs: The First Regiment Rhode Island Cavalry in the Civil War, 1861–1865* (Central Falls, RI: E.L. Freeman, 1876), 381.

[27] Entry for August 17, 1864, Henry Keiser Diary, HCWRTC, USAMHI; William H. Martin to his wife, October 11, 1864, William H. Martin Papers, HCWRTC, USAHMI.

Yet despite the provocation of Chambersburg, most Union troops adhered to orders and destroyed only barns. Some found the work actively distasteful. Instructed to assist in the barn-burning and seizures of livestock in the Shenandoah Valley, Major James M. Comly of the 23rd Ohio demanded written orders. "We executed the orders as carefully and tenderly as possible," he wrote in his diary, "burning and destroying only what we were imperatively commanded to do." Although Comly conceded that it was proper to destroy the enemy's supplies, he hated it. "It does not seem real soldierly work. We ought to enlist a force of scoundrels for such work."[28]

Sometimes even the barn-burning did not occur. Hoping to drive John S. Mosby's partisans from the area, in November 1864 Sheridan ordered the destruction of barns and mills in Loudoun County, Virginia. The region contained many Unionists. Aware of Sheridan's intent, some of them bore the ordeal stoically. "Burn away, burn away, if it will prevent Mosby from coming here," two young women sang out gaily. It still struck some Union soldiers as unjust. Brigadier General Thomas C. Devin went to the residence of a known Unionist with orders to destroy his flour mill. The owner invited him to take some refreshments, but Devin declined. "No, *sir*, the food would *choke* me." He then instructed his adjutant to fire the mill, told the owner advisedly that he should have some buckets of water ready "in case your *house* should catch fire," and promptly spurred away. The adjutant dutifully piled wood against the side of the barn, ignited it and rejoined the general. The owner promptly took the buckets of water and extinguished the flames.[29]

Even reprisals for guerrilla activity could provoke misgivings. William T. Patterson, an Ohio sergeant in Sheridan's army, reflected the anguish that attended Sheridan's decision to burn private homes in retaliation for the murder of Lieutenant Meigs. "This will include the city of Harrisonburg, the towns of Bridgewater and Dayton," he scrawled in his diary, and he kept a running account as the episode unfolded.

"This evening the citizens are removing their goods," Patterson wrote. "The work of destruction is commencing in the suburbs of the town. Now it is dark a squad of cavalry has just passed coming from the country where they have been carrying out the General's order. The whole country around is wrapped in flames, the heavens are aglow with the light thereof." He went on to describe the civilians' reactions: "such mourning, such lamentations, such crying and pleading for mercy. I never saw nor never want to see again, some were wild, crazy, mad, some cry[ing] for help while others would throw their arms around yankee soldiers necks and implore mercy." Then a report came that the order had been countermanded. "I hope it will not be enforced," Patterson wrote.[30]

Patterson's brigade commander, Brigadier General Thomas F. Wildes, shared his distress. He went in person to ask Sheridan to revoke the order – "begged and prayed"

[28]Entry for October 8, 1864, Ms. Diary, James M. Comly Papers, OHS.

[29]Hillman A. Hall, *History of the Sixth New York Cavalry* . . . (Worcester, MA: Blanchard Press, 1908), 391–393.

[30]Entry for October 4, 1864, William T. Patterson Diary, OHS.

is the phrasing used in a postwar account. Sheridan, who respected Wildes for his fighting qualities, heeded the request. The officer who was to execute the burning received the counterorder five minutes before his men were to apply the torch. "When I announced the order," the officer recalled, "there was louder cheering than there ever was when we made a bayonet charge." A short time later, Patterson recorded, a couple of cavalrymen rode by, loaded with plunder, only to be halted by Patterson's outraged colonel and arrested.[31]

"Truly," the Ohio sergeant believed, "war is cruelty." But his reluctance to see the population around him de-housed stemmed less from soft-heartedness than a desire to see justice done. While awaiting definite word that the order had been countermanded, he had written, "If it was at Berryville, Charlestown or Winchester [towns in the secessionist lower Valley] I would say burn in retaliation of Chambersburg, but this place is the most loyal or at least most innocent of any I have seen in the Valley." Such considerations mattered to Federal soldiers. Even in 1864, after years of warfare, most of them still retained a basic morality. Although not averse to destruction, they wanted to see the hard hand of war descend on those who deserved it, and usually only in rough proportion to the extent of their sins.[32]

This element of morality is critical to understanding the combination of severity and restraint that marked Union conduct during the war's final year. It clearly did not prevent destruction on a scale that desolated much of the South, but it channeled it in some directions and away from others. Public and quasipublic property like railroads, warehouses, and factories received the rough ministrations of Federal troops more often than private property. Plantations – the lairs of the slaveholding aristocracy – were targeted far more often than small farms. Policy dictated that the Southern population be divided according to the loyal, neutral, and actively disloyal, with different standards of conduct for each. The policy worked because the rank and file recognized and understood such distinctions. Not only was the Northern soldier a member of one of the most politically aware societies on earth, he was also strongly tied to his community – representatives of which marched and fought beside him – and to the values of the society that bred him.[33]

In 1866, a Northern war correspondent, William Swinton, wrote a history of the Army of the Potomac that included an account of Sheridan's devastation of the Shenandoah Valley. "The desolation of the Palatinate by Turenne was not more complete," he remarked. Although Swinton deserves credit for a learned analogy, his choice of comparison was quite inappropriate. The mistake, however, is instructive. The event he alluded to occurred on the eve of the War of the League of Augsburg in the late seventeenth century. Faced with imminent hostilities, Louis XIV and his

---

[31]S. Tschappat to John Wayland, March 16, 1912, in John Wayland, *A History of Rockingham County, Virginia* (Staunton, VA: McClure, 1943), 149–150; entry for October 5, 1864, William T. Patterson Diary, OHS.

[32]Entry for October 4, 1864, William T. Patterson Diary, OHS.

[33]For more on this point, see Michael Barton, *Goodmen: The Character of Civil War Soldiers* (State College: Pennsylvania State University Press, 1981).

advisers concluded that the Palatinate should be systematically devastated so that France's enemies could not use it as a base for operations against France. During the winter and spring of 1689, a number of major cities were put to the torch, as well as hundreds of smaller communities. Over a thousand towns and villages in the Palatinate were devastated in this manner. The contrast with Sheridan in the Shenandoah Valley could not have been sharper, for Sheridan's operations concentrated on crops, livestock, mills, and barns, not entire communities. The Devastation of the Palatinate was simplified by the fact that *ancien régime* soldiers were brutalized, wretched men, divorced from their communities and devoid of any stake in the fighting, held in the ranks only by ferocious discipline. Ordered to level cities, towns, and villages, they were scarcely bothered by the moral enormity of the pain and suffering thus visited on the population. Such men were nothing like the common soldiers who fought for the Union (or for that matter those who fought for the Confederacy).[34]

It is unlikely, for example, that the French soldiers who desolated the Palatinate had qualms of the sort that beset a detachment of the 2nd Ohio Cavalry. These men were asked to burn not towns but only barns. And yet, as one of them recalled, "many barns . . . were not burned; I know also for I saw it, that [Company] D often helped the folks that afternoon remove their furniture when the barn stood so near the house as to endanger the latter." One squad that helped an old woman with her furniture had received orders, of course, to destroy her barn. But evening fell, the officer in charge departed, and "the boys all left, not one of them would fire the barn."[35]

SEVERITY AND RESTRAINT: THE EVACUATION OF ATLANTA

Nowhere was the moral balance between severity and restraint more in evidence than during the forced evacuation of Southern civilians from Atlanta, hard on the heels of Sherman's capture of that city in September 1864. Having wrested Atlanta from Confederate control, the Federals faced the ticklish job of holding it, protecting the railroad that connected it with Nashville, and maintaining enough offensive punch to continue the thrust into Georgia. "I've got my wedge in pretty deep," Sherman would explain to a friend, "and must look out that I don't get my fingers pinched." His solution to the problem was to expel the population of Atlanta.[36]

The decision shocked Atlantans, the Confederacy at large, and even some of Sherman's own men, who expected him to conduct a more traditional occupation of the

[34]William Swinton, *Campaigns of the Army of the Potomac* (reprint ed., Secaucus, NJ: Blue and Grey Press, 1988 [1866], 560; John Childs, *Armies and Warfare in Europe, 1648–1789* (New York: Holmes and Meier, 1982), 152.

[35]Roger Hannaford, "Reminiscences," 179(d)-180(a), quoted in Stephen Z. Starr, *The Union Cavalry in the Civil War*, 3 vols. (Baton Rouge: Louisiana State University Press, 1979–1985), vol. 2, 302. Starr offers several similar comments by Union troopers. Ibid., 302–303.

[36]Sherman to ?, September 22, 1864, Silas F. Miller Papers, in Doubleday and Company Collection: Research Notes for Bruce Catton's Centennial History of the Civil War, LC.

city. When Mayor James M. Calhoun surrendered the city on the morning of September 2, for example, he was assured by Union Colonel John Coburn, "We do not come to make war upon non-combatants or private property; both shall be protected and respected by us." The colonel spoke honestly, for he did not know that Sherman had very different plans for Atlanta.[37]

In his postwar memoirs, Sherman explained that he wanted to make the city an example to the rest of the Confederacy. "I knew that the people of the South would read in this measure two important conclusions: one, that we were in earnest; and the other, if they were sincere in their common and popular clamor 'to die in the last ditch,' that the opportunity would soon come." At the time, however, Sherman emphasized another factor: his unusual logistical situation.[38]

Dangling from the end of a lengthy, vulnerable railroad that led back into Tennessee, Sherman's armies had conducted the entire Atlanta Campaign with the keen awareness that their regular supply line was tenuous at best. The letters of Captain James R. Stillwell, chaplain of the 79th Ohio, for that period are full of comments about reduced baggage and logistical austerity. When Atlanta fell, Stillwell's main reaction was that, while the wealthy citizens had apparently left, many people remained to be fed "at Uncle Sam's crib." He added that he almost wished the rest had left as well: "[T]hen [the] rebel army would have to feed them, not us."[39]

Sherman felt much the same way. He emphasized the logistical aspect when he first broached the subject of evacuation to Halleck: "I propose to remove all inhabitants of Atlanta. . . . I will allow no trade, manufactories, nor any citizens there at all, so that we will have the entire use of [the] railroad back, as also such corn and forage as may be reached by our troops." To a subordinate at Nashville he wrote, "Don't let any citizens come to Atlanta, not one." There was also the matter of the need to construct new fortifications. "The present rebel lines would require a garrison of 30,000 men," Sherman explained to Halleck, "whereas we must contract it to the vital points, viz, the railroads and necessary storehouses – all of which can be embraced in a circle of quarter the radius and requiring less than a sixth part of that number." This would require the demolition of a number of buildings in order to make way for trenches and to create fields of fire. With the population evacuated, Sherman would not have "to engage in a ceaseless wrangle every time we need a house or a site for a battery." But he could not explain this publicly: "I can't use this line of reasoning to a people who have no right to gain such a clue to our future plans and purposes."[40]

Such a disclosure would not have saved him from receiving loud protests anyway. He had anticipated this, and had already written Halleck that "if people raise a howl against my barbarity and cruelty I will answer that war is war, and not popularity-

---

[37]Quoted in A.A. Hoehling, *Last Train From Atlanta* (New York and London: Thomas Yoseloff, 1958), 417.

[38]Sherman, *Memoirs* 2:111–112.

[39]Stillwell to his wife, September 3, 1864, James R. Stillwell Papers, OHS.

[40]Sherman to Halleck, September 4, 1864, OR 38, pt. 5:794; Sherman to Joseph D. Webster, September 8, 1864, ibid., 830; Sherman to Halleck, September 13, 1864, ibid. 39, pt. 2:370.

seeking." But in fact he did not regard the measure as barbaric or cruel, and its execution was carried out with as much regard for the civilians as circumstances allowed. Nor should it be imagined that the evacuation involved the exodus of teeming thousands. Although the city had swollen to a wartime high of 22,000 prior to the summer of 1864, the battles around the city had steadily reduced the population so that no more than 3,000 were affected by Sherman's order. In the event, only 446 families left the city: 705 adults, 860 children, and 79 Negro servants, a total of 1,644 people in all. Each family was given one-fourth of a boxcar in which to stack its belongings, and each took with it an average of 1,654 pounds of furniture and household goods. Thus, while severe, the expulsion was hardly devoid of humanity. And ironically it was far from total; a colonel who helped supervise the move reported that "not more than half the people of Atlanta obeyed the order, and no force was used to compel obedience."[41]

Even so, the expulsion generated Sherman's predicted howl of protest. As it got underway, he received a petition from Atlanta's mayor, James M. Calhoun, and two city councilmen urging him to reconsider his decision. Arguing from a traditionalist view of noncombatant immunity, they observed that no similar order had ever been given in the history of the United States, and inquired, "[W]hat has this helpless people done, that they should be driven from their homes to wander strangers and outcasts and exiles, and to subsist on charity?"[42]

Sherman's response has since become a classic, constantly quoted as an example of the "realist" approach to war, and it combined all three of the arguments increasingly used by Federal commanders to justify their actions against civilians. First, he pleaded military necessity: "[M]y orders . . . were not designed to meet the humanities of the case, but to prepare for the future struggles. . . ." Second, he alleged the lack of restraint implicit in war: "You cannot qualify war in harsher terms than I will. War is cruelty, and you cannot refine it. . . . You might as well appeal against the thunderstorm as against these terrible hardships of war. They are inevitable." And finally, he emphasized that the Southern people deserved what they got, and must call a halt to the war:

[T]he only way the people of Atlanta can hope once again to live in peace and quiet at home, is to stop the war, which can only be done by admitting that it began in error and is perpetuated in pride. We don't want your negroes, or your horses, or your houses, or your lands, or anything you have, but we do want and will have a just obedience to the laws of the United States. That we will have, and if it involves the destruction of your improvements, we cannot help it.

---

[41]Sherman to Halleck, September 4, 1864, ibid. 38, pt. 5:794; Special Orders No. 67, September 8, 1864, ibid., 837; "Notice to the Citizens of Atlanta," September 8, 1864, ibid., 838; Walter G. Cooper, *Official History of Fulton County* (n.p., 1934), 180. Special Field Orders No. 70, September 10, 1864, OR 39, pt. 2, 356–357, called upon the chief quartermaster at Atlanta to afford the evacuated civilians "all the facilities he can spare to move them comfortably and safely, with their effects. . . . " Colonel Willard Warner of Sherman's staff, quoted in Samuel Carter III, *The Siege of Atlanta, 1864* (New York: St. Martins Press, 1973), 339.

[42]Calhoun et al. to Sherman, September 11, 1864, OR 39, pt. 2:417.

Then, with the almost compulsive movement from severity to gentleness that characterized much of Sherman's correspondence concerning Southern civilians, he pointed out that in Memphis and Mississippi the Union army had fed "thousands upon thousands of the families of rebel soldiers left on our hands, and whom we could not see starve." He chided the Atlantans for deprecating the horrors of war now after having helped to visit them on others in Kentucky and Tennessee, thereby desolating the homes of "hundreds and thousands of good people who only asked to live in peace at their old homes and under the Government of their inheritance."[43]

But such comparisons, Sherman went on, were idle:

I want peace, and believe it can now only be reached through union and war, and I will ever conduct war with a view to perfect an early success. But, my dear sirs, when that peace does come, you may call on me for anything. Then will I share with you the last cracker, and watch with you to shield your homes and families against danger from every quarter.[44]

This was not mere rhetoric. Even as Sherman ejected the Atlantans from their city, he pursued tantalizing hints that Georgia might be interested in making a separate peace with the Federal government. "Governor [Joseph] Brown [of Georgia] has disbanded his militia," Sherman informed Halleck on September 15, "to gather the corn and sorghum of the State. I have reason to believe that he and [Confederate Vice President Alexander] Stephens want to visit me, and I have sent them a hearty invitation." Lincoln himself perked up his ears at that, and wired Sherman of his great interest in the matter. Sherman explained to the President that two prominent Georgia citizens were currently acting as back-channel contacts between himself and Governor Brown. He said that he had suggested that Georgia could save itself from the devastation of war by withdrawing its troops from the Confederate army and in effect switching sides, for he would also expect them to help repel Hood's army from the state's borders. If they did so, he continued, "instead of desolating the land as we progress, I will keep our men to the high roads and commons and pay for the corn and meat we need and take."[45]

The looked-for visit from Brown and Stephens failed to materialize, however.

---

[43]Sherman to Calhoun et al., September 12, 1864, ibid., 418–419. It is worth noting that Sherman also became involved in an acrid exchange with his Confederate counterpart, John Bell Hood, concerning the expulsion order, albeit one that generated more heat than light. See Hood to Sherman, September 9, 1864, ibid., 415; Sherman to Hood, September 10, 1864, ibid., 416; Hood to Sherman, September 12, 1864, ibid., 419–422; and Sherman to Hood, September 14, 1864, ibid., 422. An interesting critique of the ethical implications of the expulsion order is in Walzer, *Just and Unjust Wars,* 32–33. See also Best, *Humanity in Warfare,* 209–210.

[44]Ibid., 419. Interestingly, the Democratic press seized on Sherman's letter as an implicit expression of its Chicago platform. The *New York World* (September 26, 1864) viewed Sherman (tongue in cheek) as a "Copperhead" because of the lines about not wanting Southern Negroes, but only a just obedience to the Constitution. Another paper opined that "although the measure insisted upon by him is severe and in our opinion needless, the tone and spirit of his letter is conciliatory and humane." See *The Courier,* September 27, 1864, clipping in the George Brinton McClellan, Sr. Papers, LC.

[45]Sherman, *Memoirs* 2:137–140; Sherman to Halleck, September 15, 1864, OR 39, pt. 2:381; Lincoln to Sherman, September 17, 1864, Basler (ed.), *Collected Works of Lincoln* 8:9; Sherman to Lincoln, September 17, 1864, OR 39, pt. 2:395–396.

Georgia remained in the war, and Sherman's armies spent the next several weeks fruitlessly chasing Hood's army as it bedeviled the tenuous Union supply line through the northern part of the state. Much to Sherman's frustration, the Federals were in effect fighting twice for the same real estate. He wanted to cut loose from the Western and Atlanta Railroad entirely, abandon Atlanta, and strike out for a new base on the coast.

He was going to abandon something else as well – namely, any further attempts to spare Georgia from the desolating effects of war. On October 9 he wrote Grant, "I propose that we break up the railroad from Chattanooga forward, and that we strike out with our wagons for Milledgeville, Macon, and Savannah." The mere occupation of Georgia, he argued, was useless given the hostile population. "[B]ut the utter destruction of its [rail]roads, houses, and people, will cripple their military resources. . . . I can make the march, and make Georgia howl!"[46]

SHERMAN'S MARCHES: THE AIMS AND LIMITS OF DESTRUCTION

What Sherman had in mind, in essence, was a new *chevauchée*. The original *chevauchées* dated back to the Hundred Years' War, and were massive raiding expeditions in which the English systematically pillaged or destroyed everything in their path. In its first great raid of that late medieval conflict, the army of Edward III had burned villages, churches, monasteries, and hospitals, devastated grainfields, and slaughtered French civilians by the hundred. Thousands more had fled to the relative safety of the fortified cities, only to perish from famine and disease. Subsequent *chevauchées* had sometimes been even larger in scale. When conducting these raids, the English army resembled an ambient, marauding city, complete with its own facilities to process what it plundered. The chronicler Froissart described one such expedition in 1359:

[O]n this campaign the great English lords and men of substance took with them tents of various sizes, mills for grinding corn, ovens for baking, forges for shoeing the horses and all other necessities. To carry this, they had fully eight thousand wagons, each drawn by good, strong rounseys which they had brought over from England. . . . They also carried on the wagons a small number of boats. Each could take three men over the biggest lake or pond to fish whatever part of it they liked. . . . Their army was always divided into three bodies, each moving independently with its own vanguard and rearguard and halting for the night three miles behind the preceding one. . . . They kept this formation the whole way from Calais until they reached the city of Chartres [a distance of nearly 200 miles].[47]

[46]Sherman to Grant, October 9, 1864, ibid., pt. 3:660.

[47]Froissart, *Chronicles*, trans. and ed. by Geoffrey Brereton (abridged edition; Harmondsworth, Middlesex, England: Penguin, 1968), Bk. 1, p. 164–65. For background on the *chevauchées*, see Desmond Seward, *The Hundred Years War: The English in France, 1337–1453* (London: Constable, 1978), 38–39, and Philippe Contamine, *War in the Middle Ages*, trans. by Michael Jones (London: Basil Blackwell, 1984), 222–225.

Although *chevauchées* provided sustenance for the army and gave the soldiers a motive to fight, their chief strategic purpose was frequently political and psychological. They demoralized a hostile peasantry and punished a subjugated one. They also undermined the authority of the French crown, as in 1346 when Edward III conducted an extensive raid, "burning, laying waste, and driving out the inhabitants, until the French were full of sorrow, and exclaimed: 'Where is Philip, our King?'"[48]

The logic at work here exactly anticipated part of Sherman's rationale for his March to the Sea:

> If we can march a well-appointed army right through his territory, it is a demonstration to the world, foreign and domestic, that we have a power which [Confederate President Jefferson] Davis cannot resist. This may not be war but rather statesmanship; nevertheless it is overwhelming to my mind that there are thousands of people abroad and in the South who reason thus: If the North can march an army right through the South, it is proof positive that the North can prevail. . . .

Sherman's reasoning here emphasized the march as an adroit maneuver, a way of showing, as he put it elsewhere, that if you pierced the shell of the Confederacy you found hollowness within. And, as we have already seen, his instructions for the operation, although they enjoined extensive foraging as the only practical means of securing adequate rations, also directed that the job be done in an orderly, controlled manner with a minimum of waste and wanton destruction.[49]

Even so, Sherman clearly knew that those instructions would be imperfectly carried out – that some soldiers would pillage and plunder and vandalize. And many people, then and later, have suspected that Sherman secretly (or not so secretly) wanted that to happen. His comments about "desolating the land as we progress" and "making Georgia howl" suggest as much. So too does the grim relish with which he greeted the destruction of Atlanta's war resources, a task that got out of hand and resulted in considerable destruction to the city's residential quarter. Although Sherman personally supervised efforts to contain the flames, his general attitude came through in a comment to his adjutant:

> [T]his city has done and contributed probably more to carry on and sustain the war than any other, save perhaps Richmond. We have been fighting *Atlanta* all the time in the past: have been capturing guns, wagons, etc., etc., marked *Atlanta* and made here, all the time: and now since they have been doing so much to destroy us and our Government we have to destroy them, at least enough to prevent any more of that.

The same officer would soon complain to his diary, "I am bound to say that I think Sherman lacking in enforcing discipline. Brilliant and daring, fertile, rapid and terrible, he does not seem to me to carry things out in this respect. . . ."[50]

[48]Chandos Herald in Richard Barber (ed.), *The Life and Campaigns of the Black Prince* (London: Boydell Press, 1986), 88.

[49]Sherman to Grant, November 6, 1864, OR 39, pt. 3:660.

[50]M.A. DeWolfe Howe (ed.), *Marching With Sherman: Passages From the Letters and Campaign Diaries of Henry Hitchcock . . .* (New Haven, CT: Yale University Press, 1927), 58, 157.

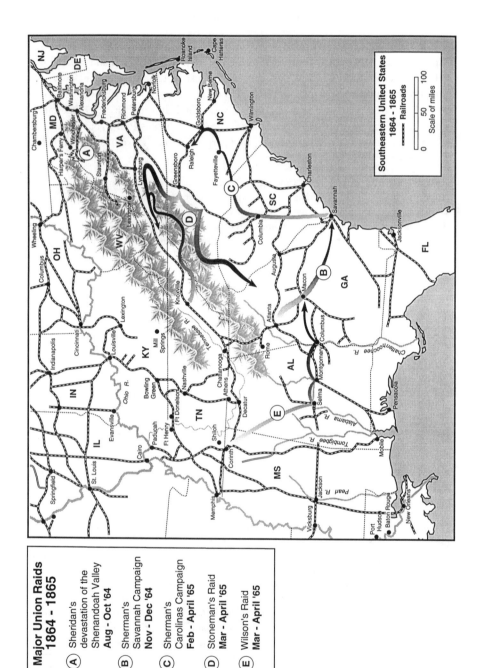

**Major Union Raids
1864 - 1865**

(A) Sheridan's
devastation of the
Shenandoah Valley
Aug - Oct '64

(B) Sherman's
Savannah Campaign
Nov - Dec '64

(C) Sherman's
Carolinas Campaign
Feb - April '65

(D) Stoneman's Raid
Mar - April '65

(E) Wilson's Raid
Mar - April '65

**Southeastern United States
1864 - 1865**

╌╌╌ Railroads

0   50   100
Scale of miles

The whole issue turns on two questions: first, whether Sherman really intended his troops to exercise restraint, and second, whether he and his officers were actually capable of enforcing the discipline that the adjutant and subsequent critics thought they should. The first question requires us to get inside the head of a man who has been dead for over a century. We cannot do it; we can only weigh and evaluate the evidence of the words he left behind. These words – despite Sherman's occasionally dire rhetoric – indicate on the whole a conservative man who possessed a deep respect for order coupled with a need to explain the justice of his actions unusual in someone of his position. Grant could order Sheridan to leave the Shenandoah Valley "a barren waste," and Sheridan could do it, both without the sermonettes that make Sherman so endlessly fascinating for historians and others. Sherman seems never to have quite become comfortable with hard war. It bothered him that soldiers would not confine themselves simply to authorized destruction. But he grew resigned to it. As he explained to a friend long after the war:

> I know that in the beginning I, too, had the old West Point notion that pillage was a capital crime, and punished it by shooting, but the Rebels wanted us to detach a division here, a brigade there, to protect their families and property while they were fighting. . . . This was a one-sided game of war, and many of us, kind-hearted, fair, just and manly . . . ceased to quarrel with our own men about such minor things, and went in to subdue the enemy, leaving minor depredations to be charged up to the account of the rebels who had forced us into the war, and who deserved all they got and *more*.[51]

Other officers grew resigned as well, sometimes under circumstances that shed light on the second question – the extent to which Sherman and his subordinates could enforce discipline. Even in the old days of conciliation, officers had found it difficult to prevent the men from acts of petty theft and vandalism. The problem was far more acute now that they were asking the men, as part of their normal duties, to live off the countryside, heat and bend railroad iron, burn mills, and confiscate horseflesh. Shortly before the Savannah Campaign began, Major James Connolly accompanied troops on a fatigue detail to wreck the Western and Atlantic Railroad. The men destroyed their assigned portion of the road, then some of them went on to burn the village of Acworth – "*without orders.*" Acworth, he noted in his diary, "has been a thriving R.R. village, but to-night it is a heap of ruins. I was the only one of the General's staff in the town when the fires first began, and I tried to prevent the burning." But while he watched one house to keep it from being fired, the soldiers simply set the torch to another. The major succeeded in saving only a handful of houses, and only those occupied by women and their families.

It is easy to understand the major's frustration. He was apparently the sole officer present – at least the only one interested in preventing the arson – and physically incapable of riding herd over the full complement of soldiers in the village. One supposes he might have drawn his revolver and shot a few of the offenders, but that was hardly a live option. He did the best he could. It was not enough, and so his diary

[51]Sherman to J.B. Fry, September 3, 1884, Letterbook, William T. Sherman Papers, LC.

entry concluded with a prediction, a rationalization, and a cautionary memorandum to himself: "It is evident that our soldiers are determined to burn, plunder and destroy everything in their way on this march. Well, that shows that they are not *afraid* of the South at any rate, and that each individual soldier is determined to strike with all his might against the rebellion, whether we ever get through or not. If we are to continue our devastation as we began to-day I don't want to be captured on this trip, for I expect every man of us the rebels capture will get a 'stout rope and a short shrift.'"[52]

Perhaps Connolly read the *Army and Navy Journal,* an impressive professional military newspaper that had begun publication the previous year. If he did he would have found a word of advice awaiting him when he and Sherman's armies reached Savannah in December 1864. The issue for the week of the 24th offered an article entitled, "The Essential Principle of Discipline." Preceding the piece was a lengthy quotation in French, which, assuming the former Illinois lawyer could read that language, would have informed Connolly that the way to deal with a soldier's faults was to punish his immediate superior.[53] The article itself began, "It is said that in some of the expeditions made from our army, private homes have been *causelessly* burned by stragglers."

How to prevent this? The author had three answers. The first, suggested by the epigram, was for private soldiers to be always in the presence of a noncommissioned officer, who would know the men well, keep tabs on them through frequent roll calls, and "find means with his bayonet, if in no other way, to keep them in their places." Lieutenants and captains had only a few sergeants to keep track of, and could always see where the fault lay when privates turned up missing. Colonels and majors, in turn, would keep an eye on their junior officers, and "for every straggler picked up, the commanding officer of his regiment should be called to a heavy account." Any officer or sergeant who, after two months at his job, could not prevent straggling, was "either culpable or incapable. . . . If, therefore, discipline has been established beforehand, outrages will not be committed."

The author had two other recommendations – the first for a hand-picked police force, mounted on fleet horses, to keep order; the second for the organization of "discipline companies" to handle recidivist offenders. The author assumed that "[i]n straggling, plundering, and setting fire to buildings, the *active ones* are almost always the same men." "Shooting or hanging," he wrote, "would undoubtedly be the proper radical remedy," and the army would be better off if such punishment were summarily applied (as several of Sherman's subordinate generals, in fact, threatened to do). Unfortunately, from a "false sense of humanity, or other causes, these appropriate means are scarcely ever employed in the 'nick of time'" – hence the need for "discipline companies" into which suspected offenders could be placed without the

---

[52]Diary entry for November 13, 1864, Paul M. Angle (ed.), *Three Years in the Army of the Cumberland: The Letters and Diary of Major James A. Connolly* (Bloomington: Indiana University Press, 1959), 298.

[53]If he could not, an English translation appeared at the foot of the article.

guilt of having executed a possibly innocent man. But the really critical thing, the author concluded, was his first subject: Officers had to be held accountable.[54]

Thus we have a detailed contemporary estimate of the sort of discipline possible in the Union army. But it is fair to ask how someone like Major Connolly would have regarded it. Certainly from the distance of more than a century, knowing what we know about the makeup of Civil War regiments, the *Army and Navy Journal* scheme has an air of unreality to it. The article expected sergeants, lieutenants, captains, majors, and colonels to behave impersonally toward one another, following the book, when in fact most of them – like the men they led – came from the same communities, often knew each others' families, and expected to live in the same communities when the war ended. Could they really have applied the unyielding system the article prescribed? Exceptionally conscientious men sometimes attempted it and were ostracized for their pains. Moreover, such a system assumed that all sergeants and officers would evaluate matters in a fairly rigid, dogmatic manner. The author of the piece, for example, presumed that all stragglers were deliberate shirkers, whereas in fact any number of extenuating circumstances – fatigue, blistered feet – could make a man lag behind his comrades. Where did one draw the line? How could an officer in charge of a foraging party simultaneously ask his troops to strip corn, hams, and other victuals from a squalling, wretched Georgia family and at the same time maintain complete decorum? Then, too, as Joseph T. Glatthaar has observed, "Vigorous control, the only solution to the problem, would have stifled the independence of the troops and detracted from the overall effectiveness of the campaign, and possibly would even have endangered its success."[55]

Finally, the system depended on most, if not all, sergeants and officers reforming their lax ways at once. Until that happened, an officer like Major Connolly would have a lot in common with King Canute. After the march, one brigade commander complained that a number of his officers, "in spite of their long experience and in face of positive orders to the contrary, suffer, nay, by their passiveness encourage, their men to throw aside the restrictions of discipline, and become outlaws and brigands." Like the author of the *Army and Navy Journal* article, he laid stress on the role officers could play in preventing such mischief, and emphasized especially the importance of the company commander, whose position, "so immediately connecting him with the rank and file, makes him a conservator of the peace and good order of the army." Officers who could not enforce discipline, he concluded – and he identified several of this sort in his brigade – ought to be dismissed.[56]

---

[54]"The Essential Principle of Military Discipline," *Army and Navy Journal* 2 (December 24, 1864), 276. For orders threatening capital punishment, see General Order No. 25 [17th Army Corps], November 17, 1864, OR 44:482; Circular [14th Army Corps], November 18, 1864, ibid., 489; Special Field Orders No. 172 [Army of the Tennessee], November 19, 1864, ibid., 493; and Special Orders No. 177 [15th Army Corps], November 20, 1864, ibid., 498.

[55]Glatthaar, *The March to the Sea and Beyond,* 147.

[56]Report of Lieutenant Colonel James W. Langley, January 3, 1865, OR 44:201.

Numerous accounts of Sherman's March survive, and as one might expect, they vary widely according to the observer's personal status and angle of vision. For the civilians in Sherman's path, a disproportionate number of whom were women, the experience was terrifying. What happened to Dolly Lunt Burge was fairly typical. She lived on a 900-acre plantation nine miles east of Covington, Georgia. She first heard the Yankees were coming the day Sherman left Atlanta. Two nights later, apprehensive and restless, she went outdoors several times and saw large fires in the distance. She thought perhaps the army would pass her by, but the soldiers overran her home the next day. That evening, Dolly Burge poured her shock and rage into the diary she meticulously kept. Understandably, the entry emphasizes the magnitude of her loss: "I . . . went to the gate to claim protection & a guard. But like Demons they rush in! My yards are full. To my smoke-house, my Dairy, Pantry, Kitchen & Cellar, like famished wolves they come, breaking locks & whatever is in their way." Within a few minutes the foragers had grabbed half a ton of meat from her smokehouse and shot down her turkeys, chickens, and pigs. Much to her dismay, the guard did nothing to stop them. "I cannot help you, Madam; it is the orders."[57]

A close reading of the entry discloses that the guard did in fact protect her. Aside from the taking of provisions, the main house was not disturbed. Burge's slaves were not so fortunate. With the utter disregard for blacks that was the norm among Union troops, the soldiers ransacked the slave cabins, taking whatever they liked until the guard ordered Burge to let her slaves move their remaining belongings to the sanctuary of the main house. That evening, two "Dutch" soldiers relieved the guard and remained overnight. Burge feared the Yankees would burn her house, but they did not. The next day the army marched on, leaving her to rejoice that her home was still intact and vowing, "Such a day, if I ever live to the age of Methuselah, may God spare me from ever seeing again."[58]

Some civilians fared worse. Burge was probably wise to have remained, for one of Sherman's troops asserted that about three-quarters of the families along his unit's line of march did flee, "and in such instances the buildings and the contents rarely escaped the torch of straggling troops." Apparently these were outbuildings, for he added, "Strict orders restrained, though they did not entirely prevent, arson and pillage of dwellings." A number of private homes were destroyed, sometimes deliberately and sometimes because of their proximity to authorized targets. Something like that may have occurred in Hillsboro, Georgia. An Iowa soldier noted that "the place was almost destroyed as it was a manufacturing town."[59]

[57]Entries for November 16, 18, 19, 1864, James I. Robertson, Jr. (ed.), "The Diary of Dolly Lunt Burge, Part VII," *Georgia Historical Quarterly* 45 (1961):371.

[58]Entry for November 19, 1864, ibid., 372–373. A useful compendium of other civilian accounts is Jones, *When Sherman Came*. It contains eighteen accounts of the Savannah Campaign, including Burge's. A few are by women as they anticipated Sherman's arrival or witnessed the aftermath, but of the fifteen that record actual encounters with Union troops, all but three report having received protection at one time or another. None lost their homes, although some knew of others that did.

[59]George W. Pepper, *Personal Recollections of Sherman's Campaign in Georgia and the Carolinas* (Zanesville, OH: Hugh Dunne, 1866), 246; entry for November 21, 1864, Abijah F. Gore Diary, CWMC, USAMHI.

For the most part, however, Georgia whites suffered primarily the loss of crops and livestock. "When we passed through there was but little left for Rebel troops to live on," an Ohio soldier told his father. "Families have enough to see the winter through but nothing to give away to their friends." Some troops found slim pickings, but most fared sumptuously; as a German-born private enthused to his family, "we lived like God in France." A good deal of looting also took place, especially by the foraging parties who operated with little supervision. "If money, watches or jewelry was found it was inevitably confiscated," recalled a New York veteran after the war, adding that the rampant thievery had "a very demoralizing effect on the men." Even men of good reputation began to steal. There were men in prisons all over the country, the old veteran believed, "who took their first lessons in theiving [sic] while acting as one of Sherman's foragers."[60]

Plenty of men regretted the hardship they and their comrades visited on civilians. During the destruction of railroads preceding the march, an Ohio soldier, drafted into the army only weeks before, scrawled in his diary: "There is great destruction of property about here. Much of it unnecessary. It is a pity to see homes of comfort destroyed thus. I think of my own house and wife and I can estimate the feelings of the enemy when I think how I would feel if served thus." Colonel Orlando M. Poe, the Union engineer who presided over the authorized destruction of Atlanta's war resources, complained to his own diary of the damage wrought by vandals, "to the great scandal of our Army, and marked detriment to its discipline." As the army neared the coast, a captain came upon four houses set afire "by some dirty rascal from our army." He made extensive but fruitless efforts to identify the arsonist. "I am ashamed to see such outrages committed," he fumed, "and made up my mind to shot [sic] the first scoundrel whom I may catch."[61]

Eight days into the Savannah Campaign, Major Thomas Taylor of the 47th Ohio — the same Taylor who had tried to save Jackson, Mississippi, from the flames the previous year — came upon a family who had been abused by a renegade party of foragers. After stripping them of everything edible, the "bummers" had smashed jars and dishes, vandalized furniture, scattered clothing, cut open mattresses, and threatened to burn the house down around their ears if they did not leave.

"Such an act of barbarity," Taylor wrote, "I have never witnessed in all the service, yet these fiends wore the Federal uniform." He tried but failed to gain a clue to the malefactors' identities, then did what little he could to "adjust affairs — but it was impossible to leave the family in any manner comfortable." Taylor's colonel sent a guard to the house, and a surgeon somehow materialized to succor the family, but

[60]Charles Ewing to his father, December 15, 1864, George C. Osborn (ed.), "Sherman's March Through Georgia: Letters from Charles Ewing to his Father Thomas Ewing," *Georgia Historical Quarterly* (1958), 326; Wilhelm Möbus to his family, January 1, 1865, David L. Anderson (ed.), "The Life of 'Wilhelm Yank': Letters From a German Soldier in the Civil War," *Michigan Historical Review* 16 (Spring 1990):83; typescript memoir, William B. Westervelt Memoir and Diary, CWMC, USAMHI.

[61]Entry for November 12, 1864, typescript diary of John Vail, OHS; entry for November 15, 1864, Ms. diary, Orlando M. Poe Papers, LC; entry for November 28, 1864, David J. De Laubenfels (ed.), "With Sherman Through Georgia: A Journal," *Georgia Historical Quarterly* 41 (1957), 297.

Taylor could locate neither blankets nor rations. Finally he wrapped a comforter around one of the children and left to rejoin his regiment, fuming, "What a black page for American history!" The issue was not that a good number of soldiers felt this way, but rather that their influence could not restrain everyone.[62]

If the diaries of Vail and Taylor testify to the excesses of the march, they also implicitly suggest that such incidents were relatively limited. Both were men who regularly noticed civilians and what happened to them, yet the incident described here is the only one Taylor recorded after the army left Atlanta. Vail, for his part, reported only his difficulty in keeping up with the veterans into whose company he had been thrown. Other accounts are more direct:

Passed through Madison, the seat of Morgan County. This is indeed a fine town, evidently a wealthy place. Many fine dwellings, abodes of luxury & ease! Town not damaged. Calaboose only burned. . . .

I have inquired closely as far as I could and repeatedly inquired. . . . I cannot learn of any outrage by any one, or the burning of any dwelling. . . .

Early in the day, passed [Eatonton]. Quite a town. People were surprised & alarmed. Private property respected except where Soldiers wanted to eat etc. A small lot of cotton & cotton yarn burned. . . .

Private homes were respected everywhere, even those of noted Rebels, and I heard of no instance of pillage or insult to the inhabitants. . . .

Except in a few instances, private residences have not been destroyed by the soldiers. . . .

Still other accounts routinely report the destruction of railroad stations, mills, cotton gins, and other public and quasipublic property, but make no mention of depredations against civilians.[63]

During this campaign, Captain John Rhiza, a topographical engineer in the 14th Corps, drew a meticulous series of maps of the terrain through which the corps passed, showing houses, barns, and outbuildings along the line of march. The maps for a 60-mile stretch still survive. Two houses bear the notation "ruined;" a third was "on fier [sic]" as Rhiza passed by. In 1955 an amateur historian, David J. De Laubenfels, revisited the corps' line of march. He was able to locate the sites of 72 of the houses shown on Rhiza's maps, including the three that had been destroyed. "Among these," De Laubenfels wrote, "no less than 22 were still there in 1955 while it was possible to establish with certainty that nine others had been torn down or burned at some time

[62]Entry for November 23, 1864, ms. diary, Thomas T. Taylor Papers, OHS.

[63]Entry for November 19, 1864, typescript diary, Lyman D. Ames Papers, OHS; entry for November 20, 1864, Howe (ed.), *Marching With Sherman*, 76; entry for November 21, 1864, typescript diary Lyman D. Ames Papers, OHS; entries for November 24, December 6, 1864, George Ward Nichols, *The Story of the Great March, From the Diary of a Staff Officer* (Reprint ed.; Williamstown, MA: Conner House, 1984 [1865]), 57, 83. For accounts that mention only authorized foraging and destruction, see, for example, entries for November 15-December 10, 1864, Nathaniel Parmeter Diary, OHS; entries for November 15-December 10, 1864, Ephraigm Franklin Brower Diary, CWMC, USAMHI; entries for November 15-December 10, 1864, typescript diary, and Albion Gross to his wife, December 14, 1864, Albion Gross Letters and Diary, CWMC, USAMHI.

since the War Between the States!" Since De Laubenfels had begun with a belief in the all-destructive fury of Sherman's March, he was quite surprised. He nevertheless assumed that many of the 41 dwellings unaccounted for must have been burned by Sherman's men, although he could find no evidence of it. Indeed, he could confirm the destruction only of the three houses on Rhiza's map – one of which actually proved to be a grist mill.[64]

The extent to which houses and towns were burned during Sherman's March to the Sea thus turns out to be much exaggerated. And what of the murdered civilians supposedly sprawled in Sherman's wake? What of the violated women? Among whites, we know of no murders and have only a few sketchy reports of rapes. The Southern legends are not completely wrong, however. Similar atrocities did occur, but the victims were African Americans. Numerous blacks were physically abused and at least one black man reported that a soldier tried to rape his wife. The worst incident occurred on December 9, when Major General Jefferson C. Davis marched his 14th Corps across rain-swollen Ebenezer Creek, then abruptly removed the pontoon bridges so as to strand hundreds of fugitive slaves on the opposite shore, closely followed by Confederate cavalry. Frantic to see their dream of freedom snatched away and terrified of what the rebel horsemen might do, hundreds of blacks plunged into the water and tried to swim across. Many drowned; just how many, no one knows. Even Sherman's hardened troops were indignant at Davis's act, and an Indiana surgeon wrote bitterly, "If I had the power I would [hang] him as high as Haman."[65]

While Georgia blacks grappled with their tenuous escape from slavery, whites endured the shock of Sherman's passing. As Major Connolly recorded, "Citizens everywhere look paralyzed and as if stricken dumb as we pass them. Columns of smoke by day, and 'pillars of fire' by night, for miles and miles on our right and left indicate to us daily and nightly the route and location of the other columns of our army." Every gin house and every grain-filled barn was destroyed: "[I]n fact everything that can be of any use to the rebels is either carried off by our foragers or set on fire and burned."[66]

It is impossible to say how much of the destruction during the Savannah Campaign was legitimate and how much exceeded the bounds of military necessity. Soon after the march began, one of Sherman's senior commanders, Major General Oliver O. Howard, complained that "quite a number" of abandoned residences had been fired "without official sanction," accompanied by "many instances of the most inexcusable and wanton acts, such as the breaking open of trunks, taking of silver plate, &c." The Georgians, he wrote, "are terrified, and believe us a thousand times worse than we are." After his armies reached the ocean, Sherman reported to Halleck that his troops

---

[64]De Laubenfels (ed.), "With Sherman Through Georgia: A Journal," 288–300.

[65]Entry for December 11, 1864, Robert G. Athearn (ed.), "An Indiana Doctor Marches With Sherman: The Diary of James Comfort Patten," *Magazine of Indiana History* 49 (1953):419. For the conduct of Sherman's men toward blacks, see Glatthaar, *March to the Sea and Beyond*, 52–65. The incident at Ebenezer Creek is described in Marszalek, *Sherman*, 312–313.

[66]Entry for November 21, 1864, Angle (ed.), *Three Years in the Army of the Cumberland*, 314.

had torn up over a hundred miles of railroad. They had also "consumed the corn and fodder in the region of country thirty miles on either side of a line from Atlanta to Savannah, as also the sweet potatoes, cattle, hogs, sheep and poultry, and have carried away more than 10,000 horses and mules, as well as a countless number of their slaves."[67]

All in all, he estimated "the damage done to the State of Georgia and its military resources at $100,000,000." Of that total, at least $20,000,000 worked to the Union's military advantage. The rest, he confessed, "is simple waste and destruction." Such an estimate is interesting but could hardly be authoritative, since the general seems to have offered it only as a rough approximation, and we cannot be sure what qualified in his mind as militarily advantageous and what did not. Sherman, for example, may have included the value of the "countless number of slaves" who trailed after the armies and whose presence he did not consider useful. He may also have included the considerable but largely accidental damage caused by the burning of war resources in Atlanta. But on the whole, the March to the Sea was probably no more destructive, in proportion to its length, than the two raids on Jackson, the Meridian expedition, or the burning of crops in the Shenandoah Valley.[68]

In any event, it contrasted sharply with the conduct of Sherman's men when they swung into South Carolina in February 1865. Until that time, the unauthorized destruction that attended the march was mainly, in the phrase of corps commander Major General Alpheus S. Williams, the work of "the few (ever found in large bodies of men) who were disorderly and vicious." From the moment the Federals crossed the Savannah River, however, incidents of pillaging and arson accelerated dramatically. The perpetrators were no longer the marginal soldiers alone, but included many of the best, most motivated troops. What happened to South Carolina forcefully underscored the substantially directed nature of the severity that had preceded it. It showed what a Federal army could do when it *wanted* to wreak indiscriminate havoc.[69]

The reason for this massive increase in violence – noticed and widely remarked on by contemporary observers – was simple. South Carolina had been the first state to secede. Not only that, it was almost universally believed to be filled, from one end to the other, with the most virulent, dedicated disunionists. It was an article of faith with most Northerners that South Carolina, as the cockpit of secession, bore most of the blame for the war. Sherman wrote Grant that he believed "the whole United States, North and South, would rejoice to have this army turned loose on South Carolina to devastate that State." The growls of impending vengeance began while the army was still resting near recently captured Savannah. "Threatening words were heard from soldiers who prided themselves on 'conservatism in house-burning while in Georgia,'" remembered a Union captain, "and officers confessed their fears that the coming campaign would be a wicked one." An Ohio soldier was more blunt. "We will make her [South Carolina] suffer worse than she did at the time of the Revolutionary

---

[67]Howard's report, November 23, 1864, OR 44:67; Sherman's report, January 1, 1865, ibid. 44:13.
[68]Ibid.
[69]Report of Alpheus S. Williams, January 9, 1865, ibid., 212.

War," he wrote his family. "We will let her know it isn't So Sweet to secede as She thought it would be."[70]

"The truth is," Sherman wrote Halleck, "the whole army is burning with an insatiable desire to wreak vengeance upon South Carolina. I almost tremble for her fate, but feel that she deserves all that seems in store for her." Other senior Union commanders agreed. Halleck had already written Sherman that if he captured Charleston (where the ordinance of secession had been passed), "I hope that by some accident the place may be destroyed, and if a little salt should be sown upon its site it may prevent the growth of future crops of nullification and secession." Back in November, Department of the South commander John G. Foster had written Halleck that Sherman, once based at Savannah, would then be admirably poised to "utterly destroy and devastate the whole State of South Carolina."[71]

Although the orders for the northward march remained the same as for the Savannah Campaign, a number of soldiers believed they detected a different subtext. As one soldier wrote home, "Shermans policy for South Carolina is understood to be destruction as we go." "Boys, this is old South Carolina," boomed an 89th Ohio soldier as his regiment crossed the state line, "lets give her h-ll." In contrast to what had transpired in Georgia, entire towns were regularly put to the torch. One soldier, marching with his regiment in the wake of previous units, passed through Robertsville, "a very nice little village but now there is nothing left to mark the place except about one hundred 'monuments' (Chimnies) erected to the memory of Jefferson D." At Barnwell – grimly renamed "Burnwell" by the troops – only a few buildings survived. "Those belong to the poorer class of people," noted Pennsylvania cavalryman William Pritchard. "The large residences of the planters, the Court House, jail and stores were all consumed."[72]

Pritchard wrote those words in an extended letter-journal, begun just before Sherman's army left Savannah and kept with the idea of mailing it to his parents when he got the chance. It is one of the more illuminating documents to emerge from the Carolinas Campaign. Pritchard considered the orders "less stringent" than in Georgia, and thought they enjoined the destruction of the "finer residences" as well as cotton gins and corn cribs. He disapproved of burning houses, but since higher authority apparently sanctioned it, he reluctantly acquiesced. "I think it partakes of the Barbarous," he wrote, although he thought the Southerners had started the business by burning Chambersburg, Pennsylvania. But the next day he saw the town of Blackville destroyed, and his doubts increased:

---

[70]Sherman to Grant, December 18, 1864, ibid., 743; David P. Conyngham, *Sherman's March Through the South with Sketches and Incidents of the Campaign* (New York: Sheldon and Company, 1865), 310 (Conyngham doubled as a reporter for the *New York Herald*); Bell I. Wiley, "Billy Yank Down South," *Virginia Quarterly Review* 26 (1950), 570.

[71]Sherman to Halleck, December 24, 1864, OR 44:799; Halleck to Sherman, December 18, 1864, ibid., 741; Foster to Halleck, November 14, 1864, ibid., 464.

[72]Samuel K. Harryman to "Maggie," January 22, 1865, Samuel K. Harryman Papers, Indiana State Library, Indianapolis. Entry for February 8, 1865, W. C. Johnson Diary, Miscellaneous Manuscripts Collection, LC; entry for February 5, 1865, Nathaniel Parmeter Diary, OHS; entry for February 8, 1865, William W. Pritchard Journal, CWMC, USAMHI.

I am more and more impressed with the burning business and the cruelty of it. I do not believe in it, and the more I see of it, the more I hate the principle. It is barbarous, cruel and rough and if we are defeated on this campaign, which by the way, I am afraid will be the result, I shall assign as the reason the wanton destruction of private property and the savageness in which this campaign is conducted.

The Confederate burning of Chambersburg no longer seemed a sufficient excuse, for the logic of reprisal would end in a vicious spiral of destruction: "[T]his war would soon assume the no quarter system – and I am not so sure but it will yet."[73]

Most soldiers did not share Pritchard's misgivings. After ten days of devastation, he thought he noted a reduction in the burning, especially as the army entered the South Carolina upcountry. "Where the people are mild, they do not suffer so much," Pritchard observed, "where they are rabid, they fare hard." But he never believed that "men would have the heart to devastate and waste as we do. The living things are killed; even old worn out horses are shot, and dogs cows and hogs are shot down and left. . . ."[74]

The most serious single act of destruction – and highly controversial, since it is unclear exactly who began the blaze – was the burning of Columbia.[75] But the scale of the overall devastation was enormous. "I saw property destroyed until I was perfectly sick of it," confessed a Michigan soldier, "& that, for me to say in S.C. is considerable." "You know that from the beginning I have advocated the most rigid measures," Chaplain James Stillwell wrote his wife. Until the march into South Carolina, he had been somewhat disappointed, even after participating in the Savannah Campaign. "[B]ut on this raid my desires have been *more* than gratified, for there is scarcely anything left in our *rear* or *trac{k}s* except pine forests and naked lands and Starving inhabitants. A majority of the *Cities, towns, villages* and *county houses* have been burnt to the ground. . . ." "The army burned everything it came near in the State of South Carolina," Major Connolly concurred, "not under orders, but in spite of orders. The men 'had it in' for the State, and they took it out in their own way. Our track through the State is a desert waste."[76]

But, Connolly added, "Since entering North Carolina the wanton destruction has stopped." It was true. The Tarheel State received much the same treatment as Georgia – possibly even a bit milder, since North Carolina was not part of the Deep South, was known to harbor significant Unionist sentiment, and had been one of the last states to secede. Certainly a number of Federal commanders issued directives encouraging gentler behavior. The abrupt cessation of the maelstrom that engulfed

[73]Entry for February 8, 9, 1865, William W. Pritchard Journal, CWMC, USAMHI.

[74]Entry for February 23, 1865, ibid.

[75]The most complete account of this episode is Marion Brunson Lucas, *Sherman and the Burning of Columbia* (College Station: Texas A & M University Press, 1976), which concludes judiciously that recklessness by Confederate authorities in destroying cotton, probable incendiarism by individual Union soldiers, and high winds combined to create the fire, which destroyed about a third of the city.

[76]Charles S. Brown to his "folks," [March or April 1865], Charles S. Brown Papers, DUL; Stillwell to his wife, March 12, 1865, James R. Stillwell Papers, OHS; Connolly to his wife, March 12, 1865, Angle (ed.), *Three Years in the Army of the Cumberland*, 384.

South Carolina formed one of the strongest proofs of the sense of discriminating righteousness that animated the Federal rank and file. For some it had an Old Testament flavor to it. Colonel Poe gleefully described the moment when his soldiers captured a spiked cannon inscribed, "Presented by one of her citizens to the sovereign State of South Carolina in commemoration of the passage of the Ordinance of Secession, Dec. 20th, 1860." Poe's men removed the spike, rendering it serviceable, and blasted away at the enemy in a shotted salute to Lincoln's second inaugural. "If Ever the Almighty sent just retribution to visit the heads of those who have offended him," Poe wrote, "he did it then."[77]

For Chaplain Stillwell, the religious analogy came more simply. He called the burning buildings "the sign of fire," and noted with grim relish: "We had the *'pillar of cloud* by day and *fire* by night.'"[78]

By the end of March, Sherman's armies had reached Raleigh. In early April, Grant's forces captured Richmond and brought Lee's fleeing army to bay at Appomattox Court House, where it surrendered on Palm Sunday 1865. Union cavalry under James Harrison Wilson learned of the fall of the Confederate capital while they were still raiding through central Alabama. Wilson issued new orders against looting, but continued the work of systematically destroying Southern war resources. "The fall of Richmond and defeat of Lee have deprived rebels in this section of their last hope," he wired Major General George H. Thomas from Montgomery. "If I can destroy arsenals and supplies at Columbus [Georgia] . . . they must disintegrate for lack of munitions." The strategy of raids thus persisted until the very end of the conflict.[79]

Such operations had done a great deal to defeat the Confederacy. By destroying railroads they had crippled the South's ability to transfer men and supplies from one theater to another. By eliminating arsenals, foundries, lead mines, and other factories they had ended the South's ability to create the sinews of war. And by taking livestock and burning or despoiling crops they had done great temporary harm to the South's ability to feed itself. Yet such results, important as they were, were less decisive than what the raids did to Southern morale and perceptions. Even at the end of the war, Confederate troops still possessed weapons and ammunition. Rations had been bad for a year but they still had food to eat.[80] What they did not possess was confidence that they could continue the struggle effectively. They could not prevent Union troops from roaming at will and visiting hardship and destruction upon places throughout the South. This sense of helplessness accelerated – although it did not begin – the

---

[77]Connolly to his wife, March 12, 1865, ibid., 384; for corroborating testimony, see Glatthaar, *The March to the Sea and Beyond,* 146, Nichols, *The Story of the Great March,* 222. General Order No. 8 [Slocum], March 7, 1865, OR 47, pt 2:719; Sherman to Major General Judson Kilpatrick, March 7, 1865, ibid., 721; Special Orders No. 63 [Blair], March 10, 1865, ibid., 760–761. Entry for March 4, 1865, Ms. diary, Orlando M. Poe Papers, LC.

[78]Stillwell to his wife, March 29, 1865, James R. Stillwell Papers, OHS.

[79]Report of James H. Wilson, January 17, 1867, OR 49, pt. 1:370–371; Wilson to Thomas, April 13, 1865, ibid., pt. 2:344.

[80]On this point, see Richard E. Beringer et al., *Why the South Lost the Civil War* (Athens: University of Georgia Press, 1986), passim., esp. 432–433.

wave of desertions that plagued the Confederate army during the war's final year. Many rebel soldiers, recognizing that their presence in the ranks could no longer protect their families, simply went home. Those who remained also worried. Concerns about continued Federal raids formed part of the reasoning that made Lee reject the possibility of dispersing his army to continue guerrilla resistance. Not only would the soldiers have to "plunder & rob" in order to live, but "the enemy's cavalry would pursue in the hopes of catching the principal officers, & wherever they went there would be fresh rapine & destruction."[81]

Destructive as it surely was, however, implementation of the Union hard war policy was accompanied by comparatively little "rapine." Except in South Carolina, Federal troops largely destroyed only what they were told to destroy. Their foraging activities, although liberal, usually concentrated on crops and livestock belonging to secessionist planters, and were in any case no worse than what Confederate troops and impressment agents did with regularity. The whirlwind of pillaging and arson that struck the Palmetto State was unique in scale; in common with the sort of depredations practiced all along by a few Federal units – the Seventh Kansas, for example, or the Ninth Ohio – it showed what Union soldiers could really do if they wished. If the desolation inflicted on the South possesses significance, it is also significant that it was not far worse. The America of 1864–1865 witnessed a new *chevauchée* – as systematic and extensive as anything Europe had seen, yet also more enlightened, because it was conducted not by brutes but by men from good families, with strong moral values that stayed their hands as often as they impelled retribution. But for that, the Federal policy of directed severity would not have been possible.

[81]Gary W. Gallagher (ed.), *Fighting for the Confederacy: The Personal Recollections of General Edward Porter Alexander* (Chapel Hill: University of North Carolina Press, 1989), 532. See also E. Porter Alexander, *Military Memoirs of a Confederate* (reprint ed., Bloomington: Indiana University Press, 1962 [1905]), 604–605. Lee's final dispatch to Jefferson Davis, which tacitly urged him to end the war, suggests that both material want and deficiencies in morale played a role in his belief that the South must stop fighting. "From what I have seen and learned, I believe an army cannot be organized or supported in Virginia, and as far as I know the condition of affairs, the country east of the Mississippi is morally and physically unable to maintain the contest unaided with any hope of ultimate success." Lee to Davis, April 20, 1865, Clifford Dowdey and Louis H. Manarin (eds.), *The Wartime Papers of R.E. Lee* (reprint ed., New York: Bramhall House, n.d. [1961]), 939.

9

Gestures of mercy, pillars of fire

Reading through the official reports of the Savannah Campaign, one is surprised by the brief treatment accorded the destruction that accompanied Sherman's great March to the Sea. Most of them sketch the foraging and burning in a few sentences or less, dwelling at length only on the odd skirmish with enemy militia and cavalry – or with the fairly extensive fighting required to capture Savannah itself and so reopen regular lines of supply. Finally a Pennsylvania officer, Colonel John Flynn, says outright what most of his colleagues implicitly suggest: "This campaign is, throughout its entire extent, void of interest to the soldier. . . ."[1]

The comment is startling. *Void of interest to the soldier?* Here was the operation so often considered the dawn of twentieth century total war, the desolating march that revived war upon civilians as a normal military tactic, the prototype for strategic air bombardment against national economies. Colonel Flynn, however, clearly had no inkling that he and his men had just passed from one epoch to another. Instead he noted that by and large, "the army has not had occasion to form for battle; few bloody fields have been lost or won; no sieges have been commenced and ended, as the enemy has not in one instance made a stand of sufficient length to require the necessity of such measures." As far as the colonel was concerned, the chief element of significance – the clash of opposing armies decisively engaged – had been entirely lacking.[2]

Tempting as it may be to believe that Colonel Flynn was just uncommonly short-sighted, a great deal of evidence suggests that the modern significance of Sherman's march, as well as other hard war measures, went substantially unrecognized by most contemporary observers. While Northern opinion hailed Sherman's marches as a form of divine retribution and also as a way to hit the South where it was most vulnerable, the arena of battle continued to exercise the decisive claim to attention. Sheridan's victories at the Battles of the Opequon, Fisher's Hill, and Cedar Creek, for example – which bracketed his devastation of the Shenandoah Valley – received far more press coverage than the devastation itself. The *Army and Navy Journal*, the voice of an

[1]Report of John Flynn, December 28, 1864, OR 44:290.
[2]Ibid., 290–291.

General Merritt's Raid into Loudon County.
Nov 28 - 1864

J.E. Taylor

Hard war as Northerners imagined it – and as it very often was. In this sketch by Union soldier-artist James E. Taylor, Union cavalrymen have torched the barn of a Virginia farm and are driving off the livestock, but the main residence stands unscathed. (Courtesy, Western Reserve Historical Society, Cleveland)

Hard war as Southerners recalled it. This pen-and-ink drawing by Adalbert Volck vividly conveys the anguish felt by Southerners over the loss of their property. It also anticipates the powerful mythology in which Northern soldiers were recalled as "thieves, murderers, rapists, arsonists, trespassers" who wantonly destroyed everything in their path. (M. and M. Karolik Collection, courtesy, Museum of Fine Arts, Boston)

emergent military professionalism, reported on Sherman's marches at length but emphasized the aspect of adroit maneuver far more than the attendant destruction. Similarly, although the post-war memoirs of Grant, Sherman, and Sheridan allude to the destruction of resources, they dwell far more heavily on the clash of armies, the conquest of cities and territory. None advocated economic warfare as one of the conflict's major lessons.[3]

Yet the climactic raids of 1864–1865 at once became a staple of the American pageant, seared into the memory of everyone who experienced them and millions who only heard of them. The first book on Sherman's marches appeared in the same year Lee surrendered. By 1866, it had already been through twenty-six editions, and several other books had joined it. As the years went by, Union veterans told their children about the raids and white Southerners in the path of war told theirs. Grandmothers put pen to paper and reminisced for future generations about the coming of the Yankees. Everyone struggled to answer the same question: What did it mean?

THE DYNAMICS OF ESCALATION AND RESTRAINT

Although much changed between the innocent early days of the Civil War and its fiery conclusion, Union military policy toward Southern civilians had one important continuity. Federal officials instinctively understood what political scientist Thomas C. Schelling would one day argue. "The power to hurt," Schelling wrote, "is bargaining power. To exploit it is diplomacy – vicious diplomacy, but diplomacy." The Union army's policy toward Southern civilians was one long exercise in such diplomacy. The goals changed, the methods changed, but Federal officials always sought to coax or coerce white Southerners into desired behaviors.[4]

Initially their effort primarily took the form of the conciliatory policy. Until recently, it was common among Civil War historians, especially military historians, to dismiss the policy as naive, an outgrowth of the picturebook-war delusions of the conflict's early months. In fact, proponents of the policy showed eminent good sense. Northern officials had every reason to suppose that political support for the fledgling Confederate government was shallow. The American South shared much in common with the North: the same language, the same heritage, the same republican ideals. Secessionists had tried for years to drag the South from the Union with signal lack of success. Their sudden triumph in 1860 seemed a ghastly fluke, the product, surely, of mutual misunderstanding or at worst a conspiracy hatched by an antidemocratic minority. Surely it did not express the considered will of the majority of white Southerners. Even after Lincoln's election and the defection of the Cotton South, Virginia, North Carolina, Arkansas, and Tennessee clung to the Union, seceding only

---

[3]On this point, see especially "The Peace Question," *Army and Navy Journal* (January 28, 1865), 356.
[4]Thomas C. Schelling, *Arms and Influence* (New Haven and London: Yale University Press, 1966), 2.

when it became clear that the alternative was to make war upon their sister Southern states. And it was known that pockets of Unionism persisted in each.[5]

The postwar myth of the solid South long obscured what historians have recently rediscovered: The assumptions of the proponents of conciliation were largely correct. The Confederate experiment was in trouble from the outset. White Southerners differed widely in their support for secession, the purposes they expected disunion to serve, and the means they were willing to countenance to preserve separate government. Paul Escott has described Jefferson Davis's unsuccessful bid to foster Confederate nationalism. Richard E. Beringer, Herman Hattaway, Archer Jones, and William N. Still have argued vigorously that the divisions within the Confederacy fatally undermined its will to resist. From the perspective of the late twentieth century, it would seem to us an act of criminal folly if the North had *not* pursued a conciliatory strategy.[6]

The policy proposed by Winfield Scott, George B. McClellan, and many others was brilliant in its simplicity. A federal judge in Missouri encapsulated it well in early 1862: "The exercise of power should be such as to leave no doubt of the ability to crush, yet there should be no crushing done." Confronted by the North's magisterial forbearance, white Southerners would quickly realize that the demons of tyranny and abolition were mere shadows trumped up by fire-eating politicians. Thus disabused, they would repudiate their deceivers and return to the Union fold.[7]

Up to a point, the conciliatory strategy worked. The Union offensives during the first six months of 1862 gave Southerners a dismaying sense of their weakness. Mill Springs, Roanoke Island, Forts Henry and Donelson, Pea Ridge, Shiloh, Island No. Ten, New Orleans: The list of Confederate defeats ran on and on. The territory lost to Northern might numbered in the thousands of square miles. By June 1862, the North had given a powerful demonstration of its ability to crush. And the cordial reception sometimes received by Union soldiers, coupled with widespread carping at the secessionists, suggested that loyalty to the Confederate government was indeed weak. Respect and magnanimity might indeed produce a swift reunion. Just one more victory – at Richmond – and it would all be over.

Yet even as McClellan's scouts beheld the church spires of the Confederate capital, conciliation was also under enormous strain. To be successful, sending signals with force, like any other form of communication, requires the message to be clearly received. But from the outset, the conciliatory policy was often obscured or con-

---

[5]Daniel W. Crofts, *Reluctant Confederates: Upper South Unionists in the Secession Crisis* (Chapel Hill: University of North Carolina Press, 1989).

[6]Paul D. Escott, *After Secession: Jefferson Davis and the Failure of Confederate Nationalism* (Baton Rouge: Louisiana State University Press, 1979); Richard E. Beringer et al., *Why the South Lost the Civil War* (Athens: University of Georgia Press, 1986). The literature on the Confederacy's internal divisions is large and still growing. See, for example, Durrill, *War of Another Kind;* Drew Gilpin Faust, "Altars of Sacrifice: Confederate Women and the Narratives of War," *Journal of American History* 76 (1990):1200–1228; Michael K. Honey, "The War Within the Confederacy: White Unionists of North Carolina," *Prologue: Journal of the National Archives* 18 (Summer 1986):75–93; Rable, *The Confederate Republic;* and James L. Roark, *Masters Without Slaves: Southern Planters in the Civil War and Reconstruction* (New York: Norton, 1977).

[7]Samuel Treat to Ethan Allen Hitchcock, February 12, 1862, Ethan Allen Hitchcock Papers, LC.

tradicted. Not all Northern officials embraced the policy. A tension soon emerged between those who basically thought the war a product of misplaced fears, and therefore emphasized a policy of general forbearance, and those who saw the origins of the war in a more sinister light and emphasized punishment for the guilty. Soldiers' depredations further undercut the message of conciliation, as did the necessary but sometimes draconian responses to guerrilla activity.

But perhaps the chief factor that obscured the message of conciliation was the North's unsettled policy toward slavery. The political scientist Richard Smoke, building on Schelling's work, has noted that belligerents generally signal a desire to limit their struggle by observing boundaries. A boundary may be geographical, like a river or a national border; qualitative, like the decision to employ a major weapon system previously forborne; or other things. The important criterion was that it must be understood by both sides and that its breaching should imply a change in the nature and intensity of the struggle. Once discovered and mutually recognized and observed, such boundaries become what Schelling called "salients," thresholds that define the scope and intensity of the fighting. The breaching of a salient represented escalation. In Smoke's formulation, it was an act that had "consequences and meaning for the overall pattern or nature of the ongoing war: its ground rules or limits."[8]

If one applies this concept to the Civil War, the status of slavery in Union policy leaps to mind as the classic example of a salient. At the outset of the war, the Lincoln administration explicitly renounced any intention of interfering with slavery, and the doctrine of noninterference was a major hallmark of the conciliatory policy. Subsequently the administration reversed itself with an equally explicit Emancipation Proclamation. Afterward, the conciliatory policy became a dead letter, and many observers saw the conflict as having become a "war of subjugation" or even "extermination."[9]

In one sense, the slavery question formed a clearcut qualitative boundary or salient, and it is not difficult to argue that Federal policymakers intended their circumspection about slavery as a signal of the sort of war they intended to wage: They would fight Confederate armies in the field and destroy the military power of the rebel government, but they would not touch the basic social and economic fabric of Southern society. The decisiveness with which Lincoln resisted any attempt by Union commanders and policymakers to interfere with slavery is consistent with this interpretation. Even so, one must acknowledge that by the summer of 1862, slavery had also become what Smoke would describe as a "blurred saliency" because of many incremental intrusions upon it – the First and Second Confiscation Acts, the new article of war prohibiting Union forces from enforcing the Fugitive Slave Law, the liberally interpreted "contraband" doctrine, and the unauthorized but widespread attempts by Northern soldiers to encourage slaves to abandon their masters. Because

---

[8]Richard Smoke, *War: Controlling Escalation* (Cambridge, MA: Harvard Belknap Press, 1977), 30–35.
[9]Variations on such characterizations frequently appeared in the wartime rhetoric of the Democratic Party. See Silbey, *A Respectable Minority*, 63–88.

of that, it is unlikely that the Southern people ever really understood the message of forbearance that Lincoln and other Northern moderates were trying to communicate.

McClellan's rebuff at the gates of Richmond ended whatever chance the conciliatory policy might have had to succeed. By giving the Confederacy a substantial victory at a time when one was desperately needed, it restored Southern morale and even set the stage for a major rebel counteroffensive in the summer of 1862. The ability of Federal armies to crush Confederate resistance was now repudiated. In the eyes of many Northerners, conciliation no longer communicated magnanimity, but weakness. Asked to comment on the policy, the prominent east Tennessee Unionist William G. "Parson" Brownlow offered a scathing assessment: "They [the rebels] attribute our forbearance toward them to cowardice and think that we are afraid of them."[10]

The repudiation of the mild policy, however, was less the product of considered thought than of sheer frustration. Even before the Richmond failure, soldiers and civilians alike were becoming impatient with conciliation; as one man put it: "This administration seems terribly afraid of hurting somebody." Afterward, the military stalemate made conciliation impossible to endure. "The Union men want to see the Rebels made to suffer," a Missourian candidly informed a Lincoln cabinet official. Many in the North expressed rueful admiration for the uncompromising tenacity of the rebels. "A large amount of the success of our enemies has resulted from their boldness," Sherman wrote military governor Andrew Johnson. "They have no hair-splitting."[11]

It was in such an environment that the Lincoln administration began to encourage military confiscation and moved toward emancipation. Some Confederates, mindful of the divisions within the South, actually welcomed such steps. "It is well," wrote J.B. Jones, a clerk in the Confederate War Department. "If the enemy had pursued a different course we should never have had the same unanimity. If they had made war only on men in arms, and spared private property, according to the usages of civilized nations, there would, at least, have been a *neutral* party in the South, and never the same energy and determination to contest the last inch of soil with the cruel invader."[12]

Confederate President Jefferson Davis actively exploited these evidences of the North's "barbarity" in his effort to create an ideology to sustain the Confederate cause. Since only one white Southern family in four owned slaves, protection for slavery made a poor rallying cry. He tried to argue that the Confederacy actually embodied the values of the original American republic, but as the war ground on such an approach was increasingly inadequate. So by mid-1862, his speeches began instead to

[10]Testimony of William G. Brownlow, Buell Commission, April 7, 1863, OR 16, pt. 2:674.

[11]James B. Post to his wife, May 31, 1862, James B. Post Letters, CWMC, USAMHI; F.A. Dick to Montgomery Blair, July 24, 1862, Blair Papers, LC; Sherman to Andrew Johnson, August 10, 1862, OR 17, pt. 2:162.

[12]Entry for July 4, 1862, Jones, *A Rebel War Clerk's Diary* 1:142.

stress the "malignity" of the South's enemies, "who are daily becoming less mindful of the usages of war and the dictates of humanity."[13]

Such pronouncements, of course, greatly distorted the actual nature of Federal policy. Even after Northern commanders repudiated conciliation and moved to a pragmatic policy instead, their measures remained well within the laws and usages of war applicable to international conflict. (Had they opted to apply the insurrectionary principle instead, the measures legitimately available to them were terrible to contemplate.) Still less did the Lincoln administration exploit the potentially explosive rage in the hearts of enslaved African Americans. In August 1863, the irrepressible General David Hunter suggested "a general arming of the negroes and a general destruction of the all the property of the slaveholders." In a letter to Edwin Stanton, he proposed to take an expeditionary force by sea, disembark on the Georgia coast, then march across the Deep South to New Orleans, "arming all the negroes and burning the house and other property of every slaveholder. A passage of this kind would create such a commotion among the negroes that they themselves could be left to do the rest of the work." This incendiary invitation was greeted with eloquent silence. The administration stood fast in its refusal to countenance the taking of slave vengeance.[14]

In the war's eastern theater, both official policy and actual conduct changed little from the days of McClellan. In the west, armies greatly intensified their foraging activity but tried to distinguish between three varieties of Southern civilian – Unionists, neutrals, and active secessionists – and gave different treatment to each. The goal was to encourage loyal behavior, and although most commanders no longer expected to detach Southern whites en masse from their allegiance to the Confederacy, they still attempted to do so on a more limited scale.

In the lower Mississippi River valley, for example, Union policy makers pursued a program of "calculated magnanimity" whereby planters could reenter the lucrative cotton market if they would only take the oath of allegiance. As Major General Lorenzo Thomas archly put it, "[T]he prospect of a sale of two or three hundred bales of cotton, at the present high prices, is a powerful weight in the scale of loyalties." In the wake of the summer 1863 Vicksburg and Tullahoma campaigns, Grant and Rosecrans, respectively, issued orders that extended an olive branch to citizens in Mississippi and Tennessee. Grant believed Mississippi could be "more easily governed now than Kentucky or Missouri" if rebels from other states could be kept out.[15]

---

[13]Jefferson Davis to the Confederate Congress, August 18, 1862, OR, Series IV, vol. 2, p. 52. Davis's efforts to build a Confederate ideology are examined in Escott, *After Secession*, 168–195.

[14]Hunter to Stanton, August 31, 1863, OR, Series III, vol. 2, p. 740.

[15]For the policy of "calculated magnanimity," see Lawrence N. Powell and Michael S. Wayne, "Self-Interest and the Decline of Confederate Nationalism," in Harry P. Owens and James J. Cooke, eds., *The Old South in the Crucible of War* (Jackson: University Press of Mississippi, 1983), 29–46. The Thomas quote is in Lorenzo Thomas to Edwin M. Stanton, April 22, 1863, L. Thomas Letterbook, AGO-Generals Papers, National Archives, quoted in ibid., 34–35. General Orders No. 50, August 1, 1863, OR 24, pt. 3:570–571; General Orders No. 175, July 18, 1863, ibid. 23, pt. 2:184; General Orders No. 199, August 15, 1863, ibid. 30, pt. 3:33–34. Grant to Halleck, August 10, 1863, ibid. 24, pt. 3:587.

Rampant guerrilla activity and the still-formidable rebel field armies, however, made effective wartime Reconstruction next to impossible, even on a limited basis. The Union military would have to break the strength of the Confederate armed forces, a task that by early 1864 seemed impossible to accomplish exclusively on the battlefield. Encouraged by the destructive expedition against Jackson, Mississippi, in July 1863, Grant expanded the scope of such operations into a strategy of raids that figured prominently in the Union campaigns of 1864–1865. With the advent of the hard war policy, civilian morale reemerged as a major strategic target.

The raids were intended to demonstrate two things to the Southern people – first, that they could be hurt, and second, that the Confederate government was powerless to protect them. Sherman said of his marches, "This may not be war but rather statesmanship," and Sheridan was grimly certain that white Southerners must experience firsthand the horrors of war. The civilians who waited at home "in peace and plenty," he wrote, knew little of its terrors. It was quite a different matter when "deprivation and suffering" were brought to their own doors. "Death," he continued implacably, "is popularly considered the maximum punishment in war, but it is not; reduction to poverty brings prayers for peace more surely and more quickly than does the destruction of human life, as the selfishness of man has demonstrated in more than one great conflict."[16]

Yet the hard war policy was not born from a simple desire to hurt civilians. Its genesis was more complex. Although the shift from conciliation to pragmatism (or "war in earnest") reflected frustration, and emancipation helped establish the moral groundwork for hard war, the actual policy was spawned primarily by the tyranny of logistics. In that respect, it was not an anticipation of the terror bombing campaigns of the twentieth century, but rather a rediscovery of older forms of warfare.

The armies of early modern Europe had lacked systems of regularized supply. They depended on foraging to survive, particularly when in the field, and the constant need to live off the land often exerted near-dictatorial control over strategy. Foraging was an inherently unpleasant experience for the civilians whose crops and fodder disappeared into the maw of a hungry army. Theoretically a commander might intend simply to revictual his forces and mean no harm to the civilians from whom he took supplies. In practice, however, his soldiers would not be gentle about it, and would frequently contribute their own gratuitous thefts, rapes, and assaults.[17]

The practice of living off the land had a negative corollary: If it made sense for an army to revictual itself from the regions through which it passed, it also made sense to deny that opportunity to the enemy. The result was "scorched earth" operations, sometimes inflicted as a defensive tactic on one's own territory, but at other times applied to enemy or even neutral territory as well. Such operations were usually much harder on civilians than simple foraging: Since time was frequently of the essence, and the denial of supplies must be complete, the habitual recourse was to burn and

[16]Philip H. Sheridan, *Personal Memoirs of P. H. Sheridan*, 2 vols. in 1 (New York: Da Capo Press, 1992 [1888]), vol. 1, p. 267; Sherman to Grant, November 6, 1864, OR 39, pt. 3:660.
[17]See van Creveld, *Supplying War*, 5–39.

destroy. When that occurred, the civilian population sometimes literally faced starvation, particularly in the early modern period when the peasantry generally lived at bare subsistence levels to begin with.

Foraging and area denial were in themselves so harsh that they had an intrinsic psychological effect. During the Middles Ages, peasants and townsmen, demoralized by repeated depredations, sometimes revolted against lords who proved impotent to protect them, as occurred during the *Jacquerie* of the Hundred Years War. Since extensive foraging and area denial operations could produce significant dislocations in the enemy camp, it made good sense – admittedly, reptilian good sense – to amplify the brutality as much as possible and so increase the psychological effect. The *chevauchées* were one example; similar operations liberally punctuated the Dutch Revolt and the Thirty Years' War. Destructive expeditions took place even after the return to order that marked the period after the Treaty of Westphalia. The most famous episode was the Devastation of the Palatinate, but there were others. For example, in 1704, when the Duke of Marlborough's victory at Donauworth failed to persuade the Elector of Bavaria to capitulate, Marlborough conducted an eighteenth century *chevauchée* in an effort to "destroy the country and oblige the Elector on[e] way or other to a complyance." His troops razed some 400 villages to the ground.[18]

The relevance of this earlier pattern to the American Civil War lies in two related points. First, the same logistical shortcomings that afflicted earlier European armies also affected the troops that fought the Civil War, eventually forcing them to adopt the age-old expedient of massive foraging. Second, the laws and usages of war, under which Civil War commanders operated, reflected those same logistical imperatives. They were redolent in Vattel's *Law of Nations,* which remained a standard authority on the subject in 1861 and heavily influenced both Halleck's *International Law* and Lieber's Code.

Vattel and most other Enlightenment commentators sought to minimize the burdens of war on noncombatants. Nevertheless, their laws and usages of war did permit massive foraging, "scorched earth" operations, and draconian measures to put down civilian uprisings. The crucial requirement was, of course, "military necessity." But while that plea created a potentially gigantic breach in the whole edifice of noncombatant immunity, it was neither naive on the part of Vattel and others to acknowledge military necessity nor cynical on the part of commanders to exploit it. In contrast to present-day ethicists, who sometimes seem more interested in erecting an ethical system from which to critique military operations rather than one in which they can realistically be conducted, Vattel and his generation took seriously the idea that if they expected statesmen and field commanders to embrace their work, their prescriptions must be practical. Operating within this framework, Vattel and others were bound to incorporate actual European experience into their work, particularly the recognition of the logistical imperative that armies must find ways to supply them-

[18]Quoted in David Chandler, *Marlborough as Military Commander* (2nd edition; London, Batsford, 1979), 139.

selves and by extension deny supplies to the enemy. It was this imperative, more than any other factor, that gave rise to the hard war measures of the Civil War.[19]

That is one reason why Colonel John Flynn – and more to the point, Grant, Sherman and Sheridan – did not regard the hard war operations of 1864–1865 as innovations in any important sense of the term. They might have preferred at the outset to win the war with a minimum of damage to civilian property, but when military necessity prodded them to seize goods from Southern farmers and destroy Southern railroads and factories, they scarcely had to create a new paradigm of war. All they had to do was to invoke the letter of the established laws and customs of war – rules largely developed during the seventeenth and eighteenth centuries, and, on the whole, quite well-adapted to the demands of a mid-nineteenth century American civil war.

THE LEGACY OF HARD WAR

If Grant, Sherman, and Sheridan failed to recognize the novelty of their actions (they viewed it more as a matter of applied common sense), the same was true of later military commentators as well. In this regard, a major contributing factor was the German Wars of Unification, which galvanized the attention of military men and seemed to augur the future of warfare far more than the struggle of 1861–1865. Both the Austro-Prussian *brüderkrieg* of 1866 and the Franco-Prussian War of 1870–1871 suggested the possibility of achieving decisive victory in one short campaign of maneuver. The Prussian Chief of Staff Helmuth von Moltke crushed the Austrian army at Königgrätz barely seventeen days after hostilities began. Four years later, he accomplished similar feats against the forces of Emperor Napoleon III. These triumphs stunned the world and captivated the attention of military men for the next generation.

The signature of the Prussian way of war was the *Hauptschlacht* – the decisive battle – and throughout the late nineteenth century American officers closely studied the model *Hauptschlachten* of Königgrätz, Sedan, and Metz. Sheridan served as an observer during the Franco-Prussian War, and two prominent military reformers, Emory Upton and William B. Hazen (both Civil War veterans) hoped to recast the American army along Prussian lines. Although American officers also studied Civil War campaigns, they usually emphasized aspects that resembled the *Hauptschlacht*. Thus, while they understood the importance of Fort Donelson, Vicksburg, and Atlanta to Northern victory, they paid much less attention to the Union *chevauchées*.[20]

---

[19]John Courtney Murray, "Remarks on the Moral Problem of War," *Theological Studies* 20 (1959):52.

[20]On the War of 1866, see Gordon Craig, *The Battle of Königgrätz: Prussia's Victory over Austria, 1866* (Philadelphia and New York: J.B. Lippincott Company, 1964); and Martin van Creveld, *Command in War* (London and Cambridge, MA: Harvard University Press, 1985), 103–147. The best account of the War of 1870–1871 is Michael Howard, *The Franco-Prussian War* (reprint ed.; New York: Dorset Press, 1990 [1961]). On the U.S. Army's emphasis on the *Hauptschlacht,* see Carol Reardon, *Soldiers and Scholars: The U.S. Army and the Uses of Military History, 1865–1920* (Lawrence: University Press of Kansas, 1990), 1–118 passim.

Even when they did, American commentators seldom understood the raids in the same light as late-twentieth century historians. An instructive example is the prominent military writer John Bigelow, whose *Principles of Strategy, Illustrated Mainly From American Campaigns,* first appeared in 1891. For Bigelow – a hero of the Battle of Gettysburg – war was preeminently "a fight between armies," and his work dealt primarily with the ways in which armies might best be brought to the battlefield and most effectively used when they got there. When he considered Sherman's march through Georgia and Sheridan's devastation of the Valley, it was simply as examples of "operating independently of a base," and his discussion of both incidents is cursory and nonanalytical. In these sections, when Bigelow discussed the accompanying destruction he couched it exclusively in terms of denying supplies to the Confederate army, making no mention of any impact on civilian morale. Indeed, his suggestions elsewhere about civilian policy are almost conciliatory in tone:

It need hardly be stated that the form of government held out to a people with a view to detaching it from its allegiance must be such as to be preferred by it to its own, and even a government imposed upon a hostile people for the purpose of merely controlling it during the course of operations must be made as acceptable to it as possible.

This might almost be viewed as a rebuke to the Lincoln administration's emancipation policy. Certainly it was as a criticism of the sterner wishes of the Radical Republicans.[21]

Bigelow made his closest approach to a present-day appreciation of hard war in a chapter on political strategy, which posited two forms of that strategy: attacking a rival's machinery of government (preferably by seizing his capital), and carrying the war home to his population. This second form, he continued, was often simply a continuation of normal operations against the opposing army:

Sheridan's devastation of the Shenandoah Valley was directed and executed with a single view to the destruction of those resources which could be turned into account by the Confederate armies. Nominally, at least, it was purely regular strategy; but by what name it was called mattered little. The people could not but feel the hardship of Sheridan's "burning," as the operation is called in the Shenandoah Valley to this day. Sherman's march through Georgia, on the other hand, was conducted with a view to bringing the war home to the Southern people.[22]

But while Bigelow understood that such operations had affected Southern morale, he implied that the Confederacy was essentially a military despotism, in which case an attack upon civilian morale could never be decisive. He quoted Grant approvingly:

The South was a military camp, controlled absolutely by the government, with soldiers to back it, and the war could have been protracted, no matter what extent the discontent reached, up to the point of open mutiny of the soldiers themselves.[23]

[21] John Bigelow, *The Principles of Strategy, Illustrated Mainly From American Campaigns,* 2nd ed. (reprint ed; New York: Greenwood Press, 1968 [1894]), 17, 144–148, 264.

[22] Ibid., 229.

[23] Ibid., 224.

Thus, Bigelow concluded ambiguously, "How far the idea of dispiriting a people may be advantageously carried is a function of most uncertain factors." On the whole he believed it could well be a mistake to try such a tactic, for the effort might simply embitter the enemy population and stiffen resistance.[24]

All in all, two points emerge from a study of Bigelow's *Principles of Strategy*. The first was his continued emphasis on the decisive battle, an emphasis he held in common with most pre-1914 military commentators. The second was his belief that warfare against enemy civilians, while legitimate and perhaps efficacious, was also problematic. He nowhere suggested it could produce decisive results on its own.

That suggestion remained at least a quarter century in the future, until Giulio Douhet, Hugh Trenchard, and other air power enthusiasts recommended the aerial bombardment of enemy civilians as a swift, effective alternative to the carnage of the First World War. The prolonged stalemate of 1914–1918 convinced many (although not all) that the search for decisive battlefield victory was futile. The horrifying casualties of Verdun, the Somme, and Passchendaele argued that success on the ground could come only at the end of a grinding struggle of attrition. Instead, why not leap over the battlefield with fleets of aircraft to rain destruction on the enemy homeland?

"[T]here is no reason," wrote the British military writer B. H. Liddell Hart in 1925, "why within a few hours, or at most days . . . the nerve system of the country inferior in air power should not be paralysed." He asked readers to imagine "London, Manchester, Birmingham, and a dozen other great centres simultaneously attacked, the business localities and Fleet Street wrecked, Whitehall a heap of ruins, the slum districts maddened into the impulse to break loose and maraud, the railways cut, factories destroyed." Under such an apocalypse the general will to resist would quickly evaporate.[25]

Ironically, the purpose of depicting such a bombardment was not to prophesy future horrors even greater than the First World War, but rather to point out an avenue to victory that would be swift and bloodless compared with the agony of 1914–1918. During the 1920s and 1930s, the defeat of Imperial Germany was believed to have been a product not of the defeat of its field armies but rather of the collapse of home front morale after four years of sustained economic hardship. Civilian morale thus appeared to be the Achilles' heel of the industrial nation-state. Air power promised the means to strike at it directly.

Beyond noting the limited (and mistaken) precedent of 1918, air power enthusiasts sought few other historical analogies to bolster their prescriptions. Although squarely within a tradition of European attacks on civilians stretching back hundreds of years, the case for aerial bombardment was made by men enamored of technology, not history, and their repudiation of past experience was often explicit. Thus, while advocates of strategic bombing might have been delighted to learn that Sherman's

[24]Ibid., 232.

[25]Quoted in Brian Bond, *War and Society in Europe, 1870–1970* (Bungay, Suffolk, UK: Fontana Paperbacks, 1984), 150.

Savannah Campaign offered a historical parallel for their own preferences, it was hardly a factor in shaping their thought.

Charles Royster is surely correct when he suggests that the influence of William T. Sherman on the future of American warfare was apparent less in his operations than in his rhetoric.[26] His postwar utterance, "War is hell" – a variation on his wartime statement, "War is cruelty and you cannot refine it" – has long been one of the best known American epigrams. The idea that one should do anything necessary to secure victory is deeply ingrained in the American consciousness.

At the same time, it should also be recognized that the concept of a "directed severity" – although at first blush unfamiliar – is also ingrained in the American way of war. Tellingly, this concept is sharply evident in American ideas about the use of air power. During the Second World War, for example, U.S. air forces in Europe pursued the doctrine of "precision bombing," in which the objective was not the obliteration of built-up areas but rather the destruction of well-defined targets. It aimed, in the words of General Henry H. "Hap" Arnold, "at knocking out not an entire industrial area, nor even a whole factory, but the most vital parts of Germany's war machine, such as the power plants and the most vital parts of Germany's war factories."[27]

American planners chose such targets largely in the belief that their eradication would be more fruitful than morale bombing of civilians, and it would be misleading to suggest that ethical scruples played a major factor. Even so, U.S. air commanders were willing to sustain heavy losses, in punishing daylight raids, rather than abandon their commitment to precision bombing. And some were uncomfortable with their British counterparts' emphasis on area bombing, with its deliberate infliction of massive civilian casualties. Nonplussed by the attempts of the British air ministry to lure U.S. air commanders into "morale bombing," Eighth Air Force General Carl Spaatz wrote Arnold in August 1944, "I personally believe that any deviation from our present policy, even for an exceptional case, will be unfortunate. There is no doubt in my mind that the RAF want to have the US Air Forces tarred with the morale bombing aftermath which we feel will be terrific."[28] The American preference for a directed severity – directed toward military resources and away from noncombatants – continues down to the present, as witness the enthusiasm for the effectiveness of precision guided munitions during the 1991 Gulf War.

[26]Charles Royster, *The Destructive War: William Tecumseh Sherman, Stonewall Jackson, and the Americans* (New York: Alfred A. Knopf, 1991), 350–353.

[27]Quoted in Weigley, *The American Way of War,* 337.

[28]Quoted in Best, *Humanity in Warfare,* 364n. None of this scrupulousness applies to the American fire bombing of Japan. This can be explained in part by the decentralized configuration of Japanese industry, which allegedly made a precision bombing campaign too difficult. But it is more plausible to recognize the deep strains of racism that underpinned the Pacific struggle. (On this point, see John Dower, *War Without Mercy: Race and Power in the Pacific War* [London and Boston: Faber and Faber, 1986].) Similarly, the racist element makes it quite misleading to attempt comparisons between, say, Sheridan's operations against Southern whites in the Shenandoah Valley and against American Indians in the Far West.

THE MYTHOLOGY OF HARD WAR

Since it is not at all difficult to show that Union forces exercised a directed severity during the *chevauchées* of 1861–1865, it is worth taking a moment to address the following (admittedly speculative) question: If the Union military effort against Southern property was indeed discriminate and roughly proportional to legitimate needs, why have so many interpretations insisted for so long that it was indiscriminate and all-annihilating? One likely reason such myth-making has been pervasive is that it has served a variety of agendas.

The idea that the Federals were conducting an immoral war in an immoral fashion goes back as far as the conflict itself. Fearful that "the hope of reconstruction was a latent sentiment in the bosom of the Southern community," Confederate nationalists portrayed the enemy as demons and blackguards in a bid to create an unbridgeable chasm to reunion. Jefferson Davis railed against "the savage ferocity" of Union military conduct. "The frontier of our country," he wrote in 1863, "bears witness to the alacrity and efficiency with which the general orders of the enemy have been executed in the devastation of farms, the destruction of the agricultural implements, the burning of the houses, and the plunder of everything movable."[29]

Southerners continued to level such charges after the war had ended, snarling of Northern "atrocities" and "barbarism," of "soulless raiders" and their "hellish work."[30] In the postwar South, the legend of Yankee ruffians waging campaigns of fire and vandalism was surely useful in several respects. First, it helped Redeemers convince their fellow white Southerners that a terrible wrong had been done them – a conviction that resonated well with the humiliations of military Reconstruction. Second, it played into the myth of a South beaten down by brute force, not defeated by military art and certainly not by internal divisions or a failure of national will. It also made it easier to overlook the Confederate government's tax-in-kind and impressment policies, as well as "scorched earth" practices carried out by the rebel army. When Grandpappy reminisced about how his team of prized horses had disappeared, he preferred to recall that Yankee vandals had done it – even if the real culprit had been a Confederate impressment agent.

Third, the myth of Yankee atrocities accounted for the economic disaster that gripped the South after 1865. As historians have since pointed out, the destruction of Southern crops, livestock, factories, railroads, and other infrastructure was anything but complete; much of the damage was repaired within a few years. The really serious economic losses can be traced to two things: the emancipation of slaves, which wiped out billions of dollars in Southern wealth, and the worthlessness of Confederate scrip,

---

[29]*Richmond Examiner*, November 21, 1862; Jefferson Davis to the Confederate Congress, December 7, 1863, in Rowland (ed.), *Jefferson Davis, Constitutionalist* 6, pp. 125–126.

[30]Edward Pollard, *The Lost Cause: A New Southern History of the War of the Confederates* (New York: E.B. Treat, 1867), 597–598; Alexander S. Paxton, "Sheridan's Bummers," *Southern Historical Society Papers* 32 (1904):89, 93.

bonds, and promissory notes into which many Southerners had sunk most of their savings. Both, of course, could be better traced to the South's decision to secede – and so begin the war – than to anything that Union soldiers did. Thus the emphasis on hard war, as an explanation for the economic devastation of the South, may have diverted attention from Southern responsibilities in bringing on the war, and thus for the outcome. Even if Southerners conceded their responsibility for beginning the conflict, the myth of Yankee atrocities remained useful. Southerners could assert that they themselves had inaugurated a chivalrous struggle based on honor; the Yankees were responsible for the brutal, destructive war it eventually became.[31]

The influence of this myth can hardly be exaggerated. Even educated Southerners, far removed in time from the conflict, accepted it uncritically, indeed passionately. When a fellow historian suggested that Woodrow Wilson tone down a passage about Sherman's "cruelty" in a manuscript he was writing, Wilson replied:

I have modified it a little; but really there is no more deliberately considered phrase in the book. I am painfully familiar with the details of that awful march, and I really think that the words I used concerning it ought to stand as a piece of sober history. . . . As for the treatment of prisoners in the southern prisons, that was doubtless heartless upon occasion; but the heartless-ness was not part of a system, as Sherman's was.

Eventually the murderous severity of the Union armies' attacks on civilian property became an article of faith. By the 1940s, one Southern historian could write, in a scholarly monograph, that "the invader did not limit himself to the property of people," but evidenced "considerable interest also in their persons, particularly the females, some of whom did not escape the fate worse than death" – without feeling the slightest need to document his lurid (and largely inaccurate) claim.[32]

The myth of indiscriminate Union attacks on Southern civilians has served other agendas as well. For persons revolted by the slaughter on the Western Front, Sher-man's marches and similar episodes aptly illustrated the brutalizing effects of war. Its utility in this respect has proven durable. Paradoxically, the image of a sweeping campaign of fire and sword also fits snugly into the "realist" image of war. The Union hard war measures resonate well with those who believe that in war one must do

---

[31]This point is suggested in Robert M. McKenzie, "The Economic Impact of Federal Operations in Alabama During the Civil War," *Alabama Historical Quarterly* 20 (1976):67–68. For the effect of the wartime destruction on the South's economy, see James F. Doster, "Were the Southern Railroads Destroyed by the Civil War?," *Civil War History* 7 (1961):310–320; Roger L. Ransom and Richard Sutch, *One Kind of Freedom: The Economic Consequences of Emancipation* (Cambridge: Cambridge University Press, 1977), 40–55; and James L. Sellers, "The Economic Incidence of the Civil War," *Mississippi Valley Historical Review* 14 (1927):179–191.

[32]Gaines M. Foster, *Ghosts of the Confederacy: Defeat, the Lost Cause, and the Emergence of the New South* (Oxford and New York: Oxford University Press, 1987), 123–124; Wilson to Albert B. Hart, December 20, 1892, quoted in Peter Novick, *That Noble Dream: The "Objectivity Question" and the American Historical Profession* (New York and Cambridge: Cambridge University Press, 1988), 79; John K. Bettersworth, *Confederate Mississippi: The People and Policies of a Cotton State in Wartime* (Baton Rouge: Louisiana State University Press, 1943), 281.

whatever is necessary to win. There is thus an admiring quality to some of the literature on William T. Sherman, the best known of the hard war advocates, whom Lloyd Lewis called a "fighting prophet." T. Harry Williams admired Grant's willingness to wage economic warfare, and called him the first of the great modern generals. Bruce Catton invariably discussed the Union war against Southern property as a case of "doing what has to be done to win."[33]

Few of these characterizations did great violence to the facts. They simply emphasized certain facts at the expense of others. The Federal effort against Southern property was indeed widespread and quite destructive. But an effort was also made to direct destructive energies toward certain targets and away from others. Neither Southerners, "realists," nor those antipathetic toward war had any reason to emphasize the substantial restraint shown by Union forces in their operations against civilian property. For Southerners, to do so would have undercut their sense of righteousness and comparative lack of responsibility for the debacle that engulfed them. For realists, it would have qualified their belief that one must do whatever must be done to gain victory in war. For those repulsed by war, it would have seemed to mitigate the brutalizing effects that war assuredly has on both societies and individuals.

But perhaps the most pervasive reason for the emphasis on the destructiveness of Union military policy has been the way in which it seemed to anticipate the sweeping struggles of the twentieth century. Especially after the Second World War, the Civil War appeared a clear prototype of modern, total war. It had witnessed the early development and use of trench warfare, ironclad warships, rapid-fire weapons, and even airships and crude machine guns. Its soldiers had traveled to the battle front aboard railroad cars and steam-driven transports; its generals had communicated with one another via endless miles of telegraph wire. It was one of the first struggles in which manufacturing and mass politics significantly affected the fighting and the outcome. The conflict's most striking modern aspect, however, was the Union attacks on Southern civilians and property. What happened to them no longer seemed merely atrocious; it foreshadowed the strategic bombardment of civilians during the two world wars.

The first historian to call attention to this was John Bennett Walters. Focusing on the Union commander most associated with attacks on Southern property, in a 1948 article Walters credited William T. Sherman with having invented total war. Sherman, he believed, had "gradually evolved his own personal philosophy of war . . . and . . . became one of the first of the modern generals to revert to the idea of the use of military force against the civilian population of the enemy." In so doing, Walters continued, Sherman demonstrated "the effectiveness of a plan of action which would destroy the enemy's economic system and terrify and demoralize the civilian population. By paralyzing the enemy's economy he destroyed its ability to supply its armies;

[33]Lloyd Lewis, *Sherman: Fighting Prophet* (New York: Harcourt, Brace, 1932); Williams, *Lincoln and His Generals*, 314; Bruce Catton, *The American Heritage Short History of the Civil War* (paperback ed.; New York: Dell, 1963 [1960]), 172.

and by despoiling and scattering the families of soldiers in the opposing army, he undermined the morale of the military forces of the Confederacy."[34]

In many respects, Walters' effort was as much polemical as analytical. His article bitterly excoriated Sherman, and in a later book on the subject he asserted that Sherman's marches "demonstrated a strange hatred – one without parallel even in World War II." That statement, could they but hear it, would ring rather oddly in the ears of the victims of the Nazi concentration camps, the Bataan death march, and the fire bombings of Hamburg, Dresden and Tokyo. Yet his connection between the Union hard war policy and the birth of total war sounded a note that other historians repeated often in the years ahead.[35]

THE PERSISTENCE OF RESTRAINT

The list of such historians is long and distinguished, and it would be grossly unfair to imply that their works perpetuate a distorted view of Northern actions against Southern civilians and property. On the contrary, they have illuminated the dynamic in a variety of ways, many of them quite insightful. But it is reasonable to note that historians have been mainly concerned with the extent and meaning of the destruction unleashed by Union armies. Mark E. Neely, Jr. observed precisely that in a provocative 1991 article entitled, "Was the Civil War a Total War?" Answering in the negative, he argued, "The *essential* aspect of any definition of total war asserts that it breaks down the distinction between soldiers and civilians, combatants and noncombatants, and this no one in the Civil War did systematically, including William T. Sherman."[36]

The question remains, however: Why did such saving distinctions persist? Certainly what had gone before was far from benign. If the hallmark of modern total war is the erosion of the barrier between combatant and noncombatant, one must recognize that the barrier itself had acquired substance barely a century before the guns spoke at Fort Sumter. Until then, invading armies routinely considered the civilians in their path as enemies to be beaten, robbed, raped, or even killed. Europe had a tradition of brutal conduct going back hundreds of years. I have already noted that the Devastation of the Palatinate in 1688–1689, to name but one incident, offered an example of systematic destruction that made Sheridan's razing of the Shenandoah

[34]John Bennett Walters, "General William T. Sherman and Total War," *Journal of Southern History* 14 (1948):447–480.

[35]Walters, *Merchant of Terror*, xviii. For more on hard war historiography, see Mark Grimsley, "A Directed Severity: The Evolution of Federal Policy Toward Southern Civilians and Property, 1861–1865" (unpub. Ph.D diss.: The Ohio State University, 1992), 1–36.

[36]Mark E. Neely, Jr., "Was the Civil War a Total War?," *Civil War History* 37, no. 1 (1991):27. Of the many works that treat the Union hard war policy, five are especially worthwhile: Weigley, *The American Way of War*, 128–152; Glatthaar, *The March to the Sea and Beyond;* Linderman, *Embattled Courage,* 180–215; James M. McPherson, "Abraham Lincoln and the Strategy of Unconditional Surrender," in his *Abraham Lincoln and the Second American Revolution* (New York: Oxford University Press, 1991), 65–92; and Royster, *The Destructive War.*

Valley seem comparatively restrained. The measures used to throttle insurgencies were even worse. An English participant wrote of a sixteenth century punitive expedition against the Irish:

We have killed, burnt and spoiled all along the lough [Lough Neagh] within four miles of Dungannon, . . . in which journeys we have killed above one hundred people of all sorts, besides such as were burnt, how many I know not. We spare none of what quality or sex soever, and it has bred much terror in the people, who heard not a drum nor saw not a fire there for a long time.

Philip II of Spain advocated a similar policy for quelling the Dutch Revolt. Even the "age of limited war" in the eighteenth century can be exaggerated. When one acknowledges the gusto with which colonists annihilated whole tribes of American Indians, to say nothing of the ease with which the western Allies as well as totalitarian regimes embraced area bombing against population centers, the restraint of Union armies in the Civil War acquires fresh salience.[37]

Any explanation must begin with the fact that official policy intended restraint to be exercised. The Federal government deliberately chose to conduct the war largely as a contest between two nations, despite the fact that it explicitly denied the Confederacy's right to exist. It applied the insurrectionary principle sparingly. Had it done so broadly and consistently, captured Confederate soldiers and civilians who gave aid and comfort to the Confederate regime might well have faced execution. Instead the Federal government threw its moral and legal authority squarely behind the preservation of distinctions between combatants and noncombatants.

Field commanders too reinforced the distinction through an endless stream of general orders that forbade pillaging and wanton destruction. Critics who cite the orders as evidence of continued depredations miss the crucial point. In war, nothing undercuts the claims of personal conscience faster than the demands of public authority. The syllogism, "If his cause be wrong, our obedience to the king wipes the crime of it out of us," has a long and melancholy history. Many soldiers, decent in themselves, have willingly performed the most sickening tasks in the name of duty.[38] By insisting on proper conduct toward civilians, Union generals encouraged rather than corroded the better angels of their soldiers' nature.

The persistence of morality among the soldiers forms a second part of the explanation. In their correspondence, both official and personal, justice is a frequent theme, a concern occasionally robust enough to balk at expedients urged by higher authority. Many soldiers would have understood the sentiments of a Union colonel in West

[37]Cyril Falls, *Elizabeth's Irish Wars* (New York: Barnes and Noble, 1970 [1950]), 277; Parker, *Army of Flanders*, 135fn. "[B]etween 1648 and 1789," writes historian John Childs, "wars in Europe accounted for the lives of hundreds of thousands of soldiers and civilians, destroyed numerous towns and villages, damaged national economies, and devastated much of Germany, Central Europe and the Low Countries. Warfare was 'limited' only when it was compared with the holocaust that had gone before and the new totality of the Napoleonic wars." Childs, *Armies and Warfare in Europe, 1648–1789*, 2.

[38]For a disturbing illustration of this point, see Christopher Browning, *Ordinary Men: Reserve Police Battalion 101 and the Final Solution in Poland* (New York: HarperCollins, 1992). The quotation is from Henry V, Act IV, scene i.

Virginia. Faced with much guerrilla activity in his district and an order from Major General David Hunter to burn houses near the sites where bushwhacking occurred, he demurred nevertheless. "To men who have taken the oath, unless charges could be made and sustained, I do not feel authorized to apply General Hunter's order. . . . I would not hesitate, but it is an important and serious matter, and should not be done hastily, or in the wrong place. . . . I would rather spare two secesh than burn up one Union man's property."[39]

A third explanatory feature was the similarity of white Southerners to their Northern counterparts. The claims of morality are stronger when one can recognize the enemy's human face. Despite regional idiosyncracies, Union soldiers and Southern civilians shared the same language, the same heritage, and much the same culture. The comments of Federal soldiers on white Southerners often noted oddities and differences, but it is misleading to suggest that these indicate a depersonalization of the enemy. Far from depicting an alien people, the soldiers' descriptions often brought enemy civilians vividly to life. Sergeant Rufus Mead, for instance, enjoyed talking to a secessionist woman: "[S]he would talk like a steamboat." Many soldiers empathized with the plight of Southern civilians even when they approved of the stern measures against them. Of Sherman's evacuation order, an Ohio army surgeon wrote his wife, "It seems very hard but serves them right for most of the *women* of the south are generally stronger secess [sic] than the men." Such sentiments did not prevent him from asking in the next sentence, "How would you like to be made to leave Marietta [Ohio] with your family and have to find a new home?"[40]

The Southern whites who least resembled Northern men were the poor, and the soldiers' comments concerning them are most unflattering. But the condition of the poor whites reflected less an alien breed than the degenerative effects of slavery, which focused attention back on the slaveholding aristocracy. A Pennsylvania cavalryman serving in northern Virginia opined that the South contained only two kinds of residence: "The one are the mansions of the wealthy and are generally fine and elegant and the other are the huts of the poorer classes and the slaves which are wretched houses. The neat little home of the northern laborer is nowhere to be found in the south." Another soldier wrote, "The poor class are all loyal or would be if they dared, but they are really more enslaved than the negroes. . . ."[41]

Such observations introduce the final component that helps explain the persistence of restraint: the Union soldiers' political sensitivity. As Lincoln maintained, they were "thinking bayonets," the product of universal white male suffrage, stump speeches, torchlight political rallies, and unabashedly partisan newspapers – in short, members of one of the most politically aware societies on earth. They debated politics around

---

[39]Col. A.D. Jaynes to Maj. John Witcher, June 21, 1864, OR 37, pt. 1:659.

[40]Rufus Mead to "folks at home," July 4, 1862, Rufus Mead Papers, LC; J. Dexter Cotton to his wife, September 17, 1864, J. Dexter Cotton Papers, LC.

[41]Entry for April 27, 1862, William Penn Lloyd diary, SHC; George W. Landrum to his sister, April 27, 1862, George W. Landrum Letters, WRHS. See also Reid Mitchell, *Civil War Soldiers: Their Expectations and Their Experiences* (New York: Viking, 1988), 109–112.

the campfire and in their letters home. Not content with that, a considerable number bombarded local newspapers with epistles on the conduct of the war. They rejected conciliation because it did not accord with their opinion of what was really required to end the rebellion. But by and large they observed the distinctions, not only between combatants and noncombatants but also between Unionist, passive, and secessionist civilians, because such distinctions made political as well as moral sense to them.[42]

When considering the evolution of Federal policy toward Southern civilians and property, several points stand out. First, although the North began the war committed to an informal policy of conciliation, that policy represented a deliberate restriction of effort. It was not merely the result of a view that saw war exclusively in terms of a clash between rival armies, though dominant conceptions of war lent credibility to the hope that the rebellion could be suppressed in this manner. Second, when attacks on Southern property did emerge, the continuities of Federal practice with previous European experience were more striking than the contrasts – in contradiction to the view that this brand of warfare represented something novel and modern. Finally, if the Union's hard war effort displayed a novel element, it lay primarily in the linkage with a democratic society. That made it possible to blame Southerners for the outbreak and continuation of the war, and so justify the destruction. But it also made possible a politically and morally aware citizen-soldiery capable of discrimination and restraint as well as destruction. The Union volunteer who marched under Grant, Sherman, and Sheridan was a very different instrument than the *ancien régime* soldier under Turenne, Marlborough, or Frederick the Great; for that matter, a different instrument even than contemporary European soldiers. It was the peculiar nature of the Federal citizen-soldier – his civic-mindedness, his continued sense of connection with community and public morality – that made possible the "directed severity." The Federal rank-and-file were neither barbarians, brutalized by war, nor "realists" unleashing indiscriminate violence. Their example thus holds out hope that the effective conduct of war need not extinguish the light of moral reason.

[42]For the ideological awareness of Civil War soldiers, Confederate as well as Union, see McPherson, *What They Fought For.*

Works cited

Manuscript collections

Duke University, Durham, North Carolina
    Charles S. Brown Papers
    Robert B. Hoadley Papers
    Eugene Marshall Diary
    George P. Metz Papers
    Charles Brown Tompkins Papers

Houghton Library, Harvard University, Cambridge, Massachusetts
    Robert G. Shaw Letters

Huntington Library, San Marino, California
    Samuel L. M. Barlow Papers
    D.P. Chapman Papers
    George Lowe Papers

Illinois Historical Society, Springfield, Illinois
    Salmon P. Chase Papers

Indiana State Library, Indianapolis
    Samuel K. Harryman Papers

Library of Congress, Washington, DC
    Blair Family Papers
    Benjamin F. Butler Papers
    Salmon P. Chase Papers
    J. Dexter Cotton Papers
    John A. Dix Papers
Doubleday and Company Collection: Research Notes for Bruce Catton's Centennial History of the Civil War
    Wilbur Fisk Papers
    Thomas F. Galwey Diary
    James J. Gillette Papers
    E. N. Gilpin Papers
    John P. Hatch Papers
    Ethan Allen Hitchcock Papers
    J. W. Keifer Papers
    Robert Todd Lincoln Collection of the Papers of Abraham Lincoln
    George Brinton McClellan, Sr., Papers
    Rufus Mead Papers

Miscellaneous Manuscripts Collection
    W. C. Johnson Diary
    William G. Mills Diary
Orlando M. Poe Papers
Edward Paul Reichhelm Papers
Almon P. Rockwell Papers
Bela T. Saint John Papers
John M. Schofield Papers
William T. Sherman Papers
Edwin M. Stanton Papers
Edwin Oberlin Wentworth Papers

Todd D. Miller Collection, Jeromesville, Ohio
  Davis Halderman Letter
  Christian Zook Letter

Minnesota Historical Society, St. Paul
  Lucius Hubbard Papers

Missouri Historical Society, St. Louis
  Ethan Allen Hitchcock Papers

National Archives, Washington
  Record Group 393

New York Historical Society, New York
  War 1861–1865 Papers

Ohio Historical Society, Columbus
  Lyman D. Ames Diary
  James M. Comly Papers
  Hugh B. Ewing Papers
  DeWitt Clinton Loudon Papers
  Nathaniel Parmeter Diary
  William T. Patterson Diary
  James R. Stillwell Papers
  Thomas T. Taylor Papers
  John Vail Diary

Southern Historical Collection, University of North Carolina at Chapel Hill
  Samuel A. Agnew Diary
  John Houston Bills Diary
  Elias Brady Papers
  George Hovey Cadman Letters
  William Penn Lloyd Diaries
  William H. Stewart Papers
  Abraham Welch Letter

United States Army Military History Institute, Carlisle Barracks, Pennsylvania
  Civil War Miscellaneous Collection
    Boucher Family Papers
    Ephraigm Franklin Brower Diary
    Abijah F. Gore Diary
    Albion Gross Letters and Diary
    William W. McCarty Letters
    Curtis C. Pollack Letters

James B. Post Letters
William W. Pritchard Journal
William Henry Walling Letters
Richard C. Watson Letters
John S. Weiser Letters
William B. Westervelt Memoir and Diary
Civil War Times Illustrated Collection
Joseph J. Scroggs Diary
Harrisburg Civil War Round Table Collection
Aaron E. Bachman Memoir
John Brown Diary
James W. Denver Letter
Alva C. Griest Diary
Henry Keiser Diary
William H. Martin Papers
Benjamin Franklin Seibert Papers
Philippe d'Orleans, Comte de Paris. Typescript MS Journal

University of Kentucky, Lexington
William T. Sherman Papers

University of Notre Dame, South Bend, Indiana
Sherman Family Papers

University of Washington, Seattle
Manning F. Force Papers

Virginia Historical Society, Richmond
Bowler Family Papers
Lucy (Wood) Butler Diary
William Nalle Diary

Western Reserve Historical Society, Cleveland
John Q. A. Campbell Diaries
Civil War Miscellany, William Palmer Collection
Salmon P. Chase Letter
George W. Landrum Papers
Regimental Papers of the Civil War (William Palmer Collection)
James Fenton Papers
William A. Robinson Diary
Sosman Family Papers
Edward A. Webb Papers

Newspapers

Army and Navy Journal
Boston Daily Advertiser
Boston Evening Transcript
Boston Post
Chicago Times
Chicago Tribune
Cincinnati Commercial
Cincinnati Gazette

Works Cited

New York Herald
New York Times
New York Tribune
New York World
Raleigh (N.C.) News and Observer
Richmond Examiner
Washington Daily National Intelligencer
Zanesville (Ohio) City Times
Zanesville (Ohio) Courier

Theses and dissertations

Barker, Brett. "The Forgotten Majority: The Northern Homefront During the Civil War, Zanesville, Ohio, 1860–1865." MA thesis, The Ohio State University, 1989.

Chumney, James Robert. "Don Carlos Buell: Gentleman General." Ph.D diss., Rice University, 1964.

Grimsley, Christopher Mark, "A Directed Severity: The Evolution of Federal Policy Toward Southern Civilians and Property, 1861–1865. Ph.D diss., The Ohio State University, 1992.

Harsh, Joseph L. "George Brinton McClellan and the Forgotten Alternative: An Introduction to the Conservative Strategy in the Civil War: April-August 1861." Ph.D diss., Rice University, 1970.

Syrett, John. "The Confiscation Acts: Efforts at Reconstruction During the Civil War." Ph.D. diss., University of Minnesota, 1971.

Published sources

Alexander, E[dward] Porter. *Military Memoirs of a Confederate.* Reprint edition. Bloomington: Indiana University Press, 1962 [1905].

Allen, Amory K. "The Civil War Letters of Amory K. Allen." *Indiana Magazine of History* 31 (1935):338–386.

Allen, George H. *Forty-Six Months With the Fourth Rhode Island Volunteers, in the War of 1861–1865.* Providence, RI: J.A. and R.A. Reid, 1887.

Ambrose, Stephen E. *Halleck: Lincoln's Chief of Staff.* Baton Rouge: Louisiana State University Press, 1962.

Anderson, David L., ed. "The Life of 'Wilhelm Yank': Letters From a German Soldier in the Civil War." *Michigan Historical Review* 16 (Spring 1990):73–93.

Anderson, Troyer Steele. *The Command of the Howe Brothers During the American Revolution.* New York and London: Oxford University Press, 1936.

Angle, Paul M., ed. *Three Years in the Army of the Cumberland: The Letters and Diary of Major James A. Connolly.* Bloomington: Indiana University Press, 1959.

Athearn, Robert G., ed., "An Indiana Doctor Marches With Sherman: The Diary of James Comfort Patten." *Magazine of Indiana History* 49 (1953):405–422.

Barber, Lucius W. *Army Memoirs of Lucius W. Barber, Company "D," 15th Illinois Volunteer Infantry.* Chicago: J.M.W. Jones, 1894.

Barber, Richard, ed. *The Life and Campaigns of the Black Prince.* London: Boydell Press, 1986.

Barrett, John G. *The Civil War in North Carolina.* Chapel Hill: University of North Carolina Press, 1963.

—— *Sherman's March Through the Carolinas.* Chapel Hill: University of North Carolina Press, 1956.

Works Cited

Barton, Michael. *Goodmen: The Character of Civil War Soldiers.* State College: Pennsylvania State University Press, 1981.

Basler, Roy P., ed. *The Collected Works of Abraham Lincoln,* 8 volumes and index. New Brunswick, NJ: Rutgers University Press, 1953.

Bauer, K. Jack, ed. *Soldiering: The Civil War Diary of Rice C. Bull.* Paperback edition. New York: Berkley, 1988 [1977].

Beale, Howard K. *The Diary of Edward Bates, 1859–1866.* American Historical Association Report, 1930. Washington: Government Printing Office, 1933.

Bearss, Margie Riddle. *Sherman's Forgotten Campaign: The Meridian Expedition.* Baltimore: Gateway Press, 1987.

Beatty, John. *Memoirs of a Volunteer, 1861–1863.* Ed. by Harvey S. Ford. New York: W.W. Norton, 1946 [1879].

Beringer, Richard E., et al. *Why the South Lost the Civil War.* Athens: University of Georgia Press, 1986.

Best, Geoffrey. *Humanity in Warfare: The Modern History of the International Law of Armed Conflicts.* London: Methuen, 1983.

Bettersworth, John K. *Confederate Mississippi: The People and Policies of a Cotton State in Wartime.* Baton Rouge: Louisiana State University Press, 1943.

Bicknell, George W. *History of the Fifth Maine Volunteers.* Portland, ME: K.L. Davis, 1871.

Bigelow, John. *The Principles of Strategy: Illustrated Mainly From American Campaigns.* 2nd Edition. New York: Greenwood Press, 1968 [1894].

Billias, George, ed. *George Washington's Opponents: British Generals and Admirals in the American Revolution.* New York: William Morrow, 1969.

[Black, Jeremiah.] *Mr. Buchanan's Administration on the Eve of Rebellion.* New York: D. Appleton, 1865.

Blegen, Theodore C., ed. *The Civil War Letters of Colonel Hans Christian Heg.* Northfield, MN: Norwegian-American Historical Association, 1936.

Bond, Brian. *War and Society in Europe, 1870–1970.* Bungay, Suffolk, UK: Fontana Paperbacks, 1984.

Bowen, J. R. *Regimental History of the First New York Dragoons . . .* n.p.: by the author, 1900.

Bowler, R. Arthur. *Logistics and the Failure of the British Army in America, 1775–1783.* Princeton, NJ: Princeton University Press, 1975.

Bradley, Erwin Stanley. *Simon Cameron, Lincoln's Secretary of War: A Political Biography.* Philadelphia: University of Pennsylvania Press, 1966.

Brice, Marshall Moore. *Conquest of a Valley.* Charlottesville: University Press of Virginia, 1965.

Brinsfield, John W. "The Military Ethics of General William T. Sherman: A Reassessment." *Parameters* 12 (1983):36–48.

Brown, Alonzo L. *History of the Fourth Regiment of Minnesota Infantry Volunteers During the Great Rebellion, 1861–1865.* St. Paul: Pioneer Press, 1892.

Brown, Edmund Randolph. *The Twenty-seventh Indiana Volunteer Infantry in the War of the Rebellion, 1861–1865.* Monticello, IN: n.p., 1899.

Browning, Christopher. *Ordinary Men: Reserve Police Battalion 101 and the Final Solution in Poland.* New York: HarperCollins, 1992.

Buel, Clarence C., and Robert U. Johnson, eds. *Battles and Leaders of the Civil War,* four volumes. Popular Edition. New York: Thomas Yoseloff, 1956 [1887].

Butler, Benjamin F. *Private and Official Correspondence of Gen. Benjamin F. Butler During the Period of the Civil War,* compiled by Jessie Ames Marshall, six volumes. Norwood, MA: Plimpton Press, 1917.

Byrne, Frank L., and Jean Powers, eds. *Your True Marcus: The Civil War Letters of a Jewish Colonel.* Kent, OH: Kent State University Press, 1985.

Canfield, S. S. *History of the 21st Regiment Ohio Volunteer Infantry, in the War of the Rebellion.* Toledo: Vrooman, Anderson and Bateman, 1893.

Capers, Gerald M. *Occupied City: New Orleans Under the Federals, 1862–1865.* Lexington: University Press of Kentucky, 1965.

Carp, E. Wayne. *To Starve the Army at Pleasure: Continental Army Administration and American Political Culture, 1775–1783.* Chapel Hill: University of North Carolina Press, 1984.

Carrington, Virgil I. *Gray Ghosts and Rebel Raiders.* Paperback edition. New York: Ballantine Books, 1973.

Carter, Samuel III. *The Siege of Atlanta, 1864.* New York: St. Martins Press, 1973.

Catton, Bruce. *The American Heritage Short History of the Civil War.* Paperback Edition. New York: Dell, 1963 [1960].

—— *Glory Road: The Bloody Route From Fredericksburg to Gettysburg.* Garden City, NY: Doubleday, 1952.

—— *Grant Moves South.* Boston: Little, Brown, 1960.

Chandler, David. *Marlborough as Military Commander.* 2nd Edition. London: Basford, 1979.

Childs, John. *Armies and Warfare in Europe, 1648–1789.* New York: Holmes and Meier, 1982.

Clark, Charles M. *The History of the Thirty-ninth Regiment, Illinois Volunteer Veteran Infantry (Yates Phalanx) in the War of the Rebellion, 1861–1865.* Chicago: n.p., 1889.

Contamine, Philippe. *War in the Middle Ages.* Trans. by Michael Jones. London: Basil Blackwell, 1984.

Conyngham, David P. *Sherman's March Through the South, With Sketches and Incidents of the Campaign.* New York: Sheldon and Company, 1865.

Cooper, Walter G. *Official History of Fulton County.* Atlanta: n.p., 1934.

Cope, Alex. *The Fifteenth Ohio Volunteers and Its Campaigns.* Columbus: n.p., 1916.

Cornish, Dudley. *The Sable Arm: Black Troops in the Union Army, 1861–1865.* Reprint edition. Lawrence: University Press of Kansas, 1987 [1956].

Cox, Jacob D. *The March to the Sea – Franklin and Nashville.* New York: Charles Scribner's Sons, 1883.

—— *Military Reminiscences of the Civil War,* two volumes. New York: Charles Scribner's Sons, 1900.

Craig, Gordon. *The Battle of Königgrätz: Prussia's Victory Over Austria, 1866.* Philadelphia and New York: J. B. Lippincott, 1964.

Crofts, Daniel W. *Reluctant Confederates: Upper South Unionists in the Secession Crisis.* Chapel Hill: University of North Carolina Press, 1989.

Cunliffe, Marcus. *Soldiers and Civilians: The Martial Spririt in America, 1775–1865.* Paperback 2nd Edition. New York: Free Press, 1973 [1968].

Curry, Leonard P. *Blueprint for Modern America: Nonmilitary Legislation of the First Civil War Congress.* Nashville: Vanderbilt University Press, 1968.

Davis, Burke. *Sherman's March.* New York: Random House, 1980.

Davis, Charles E., Jr. *Three Years in the Army: The Story of the Thirteenth Massachusetts Volunteers from July 16, 1861, to August 1, 1864.* Boston: Estes and Lauriat, 1894.

Davis, David Brion. *The Slave Power Conspiracy and the Paranoid Style.* Baton Rouge: Louisiana State University Press, 1969.

Davis, William C. *Battle at Bull Run: A History of the First Major Campaign of the Civil War.* Garden City, NY: Doubleday, 1977.

De Laubenfels, David J. "With Sherman Through Georgia: A Journal." *Georgia Historical Quarterly* 41 (1957):288–300.

Denison, Frederic. *Sabres and Spurs: The First Regiment Rhode Island Cavalry in the Civil War, 1861–1865.* Central Falls, RI: E.L. Freeman, 1876.

Dennett, Tyler, ed. *Lincoln and the Civil War: The Diaries and Letters of John Hay.* New York: Dodd, Mead and Company, 1939.

Donald, David, ed. *Inside Lincoln's Cabinet: The Civil War Diaries of Salmon P. Chase.* New York: Charles Scribners Sons, 1954.

—— *Lincoln Reconsidered: Essays on the Civil War Era.* Second Edition. New York: Alfred A. Knopf, 1956.

Doster, James F. "Were the Southern Railroads Destroyed by the Civil War?" *Civil War History* 7 (1961):310–320.

Douglas, Henry Kyd. *I Rode With Stonewall.* Chapel Hill: University of North Carolina Press, 1940.

Dowdey, Clifford, and Louis H. Manarin. *The Wartime Papers of R.E. Lee.* New York: Bramhall House, n.d. [1961].

Dower, John. *War Without Mercy: Race and Power in the Pacific War.* London and Boston: Faber and Faber, 1986.

DuPont, Henry A. *The Campaign of 1864 in the Valley of Virginia and the Expedition to Lynchburg.* New York: National Americana Society, 1925.

Durrill, Wayne K. *War of Another Kind: A Southern Community in the Great Rebellion.* New York and Oxford: Oxford University Press, 1990.

Early, Jubal A. *War Memoirs: Autobiographical Sketch and Narrative of the War Between the States.* Bloomington: Indiana University Press, 1960.

Eby, Cecil D., Jr., ed. *A Virginia Yankee in the Civil War: The Diaries of David Hunter Strother.* Chapel Hill: University of North Carolina Press, 1961.

Elliott, Charles Winslow. *Winfield Scott: The Soldier and the Man.* New York: Macmillan, 1937.

Escott, Paul D. *After Secession: Jefferson Davis and the Failure of Confederate Nationalism.* Baton Rouge: Louisiana State University Press, 1979.

Fahrney, Ralph Ray. *Horace Greeley and the Tribune in the Civil War.* Cedar Rapids, IA: Torch Press, 1936.

Falls, Cyril. *Elizabeth's Irish Wars.* New York: Barnes and Noble, 1970 [1950].

Faust, Drew Gilpin. "Altars of Sacrifice: Confederate Women and the Narratives of War." *Journal of American History* 76 (1990):1200–1228.

Favill, Josiah Marshall. *The Diary of a Young Officer.* Chicago: R.R. Donnelly and Sons, 1909.

Fellman, Michael. *Inside War: The Guerrilla Conflict in Missouri During the Civil War.* New York: Oxford University Press, 1989.

Fessenden, Francis. *The Life and Public Services of William Pitt Fessenden,* two volumes. Reprint edition. New York: Da Capo Press, 1971 [1907].

Foner, Eric. *Free Soil, Free Labor, Free Men: The Ideology of the Republican Party Before the Civil War.* New York and London: Oxford University Press, 1970.

Ford, Worthington Chauncey. *A Cycle of Adams Letters,* two volumes. Boston: Houghton, Mifflin, 1920.

Foster, Gaines M. *Ghosts of the Confederacy: Defeat, the Lost Cause, and the Emergence of the New South.* Oxford and New York: Oxford University Press, 1987.

Franklin, John H. *The Emancipation Proclamation.* Garden City, NY: Doubleday, 1963.

Fredrickson, George M. *The Inner Civil War: Northern Intellectuals and the Crisis of the Union.* Paperback edition. New York: Harper Torchbooks, 1968 [1965].

Freeman, Douglas Southall. *Lee's Lieutenants: A Study in Command,* three volumes. New York: Charles Scribners Sons, 1942–1944.

—— *R.E. Lee: A Biography.* New York: Charles Scribners Sons, 1935.

Freidel, Frank. *Francis Lieber, Nineteenth-Century Liberal.* Baton Rouge: Louisiana State University Press, 1947.

—— "General Orders 100 and Military Government." *Mississippi Valley Historical Review* 32 (1946): 541–556.

Froissart, *Chronicles,* trans. and ed. by Geoffrey Brereton. Abridged edition. Harmondsworth, Middlesex, England: Penguin, 1968.

Gabriel, Ralph H. "American Experience with Military Government." *American Historical Review* 49 (1944):630–643.

Gallagher, Gary W., ed. *Fighting for the Confederacy: The Personal Recollections of General Edward Porter Alexander.* Chapel Hill: University of North Carolina Press, 1989.

Genovese, Eugene D. *The Political Economy of Slavery: Studies in the Economy and Society of the Slave South.* New York: Vintage Books, 1965.

George, Mary Karl. *Zachariah Chandler: A Political Biography.* East Lansing: Michigan State University Press, 1969.

Gerteis, Louis S. *From Contraband to Freedman: Federal Policy Toward Southern Blacks, 1861–1865.* Contributions in American History No. 29. Westport, CT: Greenwood Press, 1973.

Gibson, John M. *Those 163 Days: A Southern Account of Sherman's March from Atlanta to Raleigh.* New York: Coward-McCann, 1961.

Glatthaar, Joseph T. *Forged in Battle: The Civil War Alliance of Black Soldiers and White Officers.* New York: Free Press, 1990.

—— *The March to the Sea and Beyond: Sherman's Troops in the Savannah and Carolinas Campaigns.* New York: New York University, 1985.

Grant, Ulysses S. *Personal Memoirs of U. S. Grant,* two volumes. New York: Charles L. Webster, 1885.

Grebner, Constantin. *We Were the Ninth: A History of the Ninth Regiment, Ohio Volunteer Infantry, April 17, 1861, to June 7, 1864.* Trans. and ed. by Frederic Trautmann. Kent, OH and London: Kent State University Press, 1987 [1897].

Grimsley, Mark. "Overthrown: The Truth Behind the McCellan-Scott Feud." *Civil War Times Illustrated* 19 (1980):20–29.

Hagerman, Edward. *The American Civil War and the Origins of Modern Warfare.* Bloomington: Indiana University Press, 1988.

Hall, Hillman A. *History of the Sixth New York Cavalry . . .* Worcester, MA: Blanchard Press, 1908.

Halleck, Henry W. *International Law; or, Rules Regulating the Intercourse of States in Peace and War.* New York: D. Van Nostrand, 1861.

Hammond, Harold E., ed. *Diary of a Union Lady, 1861–1865.* New York: Funk and Wagnalls, 1962.

Hannaford, E. *The Story of a Regiment: A History of the Campaigns . . . of the Sixth Regiment, Ohio Volunteer Infantry.* Cincinnati: n.p., 1868.

Harsh, Joseph L. "Battlesword and Rapier: Clausewitz, Jomini, and the American Civil War." *Military Affairs* 38 (December 1974): 133–138.

—— "On the McClellan-Go-Round." *Civil War History* 19 (June 1973): 101–118.

Hartigan, Richard S. *The Forgotten Victim: A History of the Civilian.* Chicago: Precedent Publishing, 1982.

—— *Lieber's Code and the Law of War.* Chicago: Precedent, 1983.

Hattaway, Herman, and Archer Jones, *How the North Won: A Military History of the Civil War.* Urbana and Chicago: University of Illinois Press, 1983.

Heleniak, Roman J., and Lawrence L. Hewitt, eds. *The Confederate High Command & Related Topics: Themes in Honor of T. Harry Williams.* Shippensburg, PA: White Mane Publishing, 1988.

Hess, Earl J. *Liberty, Virtue, and Progress: Northerners and Their War for the Union.* New York and London: New York University Press, 1988.

Higginbotham, Don. "The Early American Way of War: Reconnaissance and Appraisal." *William and Mary Quarterly,* 3rd Series, vol. 49 [1991]: 230–273.

—— *The War of American Independence: Military Attitudes, Policies and Practice, 1763–1789.* New York: William Morrow, 1969.

Higginson, Thomas Wentworth. *Army Life in a Black Regiment.* Boston: Beacon Press, 1962.

Works Cited

Hoehling, A. A. *Last Train from Atlanta.* New York and London: Thomas Yoseloff, 1958.

Holcombe, R. I. *History of the First Regiment Minnesota Volunteer Infantry.* Stillwater, MN: Eastern and Masterman, 1916.

Honey, Michael K. "The War Within the Confederacy: White Unionists of North Carolina," *Prologue: Journal of the National Archives* 18 (Summer 1986):75–93

Horrall, S. F. *History of the Forty-second Indiana Volunteer Infantry.* Chicago: Donahue and Henneberry, 1892.

Howard, Michael. *The Franco-Prussian War.* New York: Dorset Press, 1990 [1961].

Howe, M.A. DeWolfe, ed. *Home Letters of General Sherman.* New York: Charles Scribners Sons, 1909.

——, *Marching With Sherman: Passages From the Letters and Campaign Diaries of Henry Hitchcock . . .* New Haven, CT: Yale University Press, 1927.

Hutchinson, William T., and William M. E. Rachals. *The Papers of James Madison,* 16 volumes to date. Charlottesville: University Press of Virginia, 1962–.

Jackson, Joseph Orville, ed. *"Some of the Boys . . . ": The Civil War Letters of Isaac Jackson, 1862–1865.* Carbondale: Southern Illinois University Press, 1960.

James, C. L. R. *The Black Jacobins: Toussaint L'Ouverture and the San Domingo Revolution.* New edition. London: Allison and Busby, 1980.

Jennings, Francis. *The Invasion of America: Indians, Colonialism, and the Cant of Conquest.* New York: W. W. Norton, 1976 [1975].

Johnson, Howard Palmer. "New Orleans Under General Butler." *Louisiana Historical Quarterly* 24 (1941):434–536.

Johnson, James Turner. *Just War Tradition and the Restraint of War: A Moral and Historical Inquiry.* Princeton, NJ: Princeton University Press, 1981.

Johnson, Michael P. *Toward a Patriarchal Republic: The Secession of Georgia.* Baton Rouge: Louisiana State University Press, 1977.

Jomini, Baron Antoine de. *The Art of War,* trans. by G.H. Mendell and W.P. Craighill. Reprint Edition. Westport, CT: Greenwood Press, 1971 [1862].

Jones, Howard. *Union in Peril: The Crisis Over British Intervention in the Civil War.* Chapel Hill and London: University of North Carolina Press, 1992.

Jones, James Pickett. *Yankee Blitzkrieg: Wilson's Raid Through Alabama and Georgia.* Athens: University of Georgia Press, 1976.

Jones, John Beauchamp. *A Rebel War Clerk's Diary at the Confederate States Capital,* ed. by Howard Swiggett, two volumes. New York: Old Hickory Bookshop, 1935.

Jones, Katherine M. *When Sherman Came: Southern Women and the "Great March."* Indianapolis: Bobbs-Merrill, 1964.

Julian, George. *Political Recollections, 1840 to 1872.* Chicago: Jansen, McClurg and Company, 1884.

Kaplan, Sidney. "The 'Domestic Insurrections' and the Declaration of Independence." *Journal of Negro History* 61 (1976):243–255.

Keil, F. W. *The Thirty-fifth Ohio, A Narrative of Service from August, 1861 to 1864.* Fort Wayne, IN: Archer, Housh and Company, 1894.

Kerr, John H. *Under the Maltese Cross: Antietam to Appomattox: Campaigns of the 155th Pennsylvania Regiment.* Pittsburgh, Regimental Association, 1910.

Lamers, William M. *The Edge of Glory: A Biography of General William S. Rosecrans, U.S.A.* New York: Harcourt, Brace and World, 1961.

Lewis, C.S. *The Abolition of Man, or Reflections on Education with Special Reference to the Teaching of English in the Upper Forms of Schools.* Paperback edition; New York: MacMillan, 1955 [1947].

Lewis, Lloyd. *Sherman: Fighting Prophet.* New York: Harcourt, Brace and Company, 1932.

Lieber, Francis. *Manual of Political Ethics.* 2 volumes. Philadelphia: J.B. Lippincott, 1890 [1837].

—— *On Civil Liberty and Self Government.* Philadelphia: J.B. Lippincott, 1859 [1853].

Linderman, Gerald E. *Embattled Courage: The Experience of Combat in the American Civil War.* New York: Free Press, 1987.

Litwack, Leon F. *Been in the Storm So Long: The Aftermath of Slavery.* New York: Alfred A. Knopf, 1979.

Long, E.B. *The Civil War Day By Day: An Almanac, 1861–1865.* Reprint edition. New York: Da Capo Press, 1985 [1971].

Loving, Jerome K., ed. *Civil War Letters of George Washington Whitman.* Durham, NC: Duke University Press, 1975.

Lucas, Marion Brunson. *Sherman and the Burning of Columbia.* College Station: Texas A. & M. University Press, 1976.

[Lusk, William C., ed.] *War Letters of William Thompson Lusk.* New York: n.p., 1911.

Marszalek, John F. "The Inventor of Total Warfare." *Notre Dame Magazine* 18 (1989):28–31.

—— *Sherman: A Soldier's Passion for Order.* New York: Free Press, 1993.

McClellan, George B. *McClellan's Own Story.* New York: Charles L. Webster, 1884.

McDonald, Hunter, ed. *A Diary with Remininscences of the War and Refugee Life in the Shenandoah Valley, 1861–1865.* Nashville: Cullom and Ghertner, 1934.

McKenzie, Robert H. "The Economic Impact of Federal Operations in Alabama During the Civil War." *Alabama Historical Quarterly* 20 (1976):51–63.

McPherson, James M. *Abraham Lincoln and the Second American Revolution.* New York: Oxford University Press, 1991.

—— *The Battle Cry of Freedom: The Civil War Era.* New York and London: Oxford University Press, 1988.

—— *The Struggle for Equality: Abolitionists and the Negro in the Civil War and Reconstruction.* Princeton, NJ: Princeton University Press, 1964.

—— *What They Fought For, 1861–1865.* Baton Rouge: Louisiana State University Press, 1994.

Mead, John Gould. *History of the First-Tenth-Twenty-ninth Maine Regiment.* Portland: ME: S. Berry, 1871.

Meade, George Gordon, ed. *The Life and Letters of George Gordon Meade,* two volumes. New York: Charles Scribner's Sons, 1913.

Millett, Allan R., and Peter Maslowski. *For the Common Defense: A Military History of the United States of America.* New York: Free Press, 1983.

Mitchell, Reid. *Civil War Soldiers: Their Expectations and Their Experiences.* New York: Viking, 1988.

Morris, Richard B. *Forging of the Union, 1781–1789.* New York: Harper and Row, 1987.

Morris, Roy, Jr. "The Sack of Athens." *Civil War Times Illustrated* 24 (February 1986):26–32.

Murray, John Courtney. "Remarks on the Moral Problem of War." *Theological Studies* 20 (1959):40–61.

Neely, Mark E., Jr. "Was the Civil War a Total War?" *Civil War History* 37 (1991):5–28.

Nevins, Allan, ed. *A Diary of Battle: The Personal Journals of Colonel Charles S. Wainwright, 1861–1865.* New York: Harcourt, Brace and World, 1962.

——, and Milton Halsey Thomas, eds., *The Diary of George Templeton Strong,* four volumes. New York: MacMillan, 1952.

—— *The War for the Union,* four volumes. New York: Charles Scribner's Sons, 1959–1971.

[New York] Division of Archives and History. *The Sullivan-Clinton Campaign in 1779; Chronology and Selected Documents.* Albany: University of the State of New York, 1929.

Nichols, George Ward. *The Story of the Great March, From the Diary of a Staff Officer.* Reprint edition. Williamstown, MA: Conner House, 1984 [1865].

Works Cited

Novick, Peter. *That Noble Dream: The "Objectivity" Question and the American Historical Profession.* New York and Cambridge: Cambridge University Press, 1988.

Official Records of the Union and Confederate Navies, 27 volumes. Washington: Government Printing Office, 1927.

Osborn, George C., ed. "Sherman's March Through Georgia: Letters from Charles Ewing to his Father Thomas Ewing." *Georgia Historical Quarterly* 42 (1958):323–327.

Osborn, Hartwell. *Trials and Triumphs: The Record of the Fifty-fifth Ohio Volunteer Infantry.* Chicago: A.C. McClurg, 1904.

Owens, Harry P., and James J. Cooke, eds. *The Old South in the Crucible of War.* Jackson: University Press of Mississippi, 1983.

Palmer, Beverly Wilson, ed. *The Selected Letters of Charles Sumner,* two volumes. Boston: Northeastern University Press, 1990.

Paskins, Barrie. *The Ethics of War.* London: Ducksworth, 1979.

Paxton, Alexander S. "Sheridan's Bummers." *Southern Historical Society Papers* 32 (1904):89–93.

Pepper, George W. *Personal Recollections of Sherman's Campaign in Georgia and the Carolinas.* Zanesville, OH: Hugh Dunne, 1866.

Phillips, Christopher. *Damned Yankee: The Life of General Nathaniel Lyon.* London and Columbia: University of Missouri Press, 1990.

Pollard, Edward. *The Lost Cause: A New Southern History of the War of the Confederates.* New York: E.B. Treat, 1867.

Pond, George E. *The Shenandoah Valley in 1864.* New York: Charles Scribners Sons, 1883.

Potter, David M. *Lincoln and His Party in the Secession Crisis.* New Haven, CT: Yale University Press, 1942.

Puntenney, George H. *History of the Thirty-seventh Regiment of Indiana Infantry Volunteers. . . .* Rushville, IN: Jacksonian Book & Job Department, 1896.

Putnam, Samuel H. *The Story of Company A, Twenty-fifth Regiment, Mass. Vols. in the War of the Rebellion.* Worcester, MA: Putnam, Davis and Company, 1886.

Pyne, Harry R. *Ride to War: The History of the First New Jersey Cavalry,* ed. by Earl Schenck Miers. New Brunswick, NJ: Rutgers University Press, 1961.

Quaife, Milo M., ed. *From the Cannon's Mouth: The Civil War Letters of General Alpheus S. Williams.* Detroit: Wayne State University Press, 1959.

Quarles, Benjamin, *The Negro in the Civil War.* Boston: Little, Brown, 1953.

Rable, George C. *The Confederate Republic: A Revolution Against Politics.* Chapel Hill: University of North Carolina Press, 1994.

Randall, James G. *The Civil War and Reconstruction.* New York: D.C. Heath, 1937.

—— *The Confiscation of Property During the Civil War.* Indianapolis: Mutual Printing and Lithographing, 1913.

Ransom, Roger L., and Richard Sutch. *One Kind of Freedom: The Economic Consequences of Emancipation.* Cambridge: Cambridge University Press, 1977.

Reardon, Carol. *Soldiers and Scholars: The U.S. Army and the Uses of Military History, 1865–1920.* Lawrence: University Press of Kansas, 1990.

Reston, James, Jr. *Sherman's March and Vietnam.* New York: MacMillan, 1984.

Risch, Erna. *Supplying Washington's Army.* Center of Military History, Special Studies. Washington: Government Printing Office, 1981.

Roark, James L. *Masters Without Slaves: Southern Planters in the Civil War and Reconstruction.* New York: Norton, 1977.

Robertson, James I., Jr., ed. "The Diary of Dolly Lunt Burge, Part VII." *Georgia Historical Quarterly* 45 (1961):367–384.

—— *Soldiers Blue and Gray.* Columbia: University of South Carolina Press, 1988.

Ropes, John C. *The Army Under Pope.* New York: Charles Scribner's Sons, 1881.

Rose, Willie Lee. *Rehearsal for Reconstruction: The Port Royal Experiment.* Indianapolis: Bobbs, Merrill, 1964.

Rowland, Dunbar, ed. *Jefferson Davis, Constitutionalist: His Letters, Papers and Speeches,* ten volumes. Jackson: Mississippi Department of Archives and History, 1923.

Royster, Charles. *The Destructive War: William Tecumseh Sherman, Stonewall Jackson, and the Americans.* New York: Alfred A. Knopf, 1991.

—— *A Revolutionary People at War: The Continental Army and the American Character, 1775–1783.* New York: Norton, 1979.

Schelling, Thomas C. *Arms and Influence.* New Haven and London: Yales University Press, 1966.

Schurz, Carl. *Speeches of Carl Schurz.* Philadelphia: Lippincott, 1865.

Schutz, Wallace J. and Walter N. Trenerry. *Abandoned by Lincoln: A Military Biography of General John Pope.* Urbana and Chicago: University of Illinois Press, 1990.

Scott, H. L. *Military Dictionary.* New York: D. Van Nostrand, 1861.

Scott, Winfield. *Memoirs of Lieut.-General Scott,* two volumes. New York: Sheldon and Company, 1864.

Sears, Stephen W., ed. *The Civil War Papers of George B. McClellan: Selected Correspondence, 1860–1865.* New York: Ticknor and Fields, 1989.

—— *George B. McClellan: The Young Napoleon.* New York: Ticknor and Fields, 1988.

Sellers, James L. "The Economic Incidence of the Civil War in the South." *Mississippi Valley Historical Review* 14 (1927):179–191.

Seward, Desmond. *The Hundred Years War: The English in France, 1337–1453.* London: Constable, 1979.

Shafer, Boyd C. *Nationalism: Myth and Reality.* New York: Harcourt, Brace, 1955.

Shea, William L., and Earl J. Hess, *Pea Ridge: Civil War Campaign in the West.* Chapel Hill: University of North Carolina Press, 1992.

Sheridan, P.H. *Personal Memoirs of P. H. Sheridan,* two volumes in one. New York: Da Capo Press, 1992 [1888].

Sherman, Rachel Thorndike, ed. *The Sherman Letters: Correspondence Between General and Senator Sherman from 1837 to 1891.* New York: Charles Scribners Sons, 1894.

Sherman, William T. *Memoirs of General William T. Sherman.* Reprint Edition. Westport, CT: Greenwood Press, 1974 [1874].

Shy, John. *A People Numerous and Armed: Reflections on the Military Struggle for American Independence.* New York and London: Oxford University Press, 1976.

Silbey, Joel H. *A Respectable Minority: The Democratic Party in the Civil War Era, 1860–1868.* New York: W.W. Norton, 1977.

Simon, John Y., ed. *The Papers of Ulysses S. Grant,* 16 volumes to date. Carbondale and Edwardsville: Southern Illinois University Press, 1967-.

Simpson, Brooks D. "'The Doom of Slavery': Ulysses S. Grant, War Aims, and Emancipation, 1861–1863." *Civil War History* 36 (1990):36–56.

Smith, Everard H. "Chambersburg: Anatomy of a Confederate Reprisal." *American Historical Review* 96 (1991):432–455.

Smith, Justin H. "American Rule in Mexico." *American Historical Review* 23 (1918):287–302.

Smoke, Richard. *War: Controlling Escalation.* Cambridge, MA: Harvard Belknap Press, 1977.

Snead, Thomas. *The Fight for Missouri from the Election of Lincoln to the Death of Lyon.* New York: Charles Scribner's Sons, 1886.

Sparks, David S., ed. *Inside Lincoln's Army: The Diary of Marsena Rudolph Patrick, Provost Marshal General, Army of the Potomac.* New York: Thomas Yoseloff, 1964.

Stampp, Kenneth M. *And the War Came: The North and the Secession Crisis, 1860–1861.* Baton Rouge: Louisiana State University Press, 1950.

Starr, Stephen Z. *The Union Cavalry in the Civil War,* three volumes. Baton Rouge: Louisiana State University Press, 1979–1985.

Steele, Ian K. *Warpaths: Invasions of North America.* New York and Oxford: Oxford University Press, 1994.

Stevens, George T. *Three Years in the Sixth Corps.* 2nd edition. New York: D. Van Nostrand, 1870.

Stilwell, Leander. *The Story of a Common Soldier.* Kansas City, MO: Franklin Hudson, 1920.

Sutherland, Daniel E. "Abraham Lincoln, John Pope, and the Origins of Total War." *Journal of Military History* 56 (1992):567–586.

—— "Introduction to War: The Civilians of Culpeper County, Virginia." *Civil War History* 37 (1991):120–137.

Swinton, William. *Campaigns of the Army of the Potomac.* Reprint edition. Secaucus, NJ: Blue and Grey Press, 1988 [1866].

Sylvester, Lorna Lutes, ed. "The Civil War Letters of Charles Harding Cox." *Indiana Magazine of History* 68 (1972):24–78.

Thomas, Emory M. *The Confederate Nation, 1861–1865.* New York: Harper and Row, 1979.

Tolstoy, Leo. *War and Peace,* translated by Rosemary Edwards. Harmondsworth, Middlesex, England: Penguin, 1957.

Townsend, E.D. *Anecdotes of the Civil War in the United States.* New York: D. Appleton, 1884.

Trefousse, Hans L. *Ben Butler: The South Called Him BEAST!* New York: Twayne, 1957.

—— *The Radical Republicans: Lincoln's Vanguard for Racial Justice.* New York: Alfred A. Knopf, 1969.

Turner, Charles W., ed. "General Hunter's Sack of Lexington, Virginia, June 10–14, 1864: An Account by Rose Page Pendleton." *Virginia Magazine of History and Biography* 83 (1975):173–183.

U.S. Congress. *Congressional Globe,* 37th Congress, 1st and 2nd Sessions, six volumes. Washington: Government Printing Office, 1861–1862.

—— *Report of the Joint Committee on the Conduct of the War, 1863,* three volumes. Washington: Government Printing Office, 1863.

Utley, Robert M. *Frontiersmen in Blue: The United States Army and the Indian, 1848–1865.* New York: Macmillan, 1967.

Van Creveld, Martin. *Command in War.* London and Cambridge, MA: Harvard University Press, 1985.

—— *Supplying War: Logistics from Wallenstein to Patton.* Cambridge: Cambridge University Press, 1977.

Vandiver, Frank E. *Mighty Stonewall.* New York: McGraw-Hill, 1957.

Van Deusen, Glyndon D. *William Henry Seward.* New York: Oxford University Press, 1967.

Van Noppen, Ina Woestemeyer. *Stoneman's Last Raid.* Raleigh: North Carolina State College Print Shop, 1961.

Vattel, Emmerich de. *The Law of Nations, or, Principles of the Law of Nature Applied to the Conduct and Affairs of Nations and Sovereigns.* Revised Edition. London: G.G. and J. Robinson, 1797.

Walker, Aldace F. *The Vermont Brigade in the Shenandoah Valley.* Burlington, VT: Free Press Association, 1869.

Walker, Francis A. *A History of the Second Army Corps in the Army of the Potomac.* New York: Charles Scribners, 1886.

Walzer, Michael. *Just and Unjust Wars: A Moral Argument with Historical Illustrations.* Paperback Edition. Harmondsworth, Middlesex, England: Penguin, 1980 [1977].

Walters, John Bennett, "General William T. Sherman and Total War." *Journal of Southern History* 14 (1948):447–480.

—— *Merchant of Terror: General Sherman and Total War.* Indianapolis: Bobbs-Merrill, 1973.

War of the Rebellion: A Compilation of the Official Records of the Union and Confederate Armies, 70 volumes in 128 parts. Washington: Government Printing Office, 1880–1901.

Wayland, John W. *A History of Rockingham County, Virginia.* Staunton, VA: McClure, 1943.

Weigley, Russell F. *The American Way of War: A History of United States Military Strategy and Policy.* Paperback edition. Bloomington: Indiana University Press, 1977.

——— *Quartermaster General of the Union Army: A Biography of M.C. Meigs.* New York: Columbia University Press, 1959.

Welles, Gideon. "A History of Emancipation." *Galaxy* 14 (1872):838–851.

Wheeler, Richard. *Sherman's March.* New York: Thomas Y. Crowell, 1978.

Wiley, Bell Irvin. "Billy Yank Down South." *Virginia Quarterly Review* 26 (1950):559–575.

——— *The Life of Billy Yank: The Common Soldier of the Union.* Indianapolis and New York: Bobbs-Merrill, 1951.

——— *The Road to Appomattox.* New York: Atheneum, 1983 [1956].

——— *Southern Negroes, 1861–1865.* New Haven, CT: Yale University Press, 1965 [1938].

Williams, Frederick D., ed. *The Wild Life of the Army: Civil War Letters of James A. Garfield.* Lansing, MI: Michigan State University Press, 1964.

Williams, T. Harry. *Lincoln and His Generals.* New York: Alfred A. Knopf, 1952.

——— *Lincoln and the Radicals.* Madison: University of Wisconsin, 1941.

Wilson, James Grant. "General Halleck: A Memoir." *Journal of the Military Service Institution of the United States* 36 (1905):537–559.

Winters, John D. *The Civil War in Louisiana.* Baton Rouge: Louisiana State University Press, 1963.

Winther, Oscar O., ed. *With Sherman to the Sea: Civil War Reminiscences of Theodore F. Upson.* Bloomington: Indiana University Press, 1958.

[Winthrop, Robert C.,] *Speech By Robert C. Winthrop at the Great New York Ratification Meeting.* Boston: J.E. Farwell, 1864.

Woodward, C. Vann, ed. *Mary Chesnut's Civil War.* New Haven, CT: Yale University Press, 1981.

Wright, Henry H. *A History of the Sixth Iowa Infantry.* Iowa City: Iowa State Historical Society, 1923.

Yearns, W. Buck, and John G. Barrett, eds. *North Carolina Civil War Documentary.* Chapel Hill: University of North Carolina Press, 1980.

Index

Index

Grant, Ulysses S. (*cont.*)
164–166; and policy of calculated magnanimity, 161–162, 212; and pragmatic policy, 48, 99–101, 113–114, 117; views on slavery, 126; bars fugitive slaves from his lines, 140; on South as military camp, 216; and strategy of raids, 162, 164, 213; and Vicksburg Campaign, 101, 142, 151, 154–158

guerrillas and guerrilla warfare, 17, 18–19, 31, 37, 42, 48, 50, 51–52, 53, 94, 109, 143, 162, 168, 204, 210, 212; legal status of, 15, 16, 148, 150; overview of, 111–112; and pragmatic policy, 111–119; and reprisals, 21–22, 38–39, 79–81, 86–88, 112–119, 123, 142–143, 151, 167, 175–176, 179, 184–185, 224

Halleck, Henry W., 22, 53, 69, 73, 80, 99, 111, 115, 117, 126, 162–165 passim, 172, 187, 189, 199, 214; and hard war policy, 140–141, 144–145; hopes Charleston, S.C., will be destroyed, 201; and Hunter's raid, 180; and Lieber's Code, 148–150; on laws of war, 15–17; and Pope's orders, 88–89; and pragmatic policy, 49–52, 113–114; views on emancipation, 140–141; views on slavery, 125

"hard war": defined, 4–5; legacy of, 215–219; mythology of, 1, 219–222; pre-Civil War examples of, 17–22, 214

hard war policy: defined, 3–4; in operation, 142–144, 151–203; origins of, 142–144, 151–162; public debate concerning, 171, 180–183; rationale for, 172–174, 188–189; assessed, 203–204, 213–214, 222–225. *See also* Carolinas Campaign, Meridian Expedition, Savannah Campaign, Shenandoah Valley, Vicksburg Campaign

Harney, William S., 36–37
Harsh, Joseph, 33
Hatch, John P., 94
Hattaway, Herman, 162, 209
Hatteras Inlet (N.C.): capture of, 54, 58
Hawkins, Rush C., 54, 60–61
Hazen, William B., 215
Henderson, John B., 69
Hitchcock, Ethan Allen, 124
Hood, John Bell, 168–169, 189fn.
Hooker, Joseph, 75fn., 110
Howard, Oliver O., 199
Hundred Years War, 4; parallels with Union military policy, 214
Hunter, David, 50, 129, 172, 224; and military emancipation order, 127–128; and Shenandoah Valley raid of June 1864, 166–167, 178–181; suggests general arming of slaves, 212
Hurlbut, Stephen, 157–158, 161

Indians. *See* Amerindians
Ingalls, Rufus, 109
insurrectionary principle, 173, 223. *See also* laws of war
Irish Wars, 173, 223
Island No. 10, 66, 86

Jackson, Claiborne, 36–37
Jackson, Thomas J. ("Stonewall"), 43, 86, 91
Jackson (Miss.), Union capture in Vicksburg Campaign (May 1863), 142–143, 154–156; Sherman's raid on (July 1863), 158–161
Johnson, Andrew, 112, 211
Johnson, Reverdy, 49, 182
Johnston, Joseph E., 68, 155, 158, 166
Joint Committee on the Conduct of the War, 82, 86, 127
Jones, Archer, 162, 209

Keyes, Erasmus D., 111

Lane, James H., 49, 124
laws of war: belligerent rights, 13; insurrectionary principle, 11; and legal status of rebellion, 11–17; and noncombatants, 14–15. *See also* Lieber's Code; military necessity
Lee, Robert E., 7, 67, 74, 91–92, 109, 111, 164, 165, 167, 170, 203–204
Letcher, John, 167, 179
Lewis, C.S., 97
Lewis, Lloyd, 221
Liddell Hart, B.H., 217
Lieber, Francis, 148–151
Lieber's Code, 149–151, 178–179, 214
Lincoln, Abraham, 7, 19, 26–35 passim, 37, 49, 52, 69, 71, 74–75, 85, 89–90, 94, 105–106, 121, 126, 129, 172, 181, 189, 210–211, 224; election of (1860), 208; on nature of rebellion, 9; on legal status of rebellion, 11–12; on border states, 62; expresses impatience with conciliatory policy, 87, 92; decides on emancipation, 121, 132–133; views on slavery, 122, 130; approves "contraband order," 123; rejects military necessity as basis for emancipation, 124; reverses military emancipation orders, 124, 128; and evolution of emancipation policy, 130–133; issues preliminary Emancipation Proclamation, 92, 133; issues final Emancipation Proclamation, 134, 138; rationale for emancipation decision, 135–136; confers with Grant, 165–166; criticized for not enforcing prohibition on wanton destruction, 180, 182
Lockwood, Henry H., 54–55
Logan, John A., 99
Lovejoy, Owen, 130
Lyon, Nathaniel, 36–38, 48